HARLEY AND IVY
MEET
BETTY AND VERONICA

HARLEY AND IVY MEET BETTY AND VERONICA

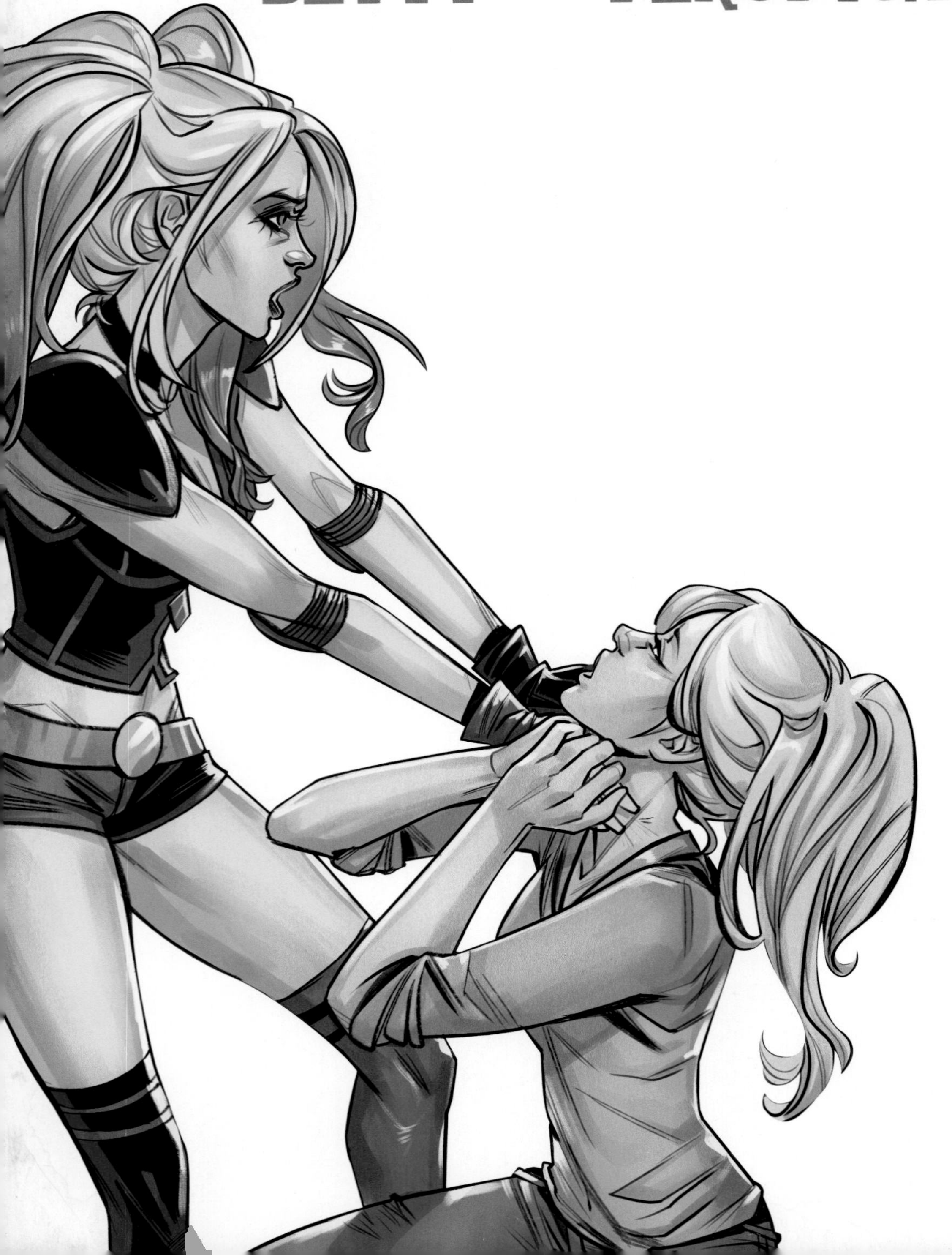

PAUL DINI
MARC ANDREYKO
—— writers ——

LAURA BRAGA
ADRIANA MELO
—— artists ——

ARIF PRIANTO
TONY AVIÑA
J. NANJAN
—— colorists ——

DERON BENNETT
—— letterer ——

AMANDA CONNER and PAUL MOUNTS
—— collection cover artists ——

HARLEY QUINN created by PAUL DINI and BRUCE TIMM

KRISTY QUINN Editor – Original Series
JEB WOODARD Group Editor – Collected Editions
ERIKA ROTHBERG Editor – Collected Edition
STEVE COOK Design Director – Books
MEGEN BELLERSEN Publication Design

BOB HARRAS Senior VP – Editor-in-Chief, DC Comics
PAT McCALLUM Executive Editor, DC Comics

DIANE NELSON President
DAN DiDIO Publisher
JIM LEE Publisher
GEOFF JOHNS President & Chief Creative Officer
AMIT DESAI Executive VP – Business & Marketing Strategy,
Direct to Consumer & Global Franchise Management
SAM ADES Senior VP & General Manager, Digital Services
BOBBIE CHASE VP & Executive Editor, Young Reader & Talent Development
MARK CHIARELLO Senior VP – Art, Design & Collected Editions
JOHN CUNNINGHAM Senior VP – Sales & Trade Marketing
ANNE DePIES Senior VP – Business Strategy, Finance & Administration
DON FALLETTI VP – Manufacturing Operations
LAWRENCE GANEM VP – Editorial Administration & Talent Relations
ALISON GILL Senior VP – Manufacturing & Operations
HANK KANALZ Senior VP – Editorial Strategy & Administration
JAY KOGAN VP – Legal Affairs
JACK MAHAN VP – Business Affairs
NICK J. NAPOLITANO VP – Manufacturing Administration
EDDIE SCANNELL VP – Consumer Marketing
COURTNEY SIMMONS Senior VP – Publicity & Communications
JIM (SKI) SOKOLOWSKI VP – Comic Book Specialty Sales & Trade Marketing
NANCY SPEARS VP – Mass, Book, Digital Sales & Trade Marketing
MICHELE R. WELLS VP – Content Strategy

HARLEY AND IVY MEET BETTY AND VERONICA

DC Comics, 2900 West Alameda Ave., Burbank, CA 91505
Printed by LSC Communications, Kendallville, IN, USA. 7/27/18. First Printing.
ISBN: 978-1-4012-8033-8

Library of Congress Cataloging-in-Publication Data is available.

PEFC Certified
Printed on paper from
sustainably managed
forests and controlled
sources

PEFC/29-31-337 www.pefc.org

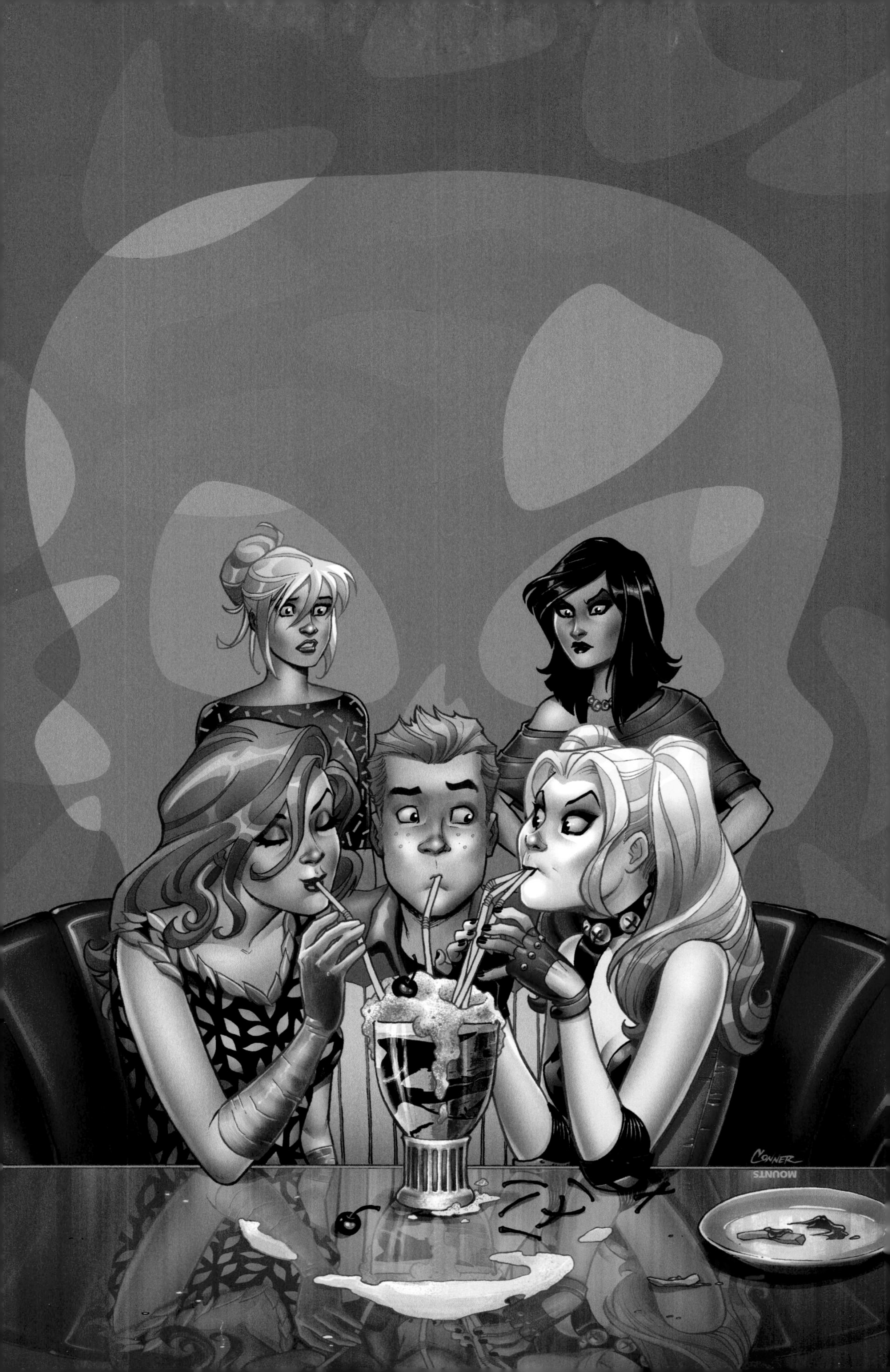
CONNER

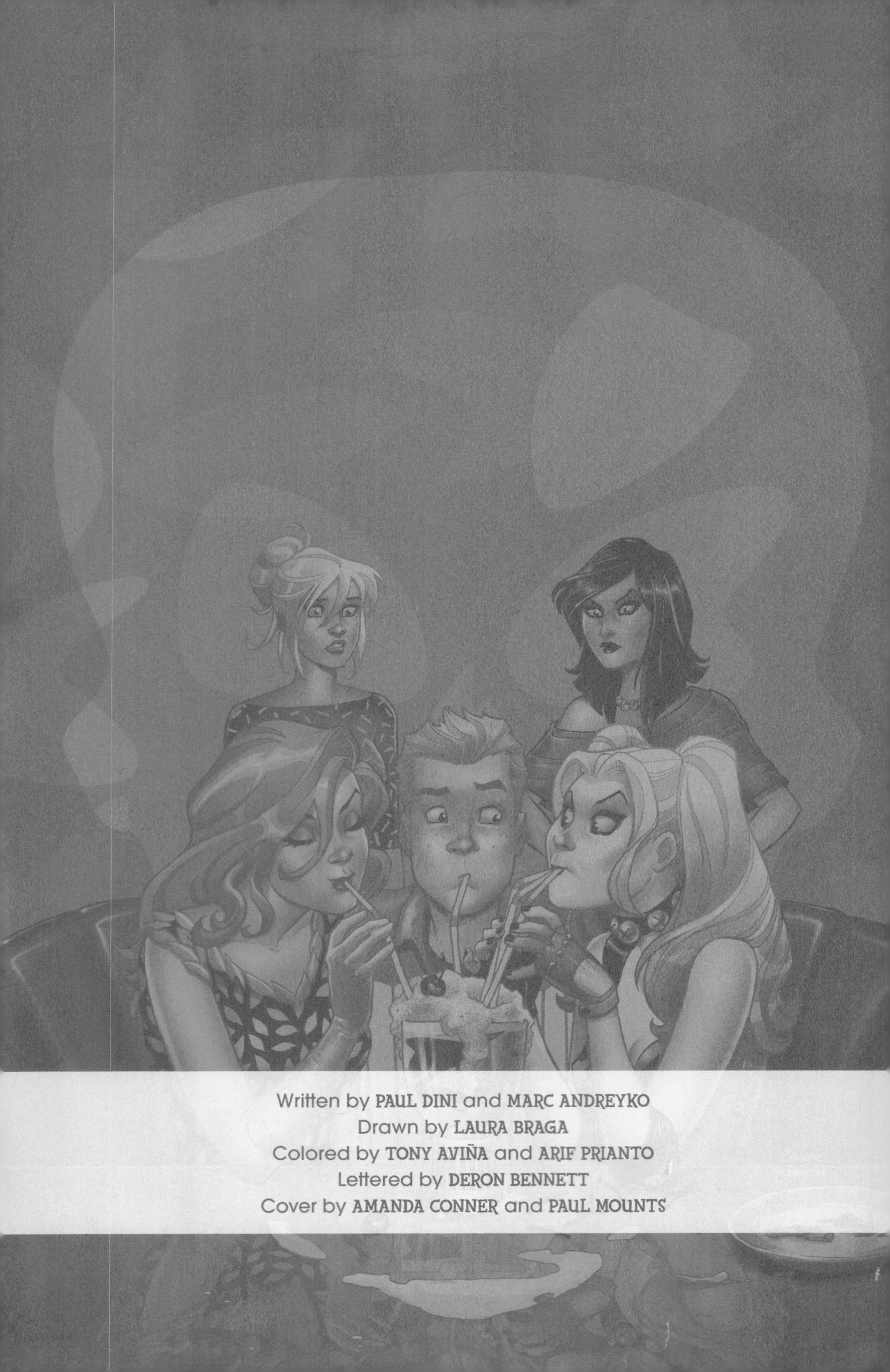

Written by PAUL DINI and MARC ANDREYKO
Drawn by LAURA BRAGA
Colored by TONY AVIÑA and ARIF PRIANTO
Lettered by DERON BENNETT
Cover by AMANDA CONNER and PAUL MOUNTS

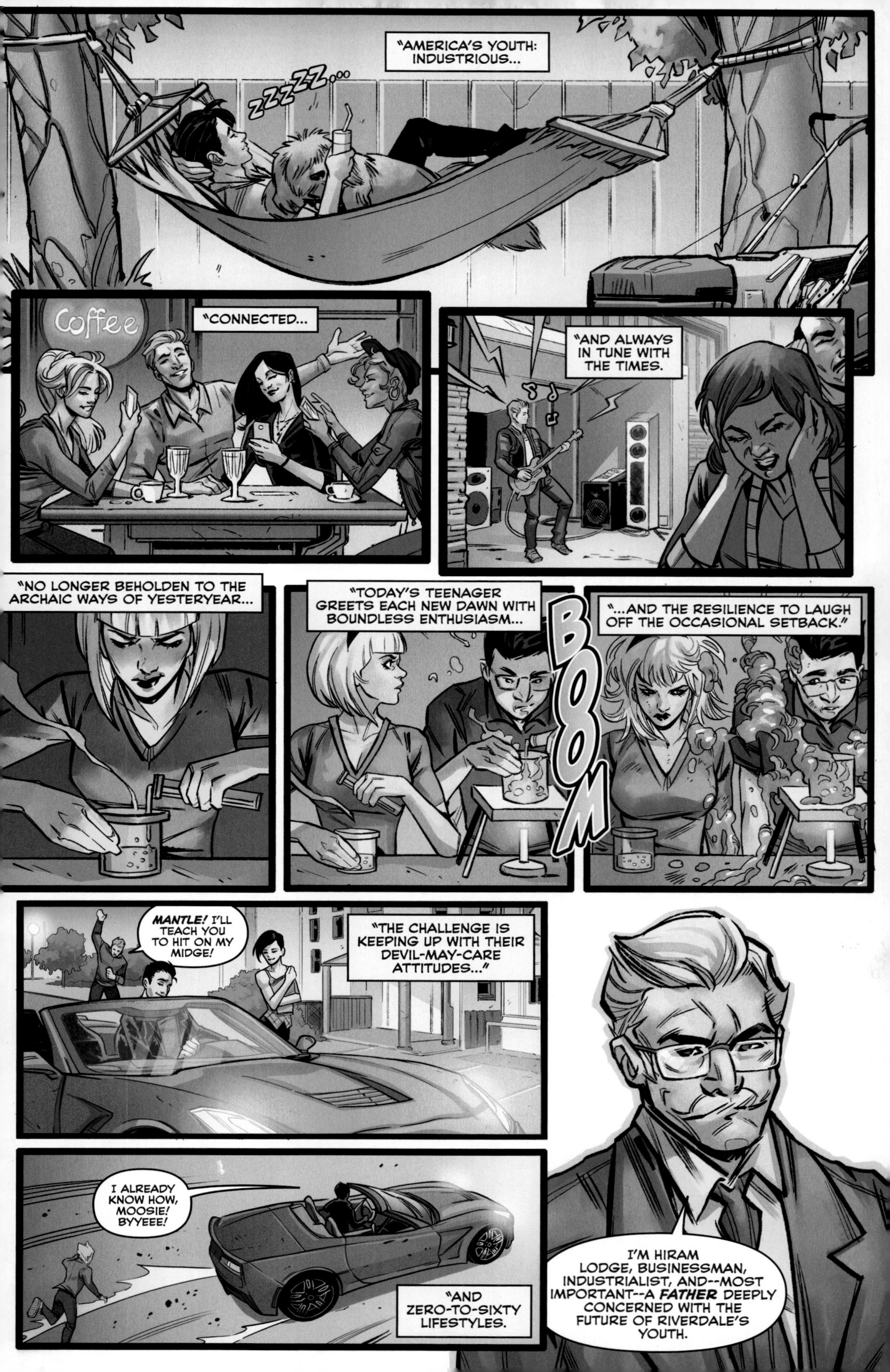
"AMERICA'S YOUTH: INDUSTRIOUS...
ZZZZZ...
"CONNECTED...
Coffee
"AND ALWAYS IN TUNE WITH THE TIMES.
"NO LONGER BEHOLDEN TO THE ARCHAIC WAYS OF YESTERYEAR...
"TODAY'S TEENAGER GREETS EACH NEW DAWN WITH BOUNDLESS ENTHUSIASM...
BOOM
"...AND THE RESILIENCE TO LAUGH OFF THE OCCASIONAL SETBACK."
MANTLE! I'LL TEACH YOU TO HIT ON MY MIDGE!
"THE CHALLENGE IS KEEPING UP WITH THEIR DEVIL-MAY-CARE ATTITUDES..."
I ALREADY KNOW HOW, MOOSIE! BYYEEE!
"AND ZERO-TO-SIXTY LIFESTYLES.
I'M HIRAM LODGE, BUSINESSMAN, INDUSTRIALIST, AND--MOST IMPORTANT--A FATHER DEEPLY CONCERNED WITH THE FUTURE OF RIVERDALE'S YOUTH.

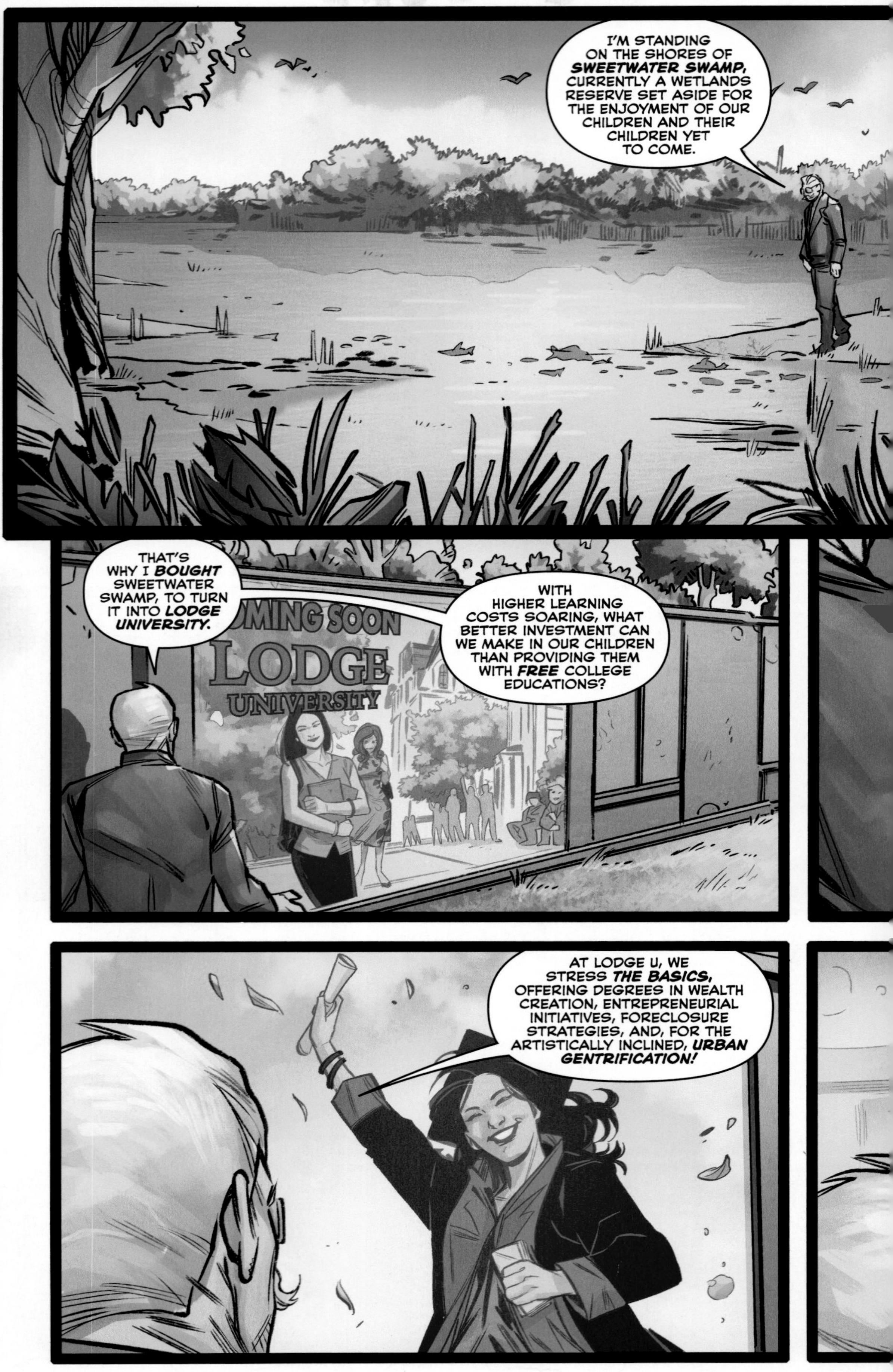
I'M STANDING ON THE SHORES OF SWEETWATER SWAMP, CURRENTLY A WETLANDS RESERVE SET ASIDE FOR THE ENJOYMENT OF OUR CHILDREN AND THEIR CHILDREN YET TO COME.
THAT'S WHY I BOUGHT SWEETWATER SWAMP, TO TURN IT INTO LODGE UNIVERSITY.
OMING SOON
LODGE
UNIVERSITY
WITH HIGHER LEARNING COSTS SOARING, WHAT BETTER INVESTMENT CAN WE MAKE IN OUR CHILDREN THAN PROVIDING THEM WITH FREE COLLEGE EDUCATIONS?
AT LODGE U, WE STRESS THE BASICS, OFFERING DEGREES IN WEALTH CREATION, ENTREPRENEURIAL INITIATIVES, FORECLOSURE STRATEGIES, AND, FOR THE ARTISTICALLY INCLINED, URBAN GENTRIFICATION!

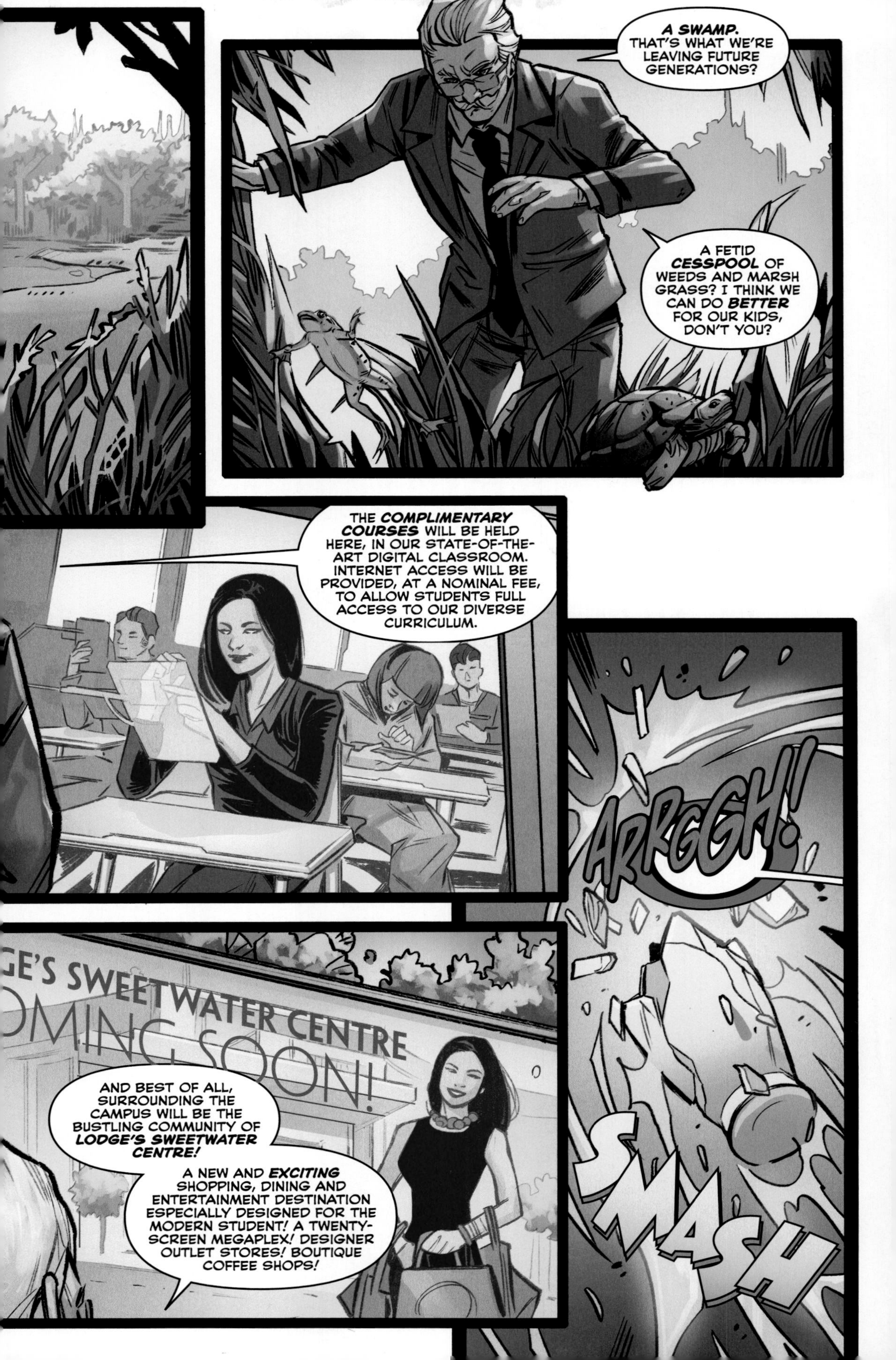
A SWAMP. THAT'S WHAT WE'RE LEAVING FUTURE GENERATIONS?
A FETID CESSPOOL OF WEEDS AND MARSH GRASS? I THINK WE CAN DO BETTER FOR OUR KIDS, DON'T YOU?
THE COMPLIMENTARY COURSES WILL BE HELD HERE, IN OUR STATE-OF-THE-ART DIGITAL CLASSROOM. INTERNET ACCESS WILL BE PROVIDED, AT A NOMINAL FEE, TO ALLOW STUDENTS FULL ACCESS TO OUR DIVERSE CURRICULUM.
ARRGGH!
SMASH
GE'S SWEETWATER CENTRE
OMING SOON!
AND BEST OF ALL, SURROUNDING THE CAMPUS WILL BE THE BUSTLING COMMUNITY OF LODGE'S SWEETWATER CENTRE!
A NEW AND EXCITING SHOPPING, DINING AND ENTERTAINMENT DESTINATION ESPECIALLY DESIGNED FOR THE MODERN STUDENT! A TWENTY-SCREEN MEGAPLEX! DESIGNER OUTLET STORES! BOUTIQUE COFFEE SHOPS!

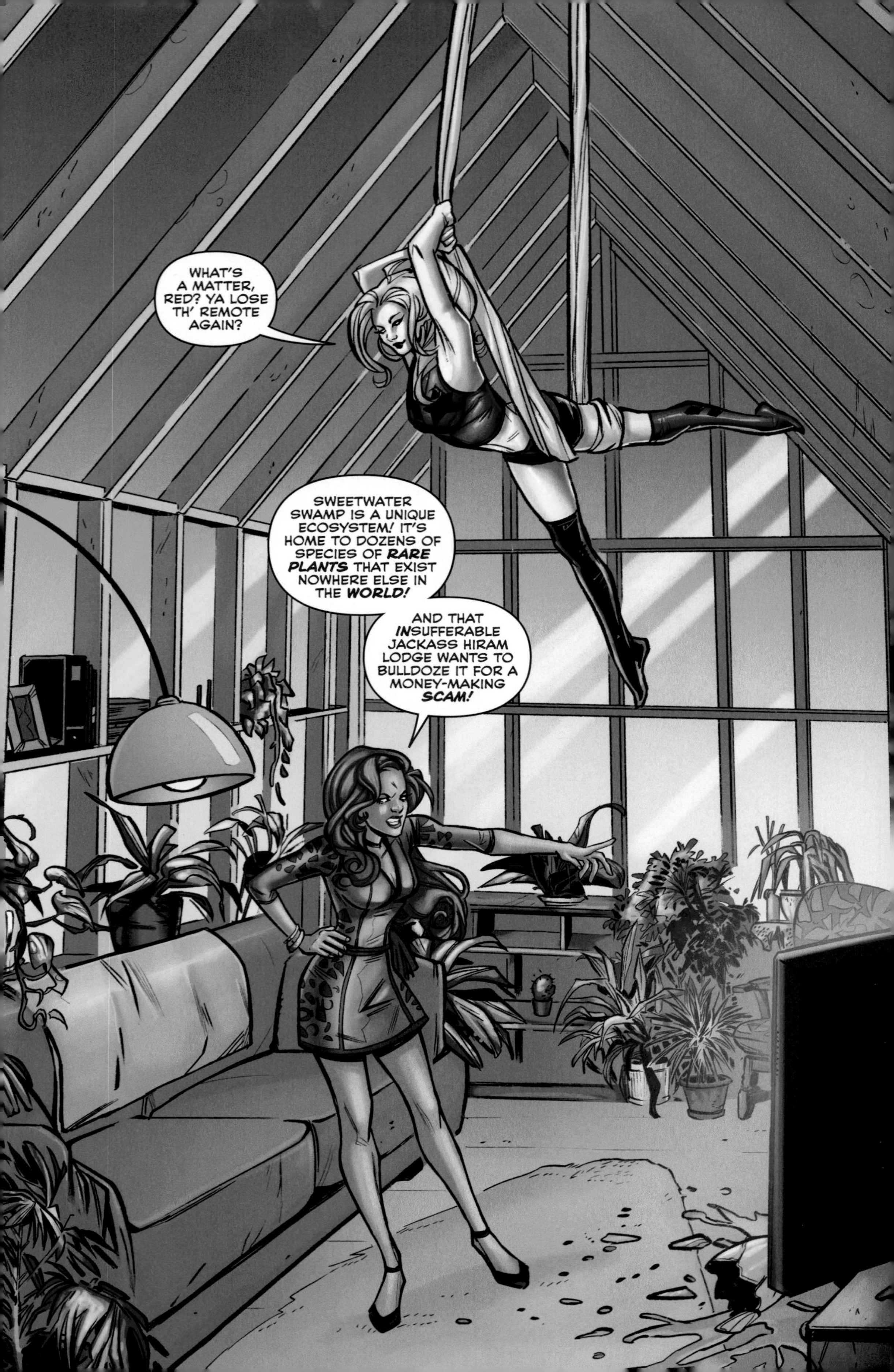
WHAT'S A MATTER, RED? YA LOSE TH' REMOTE AGAIN?
SWEETWATER SWAMP IS A UNIQUE ECOSYSTEM! IT'S HOME TO DOZENS OF SPECIES OF **RARE PLANTS** THAT EXIST NOWHERE ELSE IN THE **WORLD!**
AND THAT **IN**SUFFERABLE JACKASS HIRAM LODGE WANTS TO BULLDOZE IT FOR A MONEY-MAKING **SCAM!**

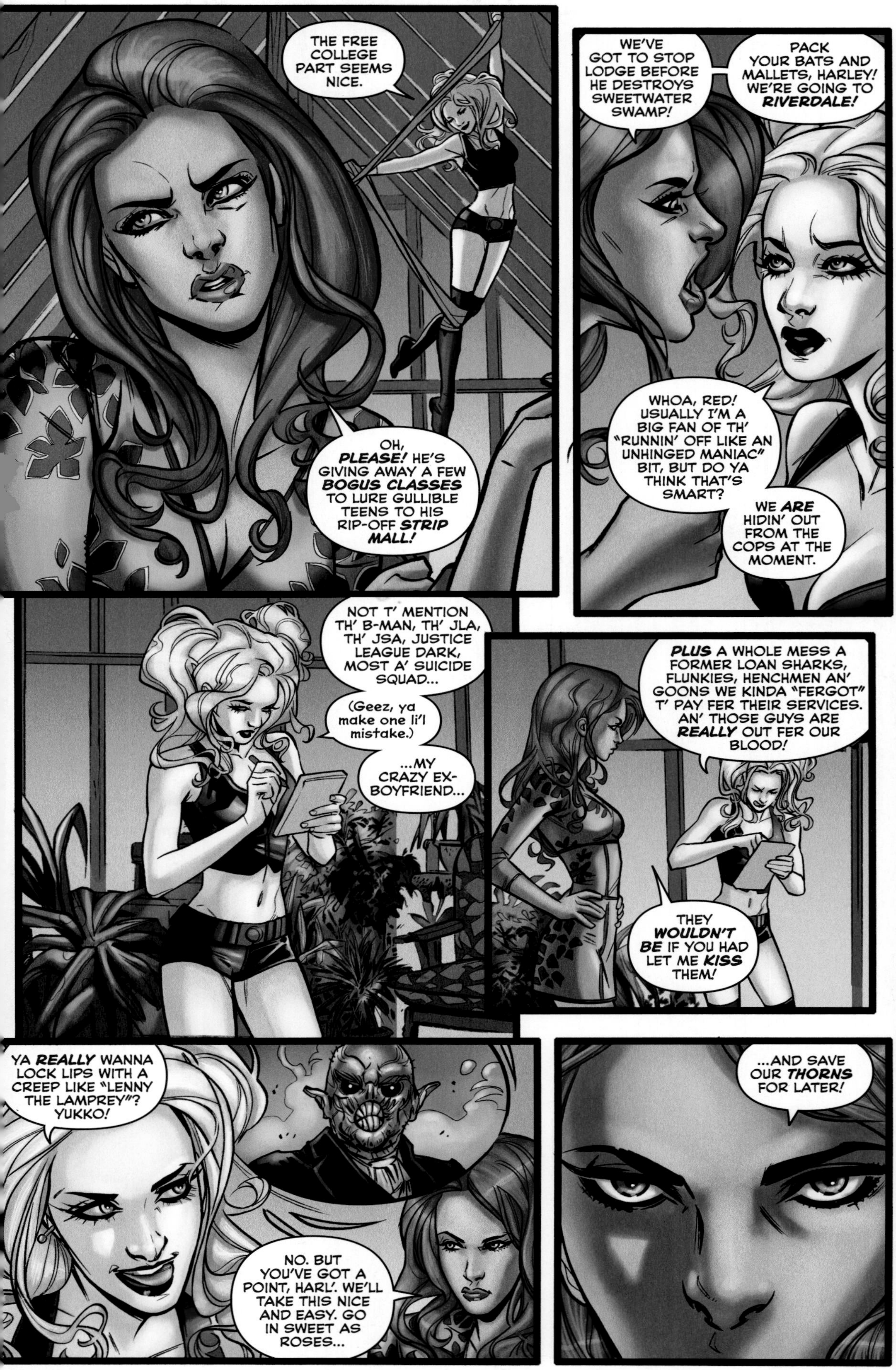
THE FREE COLLEGE PART SEEMS NICE.
OH, PLEASE! HE'S GIVING AWAY A FEW BOGUS CLASSES TO LURE GULLIBLE TEENS TO HIS RIP-OFF STRIP MALL!
WE'VE GOT TO STOP LODGE BEFORE HE DESTROYS SWEETWATER SWAMP!
PACK YOUR BATS AND MALLETS, HARLEY! WE'RE GOING TO RIVERDALE!
WHOA, RED! USUALLY I'M A BIG FAN OF TH' "RUNNIN' OFF LIKE AN UNHINGED MANIAC" BIT, BUT DO YA THINK THAT'S SMART?
WE ARE HIDIN' OUT FROM THE COPS AT THE MOMENT.
NOT T' MENTION TH' B-MAN, TH' JLA, TH' JSA, JUSTICE LEAGUE DARK, MOST A' SUICIDE SQUAD...
(Geez, ya make one li'l mistake.)
...MY CRAZY EX-BOYFRIEND...
PLUS A WHOLE MESS A FORMER LOAN SHARKS, FLUNKIES, HENCHMEN AN' GOONS WE KINDA "FERGOT" T' PAY FER THEIR SERVICES. AN' THOSE GUYS ARE REALLY OUT FER OUR BLOOD!
THEY WOULDN'T BE IF YOU HAD LET ME KISS THEM!
YA REALLY WANNA LOCK LIPS WITH A CREEP LIKE "LENNY THE LAMPREY"? YUKKO!
NO. BUT YOU'VE GOT A POINT, HARL'. WE'LL TAKE THIS NICE AND EASY. GO IN SWEET AS ROSES...
...AND SAVE OUR THORNS FOR LATER!

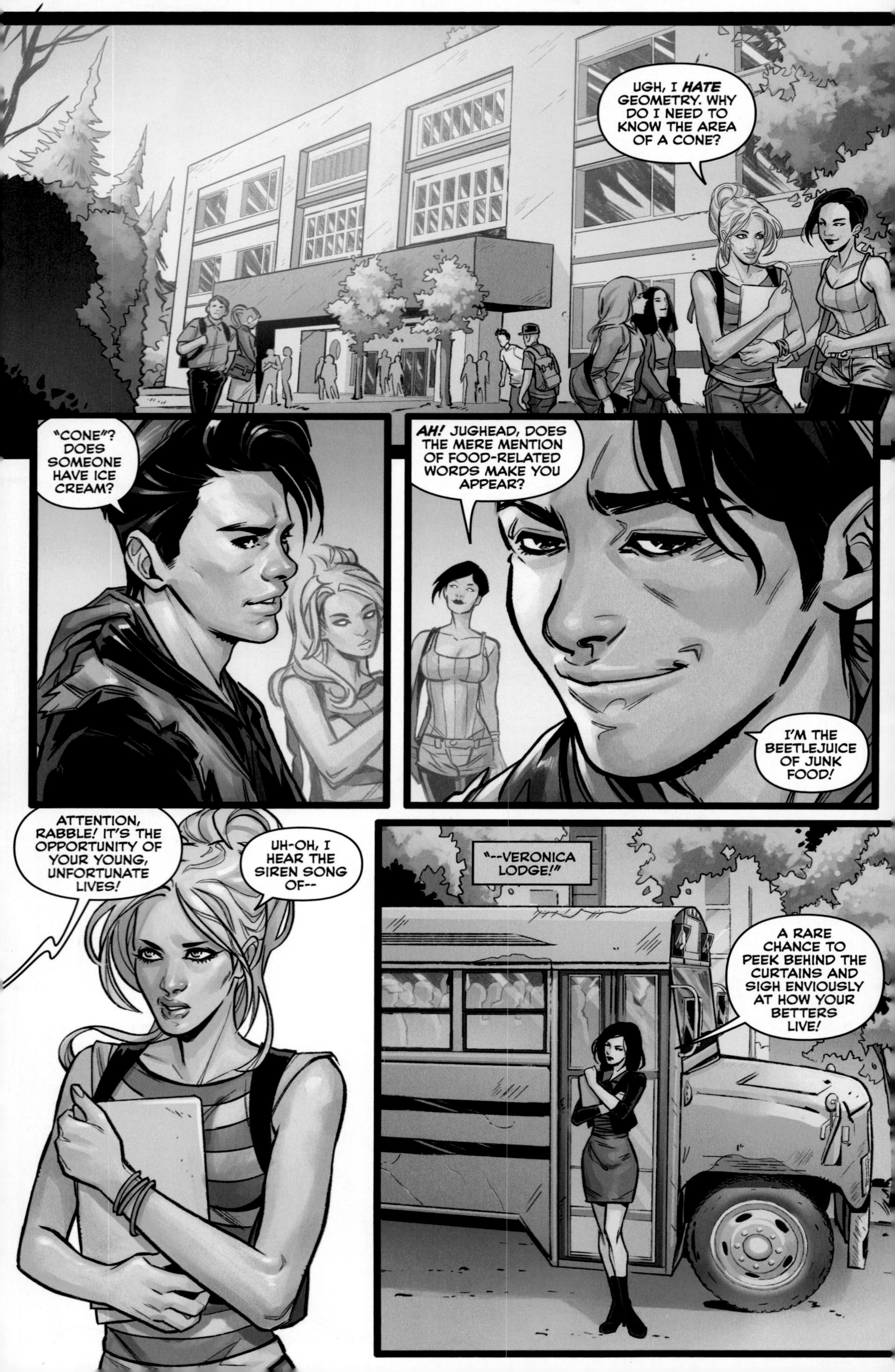
UGH, I ***HATE*** GEOMETRY. WHY DO I NEED TO KNOW THE AREA OF A CONE?
"CONE"? DOES SOMEONE HAVE ICE CREAM?
AH! JUGHEAD, DOES THE MERE MENTION OF FOOD-RELATED WORDS MAKE YOU APPEAR?
I'M THE BEETLEJUICE OF JUNK FOOD!
ATTENTION, RABBLE! IT'S THE OPPORTUNITY OF YOUR YOUNG, UNFORTUNATE LIVES!
UH-OH, I HEAR THE SIREN SONG OF--
"--VERONICA LODGE!"
A RARE CHANCE TO PEEK BEHIND THE CURTAINS AND SIGH ENVIOUSLY AT HOW YOUR BETTERS LIVE!

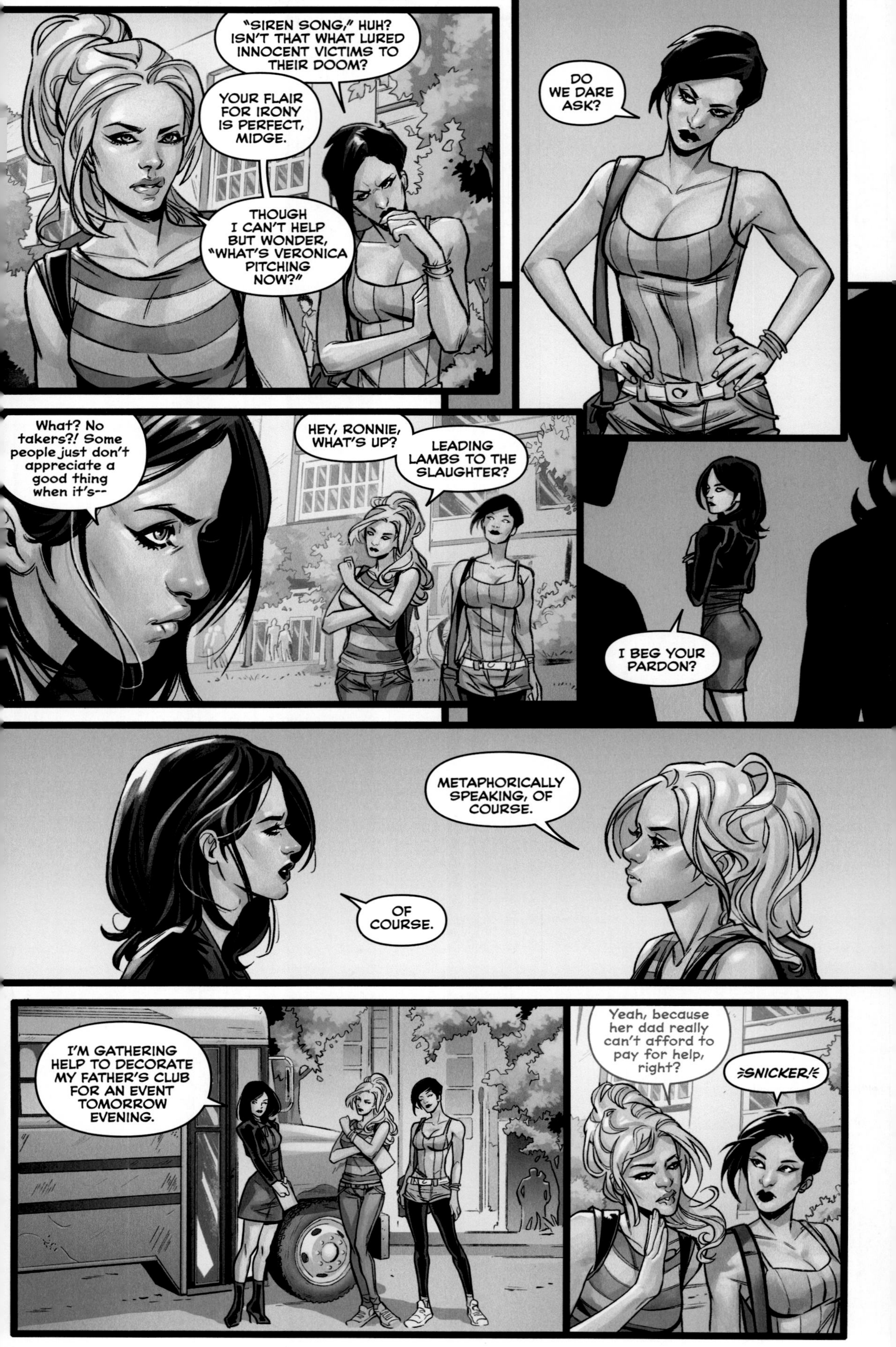
"SIREN SONG," HUH? ISN'T THAT WHAT LURED INNOCENT VICTIMS TO THEIR DOOM?
YOUR FLAIR FOR IRONY IS PERFECT, MIDGE.
THOUGH I CAN'T HELP BUT WONDER, "WHAT'S VERONICA PITCHING NOW?"
DO WE DARE ASK?
What? No takers?! Some people just don't appreciate a good thing when it's--
HEY, RONNIE, WHAT'S UP?
LEADING LAMBS TO THE SLAUGHTER?
I BEG YOUR PARDON?
METAPHORICALLY SPEAKING, OF COURSE.
OF COURSE.
I'M GATHERING HELP TO DECORATE MY FATHER'S CLUB FOR AN EVENT TOMORROW EVENING.
Yeah, because her dad really can't afford to pay for help, right?
SNICKER!

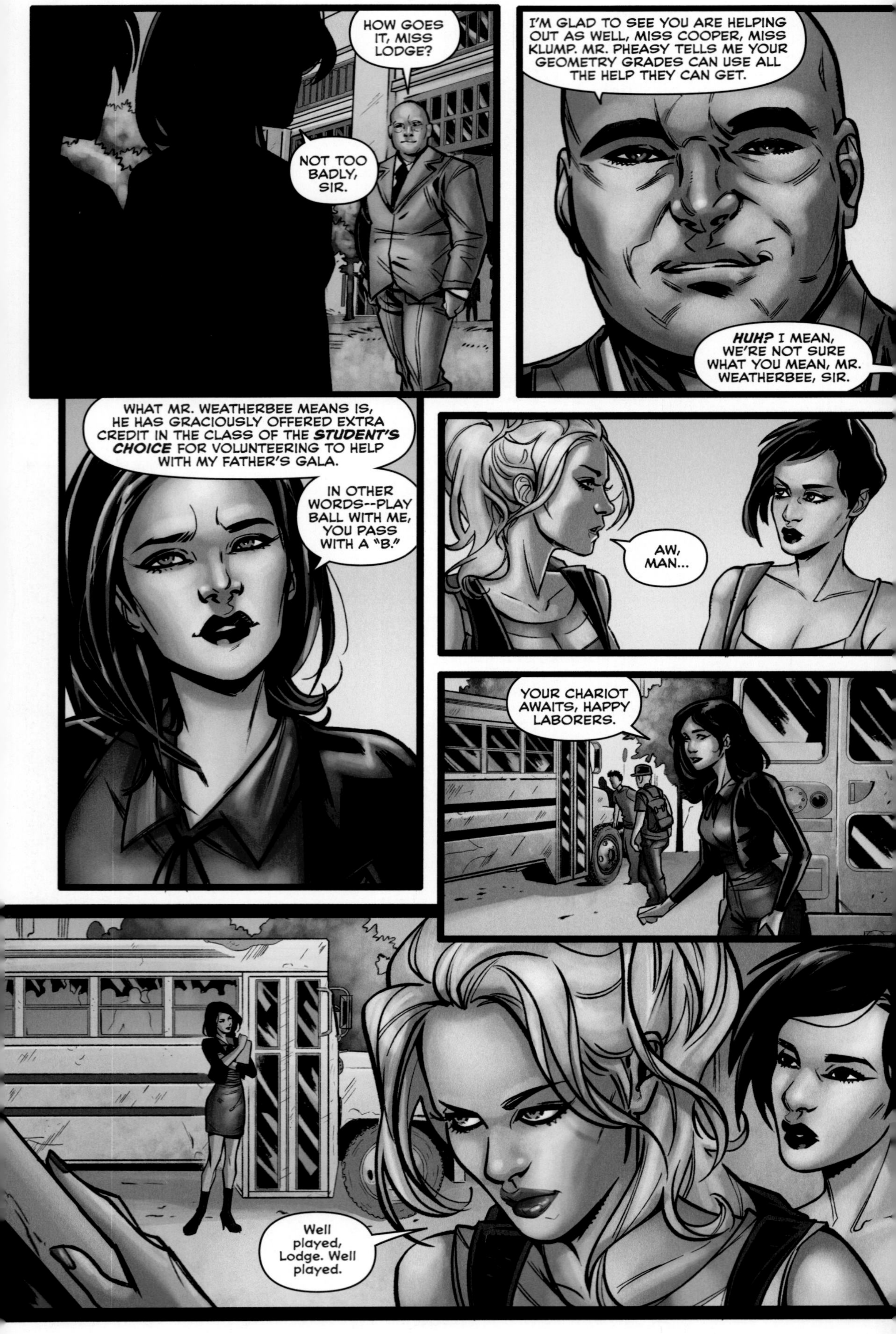
HOW GOES IT, MISS LODGE?
NOT TOO BADLY, SIR.
I'M GLAD TO SEE YOU ARE HELPING OUT AS WELL, MISS COOPER, MISS KLUMP. MR. PHEASY TELLS ME YOUR GEOMETRY GRADES CAN USE ALL THE HELP THEY CAN GET.
HUH? I MEAN, WE'RE NOT SURE WHAT YOU MEAN, MR. WEATHERBEE, SIR.
WHAT MR. WEATHERBEE MEANS IS, HE HAS GRACIOUSLY OFFERED EXTRA CREDIT IN THE CLASS OF THE STUDENT'S CHOICE FOR VOLUNTEERING TO HELP WITH MY FATHER'S GALA.
IN OTHER WORDS--PLAY BALL WITH ME, YOU PASS WITH A "B."
AW, MAN...
YOUR CHARIOT AWAITS, HAPPY LABORERS.
Well played, Lodge. Well played.

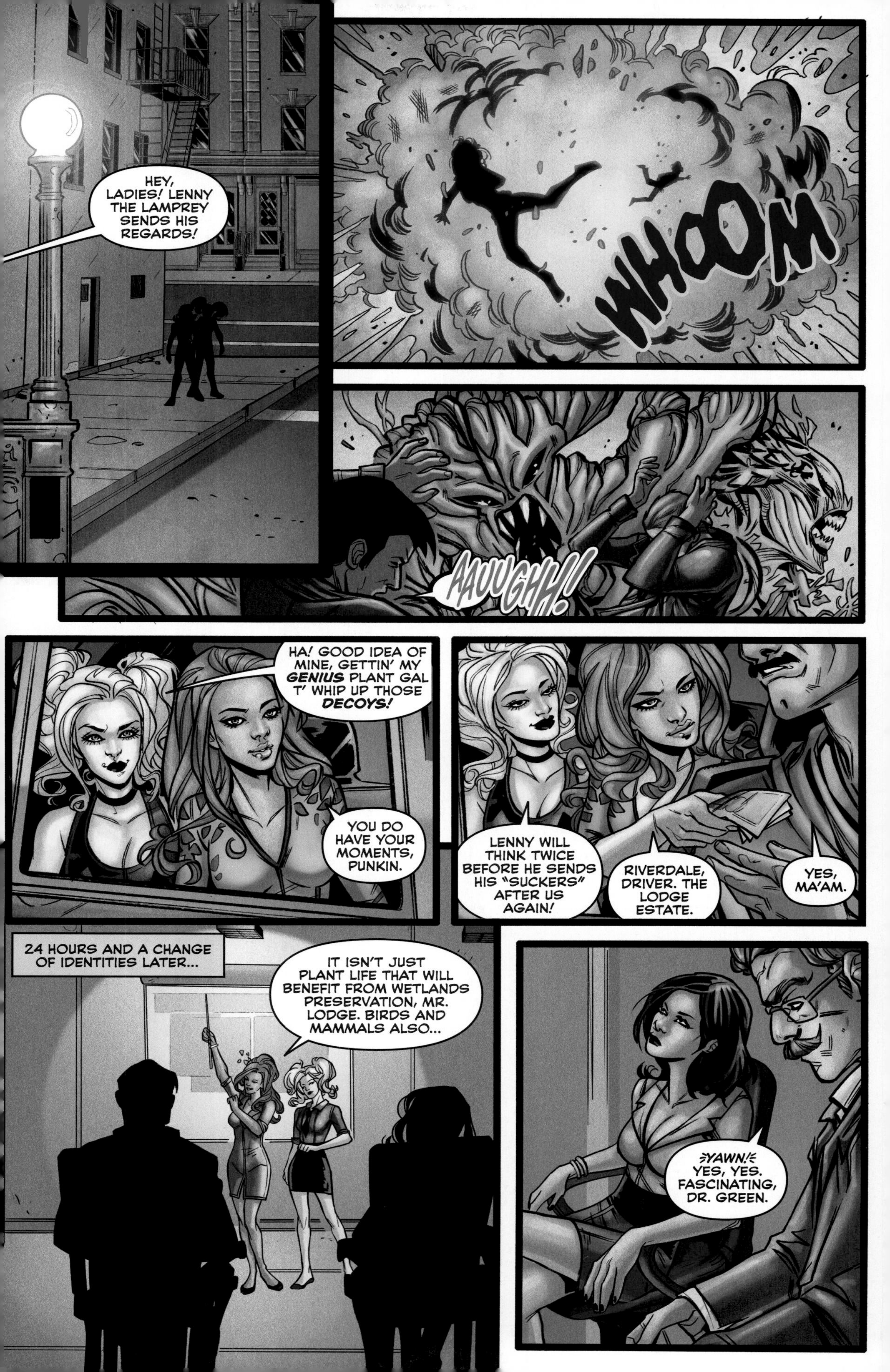

HEY, LADIES! LENNY THE LAMPREY SENDS HIS REGARDS!
WHOOM
AAUUGHH!
HA! GOOD IDEA OF MINE, GETTIN' MY GENIUS PLANT GAL T' WHIP UP THOSE DECOYS!
YOU DO HAVE YOUR MOMENTS, PUNKIN.
LENNY WILL THINK TWICE BEFORE HE SENDS HIS "SUCKERS" AFTER US AGAIN!
RIVERDALE, DRIVER. THE LODGE ESTATE.
YES, MA'AM.
24 HOURS AND A CHANGE OF IDENTITIES LATER...
IT ISN'T JUST PLANT LIFE THAT WILL BENEFIT FROM WETLANDS PRESERVATION, MR. LODGE. BIRDS AND MAMMALS ALSO...
YAWN! YES, YES. FASCINATING, DR. GREEN.

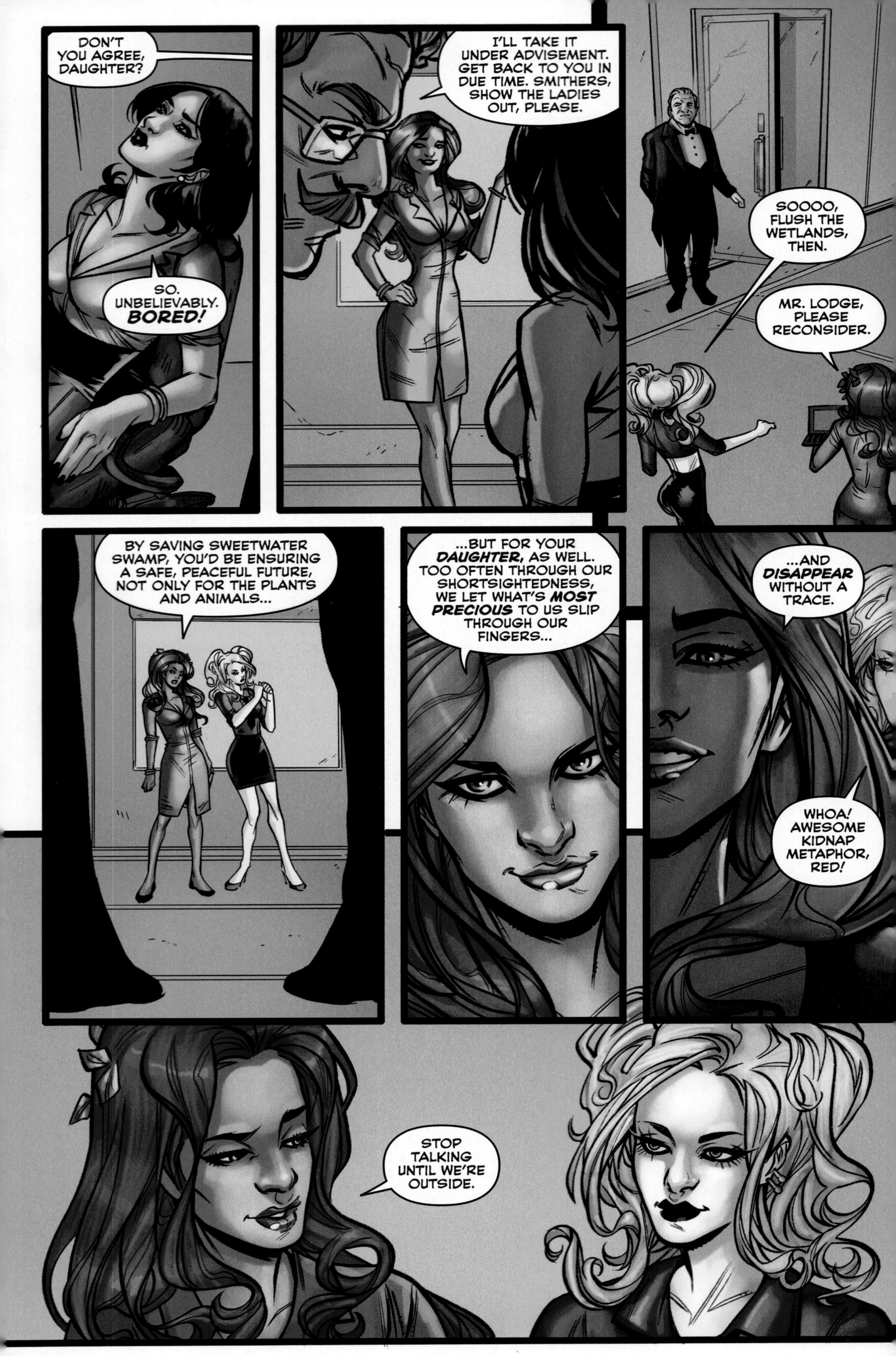
DON'T YOU AGREE, DAUGHTER?
SO. UNBELIEVABLY. ***BORED!***
I'LL TAKE IT UNDER ADVISEMENT. GET BACK TO YOU IN DUE TIME. SMITHERS, SHOW THE LADIES OUT, PLEASE.
SOOOO, FLUSH THE WETLANDS, THEN.
MR. LODGE, PLEASE RECONSIDER.
BY SAVING SWEETWATER SWAMP, YOU'D BE ENSURING A SAFE, PEACEFUL FUTURE, NOT ONLY FOR THE PLANTS AND ANIMALS...
...BUT FOR YOUR ***DAUGHTER,*** AS WELL. TOO OFTEN THROUGH OUR SHORTSIGHTEDNESS, WE LET WHAT'S ***MOST PRECIOUS*** TO US SLIP THROUGH OUR FINGERS...
...AND ***DISAPPEAR*** WITHOUT A TRACE.
WHOA! AWESOME KIDNAP METAPHOR, RED!
STOP TALKING UNTIL WE'RE OUTSIDE.

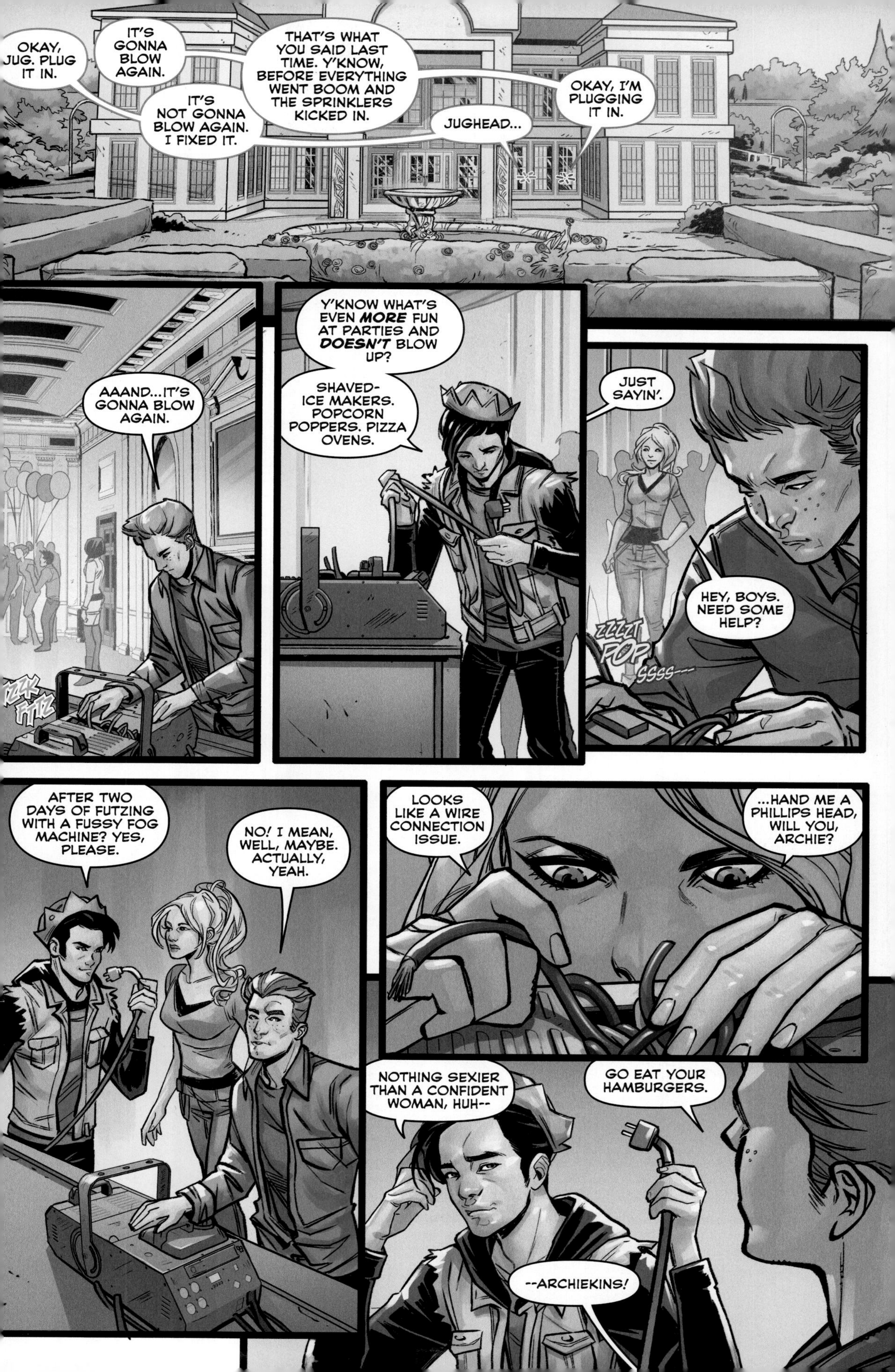
OKAY, JUG. PLUG IT IN.
IT'S GONNA BLOW AGAIN.
IT'S NOT GONNA BLOW AGAIN. I FIXED IT.
THAT'S WHAT YOU SAID LAST TIME. Y'KNOW, BEFORE EVERYTHING WENT BOOM AND THE SPRINKLERS KICKED IN.
JUGHEAD...
OKAY, I'M PLUGGING IT IN.
AAAND...IT'S GONNA BLOW AGAIN.
FTTZ
Y'KNOW WHAT'S EVEN **MORE** FUN AT PARTIES AND **DOESN'T** BLOW UP?
SHAVED-ICE MAKERS. POPCORN POPPERS. PIZZA OVENS.
JUST SAYIN'.
ZZZZT
POP
SSSS---
HEY, BOYS. NEED SOME HELP?
AFTER TWO DAYS OF FUTZING WITH A FUSSY FOG MACHINE? YES, PLEASE.
NO! I MEAN, WELL, MAYBE. ACTUALLY, YEAH.
LOOKS LIKE A WIRE CONNECTION ISSUE.
...HAND ME A PHILLIPS HEAD, WILL YOU, ARCHIE?
NOTHING SEXIER THAN A CONFIDENT WOMAN, HUH--
GO EAT YOUR HAMBURGERS.
--ARCHIEKINS!

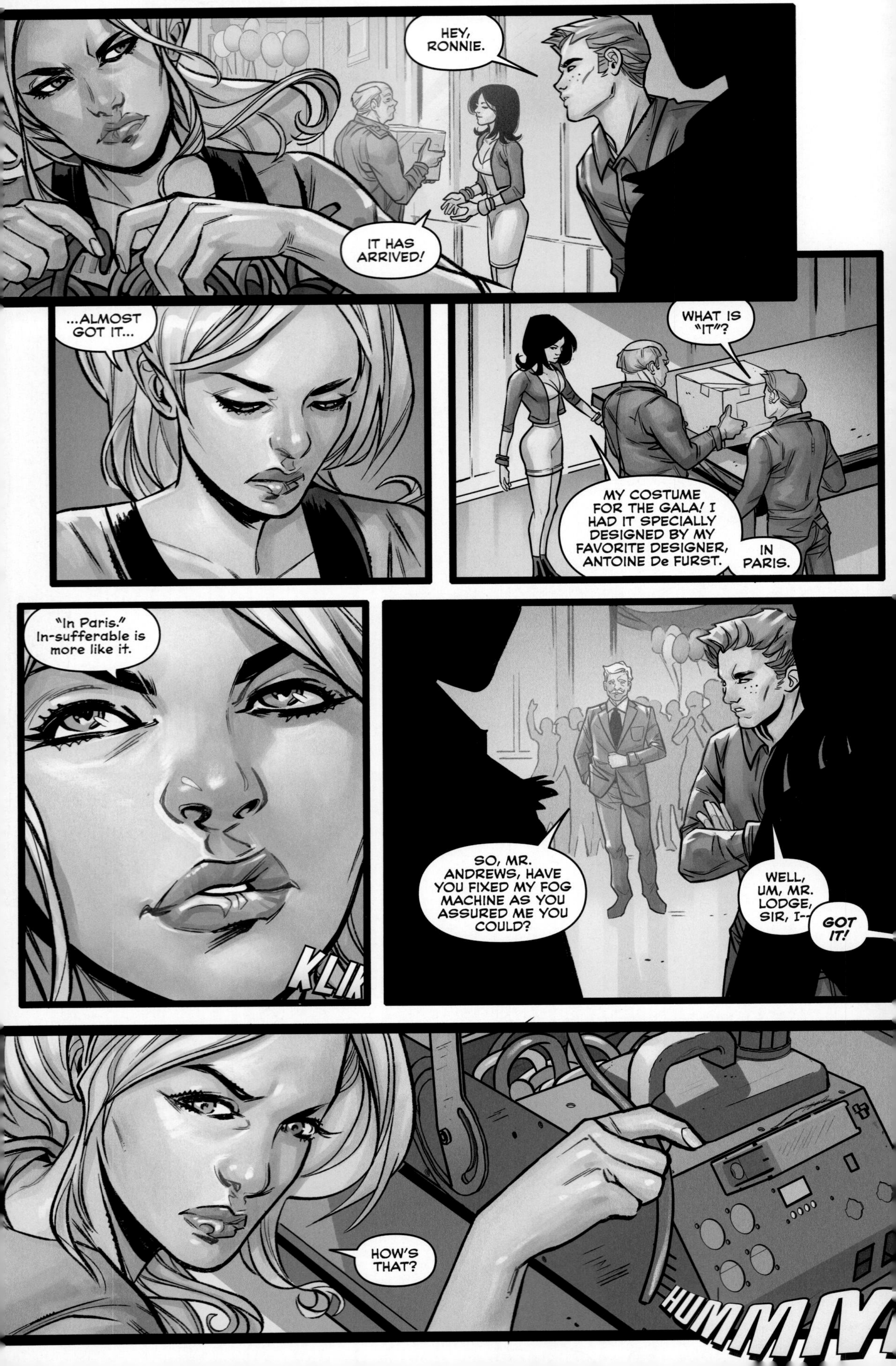
HEY, RONNIE.
IT HAS ARRIVED!
...ALMOST GOT IT...
WHAT IS "IT"?
MY COSTUME FOR THE GALA! I HAD IT SPECIALLY DESIGNED BY MY FAVORITE DESIGNER, ANTOINE De FURST.
IN PARIS.
"In Paris." In-sufferable is more like it.
KLIK
SO, MR. ANDREWS, HAVE YOU FIXED MY FOG MACHINE AS YOU ASSURED ME YOU COULD?
WELL, UM, MR. LODGE, SIR, I--
GOT IT!
HOW'S THAT?
HUMMMM

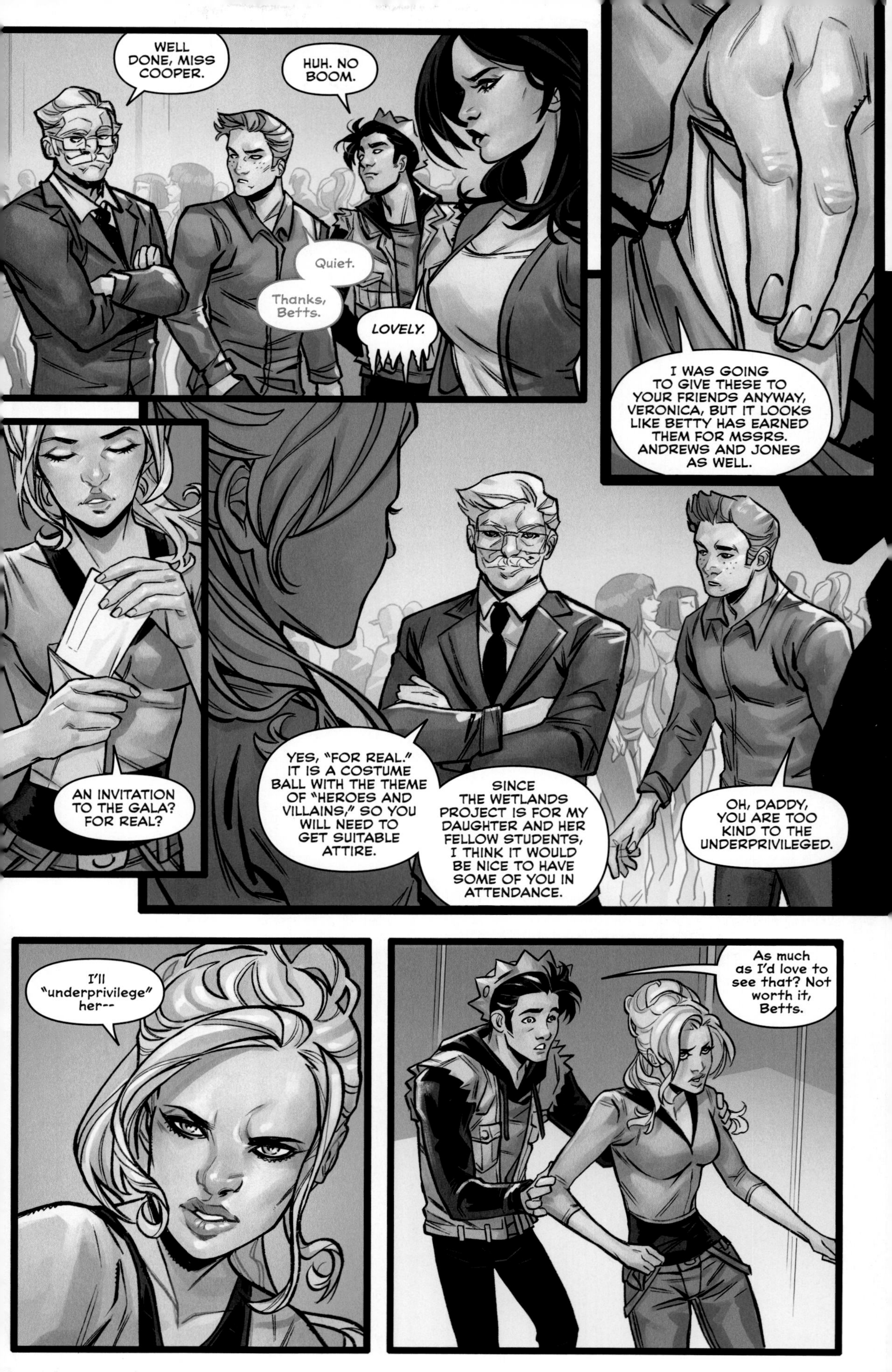
WELL DONE, MISS COOPER.
HUH. NO BOOM.
Quiet.
Thanks, Betts.
LOVELY.
I WAS GOING TO GIVE THESE TO YOUR FRIENDS ANYWAY, VERONICA, BUT IT LOOKS LIKE BETTY HAS EARNED THEM FOR MSSRS. ANDREWS AND JONES AS WELL.
AN INVITATION TO THE GALA? FOR REAL?
YES, "FOR REAL." IT IS A COSTUME BALL WITH THE THEME OF "HEROES AND VILLAINS," SO YOU WILL NEED TO GET SUITABLE ATTIRE.
SINCE THE WETLANDS PROJECT IS FOR MY DAUGHTER AND HER FELLOW STUDENTS, I THINK IT WOULD BE NICE TO HAVE SOME OF YOU IN ATTENDANCE.
OH, DADDY, YOU ARE TOO KIND TO THE UNDERPRIVILEGED.
I'll "underprivilege" her--
As much as I'd love to see that? Not worth it, Betts.

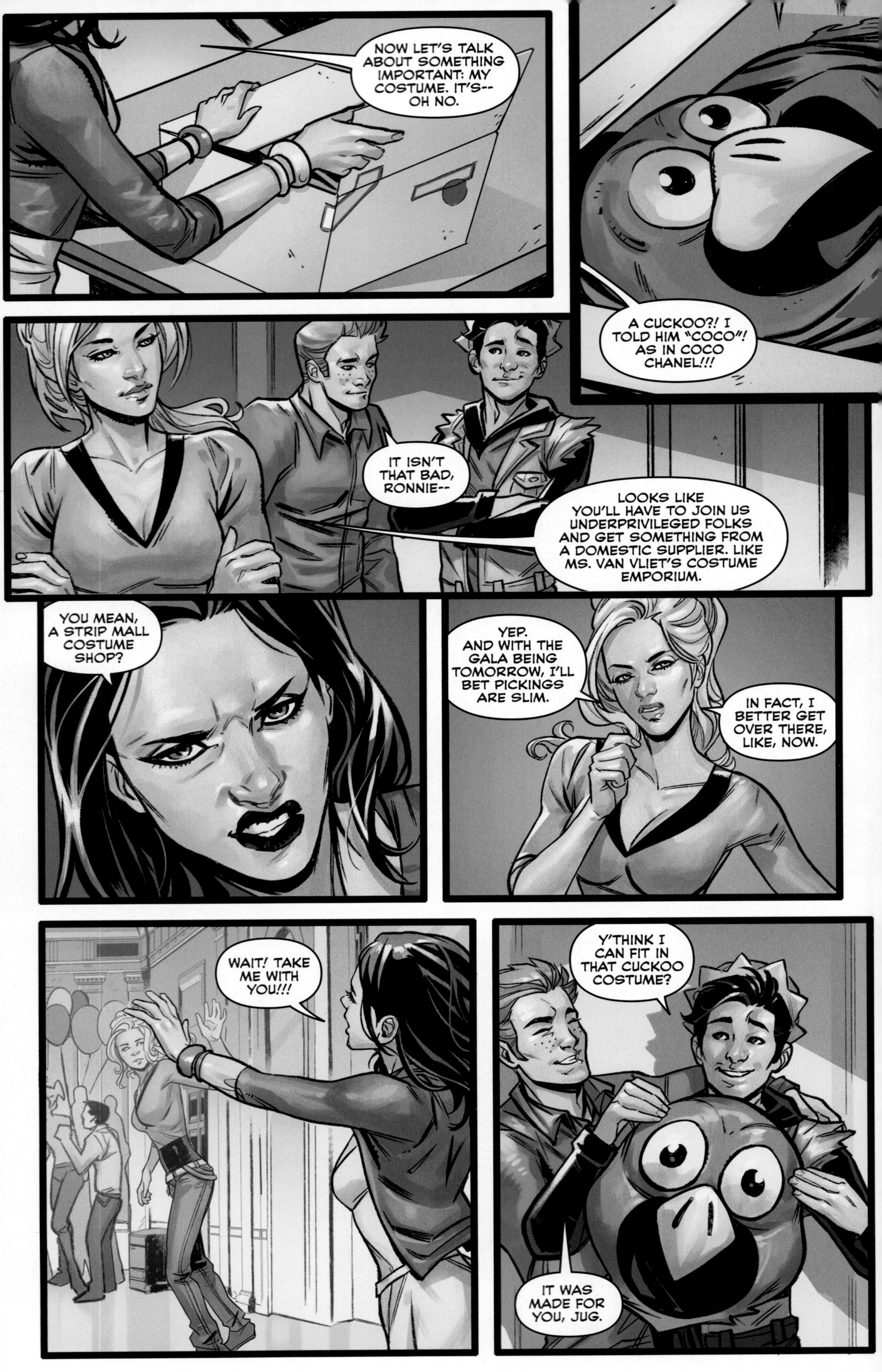
NOW LET'S TALK ABOUT SOMETHING IMPORTANT: MY COSTUME. IT'S-- OH NO.
A CUCKOO?! I TOLD HIM "COCO"! AS IN COCO CHANEL!!!
IT ISN'T THAT BAD, RONNIE--
LOOKS LIKE YOU'LL HAVE TO JOIN US UNDERPRIVILEGED FOLKS AND GET SOMETHING FROM A DOMESTIC SUPPLIER. LIKE MS. VAN VLIET'S COSTUME EMPORIUM.
YOU MEAN, A STRIP MALL COSTUME SHOP?
YEP. AND WITH THE GALA BEING TOMORROW, I'LL BET PICKINGS ARE SLIM.
IN FACT, I BETTER GET OVER THERE, LIKE, NOW.
WAIT! TAKE ME WITH YOU!!!
Y'THINK I CAN FIT IN THAT CUCKOO COSTUME?
IT WAS MADE FOR YOU, JUG.

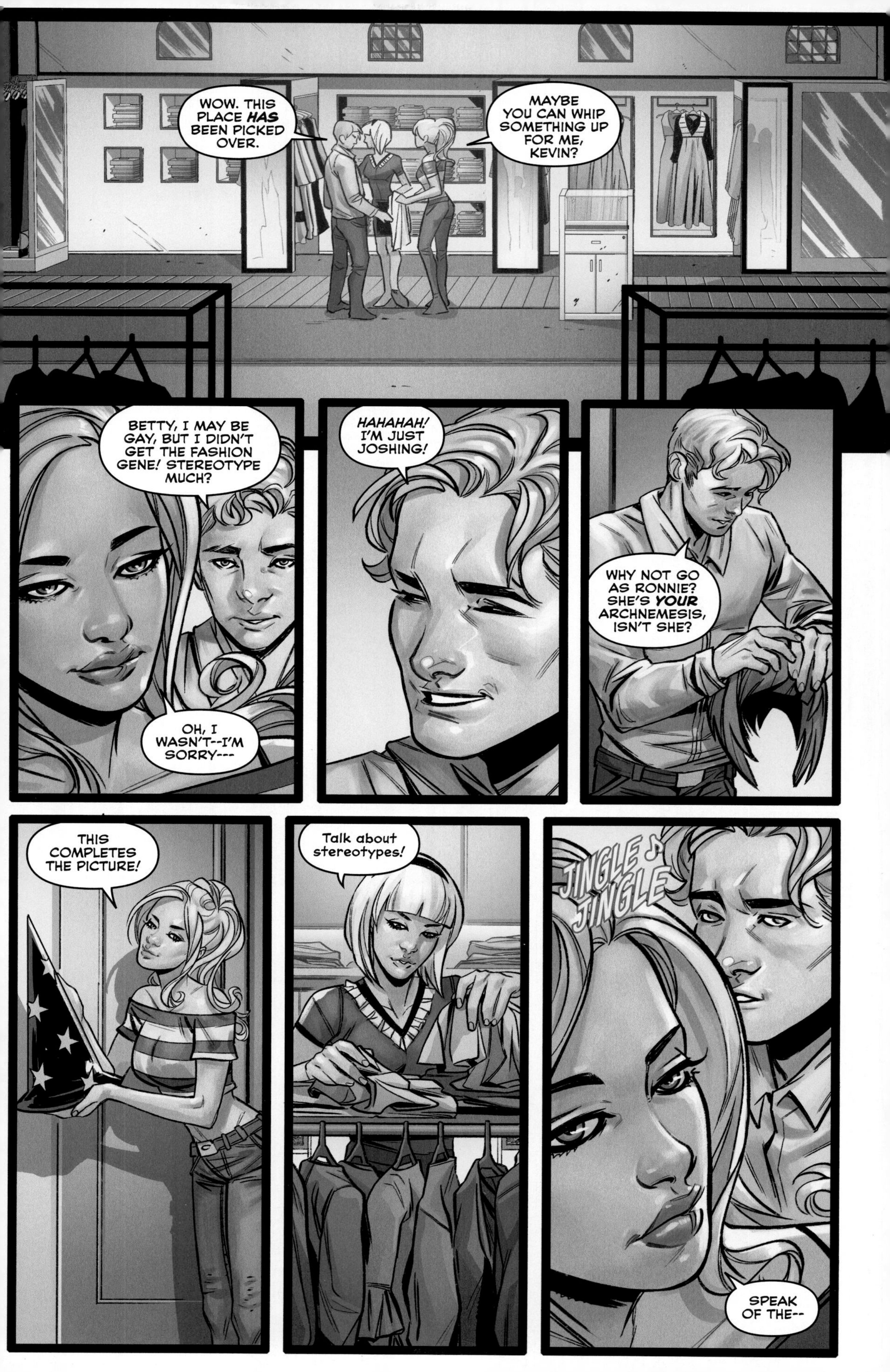
WOW. THIS PLACE **HAS** BEEN PICKED OVER.
MAYBE YOU CAN WHIP SOMETHING UP FOR ME, KEVIN?
BETTY, I MAY BE GAY, BUT I DIDN'T GET THE FASHION GENE! STEREOTYPE MUCH?
OH, I WASN'T--I'M SORRY---
HAHAHAH! I'M JUST JOSHING!
WHY NOT GO AS RONNIE? SHE'S ***YOUR*** ARCHNEMESIS, ISN'T SHE?
THIS COMPLETES THE PICTURE!
Talk about stereotypes!
JINGLE JINGLE
SPEAK OF THE--

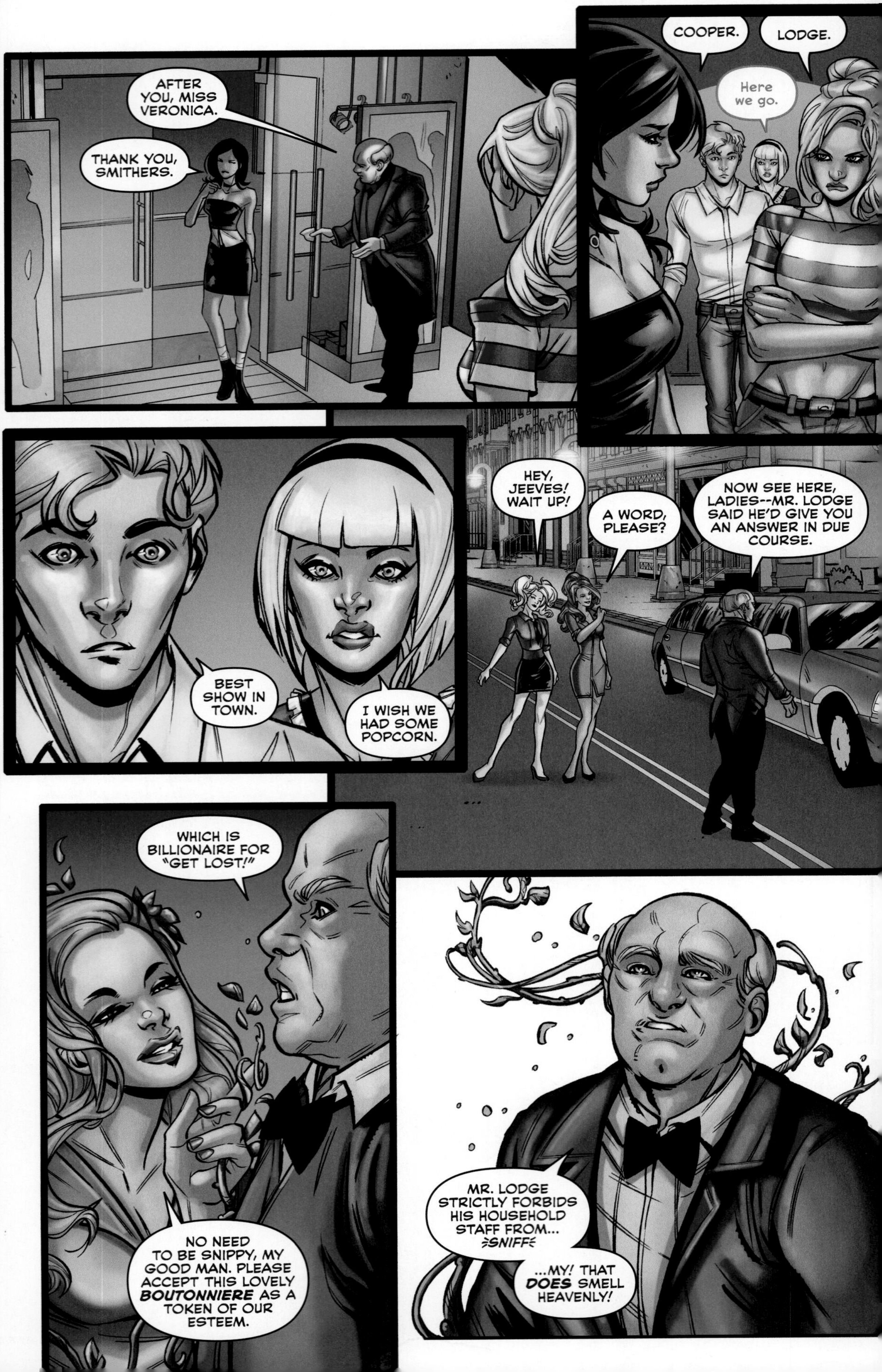
AFTER YOU, MISS VERONICA.
THANK YOU, SMITHERS.
COOPER.
LODGE.
Here we go.
BEST SHOW IN TOWN.
I WISH WE HAD SOME POPCORN.
HEY, JEEVES! WAIT UP!
A WORD, PLEASE?
NOW SEE HERE, LADIES--MR. LODGE SAID HE'D GIVE YOU AN ANSWER IN DUE COURSE.
WHICH IS BILLIONAIRE FOR "GET LOST!"
NO NEED TO BE SNIPPY, MY GOOD MAN. PLEASE ACCEPT THIS LOVELY BOUTONNIERE AS A TOKEN OF OUR ESTEEM.
MR. LODGE STRICTLY FORBIDS HIS HOUSEHOLD STAFF FROM... SNIFF
...MY! THAT DOES SMELL HEAVENLY!

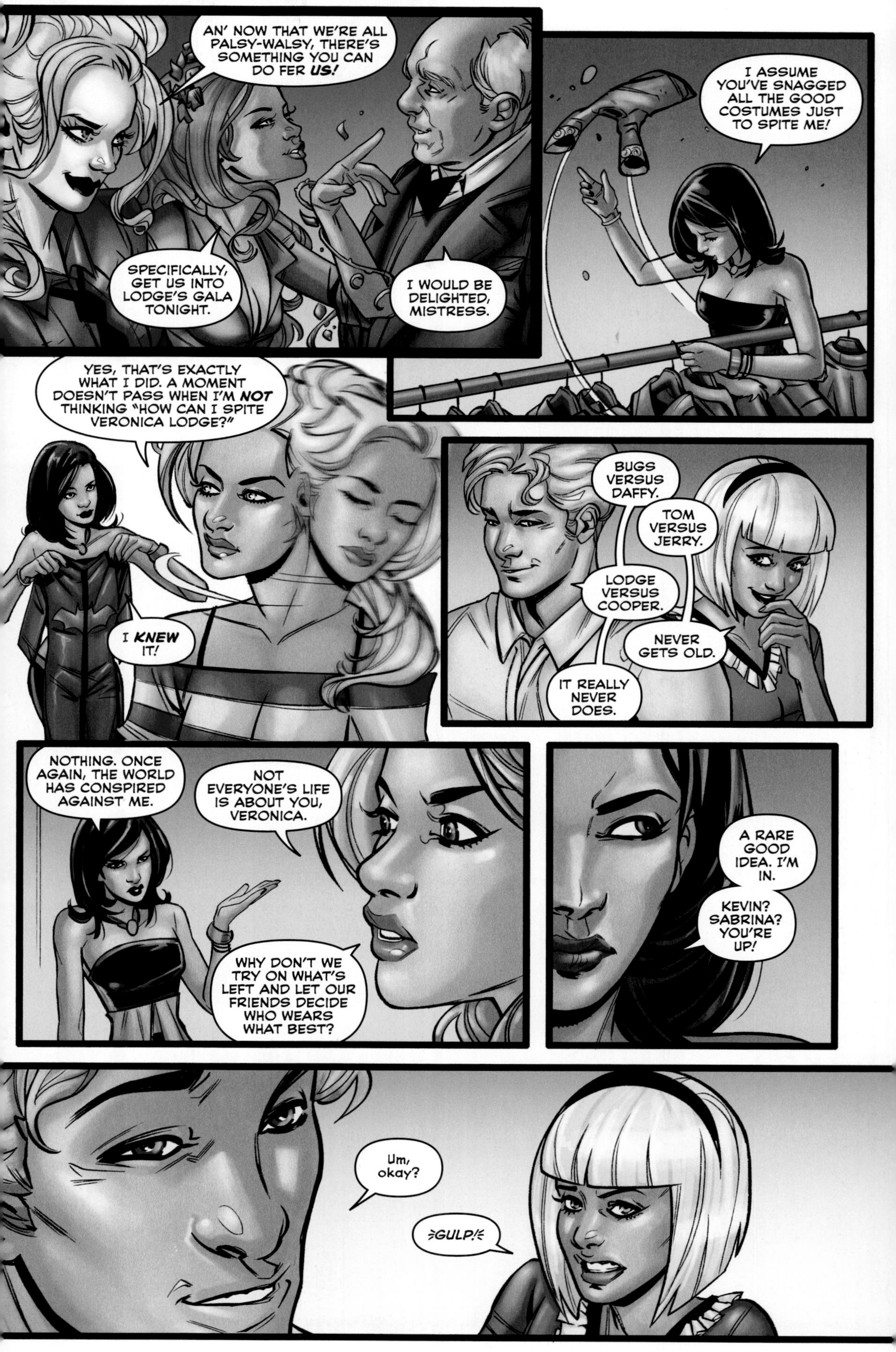
AN' NOW THAT WE'RE ALL PALSY-WALSY, THERE'S SOMETHING YOU CAN DO FER US!
SPECIFICALLY, GET US INTO LODGE'S GALA TONIGHT.
I WOULD BE DELIGHTED, MISTRESS.
I ASSUME YOU'VE SNAGGED ALL THE GOOD COSTUMES JUST TO SPITE ME!
YES, THAT'S EXACTLY WHAT I DID. A MOMENT DOESN'T PASS WHEN I'M NOT THINKING "HOW CAN I SPITE VERONICA LODGE?"
I KNEW IT!
BUGS VERSUS DAFFY.
TOM VERSUS JERRY.
LODGE VERSUS COOPER.
NEVER GETS OLD.
IT REALLY NEVER DOES.
NOTHING. ONCE AGAIN, THE WORLD HAS CONSPIRED AGAINST ME.
NOT EVERYONE'S LIFE IS ABOUT YOU, VERONICA.
WHY DON'T WE TRY ON WHAT'S LEFT AND LET OUR FRIENDS DECIDE WHO WEARS WHAT BEST?
A RARE GOOD IDEA. I'M IN.
KEVIN? SABRINA? YOU'RE UP!
Um, okay?
GULP!

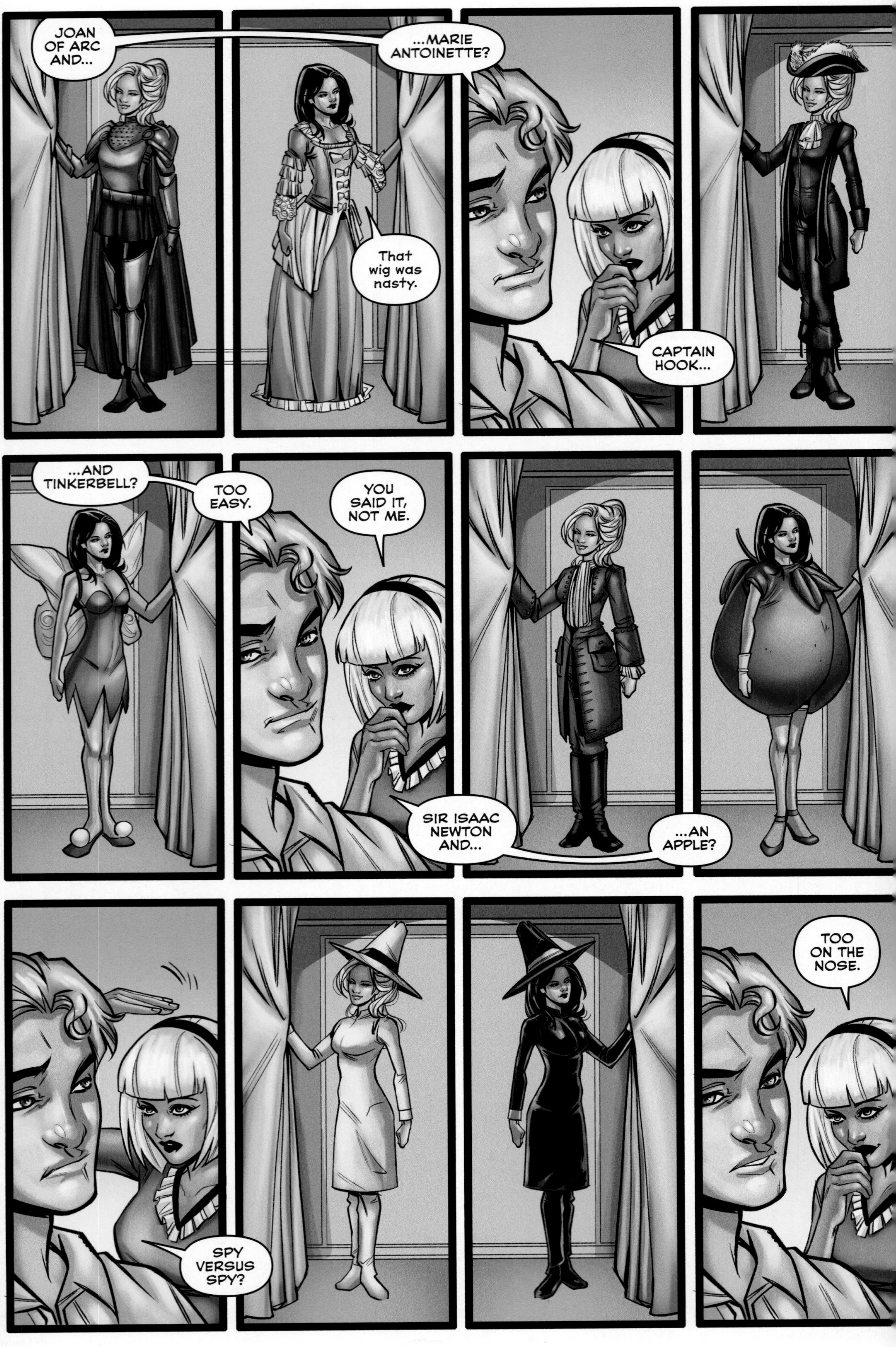
JOAN OF ARC AND...
...MARIE ANTOINETTE?
That wig was nasty.
CAPTAIN HOOK...
...AND TINKERBELL?
TOO EASY.
YOU SAID IT, NOT ME.
SIR ISAAC NEWTON AND...
...AN APPLE?
SPY VERSUS SPY?
TOO ON THE NOSE.

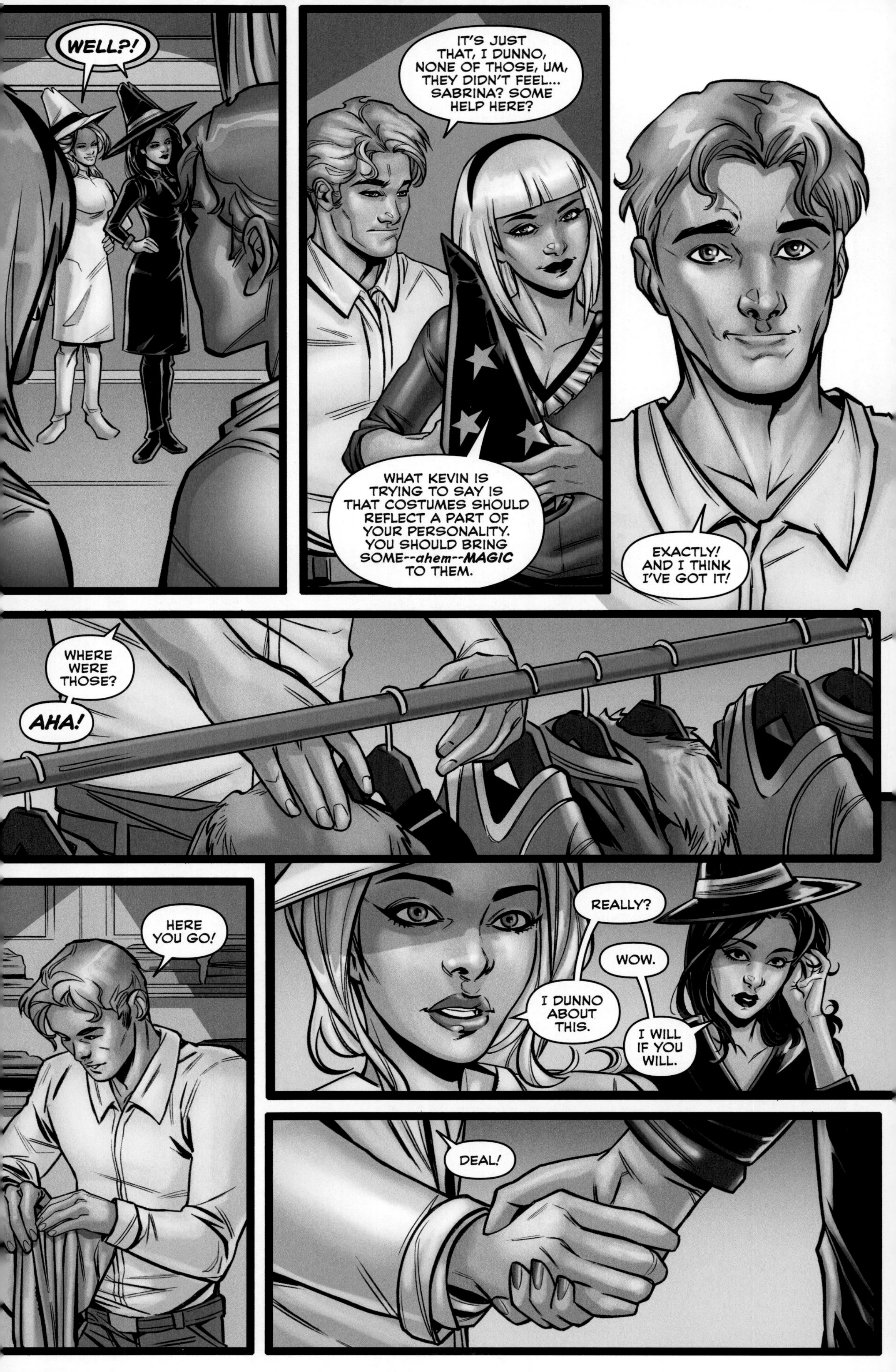
WELL?!
IT'S JUST THAT, I DUNNO, NONE OF THOSE, UM, THEY DIDN'T FEEL... SABRINA? SOME HELP HERE?
WHAT KEVIN IS TRYING TO SAY IS THAT COSTUMES SHOULD REFLECT A PART OF YOUR PERSONALITY. YOU SHOULD BRING SOME--*ahem*--*MAGIC* TO THEM.
EXACTLY! AND I THINK I'VE GOT IT!
WHERE WERE THOSE?
AHA!
HERE YOU GO!
REALLY?
I DUNNO ABOUT THIS.
WOW.
I WILL IF YOU WILL.
DEAL!

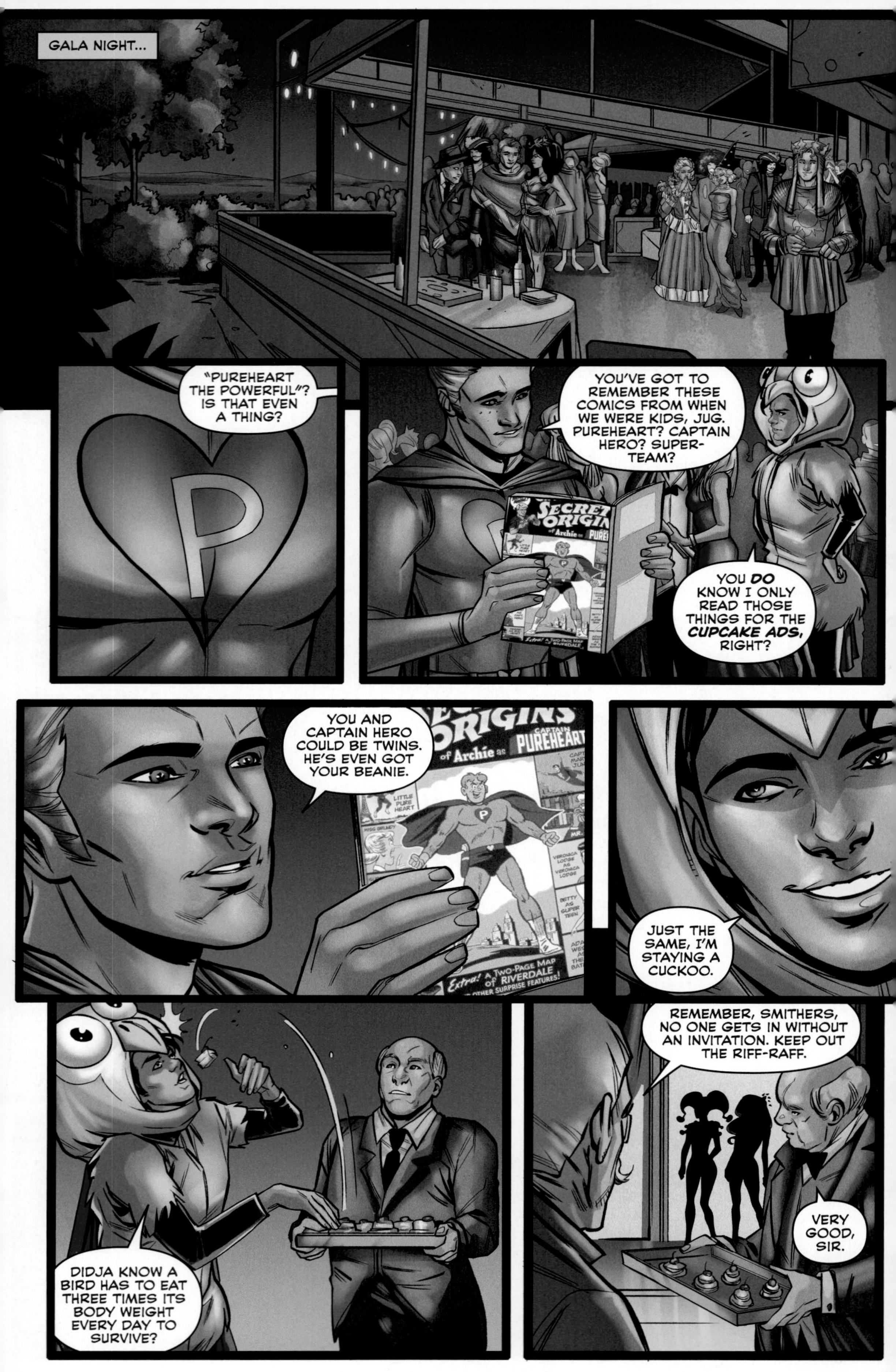
GALA NIGHT...
"PUREHEART THE POWERFUL"? IS THAT EVEN A THING?
YOU'VE GOT TO REMEMBER THESE COMICS FROM WHEN WE WERE KIDS, JUG. PUREHEART? CAPTAIN HERO? SUPER-TEAM?
YOU DO KNOW I ONLY READ THOSE THINGS FOR THE CUPCAKE ADS, RIGHT?
YOU AND CAPTAIN HERO COULD BE TWINS. HE'S EVEN GOT YOUR BEANIE.
ORIGINS of Archie as CAPTAIN PUREHEART
LITTLE PURE HEART
VERONICA LODGE AS VERONICA LODGE
BETTY AS SUPER TEEN
Extra! A TWO-PAGE MAP of RIVERDALE
OTHER SURPRISE FEATURES!
JUST THE SAME, I'M STAYING A CUCKOO.
DIDJA KNOW A BIRD HAS TO EAT THREE TIMES ITS BODY WEIGHT EVERY DAY TO SURVIVE?
REMEMBER, SMITHERS, NO ONE GETS IN WITHOUT AN INVITATION. KEEP OUT THE RIFF-RAFF.
VERY GOOD, SIR.

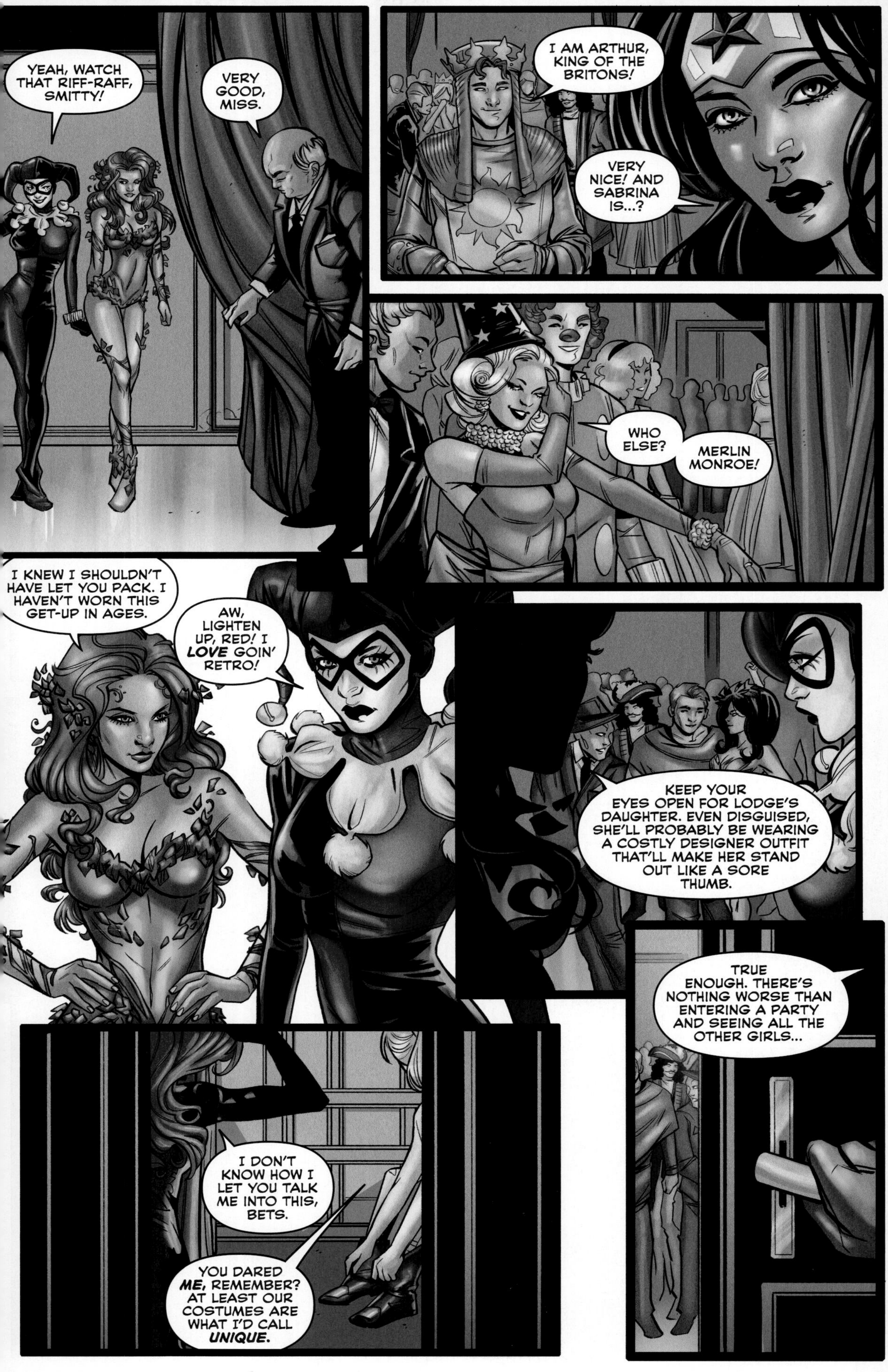
YEAH, WATCH THAT RIFF-RAFF, SMITTY!
VERY GOOD, MISS.
I AM ARTHUR, KING OF THE BRITONS!
VERY NICE! AND SABRINA IS...?
WHO ELSE?
MERLIN MONROE!
I KNEW I SHOULDN'T HAVE LET YOU PACK. I HAVEN'T WORN THIS GET-UP IN AGES.
AW, LIGHTEN UP, RED! I LOVE GOIN' RETRO!
KEEP YOUR EYES OPEN FOR LODGE'S DAUGHTER. EVEN DISGUISED, SHE'LL PROBABLY BE WEARING A COSTLY DESIGNER OUTFIT THAT'LL MAKE HER STAND OUT LIKE A SORE THUMB.
I DON'T KNOW HOW I LET YOU TALK ME INTO THIS, BETS.
YOU DARED ME, REMEMBER? AT LEAST OUR COSTUMES ARE WHAT I'D CALL UNIQUE.
TRUE ENOUGH. THERE'S NOTHING WORSE THAN ENTERING A PARTY AND SEEING ALL THE OTHER GIRLS...

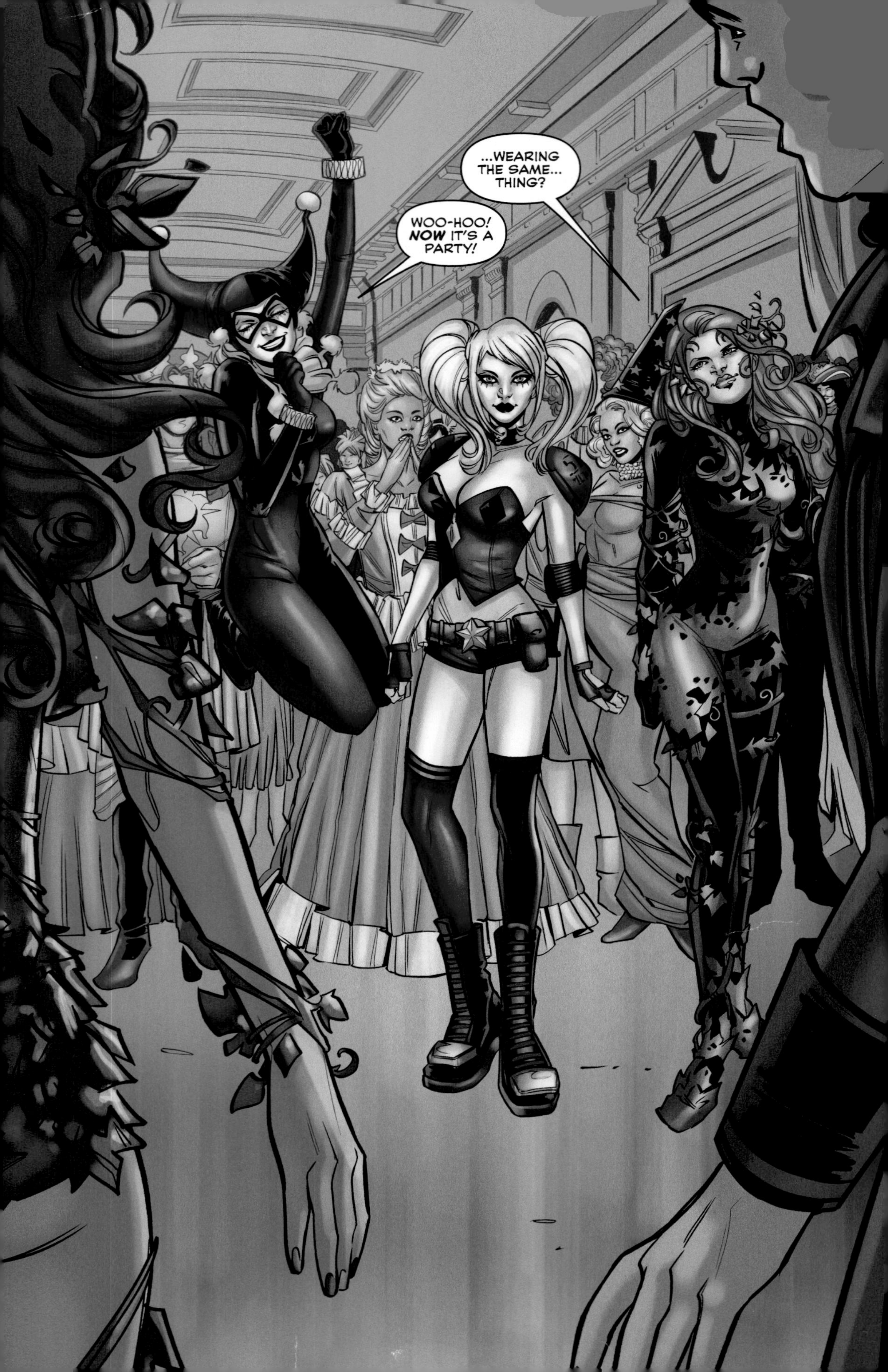
...WEARING THE SAME... THING?
WOO-HOO! **NOW** IT'S A PARTY!

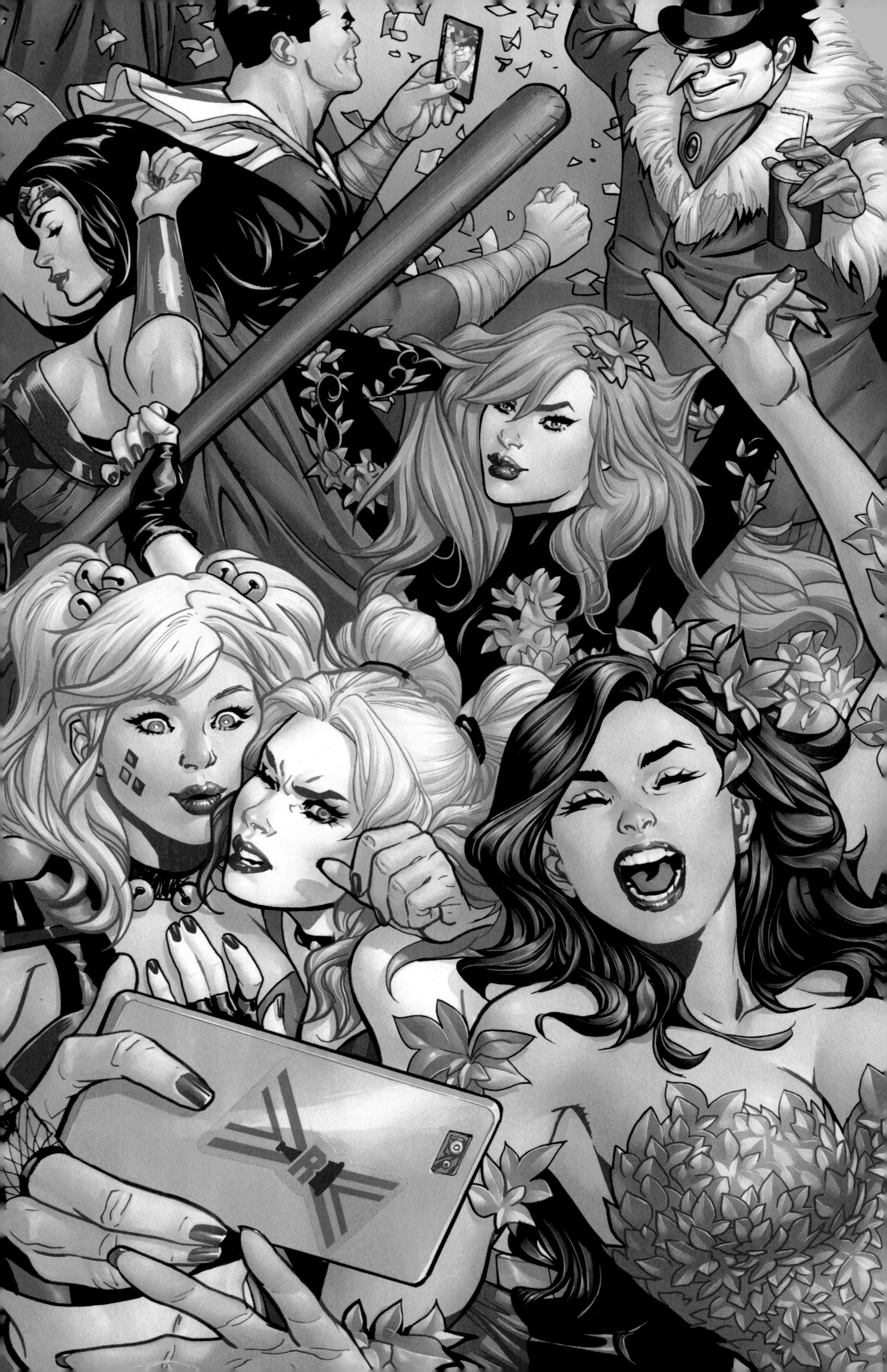

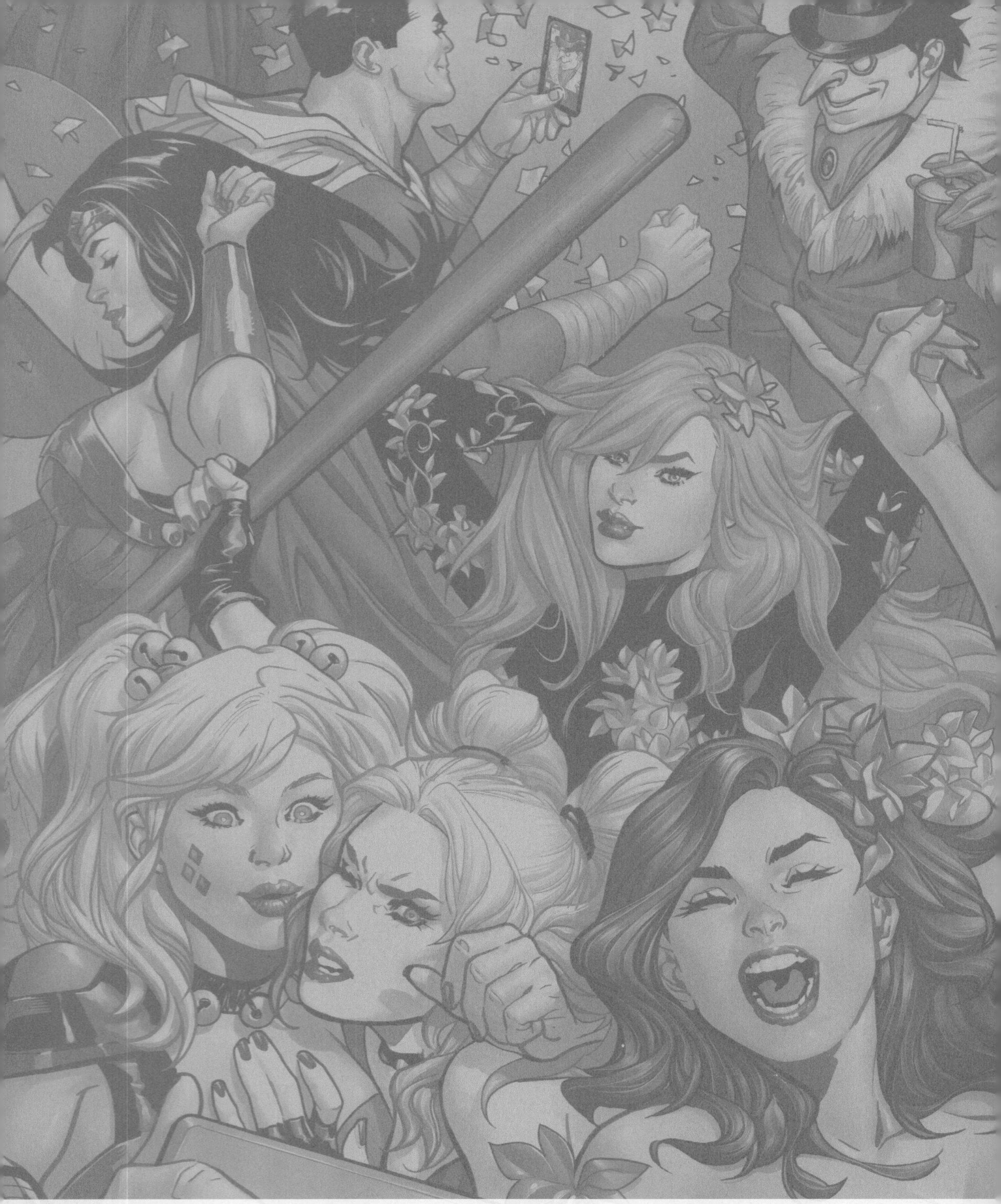

Written by MARC ANDREYKO and PAUL DINI
Drawn by LAURA BRAGA
Colored by ARIF PRIANTO with J. NANJAN
Lettered by DERON BENNETT
Cover by EMANUELA LUPACCHINO with TOMEU MOREY

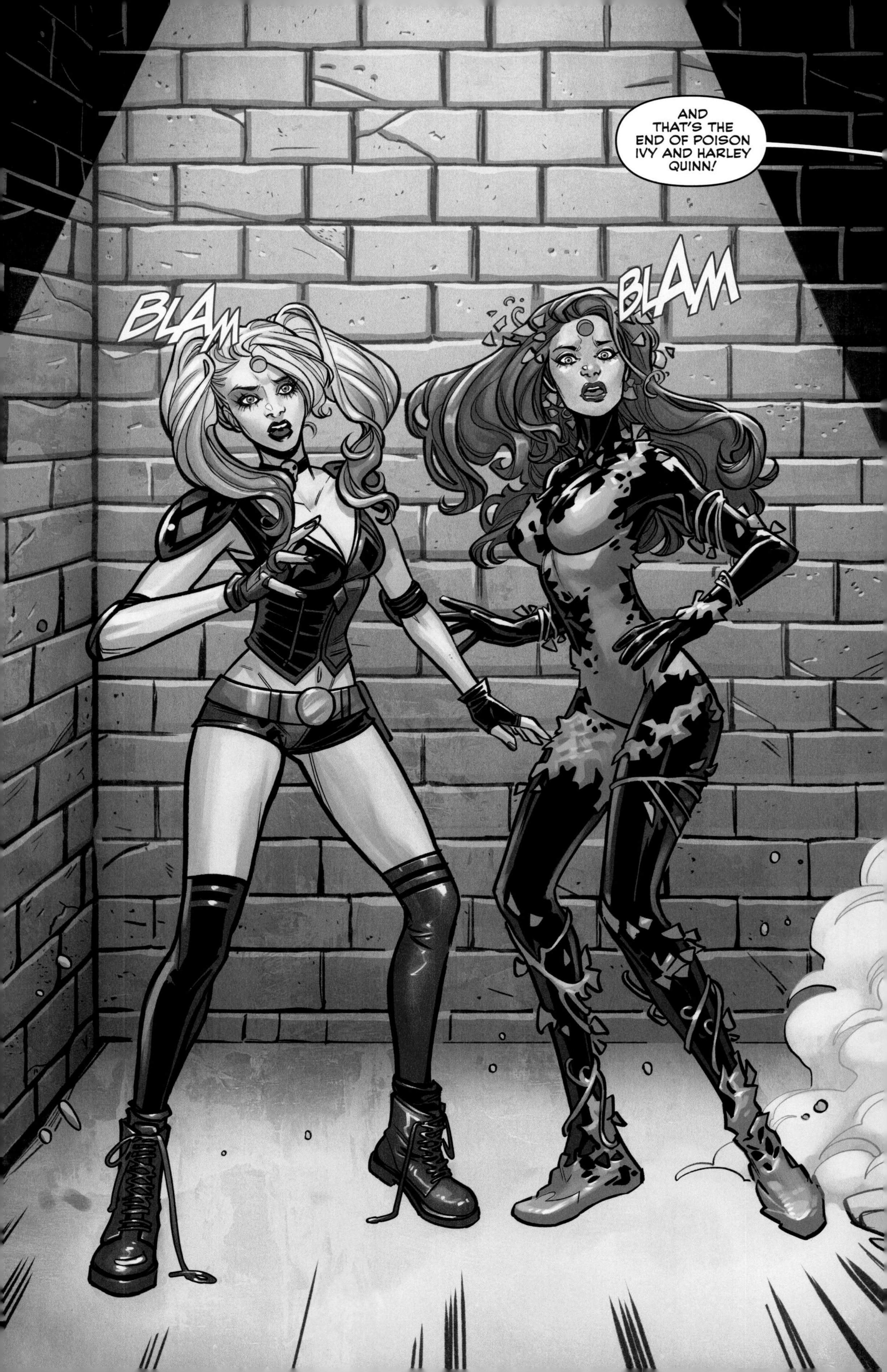
BLAM
BLAM
AND THAT'S THE END OF POISON IVY AND HARLEY QUINN!

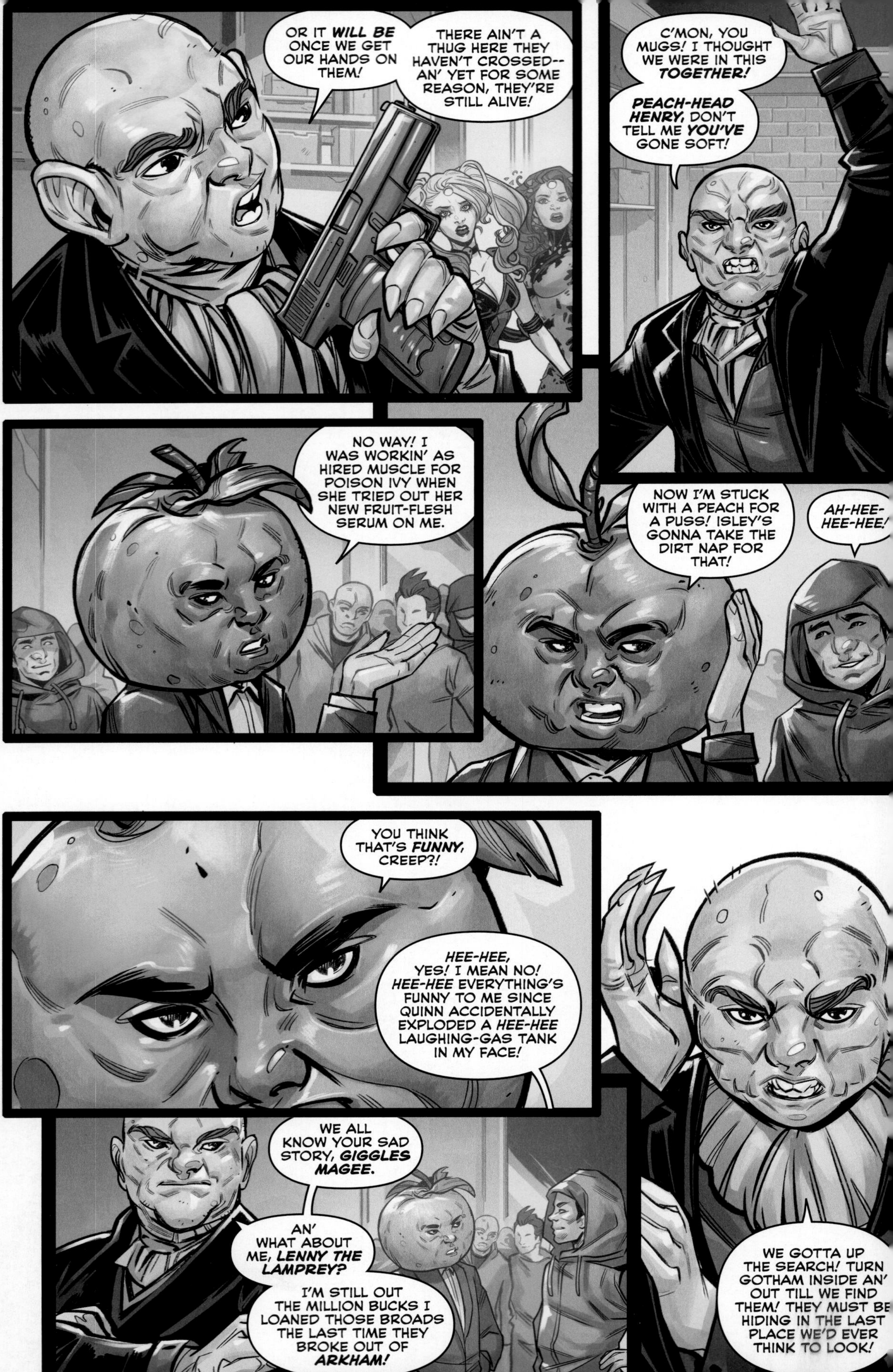
OR IT WILL BE ONCE WE GET OUR HANDS ON THEM!
THERE AIN'T A THUG HERE THEY HAVEN'T CROSSED-- AN' YET FOR SOME REASON, THEY'RE STILL ALIVE!
C'MON, YOU MUGS! I THOUGHT WE WERE IN THIS TOGETHER!
PEACH-HEAD HENRY, DON'T TELL ME YOU'VE GONE SOFT!
NO WAY! I WAS WORKIN' AS HIRED MUSCLE FOR POISON IVY WHEN SHE TRIED OUT HER NEW FRUIT-FLESH SERUM ON ME.
NOW I'M STUCK WITH A PEACH FOR A PUSS! ISLEY'S GONNA TAKE THE DIRT NAP FOR THAT!
AH-HEE-HEE-HEE!
YOU THINK THAT'S FUNNY, CREEP?!
HEE-HEE, YES! I MEAN NO! HEE-HEE EVERYTHING'S FUNNY TO ME SINCE QUINN ACCIDENTALLY EXPLODED A HEE-HEE LAUGHING-GAS TANK IN MY FACE!
WE ALL KNOW YOUR SAD STORY, GIGGLES MAGEE.
AN' WHAT ABOUT ME, LENNY THE LAMPREY?
I'M STILL OUT THE MILLION BUCKS I LOANED THOSE BROADS THE LAST TIME THEY BROKE OUT OF ARKHAM!
WE GOTTA UP THE SEARCH! TURN GOTHAM INSIDE AN' OUT TILL WE FIND THEM! THEY MUST BE HIDING IN THE LAST PLACE WE'D EVER THINK TO LOOK!

RIVERDALE.

CLASSIC VERSUS NEW. AWK. WARD.

TEN BUCKS ON LODGE THROWING THE FIRST PUNCH.

YOU'RE ON.

uh-oh.

≥SNORT!≤ PRICELESS!

IVY! LOOKIT THAT! THEY'RE DRESSED AS US! WHATTAYA KNOW? WE'VE ARRIVED!!

Ixnay on the us-ay!

EXCUSE ME, THIS IS MY FATHER'S PARTY AND WE CANNOT HAVE REPEAT CHARACTERS. ESPECIALLY "OLD" VERSIONS. IT IS JUST TOO GAUCHE.

WHAT MISS LODGE MEANS IS SHE SIMPLY CANNOT HAVE A GOOD TIME AT THIS GALA WITHOUT COMPLIMENTING YOUR AMAZING ENSEMBLES.

THAT IS NOT--

EXCUSE US, BUT MISS LODGE HAS SOME HOSTESSING OBLIGATIONS.

WAIT! SMITHERS!

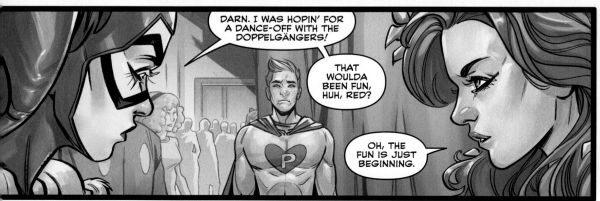

DARN. I WAS HOPIN' FOR A DANCE-OFF WITH THE DOPPELGÄNGERS!

THAT WOULDA BEEN FUN, HUH, RED?

OH, THE FUN IS JUST BEGINNING.

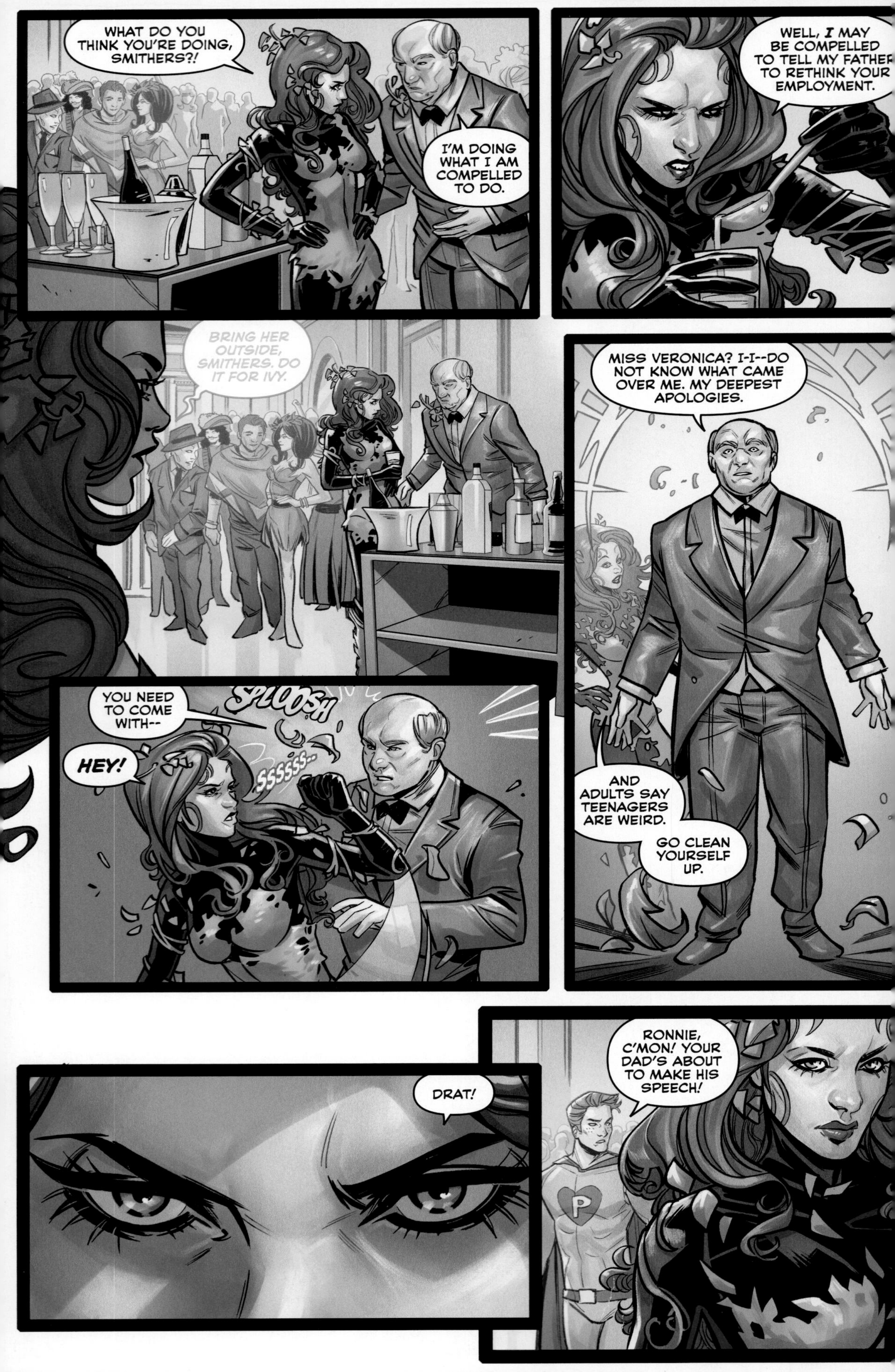
WHAT DO YOU THINK YOU'RE DOING, SMITHERS?!
I'M DOING WHAT I AM COMPELLED TO DO.
WELL, I MAY BE COMPELLED TO TELL MY FATHER TO RETHINK YOUR EMPLOYMENT.
BRING HER OUTSIDE, SMITHERS. DO IT FOR IVY.
YOU NEED TO COME WITH--
HEY!
SPLOOSH
SSSSSS...
MISS VERONICA? I-I--DO NOT KNOW WHAT CAME OVER ME. MY DEEPEST APOLOGIES.
AND ADULTS SAY TEENAGERS ARE WEIRD.
GO CLEAN YOURSELF UP.
DRAT!
RONNIE, C'MON! YOUR DAD'S ABOUT TO MAKE HIS SPEECH!

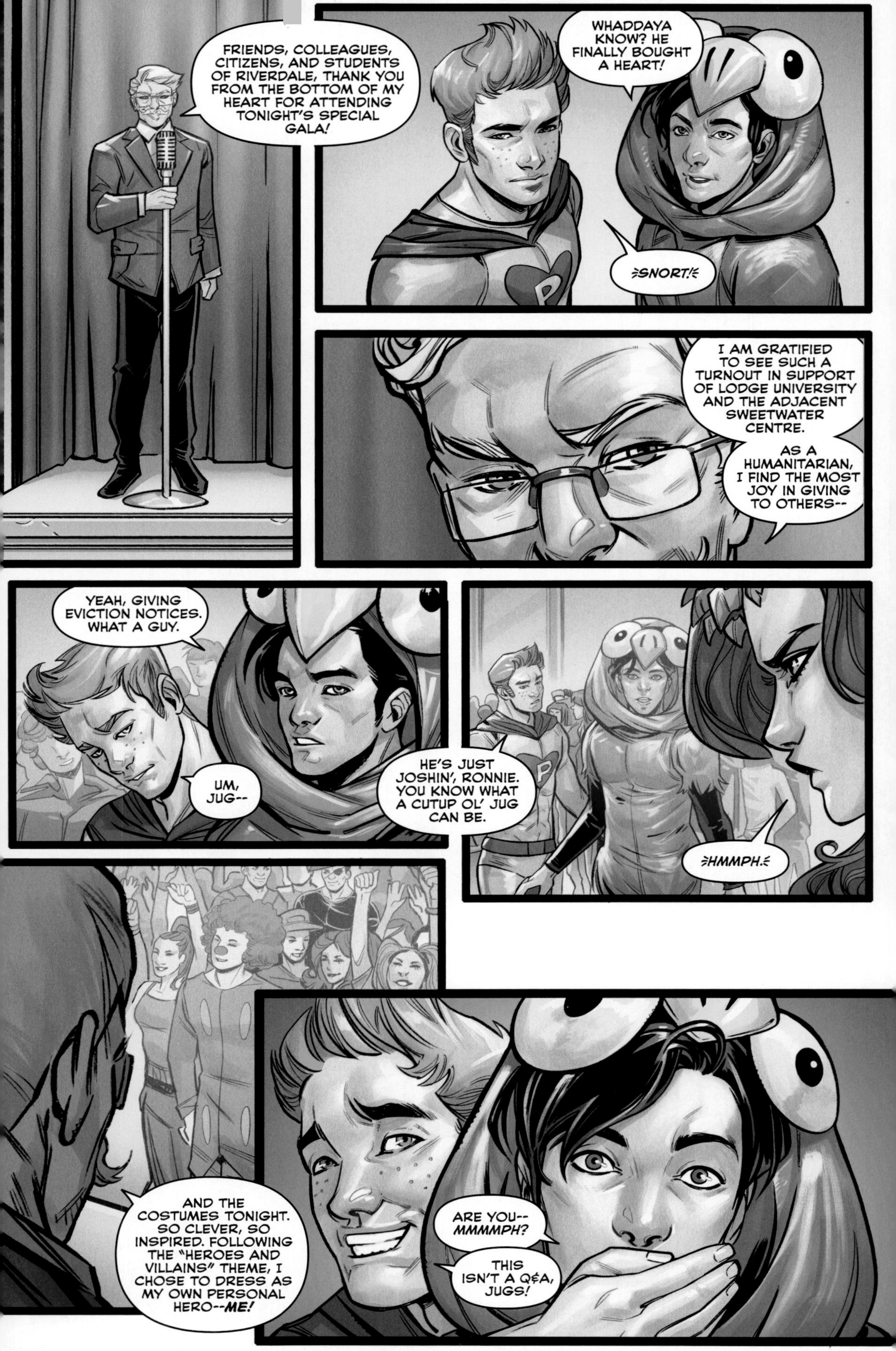
FRIENDS, COLLEAGUES, CITIZENS, AND STUDENTS OF RIVERDALE, THANK YOU FROM THE BOTTOM OF MY HEART FOR ATTENDING TONIGHT'S SPECIAL GALA!
WHADDAYA KNOW? HE FINALLY BOUGHT A HEART!
SNORT!
I AM GRATIFIED TO SEE SUCH A TURNOUT IN SUPPORT OF LODGE UNIVERSITY AND THE ADJACENT SWEETWATER CENTRE.
AS A HUMANITARIAN, I FIND THE MOST JOY IN GIVING TO OTHERS--
YEAH, GIVING EVICTION NOTICES. WHAT A GUY.
UM, JUG--
HE'S JUST JOSHIN', RONNIE. YOU KNOW WHAT A CUTUP OL' JUG CAN BE.
HMMPH.
AND THE COSTUMES TONIGHT. SO CLEVER, SO INSPIRED. FOLLOWING THE "HEROES AND VILLAINS" THEME, I CHOSE TO DRESS AS MY OWN PERSONAL HERO--ME!
ARE YOU-- MMMMPH?
THIS ISN'T A Q&A, JUGS!

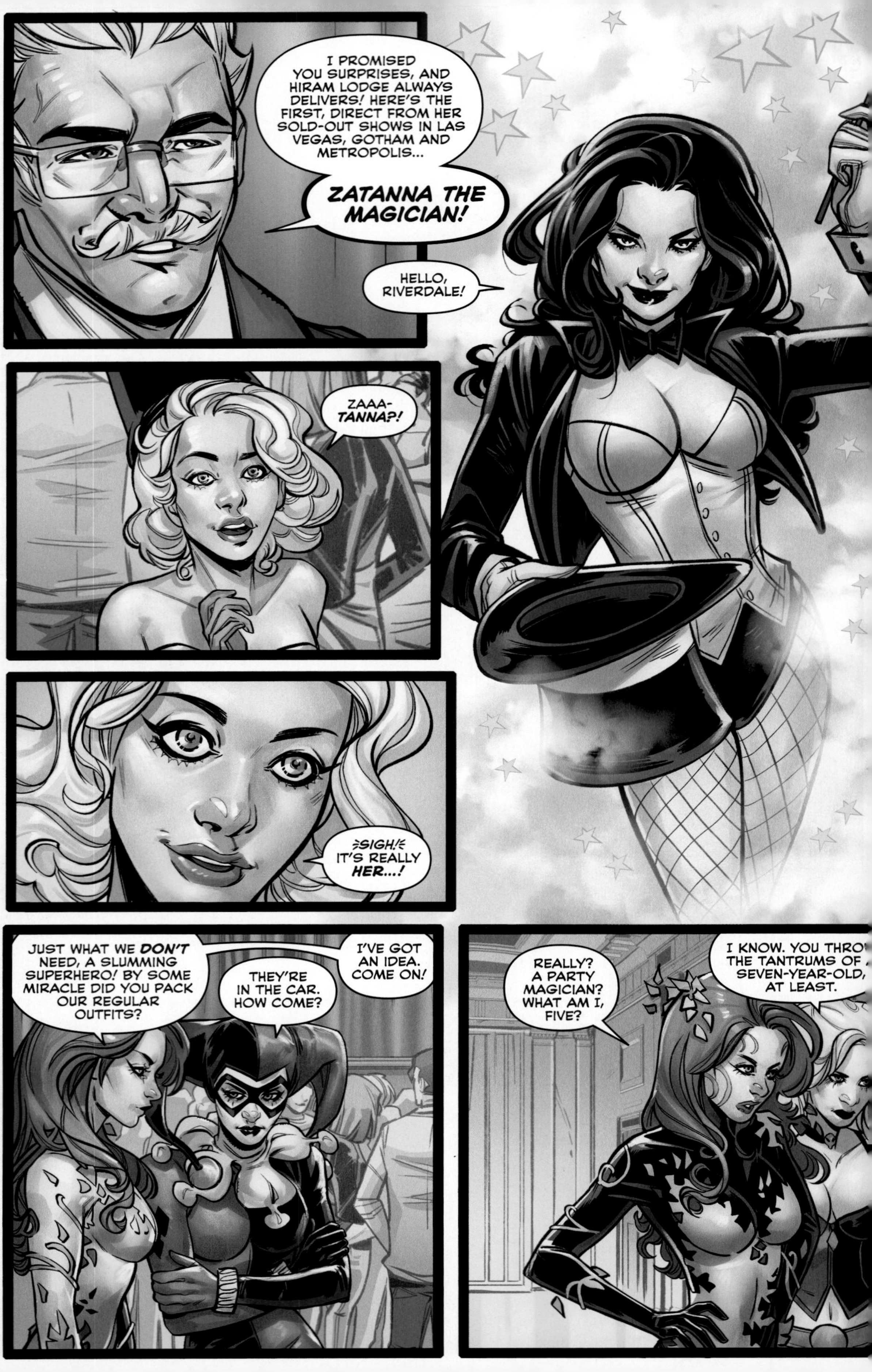
I PROMISED YOU SURPRISES, AND HIRAM LODGE ALWAYS DELIVERS! HERE'S THE FIRST, DIRECT FROM HER SOLD-OUT SHOWS IN LAS VEGAS, GOTHAM AND METROPOLIS...
ZATANNA THE MAGICIAN!
HELLO, RIVERDALE!
ZAAA-TANNA?!
SIGH! IT'S REALLY HER...!
JUST WHAT WE DON'T NEED, A SLUMMING SUPERHERO! BY SOME MIRACLE DID YOU PACK OUR REGULAR OUTFITS?
THEY'RE IN THE CAR. HOW COME?
I'VE GOT AN IDEA. COME ON!
REALLY? A PARTY MAGICIAN? WHAT AM I, FIVE?
I KNOW. YOU THROW THE TANTRUMS OF A SEVEN-YEAR-OLD, AT LEAST.

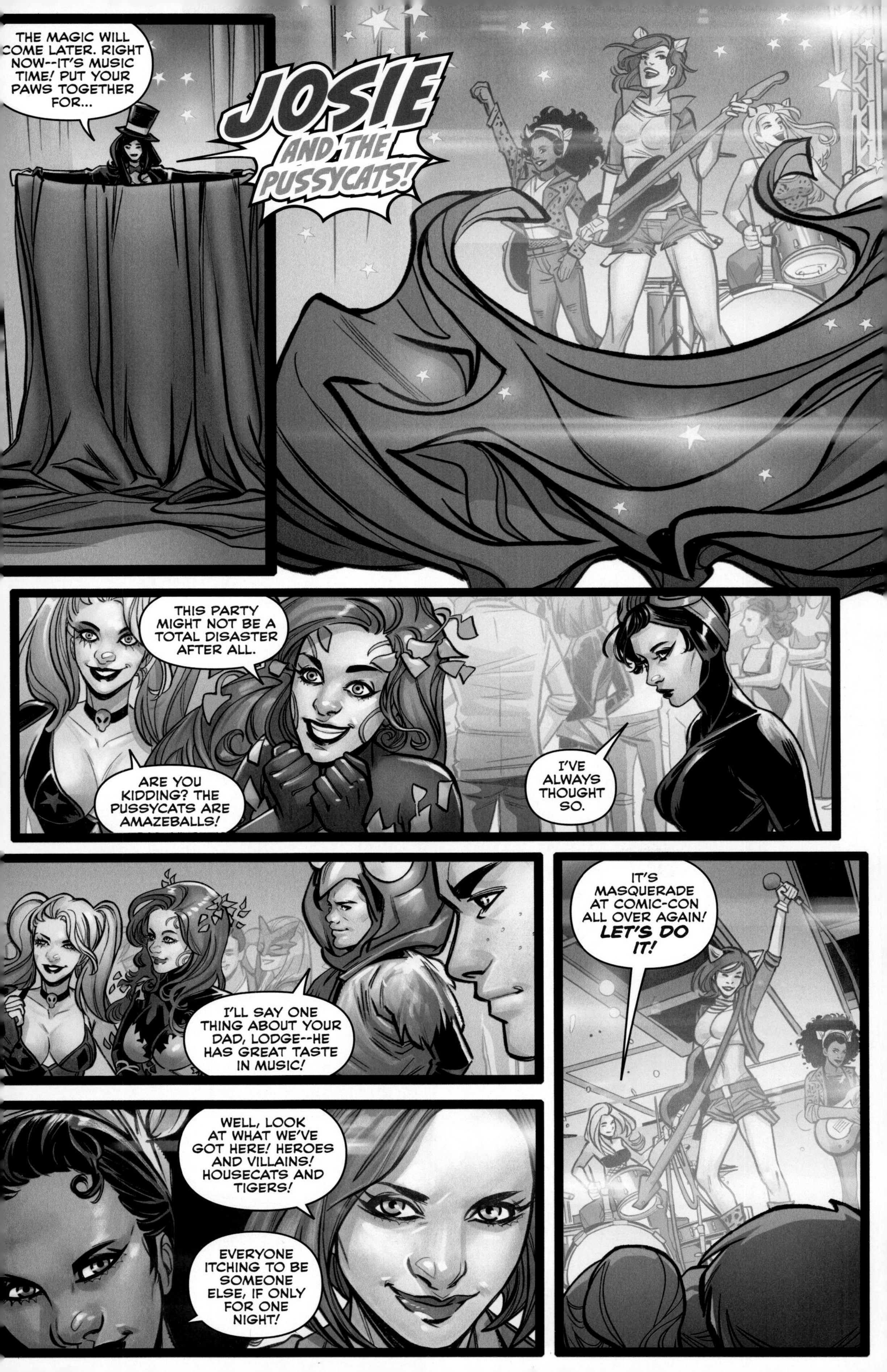
THE MAGIC WILL COME LATER. RIGHT NOW--IT'S MUSIC TIME! PUT YOUR PAWS TOGETHER FOR...
JOSIE AND THE PUSSYCATS!
THIS PARTY MIGHT NOT BE A TOTAL DISASTER AFTER ALL.
ARE YOU KIDDING? THE PUSSYCATS ARE AMAZEBALLS!
I'VE ALWAYS THOUGHT SO.
I'LL SAY ONE THING ABOUT YOUR DAD, LODGE--HE HAS GREAT TASTE IN MUSIC!
IT'S MASQUERADE AT COMIC-CON ALL OVER AGAIN! LET'S DO IT!
WELL, LOOK AT WHAT WE'VE GOT HERE! HEROES AND VILLAINS! HOUSECATS AND TIGERS!
EVERYONE ITCHING TO BE SOMEONE ELSE, IF ONLY FOR ONE NIGHT!

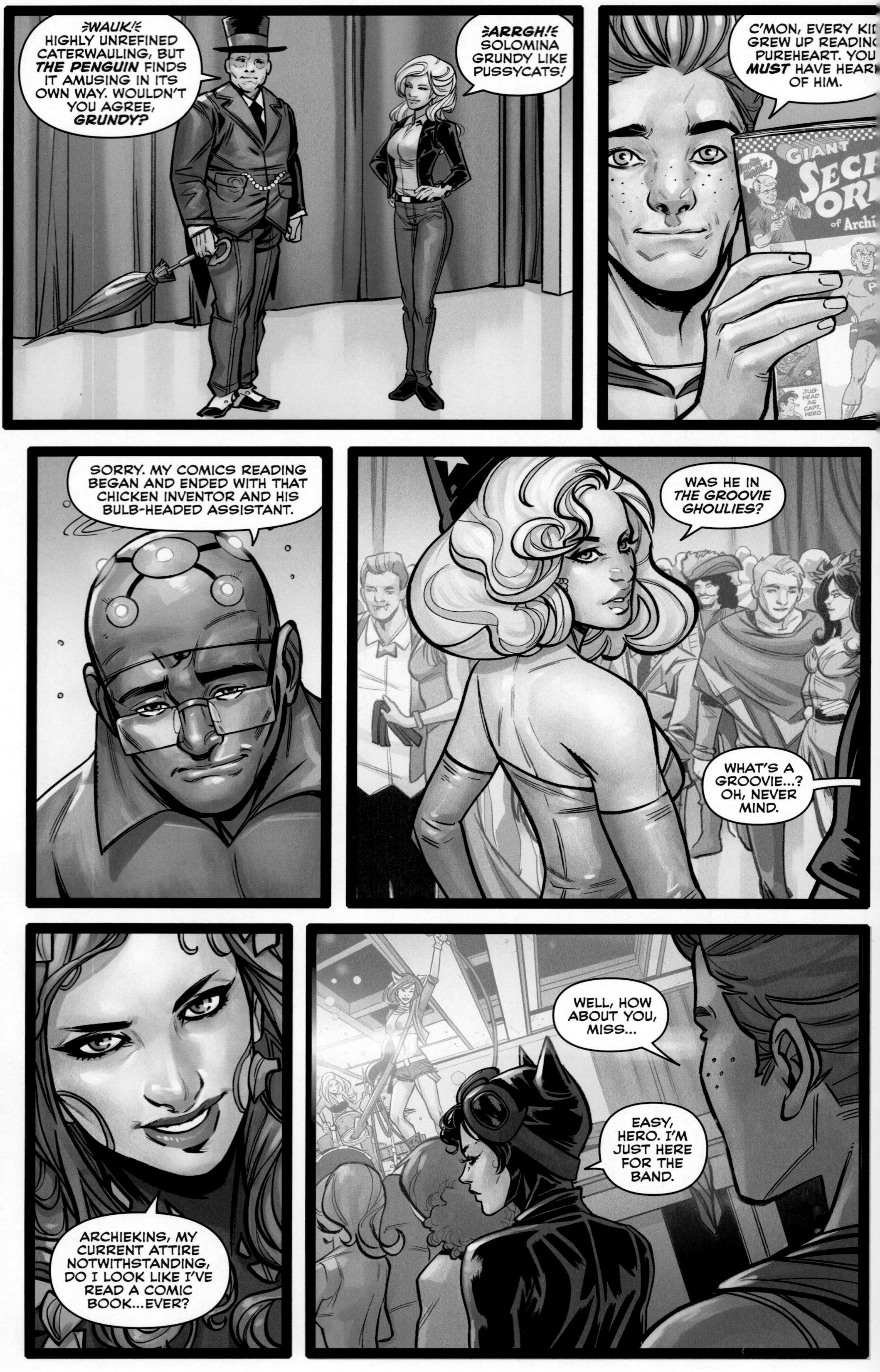

WAUK! HIGHLY UNREFINED CATERWAULING, BUT ***THE PENGUIN*** FINDS IT AMUSING IN ITS OWN WAY. WOULDN'T YOU AGREE, ***GRUNDY?***
ARRGH! SOLOMINA GRUNDY LIKE PUSSYCATS!
C'MON, EVERY KI GREW UP READIN PUREHEART. YOU ***MUST*** HAVE HEAR OF HIM.
GIANT
JUG HEAD AS CAPT. HERO
SORRY. MY COMICS READING BEGAN AND ENDED WITH THAT CHICKEN INVENTOR AND HIS BULB-HEADED ASSISTANT.
WAS HE IN *THE GROOVIE GHOULIES?*
WHAT'S A GROOVIE...? OH, NEVER MIND.
ARCHIEKINS, MY CURRENT ATTIRE NOTWITHSTANDING, DO I LOOK LIKE I'VE READ A COMIC BOOK...EVER?
WELL, HOW ABOUT YOU, MISS...
EASY, HERO. I'M JUST HERE FOR THE BAND.

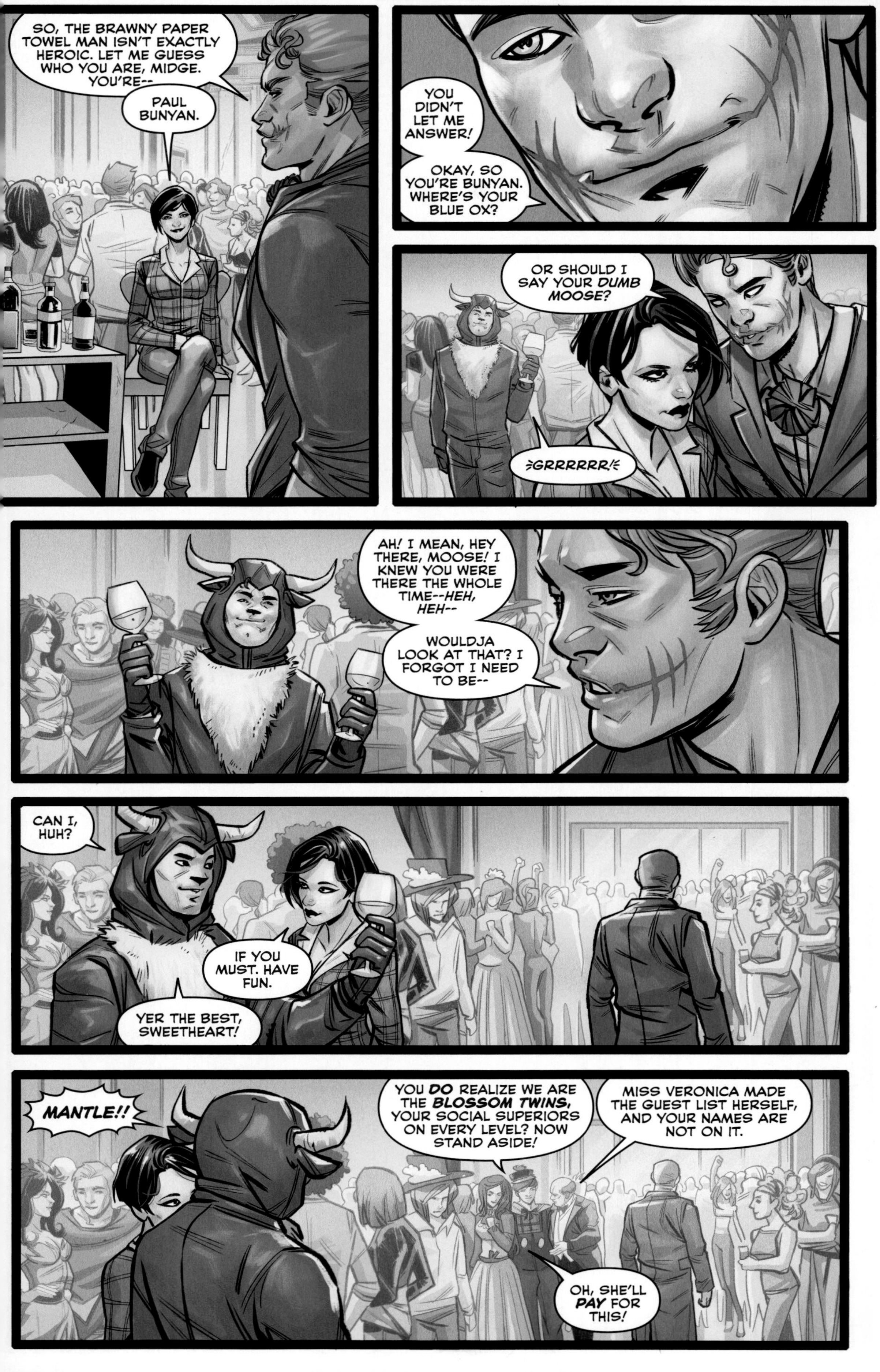
SO, THE BRAWNY PAPER TOWEL MAN ISN'T EXACTLY HEROIC. LET ME GUESS WHO YOU ARE, MIDGE. YOU'RE--
PAUL BUNYAN.
YOU DIDN'T LET ME ANSWER!
OKAY, SO YOU'RE BUNYAN. WHERE'S YOUR BLUE OX?
OR SHOULD I SAY YOUR *DUMB MOOSE*?
GRRRRRR!
AH! I MEAN, HEY THERE, MOOSE! I KNEW YOU WERE THERE THE WHOLE TIME--*HEH, HEH*--
WOULDJA LOOK AT THAT? I FORGOT I NEED TO BE--
CAN I, HUH?
IF YOU MUST. HAVE FUN.
YER THE BEST, SWEETHEART!
MANTLE!!
YOU **DO** REALIZE WE ARE THE ***BLOSSOM TWINS***, YOUR SOCIAL SUPERIORS ON EVERY LEVEL? NOW STAND ASIDE!
MISS VERONICA MADE THE GUEST LIST HERSELF, AND YOUR NAMES ARE NOT ON IT.
OH, SHE'LL **PAY** FOR THIS!

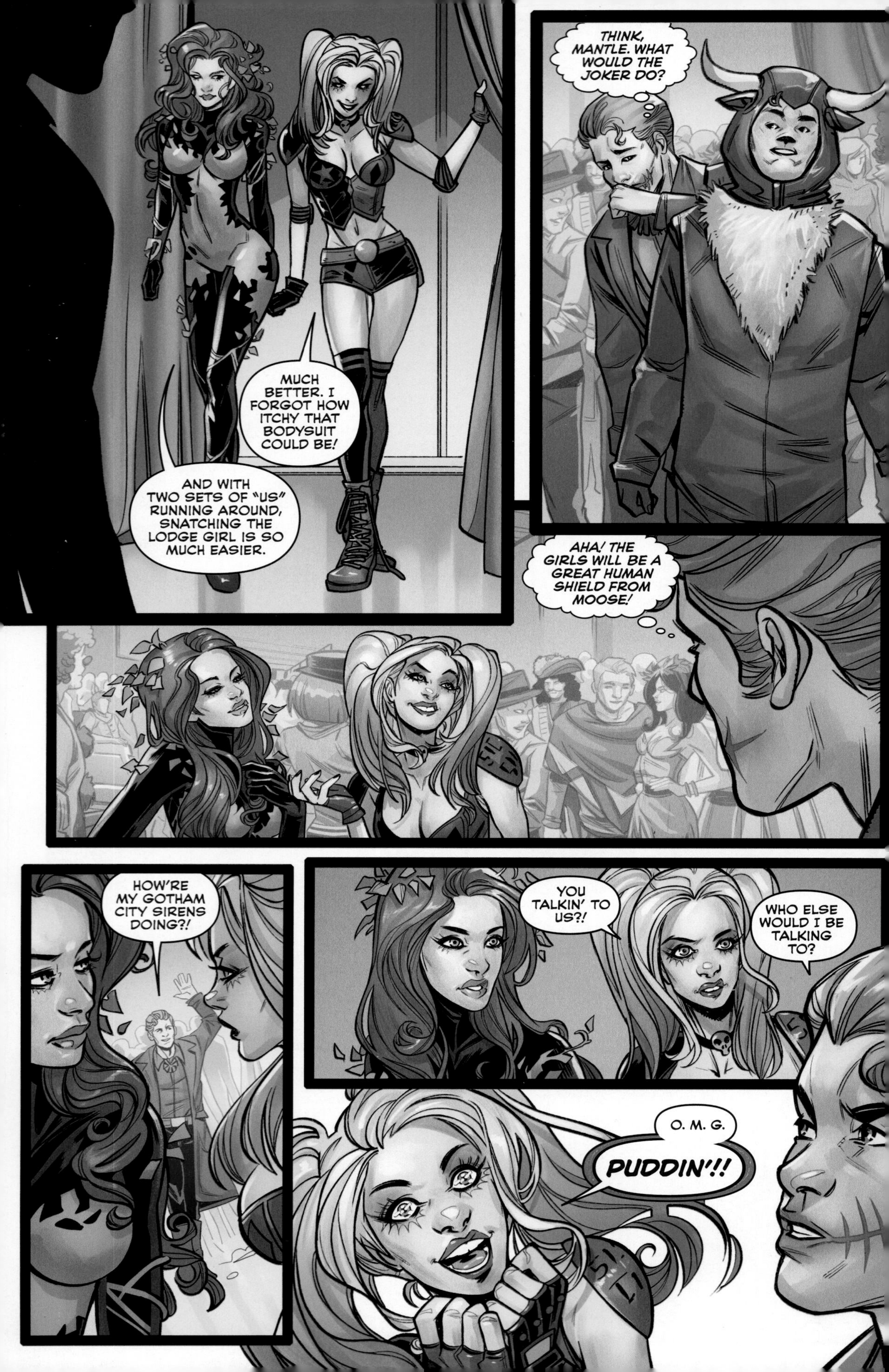
MUCH BETTER. I FORGOT HOW ITCHY THAT BODYSUIT COULD BE!
AND WITH TWO SETS OF "US" RUNNING AROUND, SNATCHING THE LODGE GIRL IS SO MUCH EASIER.
THINK, MANTLE. WHAT WOULD THE JOKER DO?
AHA! THE GIRLS WILL BE A GREAT HUMAN SHIELD FROM MOOSE!
HOW'RE MY GOTHAM CITY SIRENS DOING?!
YOU TALKIN' TO US?!
WHO ELSE WOULD I BE TALKING TO?
O. M. G.
PUDDIN'!!

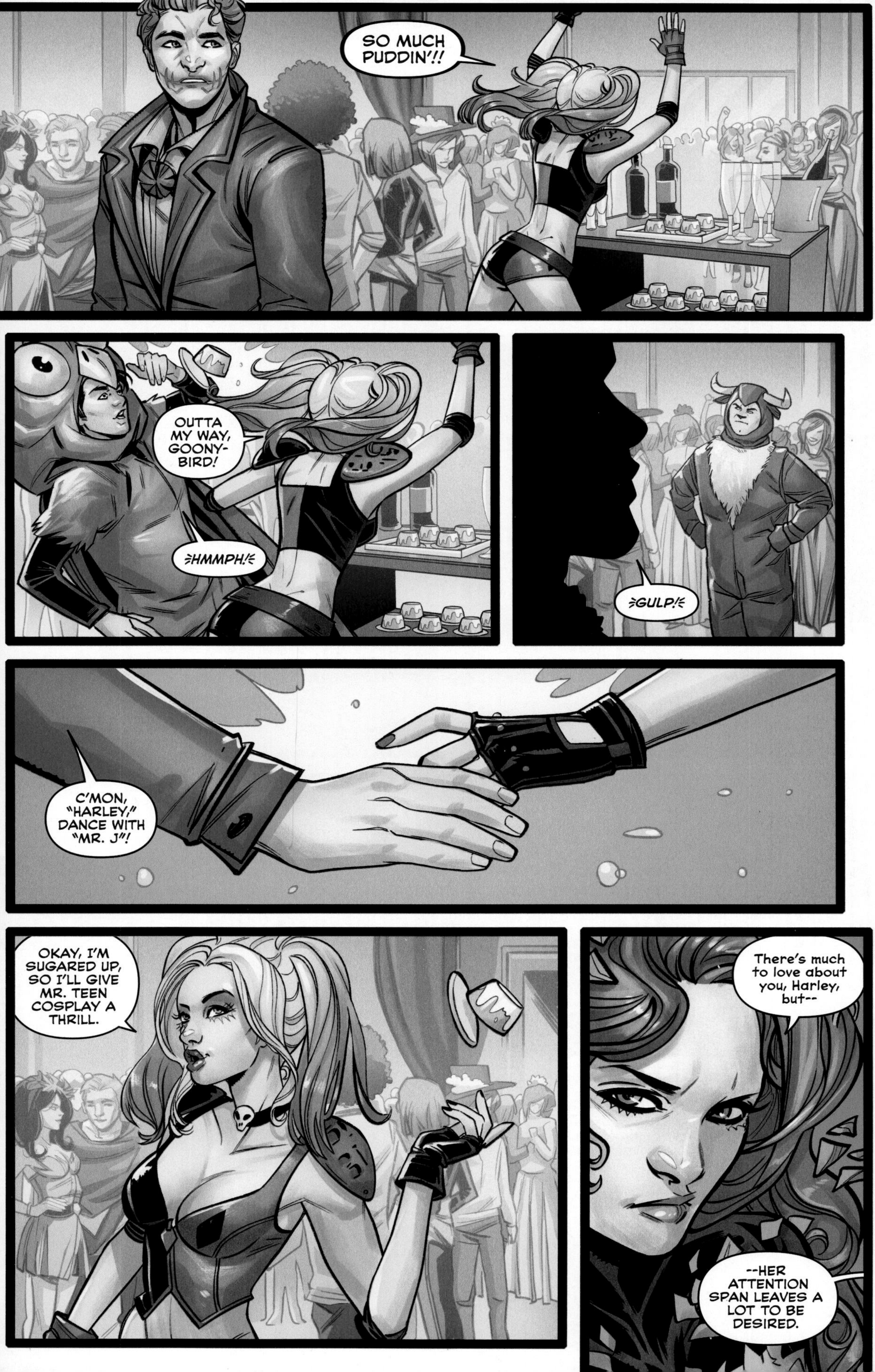
SO MUCH PUDDIN'!!
OUTTA MY WAY, GOONY-BIRD!
HMMPH!
GULP!
C'MON, "HARLEY," DANCE WITH "MR. J"!
OKAY, I'M SUGARED UP, SO I'LL GIVE MR. TEEN COSPLAY A THRILL.
There's much to love about you, Harley, but--
--HER ATTENTION SPAN LEAVES A LOT TO BE DESIRED.

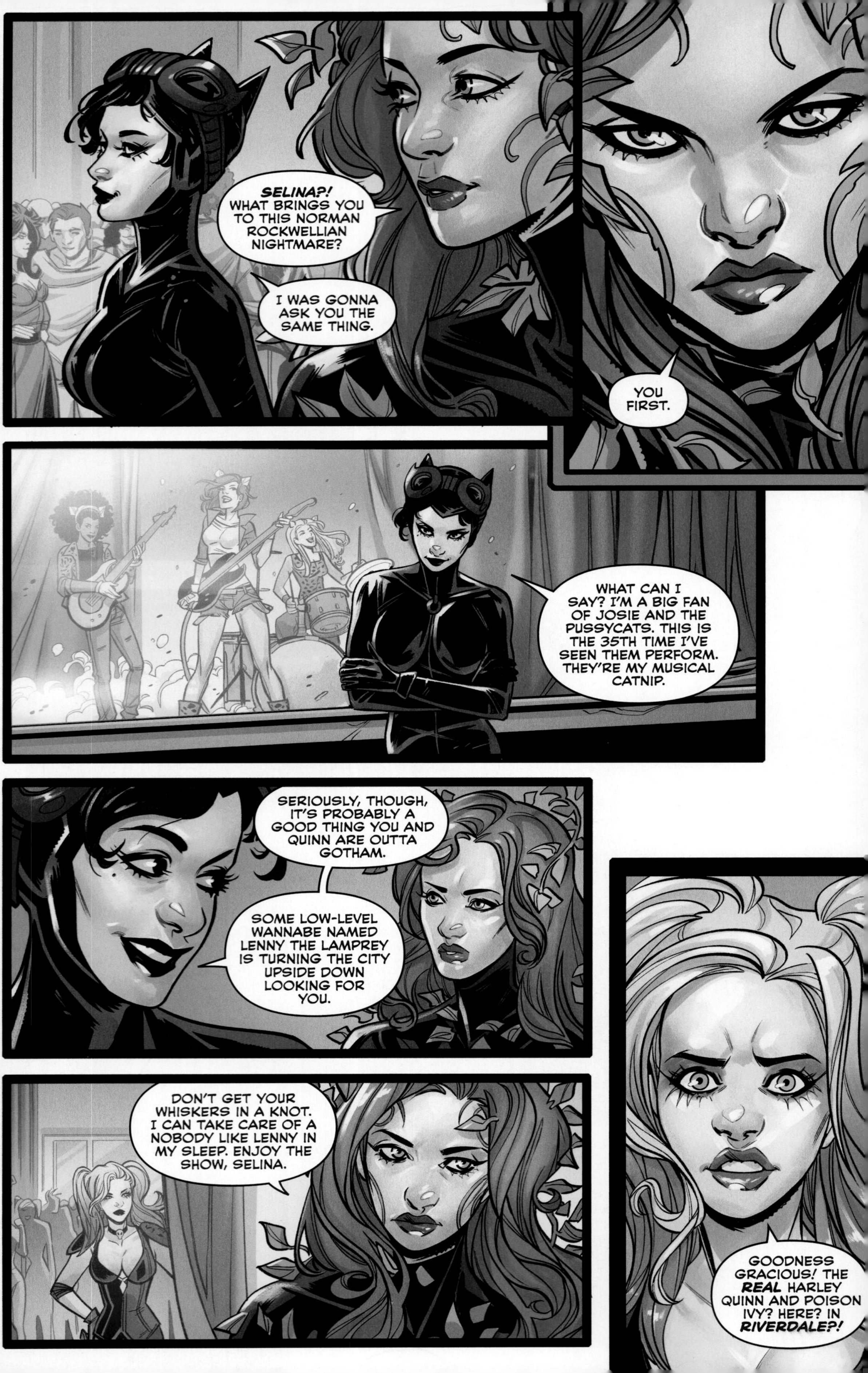
SELINA?! WHAT BRINGS YOU TO THIS NORMAN ROCKWELLIAN NIGHTMARE?
I WAS GONNA ASK YOU THE SAME THING.
YOU FIRST.
WHAT CAN I SAY? I'M A BIG FAN OF JOSIE AND THE PUSSYCATS. THIS IS THE 35TH TIME I'VE SEEN THEM PERFORM. THEY'RE MY MUSICAL CATNIP.
SERIOUSLY, THOUGH, IT'S PROBABLY A GOOD THING YOU AND QUINN ARE OUTTA GOTHAM.
SOME LOW-LEVEL WANNABE NAMED LENNY THE LAMPREY IS TURNING THE CITY UPSIDE DOWN LOOKING FOR YOU.
DON'T GET YOUR WHISKERS IN A KNOT. I CAN TAKE CARE OF A NOBODY LIKE LENNY IN MY SLEEP. ENJOY THE SHOW, SELINA.
GOODNESS GRACIOUS! THE REAL HARLEY QUINN AND POISON IVY? HERE? IN RIVERDALE?!

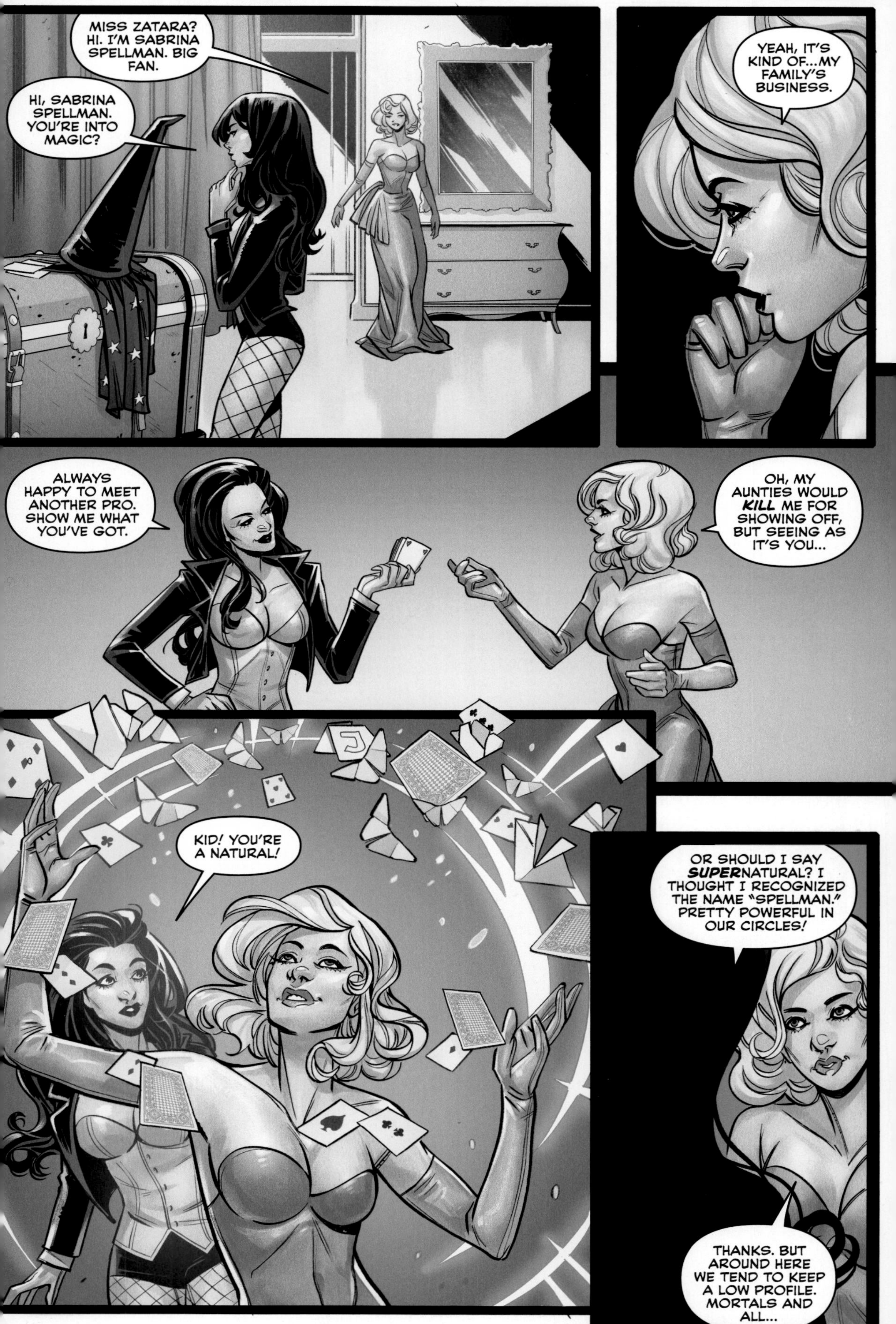
MISS ZATARA? HI. I'M SABRINA SPELLMAN. BIG FAN.
HI, SABRINA SPELLMAN. YOU'RE INTO MAGIC?
YEAH, IT'S KIND OF...MY FAMILY'S BUSINESS.
ALWAYS HAPPY TO MEET ANOTHER PRO. SHOW ME WHAT YOU'VE GOT.
OH, MY AUNTIES WOULD *KILL* ME FOR SHOWING OFF, BUT SEEING AS IT'S YOU...
KID! YOU'RE A NATURAL!
OR SHOULD I SAY *SUPER*NATURAL? I THOUGHT I RECOGNIZED THE NAME "SPELLMAN." PRETTY POWERFUL IN OUR CIRCLES!
THANKS. BUT AROUND HERE WE TEND TO KEEP A LOW PROFILE. MORTALS AND ALL...

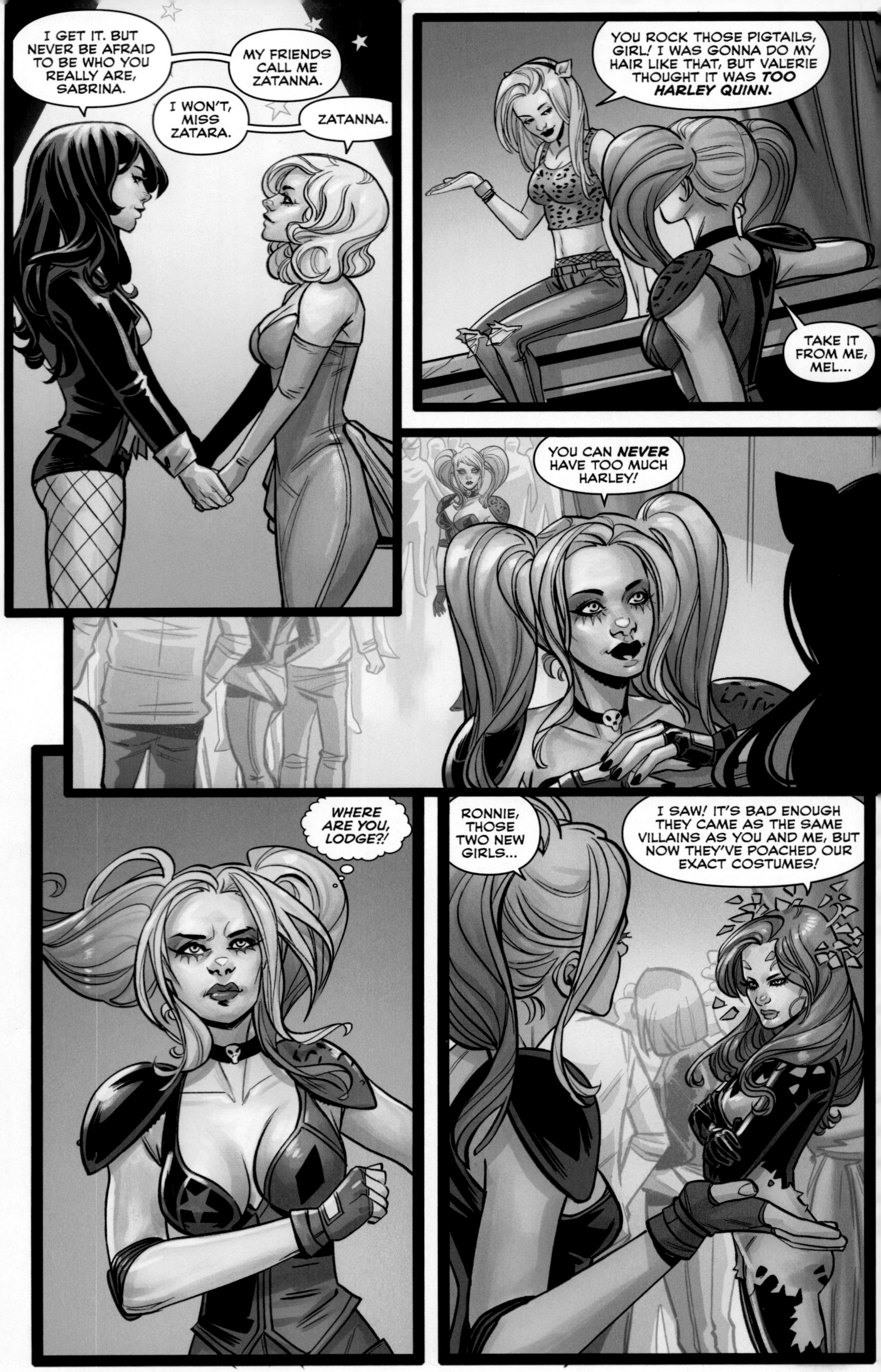
I GET IT. BUT NEVER BE AFRAID TO BE WHO YOU REALLY ARE, SABRINA.
MY FRIENDS CALL ME ZATANNA.
I WON'T, MISS ZATARA.
ZATANNA.
YOU ROCK THOSE PIGTAILS, GIRL! I WAS GONNA DO MY HAIR LIKE THAT, BUT VALERIE THOUGHT IT WAS *TOO HARLEY QUINN.*
TAKE IT FROM ME, MEL...
YOU CAN *NEVER* HAVE TOO MUCH HARLEY!
WHERE ARE YOU, LODGE?!
RONNIE, THOSE TWO NEW GIRLS...
I SAW! IT'S BAD ENOUGH THEY CAME AS THE SAME VILLAINS AS YOU AND ME, BUT NOW THEY'VE POACHED OUR EXACT COSTUMES!

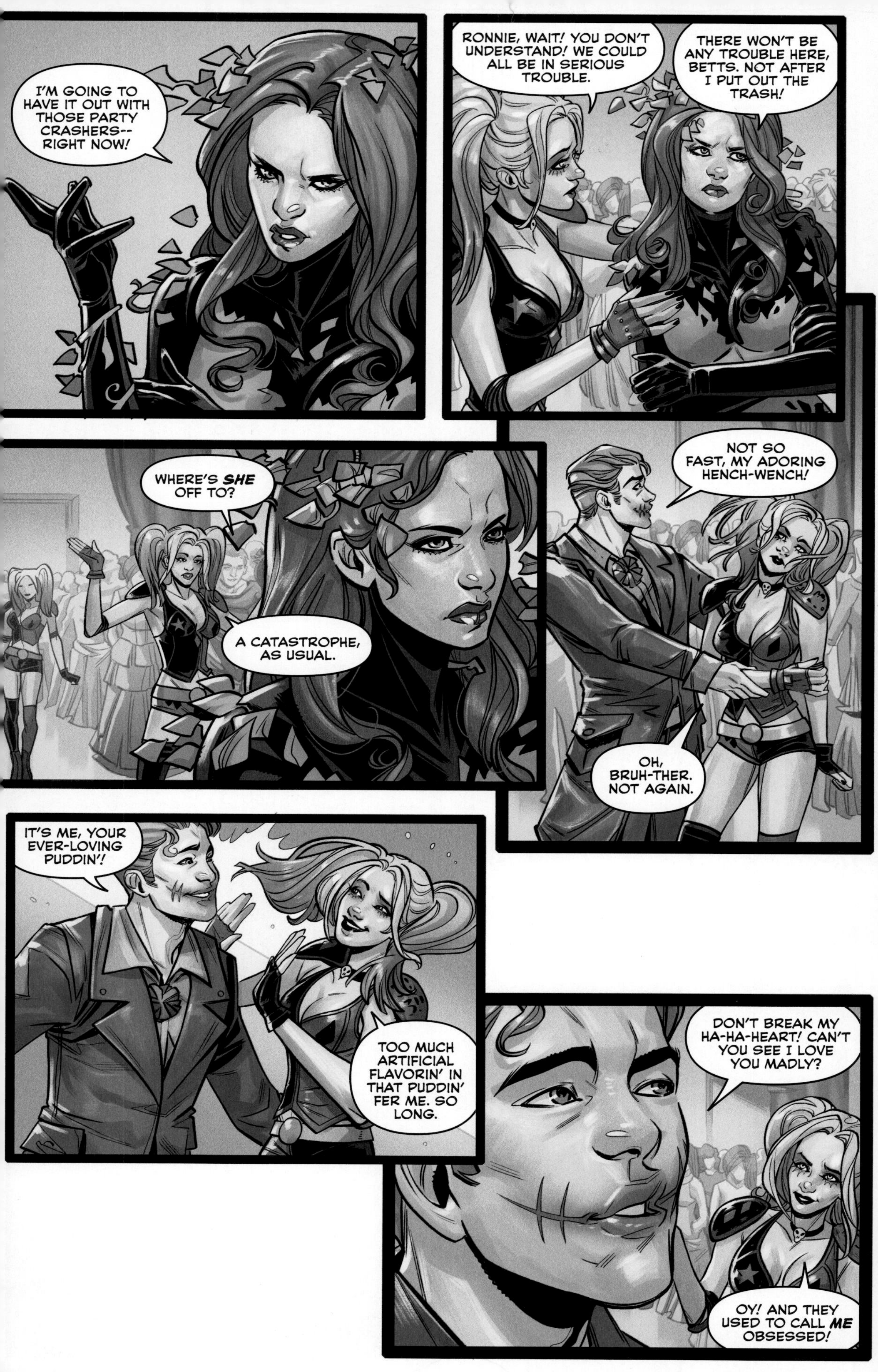
I'M GOING TO HAVE IT OUT WITH THOSE PARTY CRASHERS-- RIGHT NOW!
RONNIE, WAIT! YOU DON'T UNDERSTAND! WE COULD ALL BE IN SERIOUS TROUBLE.
THERE WON'T BE ANY TROUBLE HERE, BETTS. NOT AFTER I PUT OUT THE TRASH!
WHERE'S SHE OFF TO?
A CATASTROPHE, AS USUAL.
NOT SO FAST, MY ADORING HENCH-WENCH!
OH, BRUH-THER. NOT AGAIN.
IT'S ME, YOUR EVER-LOVING PUDDIN'!
TOO MUCH ARTIFICIAL FLAVORIN' IN THAT PUDDIN' FER ME. SO LONG.
DON'T BREAK MY HA-HA-HEART! CAN'T YOU SEE I LOVE YOU MADLY?
OY! AND THEY USED TO CALL ME OBSESSED!

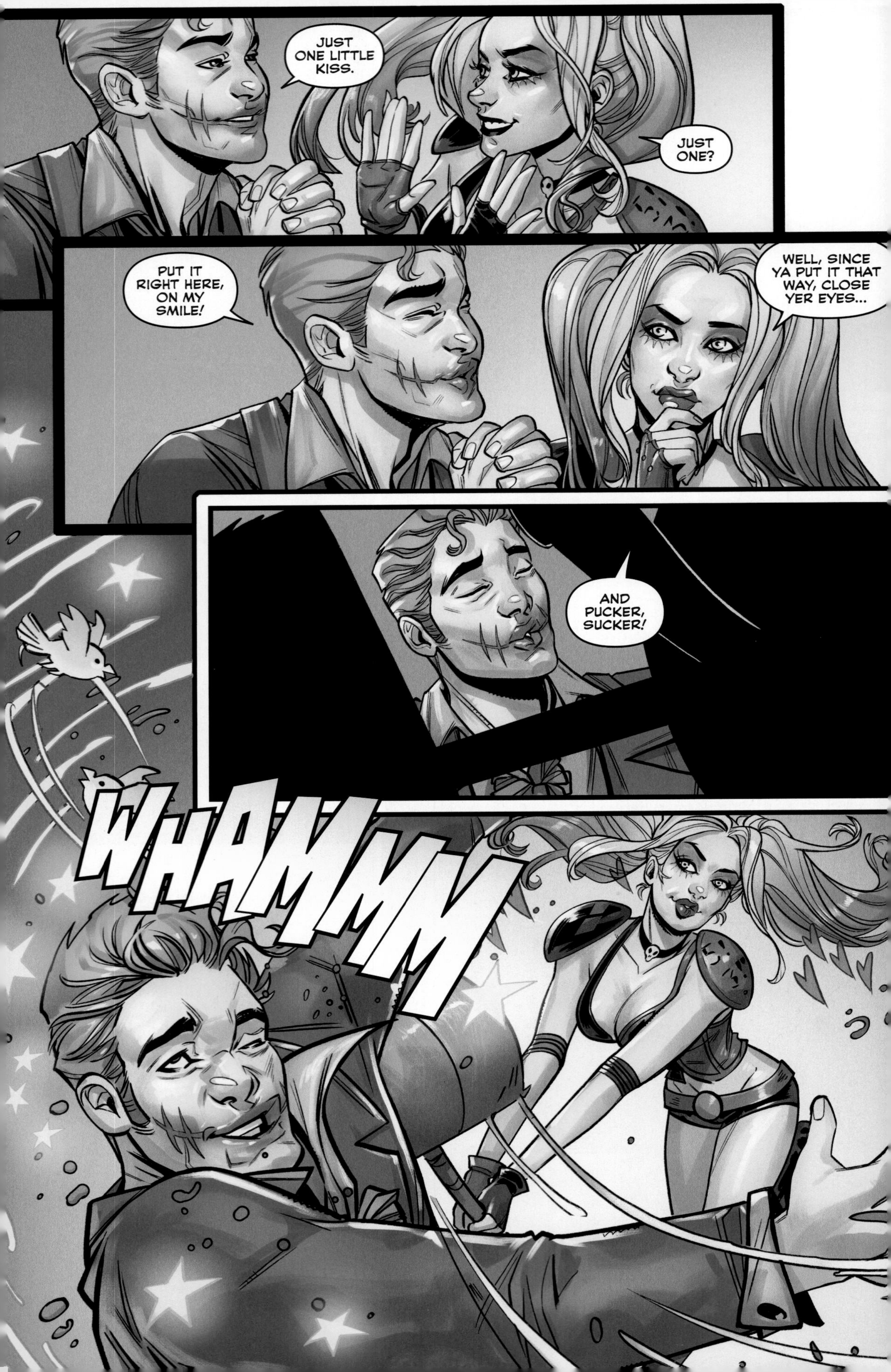
JUST ONE LITTLE KISS.
JUST ONE?
PUT IT RIGHT HERE, ON MY SMILE!
WELL, SINCE YA PUT IT THAT WAY, CLOSE YER EYES...
AND PUCKER, SUCKER!
WHAMMM

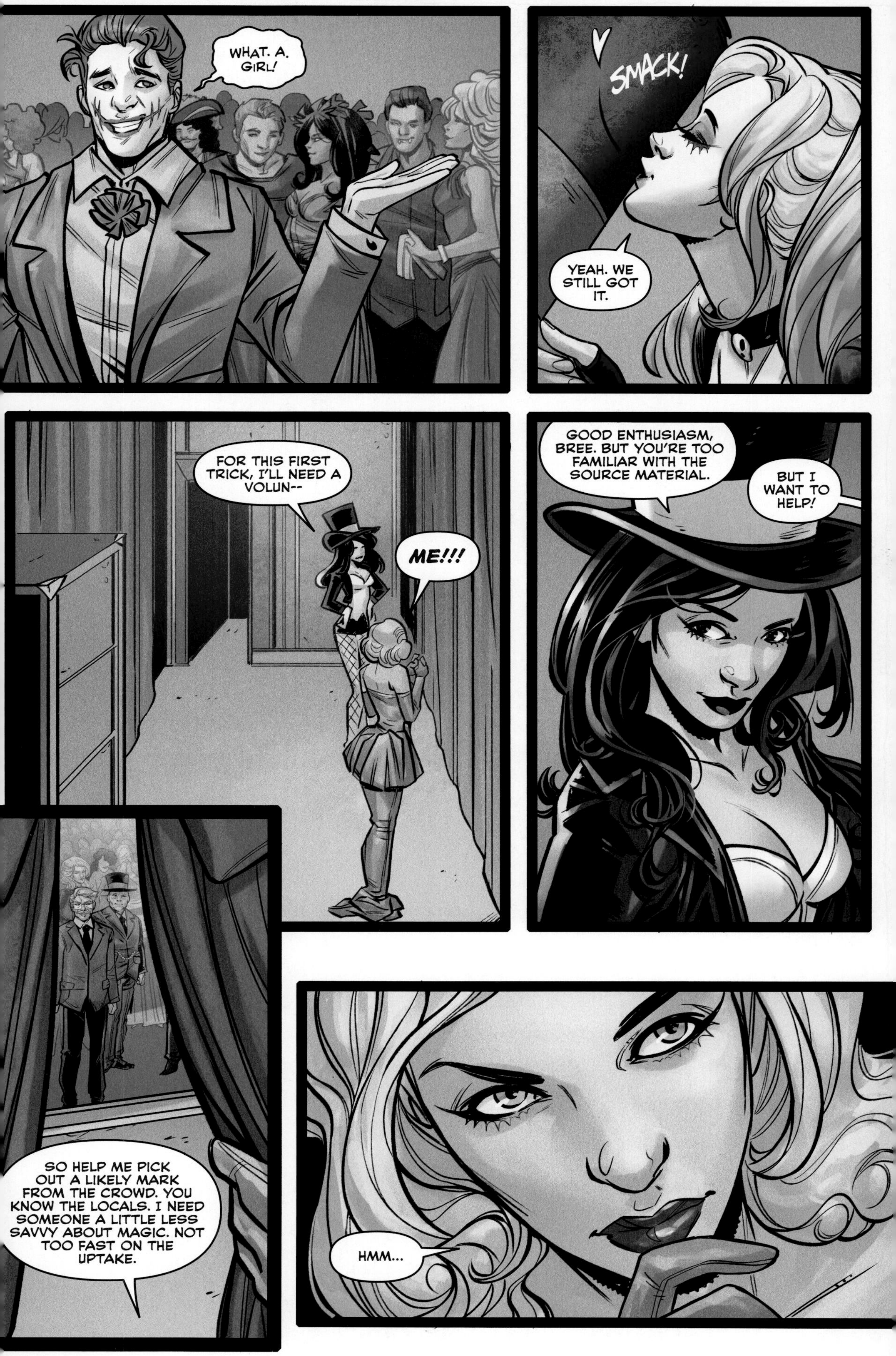
WHAT. A. GIRL!
SMACK!
YEAH. WE STILL GOT IT.
FOR THIS FIRST TRICK, I'LL NEED A VOLUN--
ME!!!
GOOD ENTHUSIASM, BREE. BUT YOU'RE TOO FAMILIAR WITH THE SOURCE MATERIAL.
BUT I WANT TO HELP!
SO HELP ME PICK OUT A LIKELY MARK FROM THE CROWD. YOU KNOW THE LOCALS. I NEED SOMEONE A LITTLE LESS SAVVY ABOUT MAGIC. NOT TOO FAST ON THE UPTAKE.
HMM...

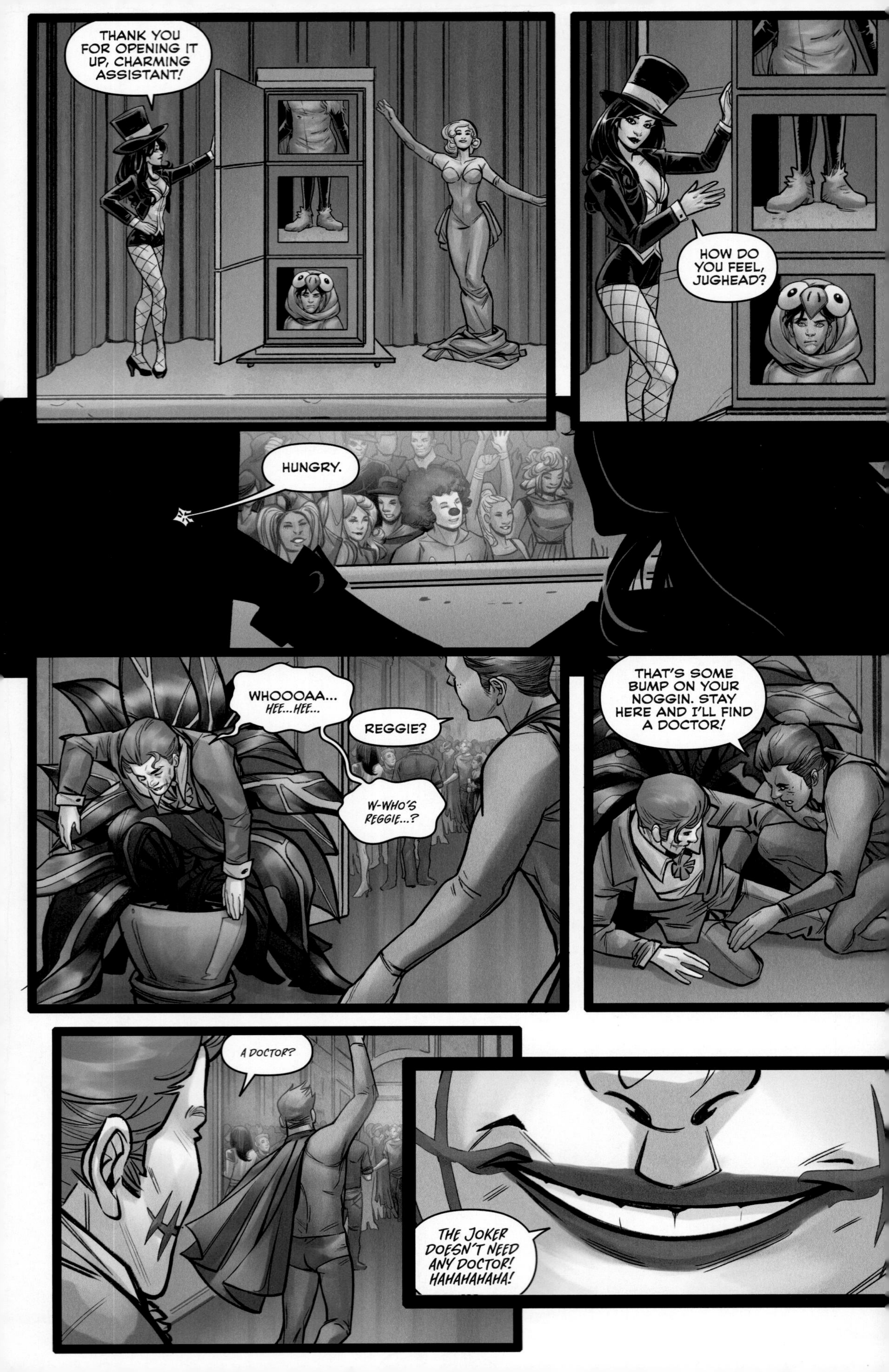
THANK YOU FOR OPENING IT UP, CHARMING ASSISTANT!
HOW DO YOU FEEL, JUGHEAD?
HUNGRY.
WHOOOAA... HEE...HEE...
REGGIE?
W-WHO'S REGGIE...?
THAT'S SOME BUMP ON YOUR NOGGIN. STAY HERE AND I'LL FIND A DOCTOR!
A DOCTOR?
THE JOKER DOESN'T NEED ANY DOCTOR! HAHAHAHAHA!

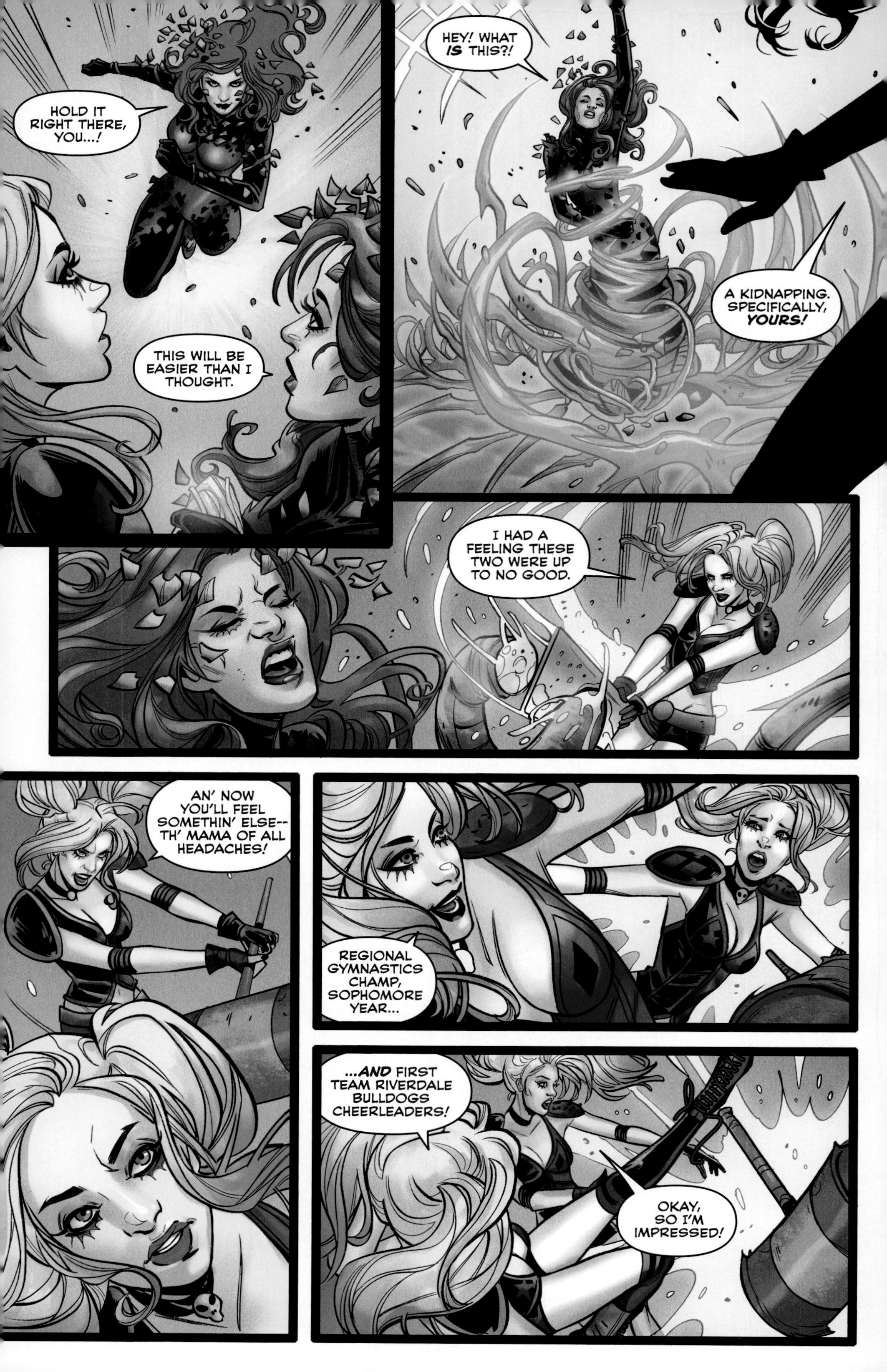
HOLD IT RIGHT THERE, YOU...!
THIS WILL BE EASIER THAN I THOUGHT.
HEY! WHAT IS THIS?!
A KIDNAPPING. SPECIFICALLY, YOURS!
I HAD A FEELING THESE TWO WERE UP TO NO GOOD.
AN' NOW YOU'LL FEEL SOMETHIN' ELSE-- TH' MAMA OF ALL HEADACHES!
REGIONAL GYMNASTICS CHAMP, SOPHOMORE YEAR...
...AND FIRST TEAM RIVERDALE BULLDOGS CHEERLEADERS!
OKAY, SO I'M IMPRESSED!

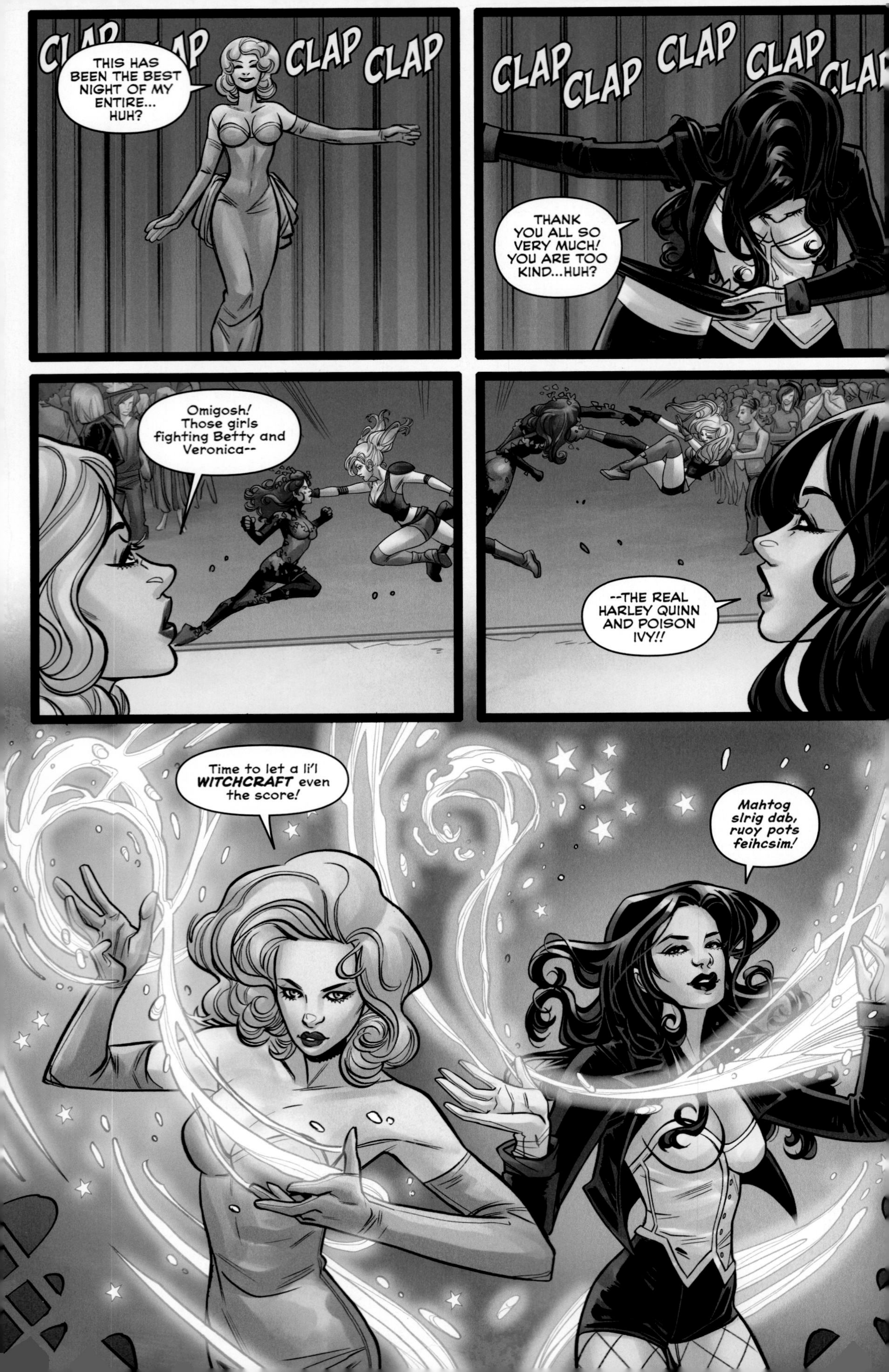
CLAP CLAP CLAP CLAP
THIS HAS BEEN THE BEST NIGHT OF MY ENTIRE... HUH?
CLAP CLAP CLAP CLAP CLAP
THANK YOU ALL SO VERY MUCH! YOU ARE TOO KIND...HUH?
Omigosh! Those girls fighting Betty and Veronica--
--THE REAL HARLEY QUINN AND POISON IVY!!
Time to let a li'l WITCHCRAFT even the score!
Mahtog slrig dab, ruoy pots feihcsim!

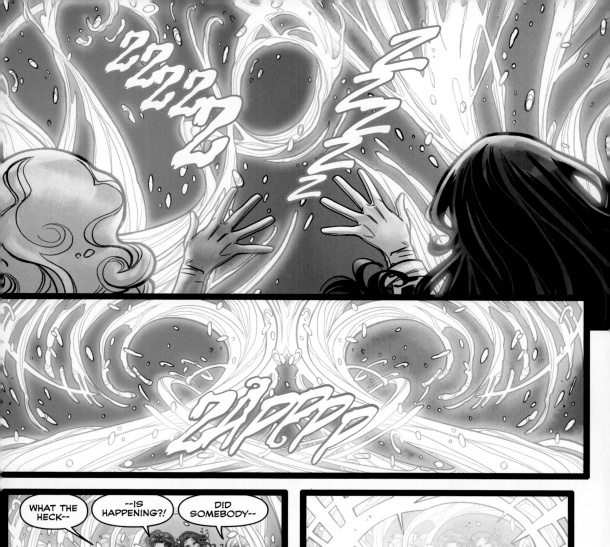

WHAT THE HECK--

--IS HAPPENING?!

DID SOMEBODY--

--SPIKE THE PUNCH?!

OOoooHHH! SWIRLY!

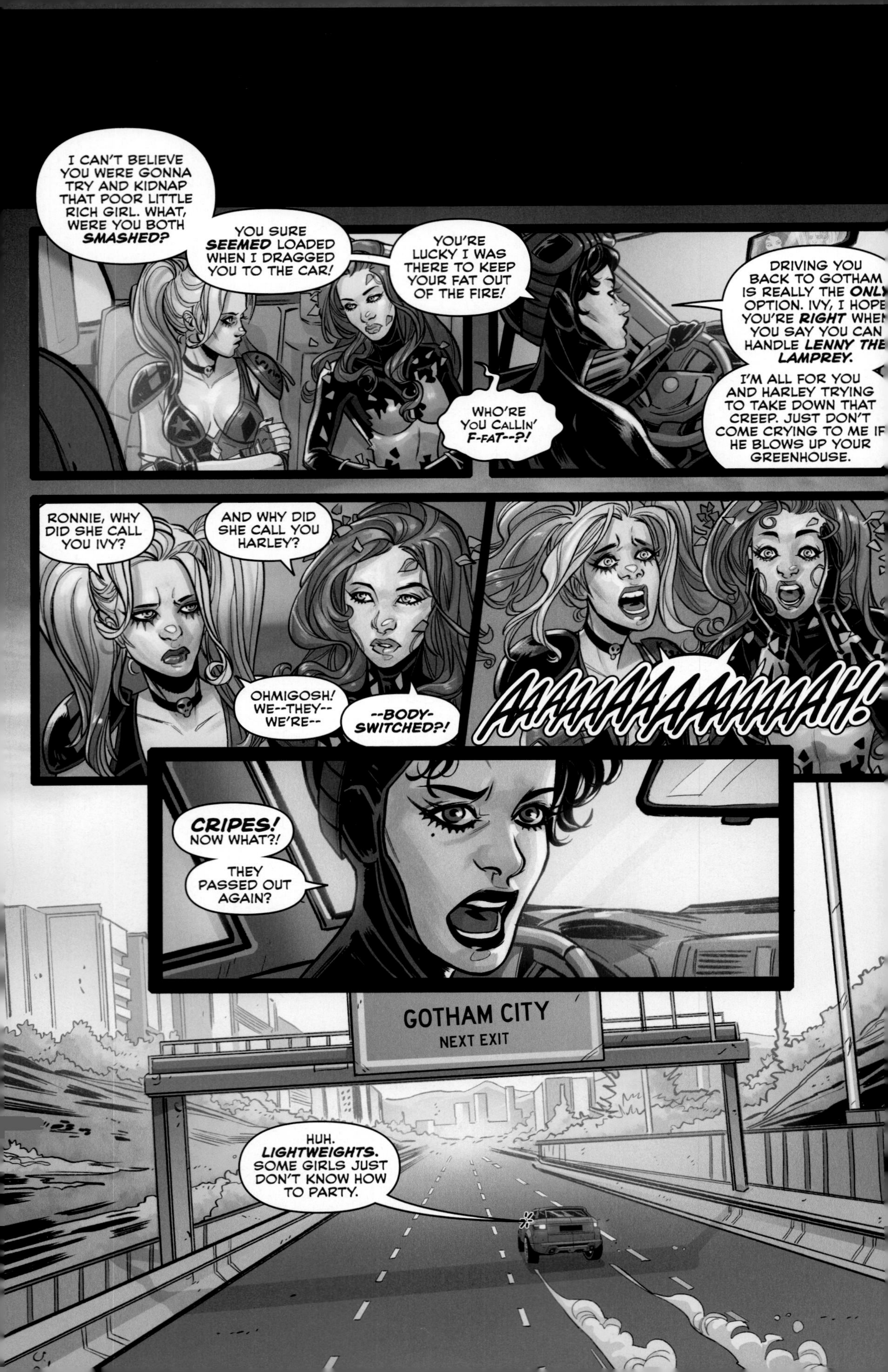

I CAN'T BELIEVE YOU WERE GONNA TRY AND KIDNAP THAT POOR LITTLE RICH GIRL. WHAT, WERE YOU BOTH SMASHED?
YOU SURE SEEMED LOADED WHEN I DRAGGED YOU TO THE CAR!
YOU'RE LUCKY I WAS THERE TO KEEP YOUR FAT OUT OF THE FIRE!
WHO'RE YOU CALLIN' F-FAT--?!
DRIVING YOU BACK TO GOTHAM IS REALLY THE ONLY OPTION. IVY, I HOPE YOU'RE RIGHT WHEN YOU SAY YOU CAN HANDLE LENNY THE LAMPREY.
I'M ALL FOR YOU AND HARLEY TRYING TO TAKE DOWN THAT CREEP. JUST DON'T COME CRYING TO ME IF HE BLOWS UP YOUR GREENHOUSE.
RONNIE, WHY DID SHE CALL YOU IVY?
AND WHY DID SHE CALL YOU HARLEY?
OHMIGOSH! WE--THEY--WE'RE--
--BODY-SWITCHED?!
AAAAAAAAAAAAAAH!
CRIPES! NOW WHAT?!
THEY PASSED OUT AGAIN?
GOTHAM CITY
NEXT EXIT
HUH. LIGHTWEIGHTS. SOME GIRLS JUST DON'T KNOW HOW TO PARTY.

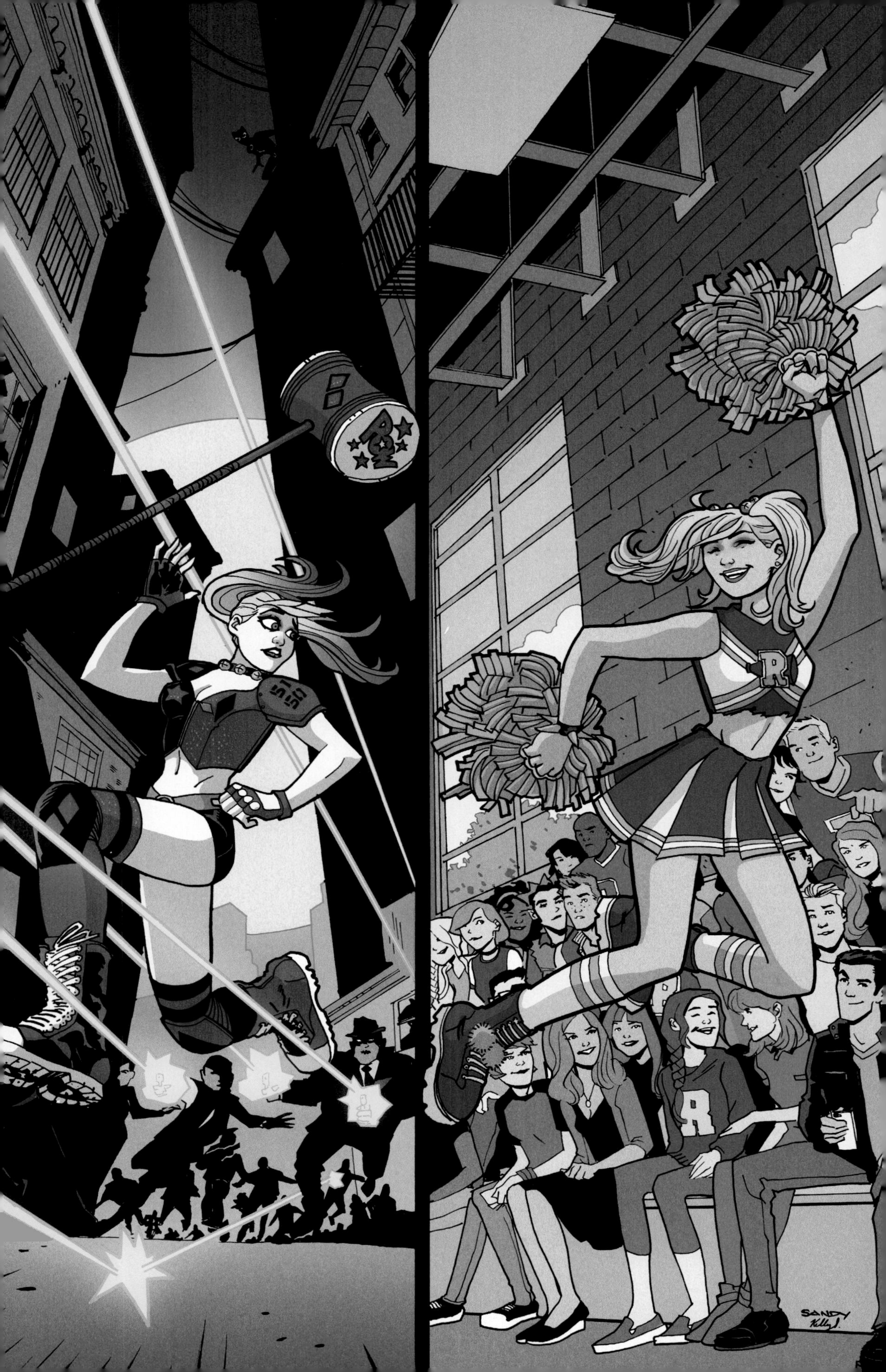

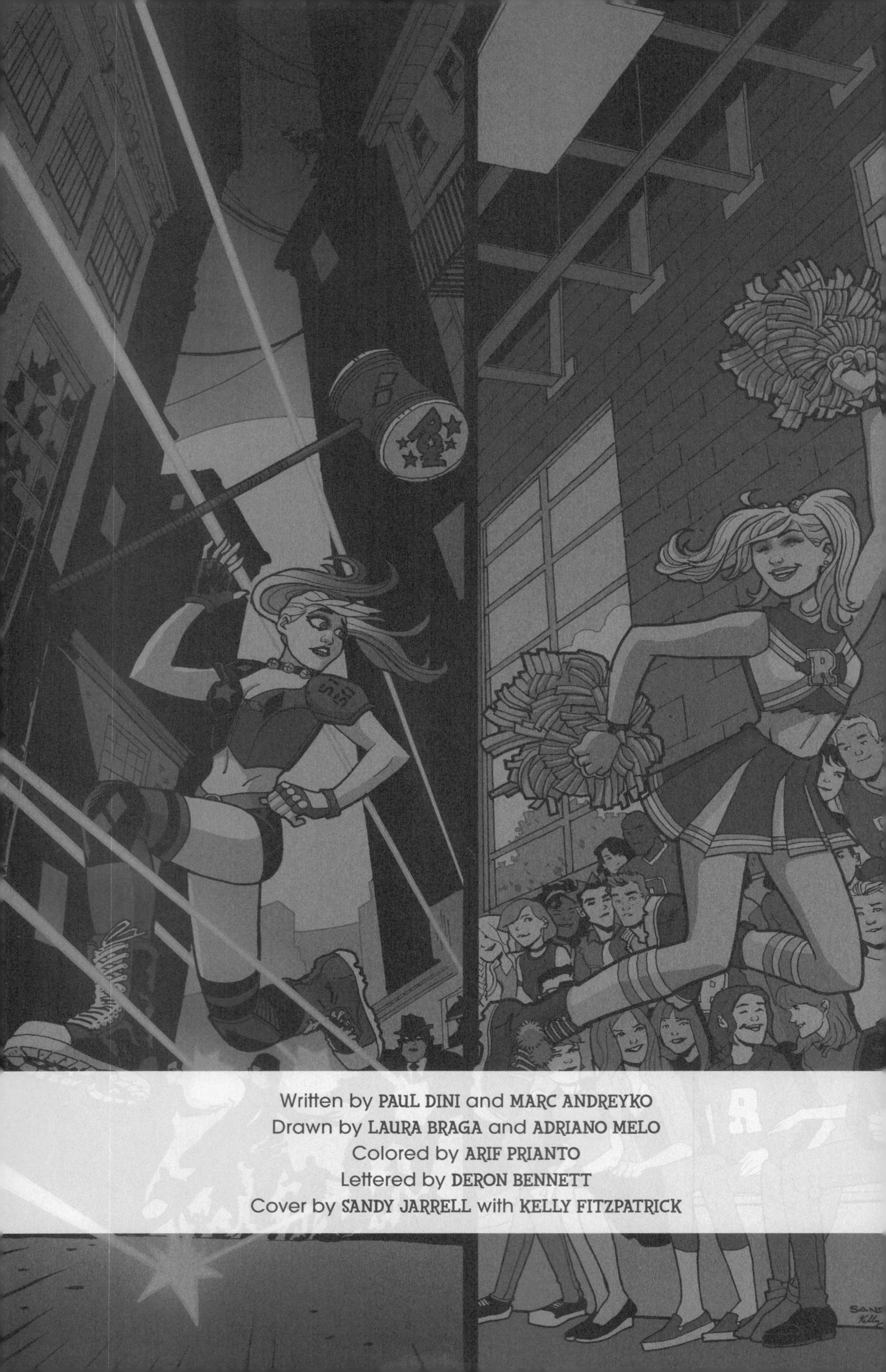

Written by **PAUL DINI** and **MARC ANDREYKO**
Drawn by **LAURA BRAGA** and **ADRIANO MELO**
Colored by **ARIF PRIANTO**
Lettered by **DERON BENNETT**
Cover by **SANDY JARRELL** with **KELLY FITZPATRICK**

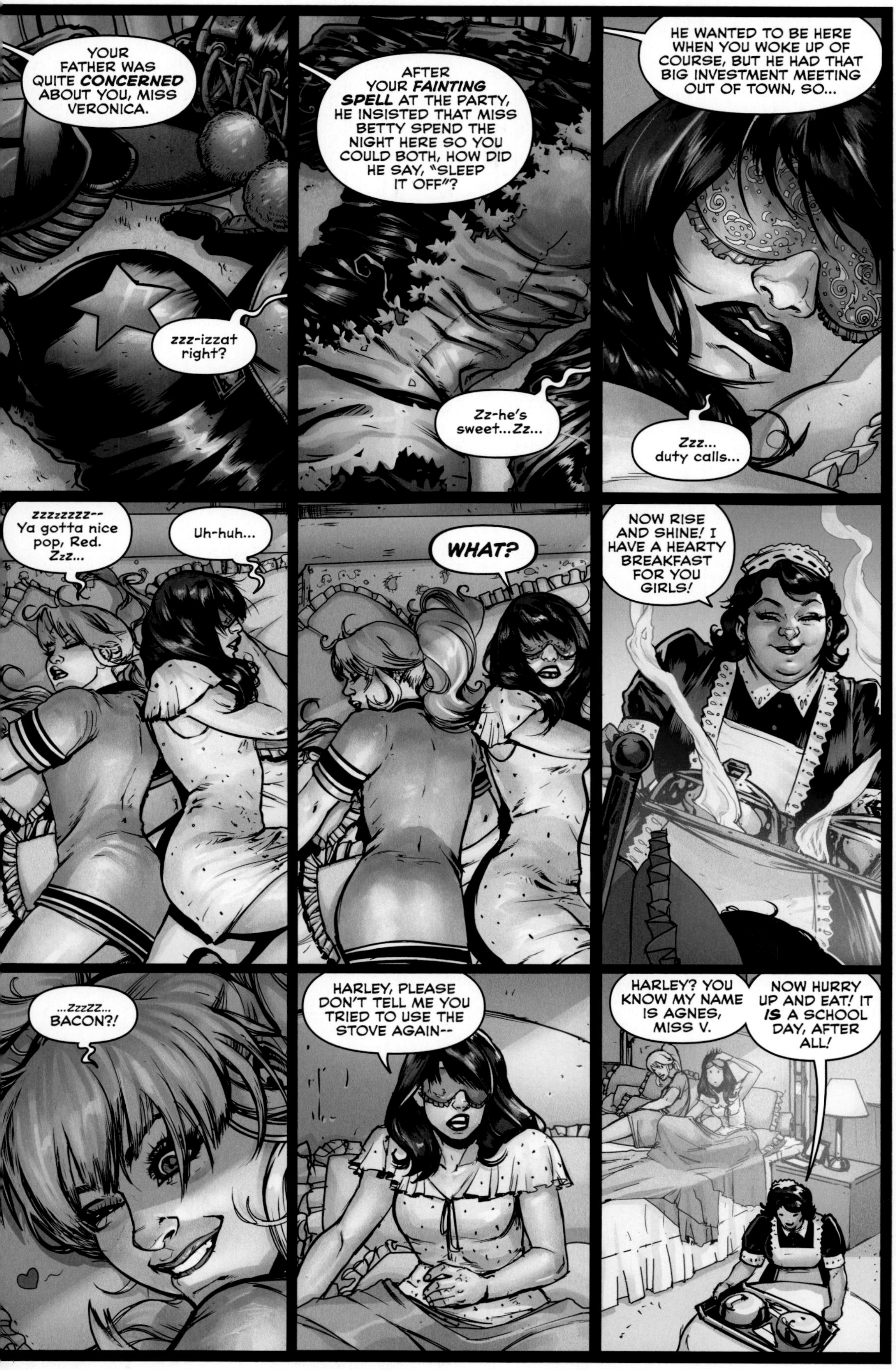
YOUR FATHER WAS QUITE CONCERNED ABOUT YOU, MISS VERONICA.
zzz-izzat right?
AFTER YOUR FAINTING SPELL AT THE PARTY, HE INSISTED THAT MISS BETTY SPEND THE NIGHT HERE SO YOU COULD BOTH, HOW DID HE SAY, "SLEEP IT OFF"?
Zz-he's sweet...Zz...
HE WANTED TO BE HERE WHEN YOU WOKE UP OF COURSE, BUT HE HAD THAT BIG INVESTMENT MEETING OUT OF TOWN, SO...
Zzz... duty calls...
zzzzzzzz-- Ya gotta nice pop, Red. Zzz...
Uh-huh...
WHAT?
NOW RISE AND SHINE! I HAVE A HEARTY BREAKFAST FOR YOU GIRLS!
...ZzzZZ... BACON?!
HARLEY, PLEASE DON'T TELL ME YOU TRIED TO USE THE STOVE AGAIN--
HARLEY? YOU KNOW MY NAME IS AGNES, MISS V.
NOW HURRY UP AND EAT! IT IS A SCHOOL DAY, AFTER ALL!

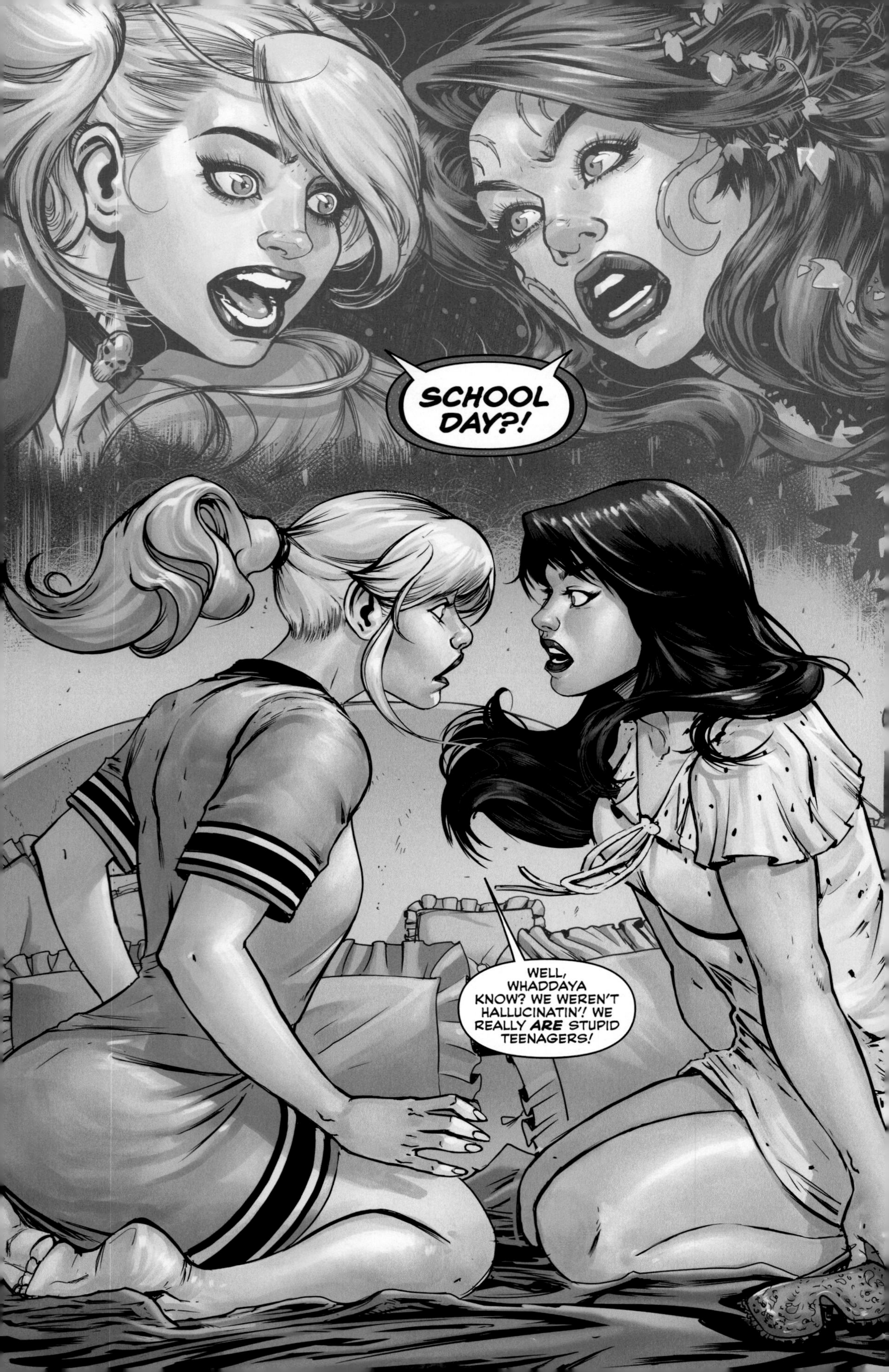
SCHOOL DAY?!
WELL, WHADDAYA KNOW? WE WEREN'T HALLUCINATIN'! WE REALLY ARE STUPID TEENAGERS!

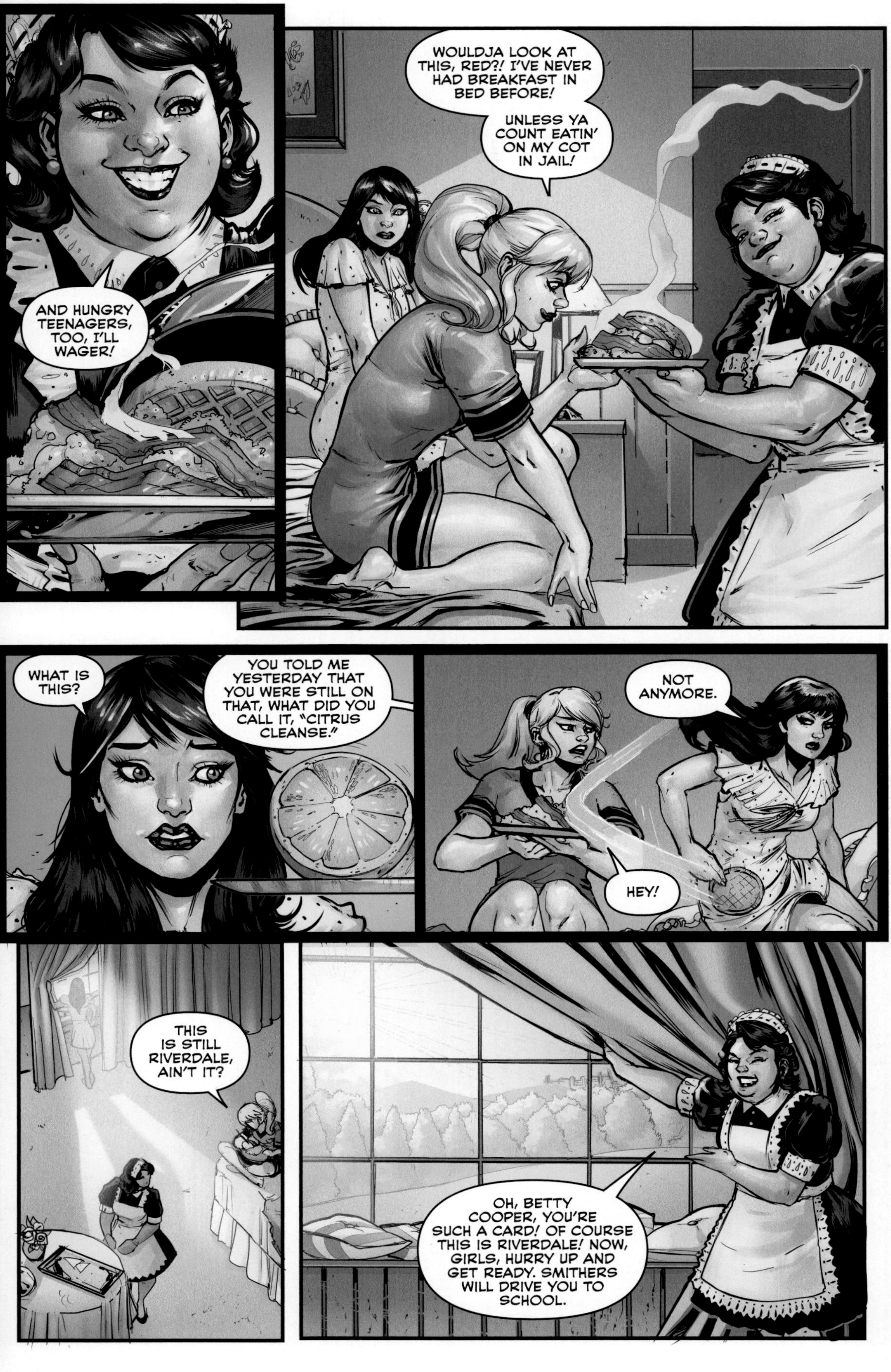
AND HUNGRY TEENAGERS, TOO, I'LL WAGER!
WOULDJA LOOK AT THIS, RED?! I'VE NEVER HAD BREAKFAST IN BED BEFORE!
UNLESS YA COUNT EATIN' ON MY COT IN JAIL!
WHAT IS THIS?
YOU TOLD ME YESTERDAY THAT YOU WERE STILL ON THAT, WHAT DID YOU CALL IT, "CITRUS CLEANSE."
NOT ANYMORE.
HEY!
THIS IS STILL RIVERDALE, AIN'T IT?
OH, BETTY COOPER, YOU'RE SUCH A CARD! OF COURSE THIS IS RIVERDALE! NOW, GIRLS, HURRY UP AND GET READY. SMITHERS WILL DRIVE YOU TO SCHOOL.

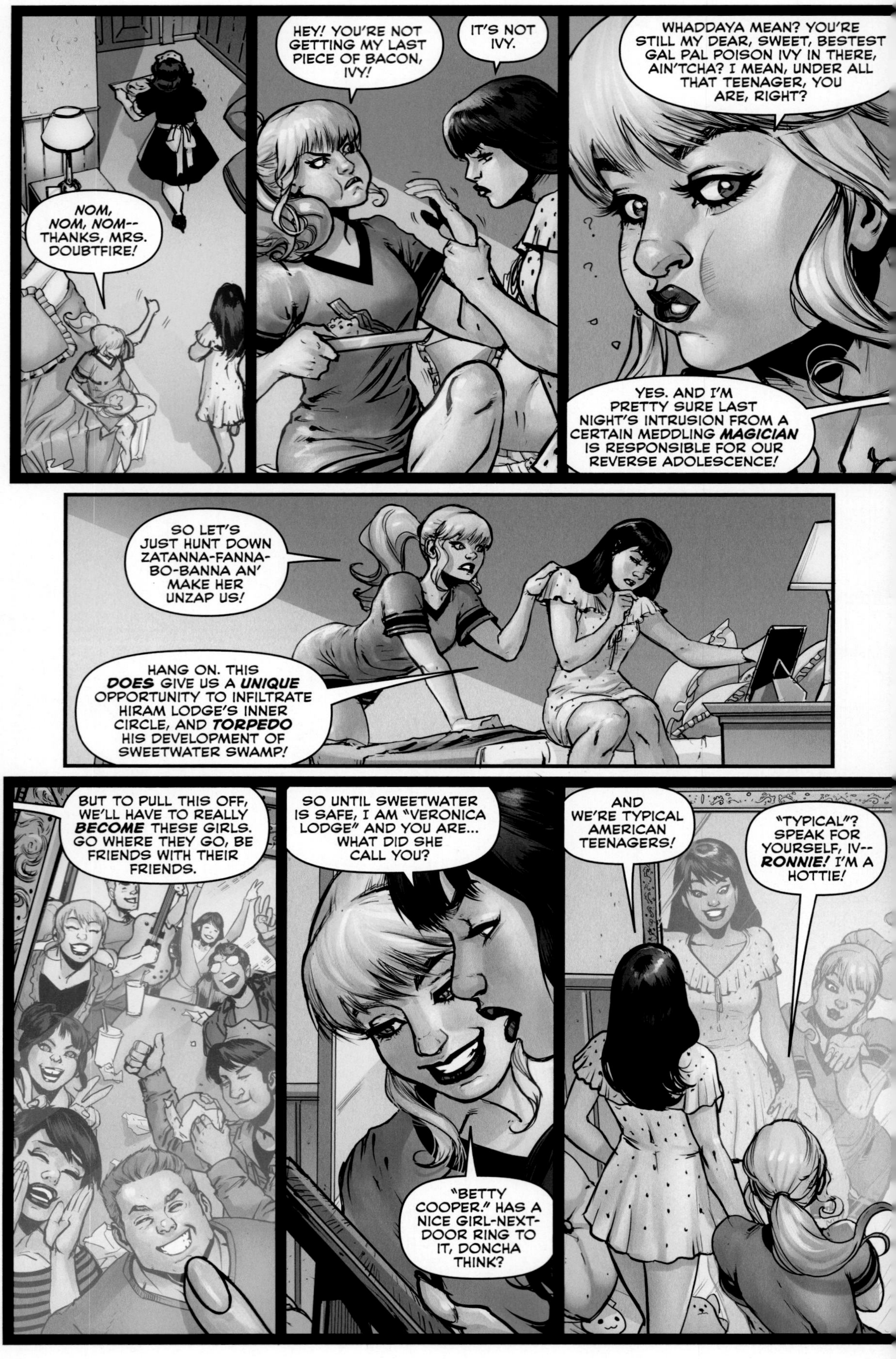

NOM, NOM, NOM-- THANKS, MRS. DOUBTFIRE!
HEY! YOU'RE NOT GETTING MY LAST PIECE OF BACON, IVY!
IT'S NOT IVY.
WHADDAYA MEAN? YOU'RE STILL MY DEAR, SWEET, BESTEST GAL PAL POISON IVY IN THERE, AIN'TCHA? I MEAN, UNDER ALL THAT TEENAGER, YOU ARE, RIGHT?
YES. AND I'M PRETTY SURE LAST NIGHT'S INTRUSION FROM A CERTAIN MEDDLING MAGICIAN IS RESPONSIBLE FOR OUR REVERSE ADOLESCENCE!
SO LET'S JUST HUNT DOWN ZATANNA-FANNA-BO-BANNA AN' MAKE HER UNZAP US!
HANG ON. THIS DOES GIVE US A UNIQUE OPPORTUNITY TO INFILTRATE HIRAM LODGE'S INNER CIRCLE, AND TORPEDO HIS DEVELOPMENT OF SWEETWATER SWAMP!
BUT TO PULL THIS OFF, WE'LL HAVE TO REALLY BECOME THESE GIRLS. GO WHERE THEY GO, BE FRIENDS WITH THEIR FRIENDS.
SO UNTIL SWEETWATER IS SAFE, I AM "VERONICA LODGE" AND YOU ARE... WHAT DID SHE CALL YOU?
"BETTY COOPER." HAS A NICE GIRL-NEXT-DOOR RING TO IT, DONCHA THINK?
AND WE'RE TYPICAL AMERICAN TEENAGERS!
"TYPICAL"? SPEAK FOR YOURSELF, IV-- RONNIE! I'M A HOTTIE!

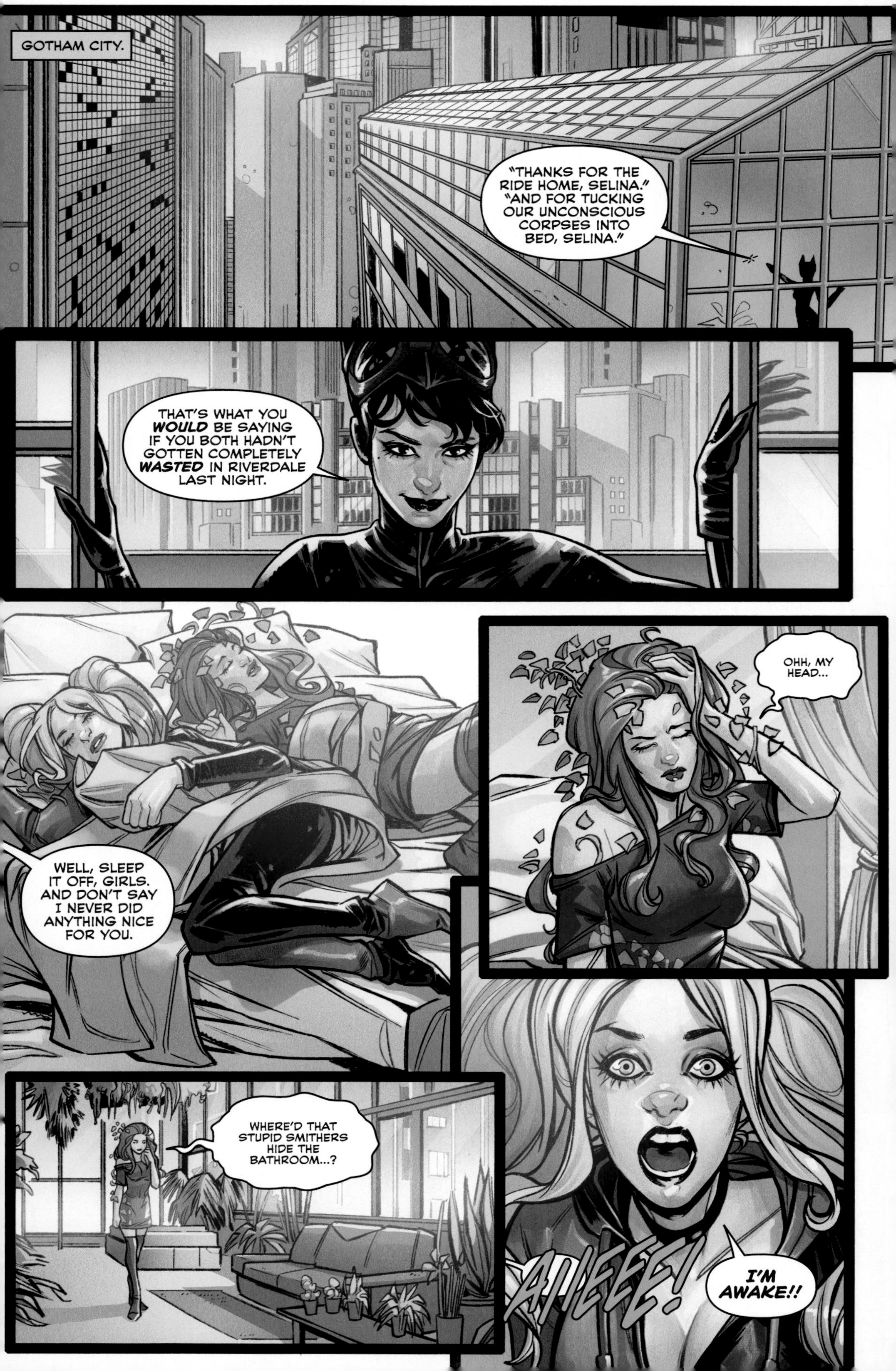
GOTHAM CITY.
"THANKS FOR THE RIDE HOME, SELINA." "AND FOR TUCKING OUR UNCONSCIOUS CORPSES INTO BED, SELINA."
THAT'S WHAT YOU **WOULD** BE SAYING IF YOU BOTH HADN'T GOTTEN COMPLETELY **WASTED** IN RIVERDALE LAST NIGHT.
WELL, SLEEP IT OFF, GIRLS. AND DON'T SAY I NEVER DID ANYTHING NICE FOR YOU.
OHH, MY HEAD...
WHERE'D THAT STUPID SMITHERS HIDE THE BATHROOM...?
AIIEEE!
I'M AWAKE!!

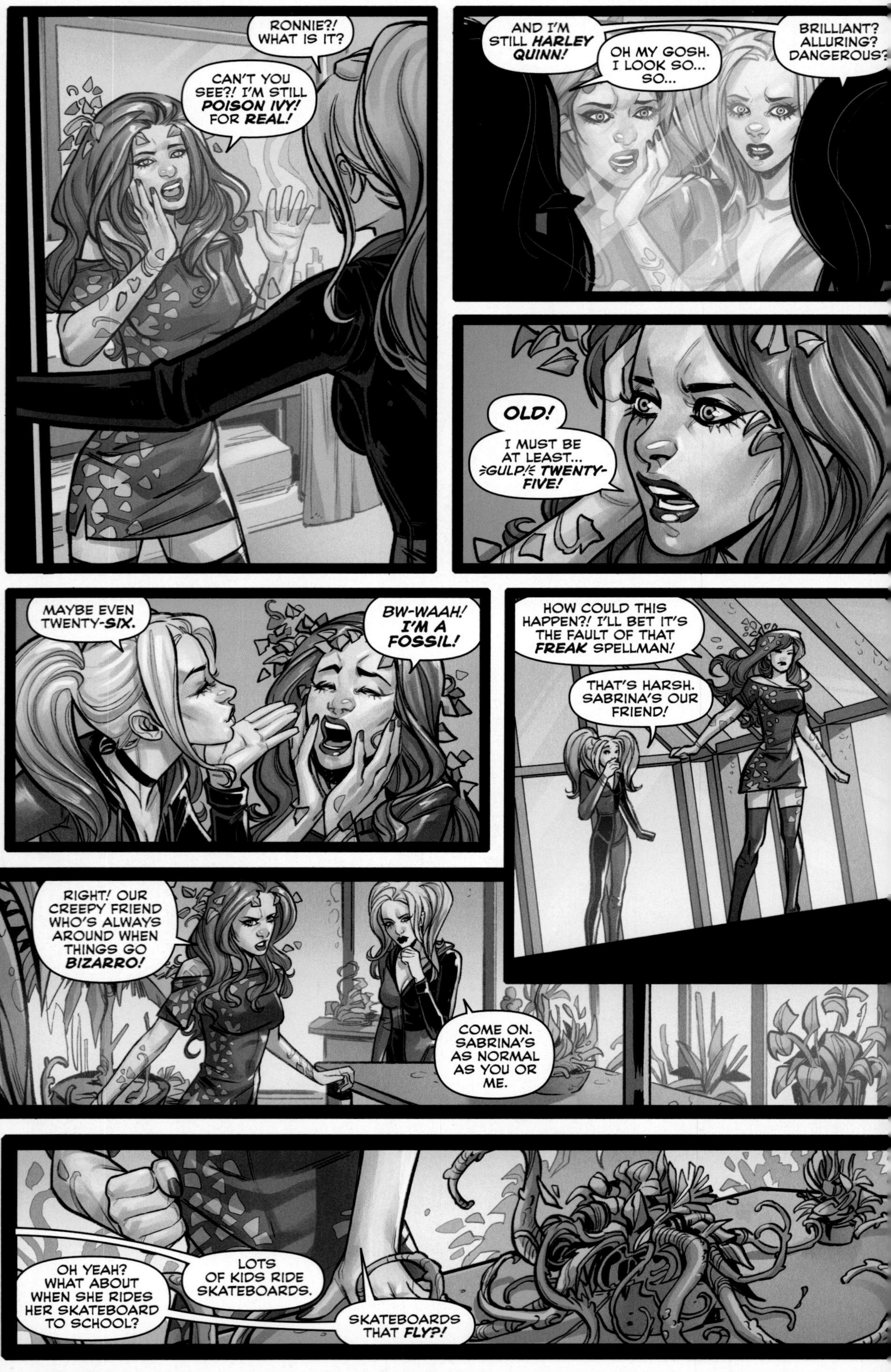
RONNIE?! WHAT IS IT?
CAN'T YOU SEE?! I'M STILL POISON IVY! FOR REAL!
AND I'M STILL HARLEY QUINN!
OH MY GOSH. I LOOK SO... SO...
BRILLIANT? ALLURING? DANGEROUS?
OLD!
I MUST BE AT LEAST... GULP! TWENTY-FIVE!
MAYBE EVEN TWENTY-SIX.
BW-WAAH! I'M A FOSSIL!
HOW COULD THIS HAPPEN?! I'LL BET IT'S THE FAULT OF THAT FREAK SPELLMAN!
THAT'S HARSH. SABRINA'S OUR FRIEND!
RIGHT! OUR CREEPY FRIEND WHO'S ALWAYS AROUND WHEN THINGS GO BIZARRO!
COME ON. SABRINA'S AS NORMAL AS YOU OR ME.
OH YEAH? WHAT ABOUT WHEN SHE RIDES HER SKATEBOARD TO SCHOOL?
LOTS OF KIDS RIDE SKATEBOARDS.
SKATEBOARDS THAT FLY?!

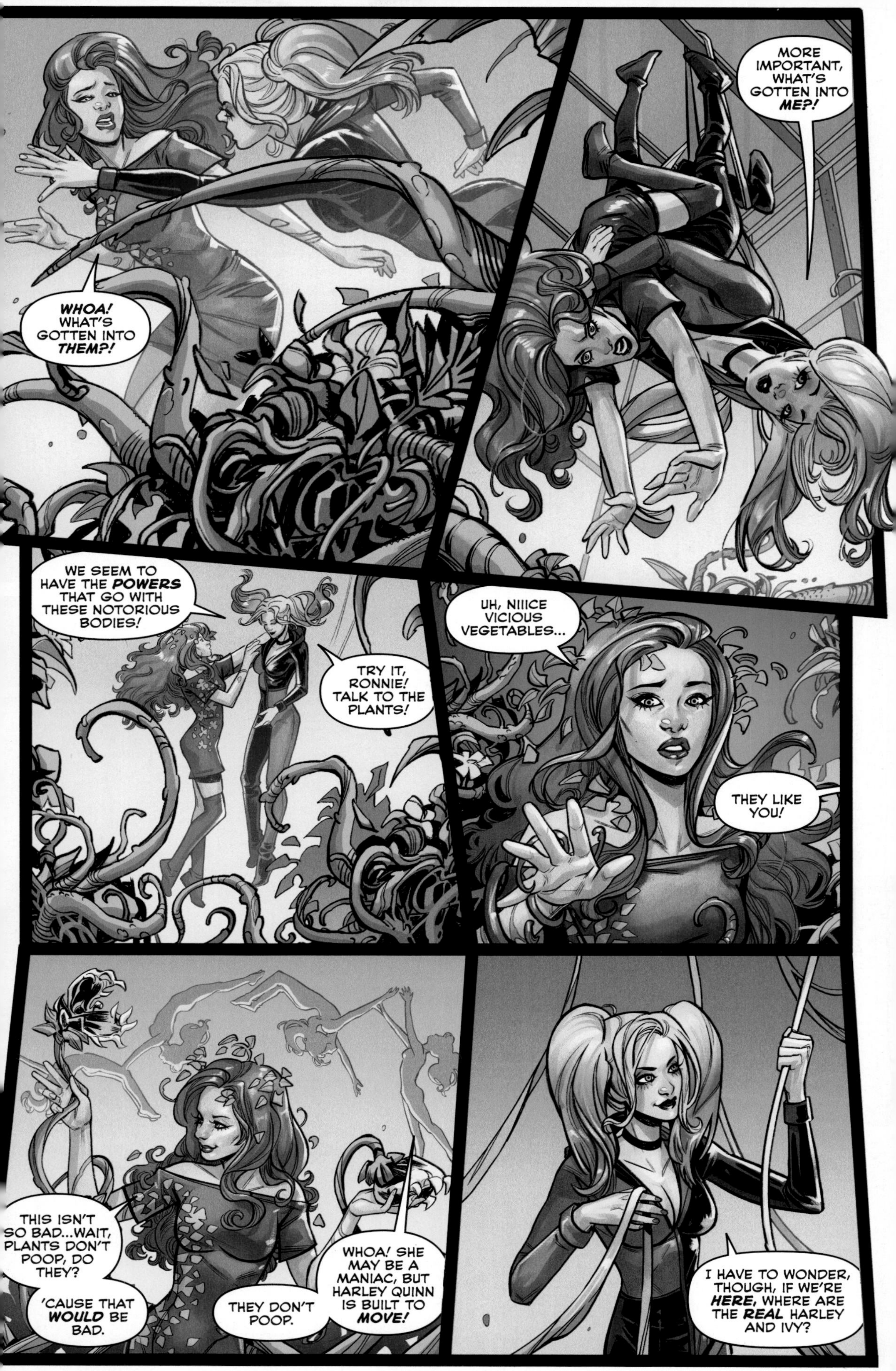
WHOA! WHAT'S GOTTEN INTO THEM?!
MORE IMPORTANT, WHAT'S GOTTEN INTO ME?!
WE SEEM TO HAVE THE POWERS THAT GO WITH THESE NOTORIOUS BODIES!
TRY IT, RONNIE! TALK TO THE PLANTS!
UH, NIIICE VICIOUS VEGETABLES...
THEY LIKE YOU!
THIS ISN'T SO BAD...WAIT, PLANTS DON'T POOP, DO THEY?
'CAUSE THAT WOULD BE BAD.
THEY DON'T POOP.
WHOA! SHE MAY BE A MANIAC, BUT HARLEY QUINN IS BUILT TO MOVE!
I HAVE TO WONDER, THOUGH, IF WE'RE HERE, WHERE ARE THE REAL HARLEY AND IVY?

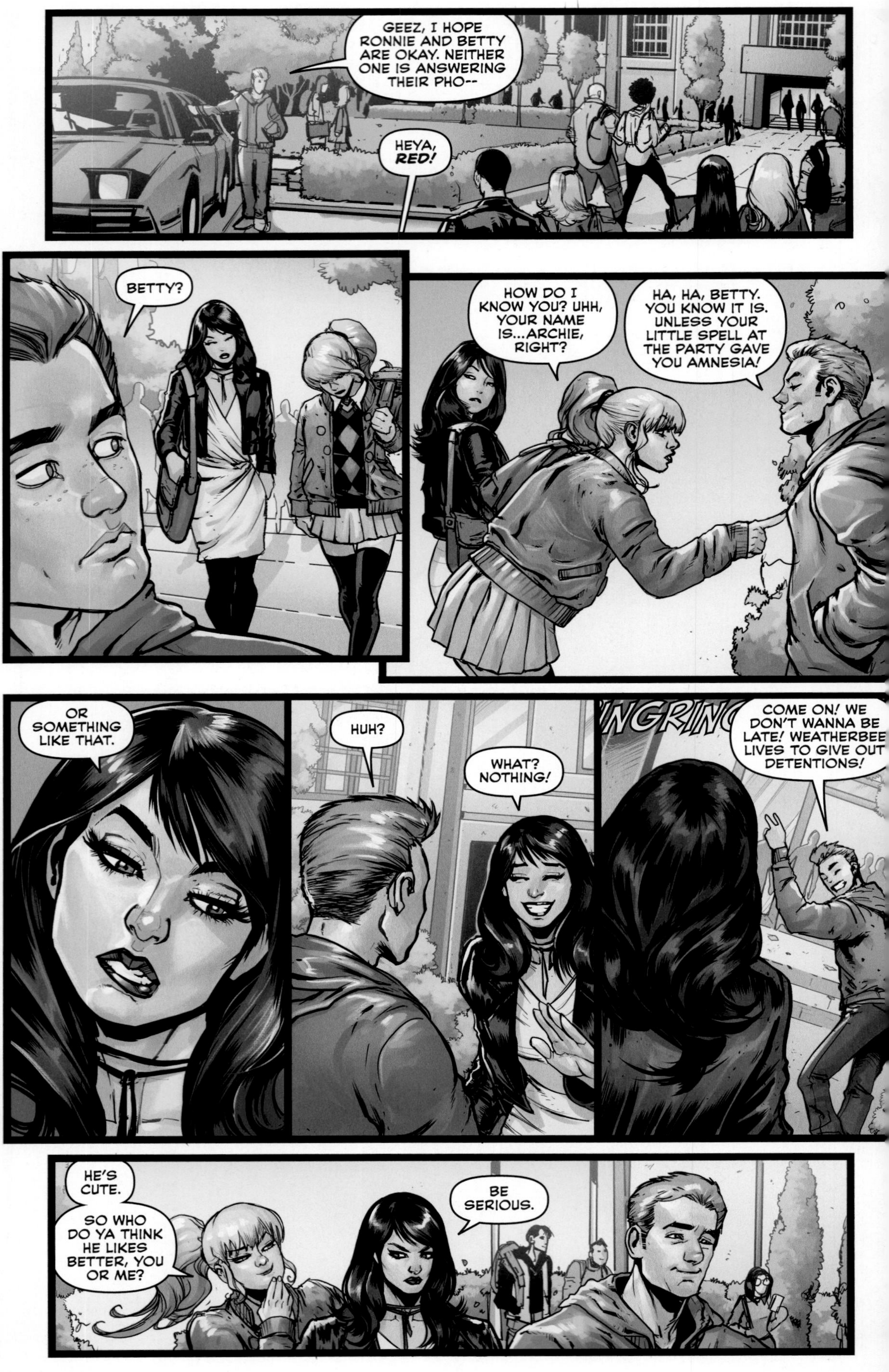
GEEZ, I HOPE RONNIE AND BETTY ARE OKAY. NEITHER ONE IS ANSWERING THEIR PHO--
HEYA, **RED!**
BETTY?
HOW DO I KNOW YOU? UHH, YOUR NAME IS...ARCHIE, RIGHT?
HA, HA, BETTY. YOU KNOW IT IS. UNLESS YOUR LITTLE SPELL AT THE PARTY GAVE YOU AMNESIA!
OR SOMETHING LIKE THAT.
HUH?
WHAT? NOTHING!
NGRING
COME ON! WE DON'T WANNA BE LATE! WEATHERBEE LIVES TO GIVE OUT DETENTIONS!
HE'S CUTE.
SO WHO DO YA THINK HE LIKES BETTER, YOU OR ME?
BE SERIOUS.

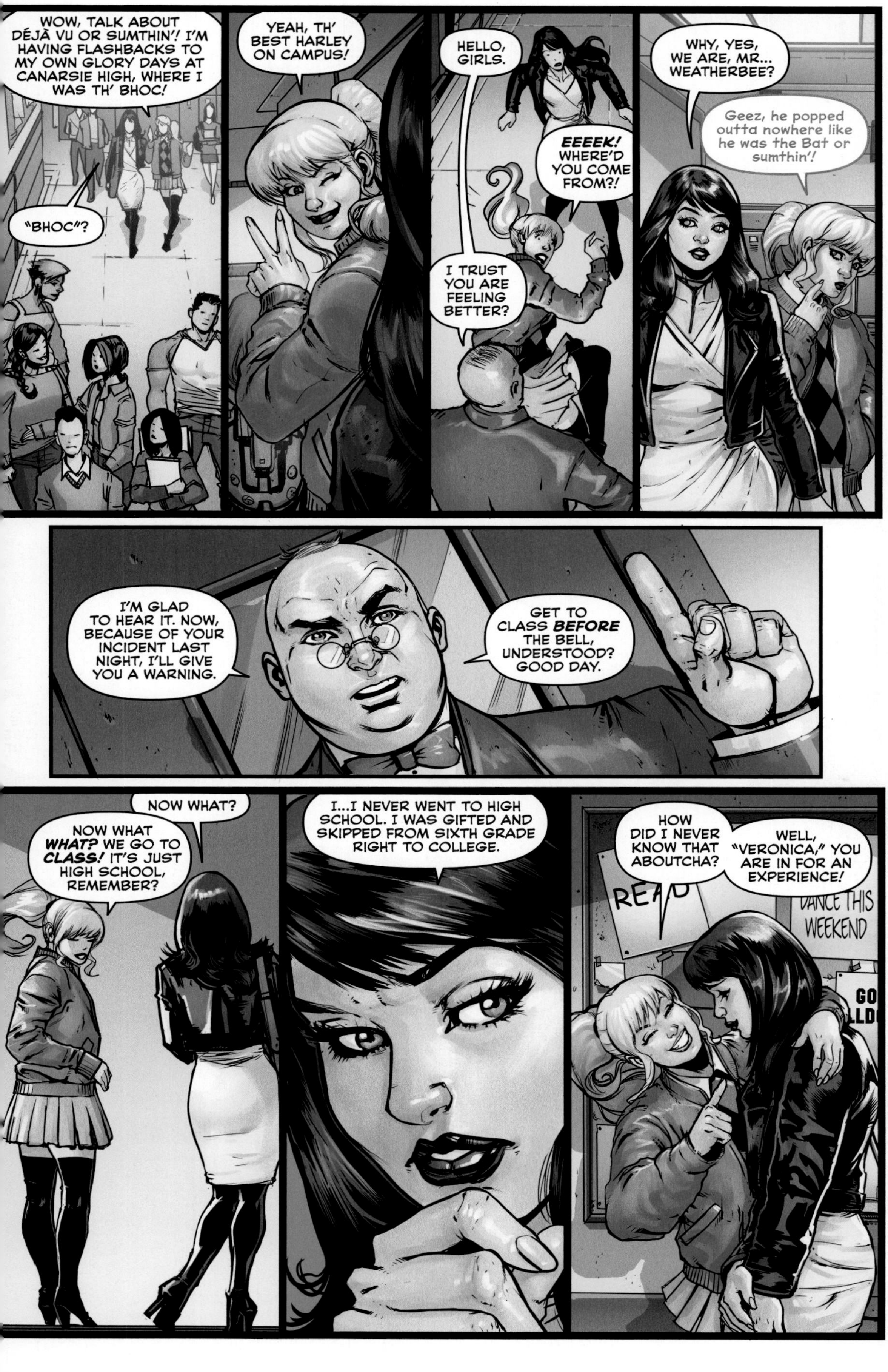
WOW, TALK ABOUT DÉJÀ VU OR SUMTHIN'! I'M HAVING FLASHBACKS TO MY OWN GLORY DAYS AT CANARSIE HIGH, WHERE I WAS TH' BHOC!
"BHOC"?
YEAH, TH' BEST HARLEY ON CAMPUS!
HELLO, GIRLS.
EEEEK! WHERE'D YOU COME FROM?!
I TRUST YOU ARE FEELING BETTER?
WHY, YES, WE ARE, MR... WEATHERBEE?
Geez, he popped outta nowhere like he was the Bat or sumthin'!
I'M GLAD TO HEAR IT. NOW, BECAUSE OF YOUR INCIDENT LAST NIGHT, I'LL GIVE YOU A WARNING.
GET TO CLASS BEFORE THE BELL, UNDERSTOOD? GOOD DAY.
NOW WHAT?
NOW WHAT WHAT? WE GO TO CLASS! IT'S JUST HIGH SCHOOL, REMEMBER?
I...I NEVER WENT TO HIGH SCHOOL. I WAS GIFTED AND SKIPPED FROM SIXTH GRADE RIGHT TO COLLEGE.
HOW DID I NEVER KNOW THAT ABOUTCHA?
WELL, "VERONICA," YOU ARE IN FOR AN EXPERIENCE!
READ
DANCE THIS WEEKEND

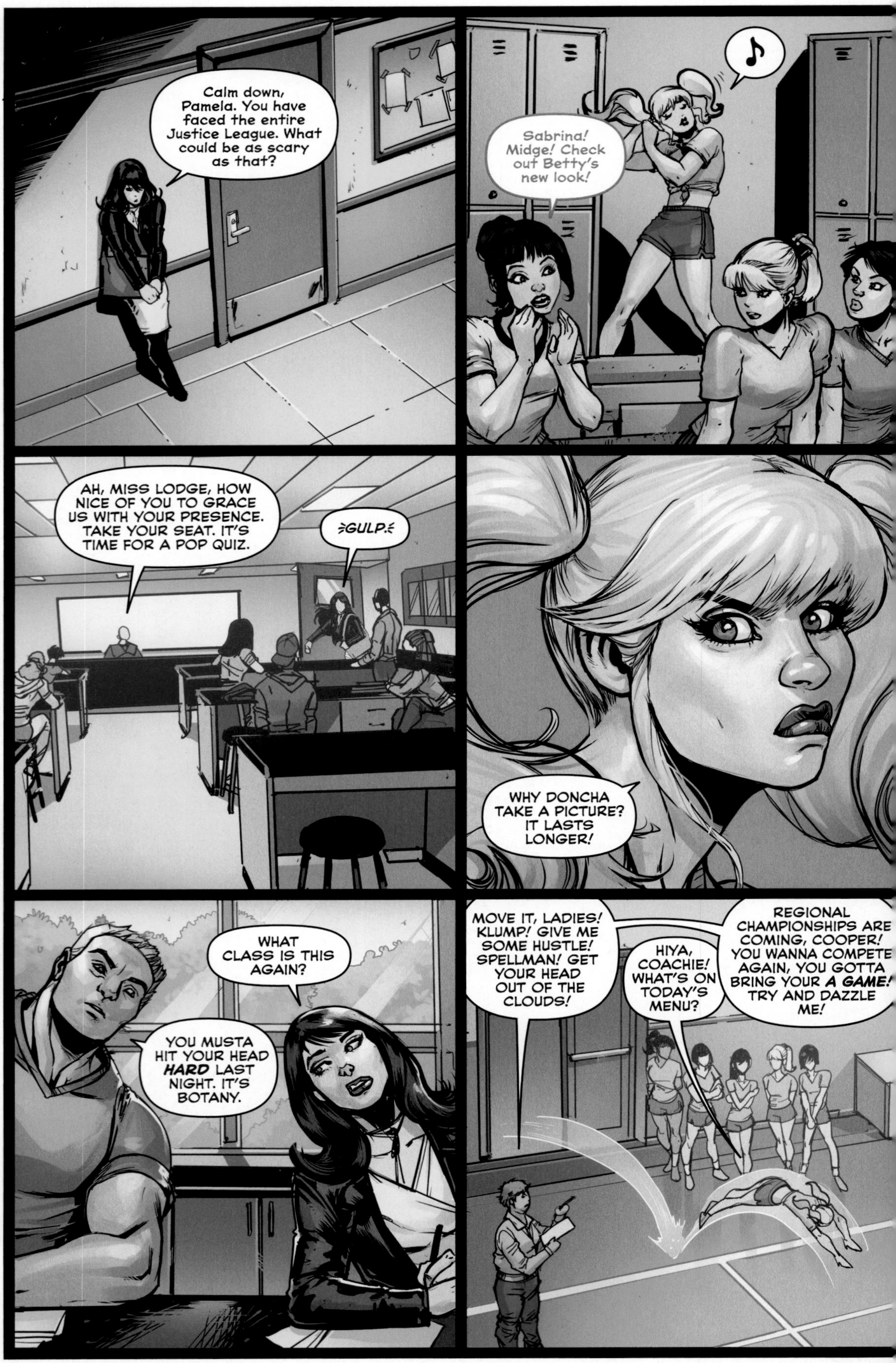
Calm down, Pamela. You have faced the entire Justice League. What could be as scary as that?
♪
Sabrina! Midge! Check out Betty's new look!
AH, MISS LODGE, HOW NICE OF YOU TO GRACE US WITH YOUR PRESENCE. TAKE YOUR SEAT. IT'S TIME FOR A POP QUIZ.
GULP.
WHY DONCHA TAKE A PICTURE? IT LASTS LONGER!
WHAT CLASS IS THIS AGAIN?
YOU MUSTA HIT YOUR HEAD HARD LAST NIGHT. IT'S BOTANY.
MOVE IT, LADIES! KLUMP! GIVE ME SOME HUSTLE! SPELLMAN! GET YOUR HEAD OUT OF THE CLOUDS!
HIYA, COACHIE! WHAT'S ON TODAY'S MENU?
REGIONAL CHAMPIONSHIPS ARE COMING, COOPER! YOU WANNA COMPETE AGAIN, YOU GOTTA BRING YOUR A GAME! TRY AND DAZZLE ME!

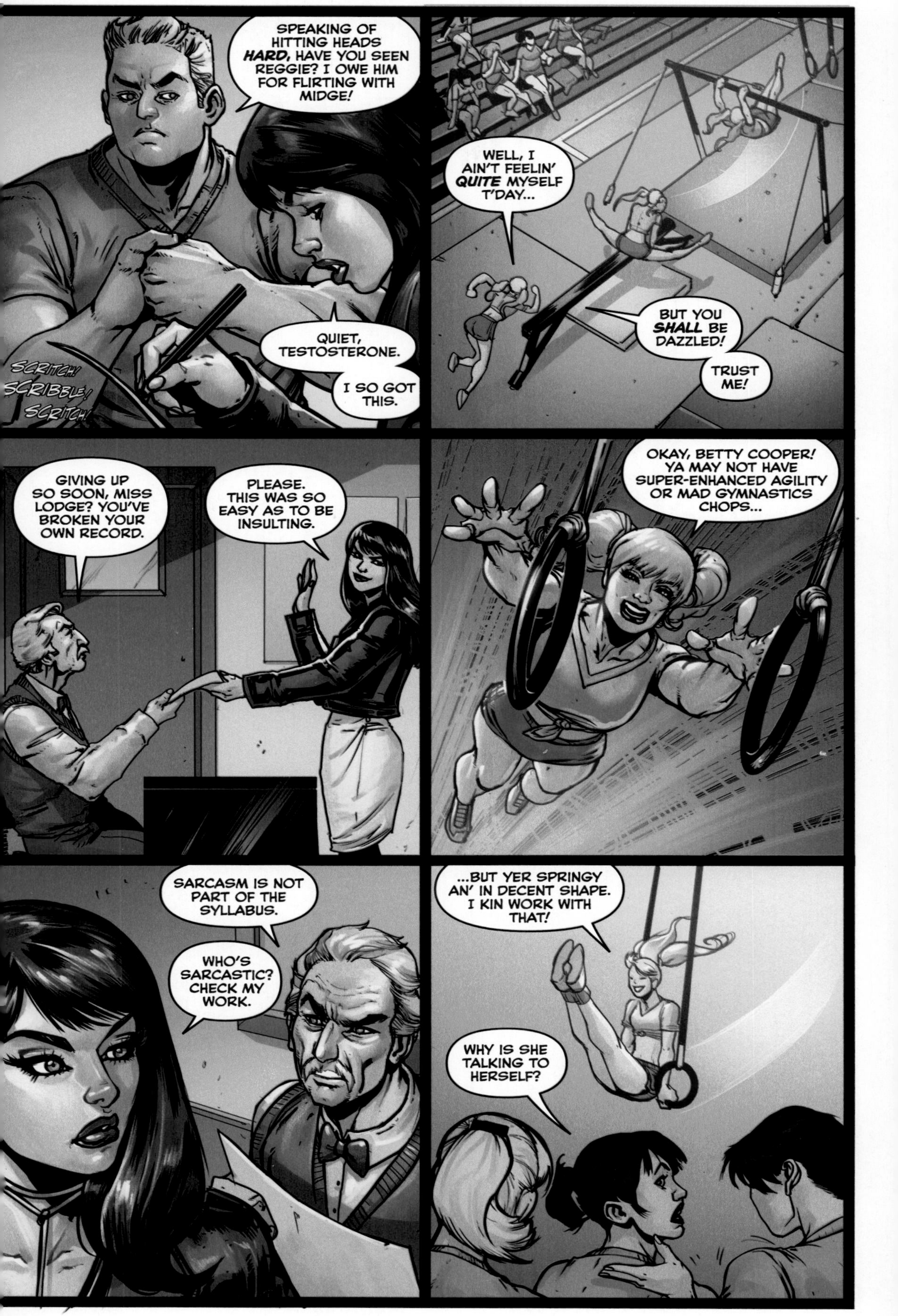
SPEAKING OF HITTING HEADS HARD, HAVE YOU SEEN REGGIE? I OWE HIM FOR FLIRTING WITH MIDGE!
QUIET, TESTOSTERONE.
I SO GOT THIS.
SCRITCH! SCRIBBLE! SCRITCH!
WELL, I AIN'T FEELIN' QUITE MYSELF T'DAY...
BUT YOU SHALL BE DAZZLED!
TRUST ME!
GIVING UP SO SOON, MISS LODGE? YOU'VE BROKEN YOUR OWN RECORD.
PLEASE. THIS WAS SO EASY AS TO BE INSULTING.
OKAY, BETTY COOPER! YA MAY NOT HAVE SUPER-ENHANCED AGILITY OR MAD GYMNASTICS CHOPS...
SARCASM IS NOT PART OF THE SYLLABUS.
WHO'S SARCASTIC? CHECK MY WORK.
...BUT YER SPRINGY AN' IN DECENT SHAPE. I KIN WORK WITH THAT!
WHY IS SHE TALKING TO HERSELF?

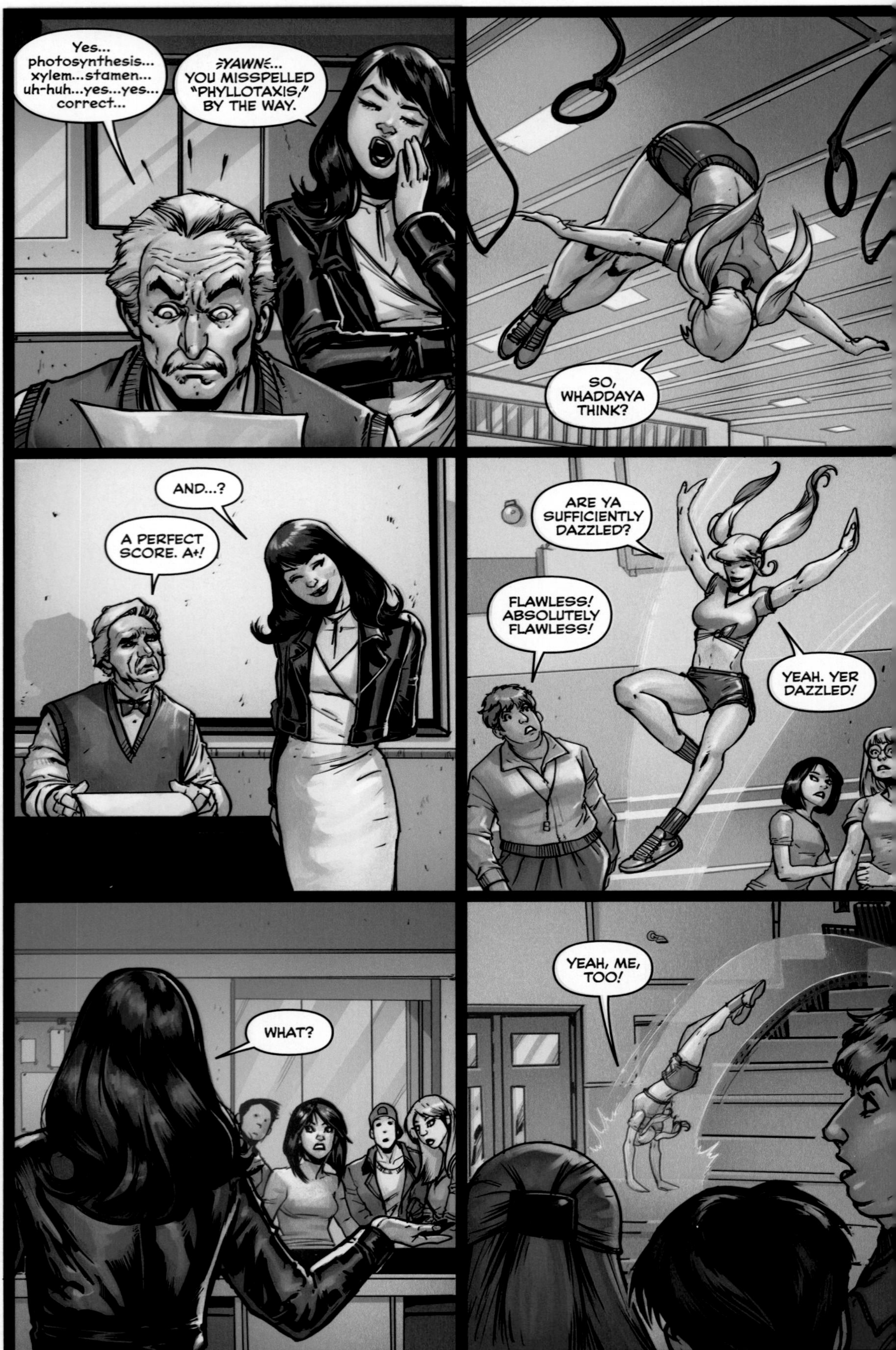
Yes... photosynthesis... xylem...stamen... uh-huh...yes...yes... correct...
YAWN... YOU MISSPELLED "PHYLLOTAXIS," BY THE WAY.
SO, WHADDAYA THINK?
AND...?
A PERFECT SCORE. A+!
ARE YA SUFFICIENTLY DAZZLED?
FLAWLESS! ABSOLUTELY FLAWLESS!
YEAH. YER DAZZLED!
WHAT?
YEAH, ME, TOO!

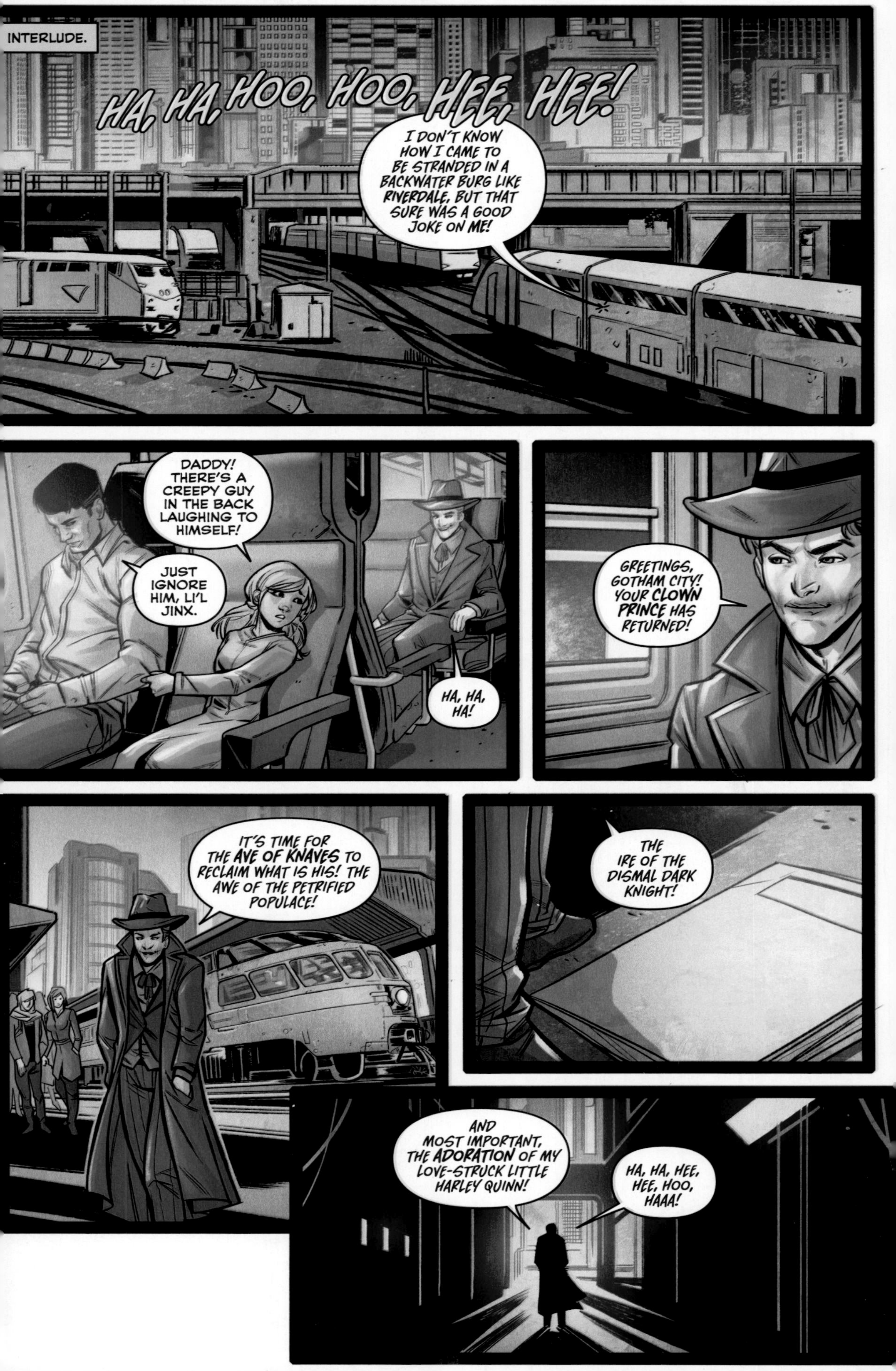

INTERLUDE.
HA, HA, HOO, HOO, HEE, HEE!
I DON'T KNOW HOW I CAME TO BE STRANDED IN A BACKWATER BURG LIKE RIVERDALE, BUT THAT SURE WAS A GOOD JOKE ON ME!
DADDY! THERE'S A CREEPY GUY IN THE BACK LAUGHING TO HIMSELF!
JUST IGNORE HIM, LI'L JINX.
HA, HA, HA!
GREETINGS, GOTHAM CITY! YOUR CLOWN PRINCE HAS RETURNED!
IT'S TIME FOR THE AVE OF KNAVES TO RECLAIM WHAT IS HIS! THE AWE OF THE PETRIFIED POPULACE!
THE IRE OF THE DISMAL DARK KNIGHT!
AND MOST IMPORTANT, THE ADORATION OF MY LOVE-STRUCK LITTLE HARLEY QUINN!
HA, HA, HEE, HEE, HOO, HAAA!

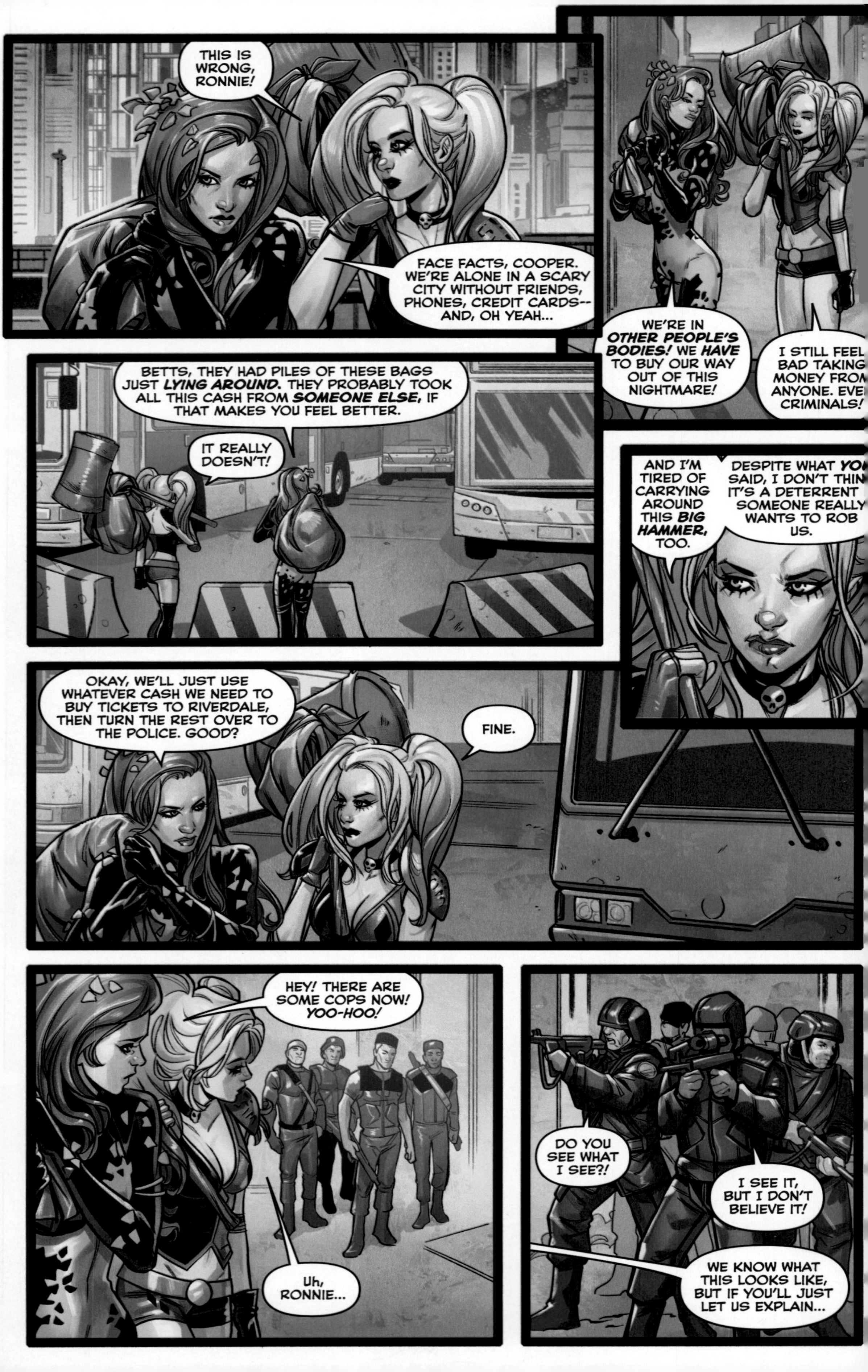

THIS IS WRONG, RONNIE!
FACE FACTS, COOPER. WE'RE ALONE IN A SCARY CITY WITHOUT FRIENDS, PHONES, CREDIT CARDS-- AND, OH YEAH...
WE'RE IN OTHER PEOPLE'S BODIES! WE HAVE TO BUY OUR WAY OUT OF THIS NIGHTMARE!
I STILL FEEL BAD TAKING MONEY FROM ANYONE. EVEN CRIMINALS!
BETTS, THEY HAD PILES OF THESE BAGS JUST LYING AROUND. THEY PROBABLY TOOK ALL THIS CASH FROM SOMEONE ELSE, IF THAT MAKES YOU FEEL BETTER.
IT REALLY DOESN'T!
AND I'M TIRED OF CARRYING AROUND THIS BIG HAMMER, TOO.
DESPITE WHAT YOU SAID, I DON'T THINK IT'S A DETERRENT IF SOMEONE REALLY WANTS TO ROB US.
OKAY, WE'LL JUST USE WHATEVER CASH WE NEED TO BUY TICKETS TO RIVERDALE, THEN TURN THE REST OVER TO THE POLICE. GOOD?
FINE.
HEY! THERE ARE SOME COPS NOW! YOO-HOO!
Uh, RONNIE...
DO YOU SEE WHAT I SEE?!
I SEE IT, BUT I DON'T BELIEVE IT!
WE KNOW WHAT THIS LOOKS LIKE, BUT IF YOU'LL JUST LET US EXPLAIN...

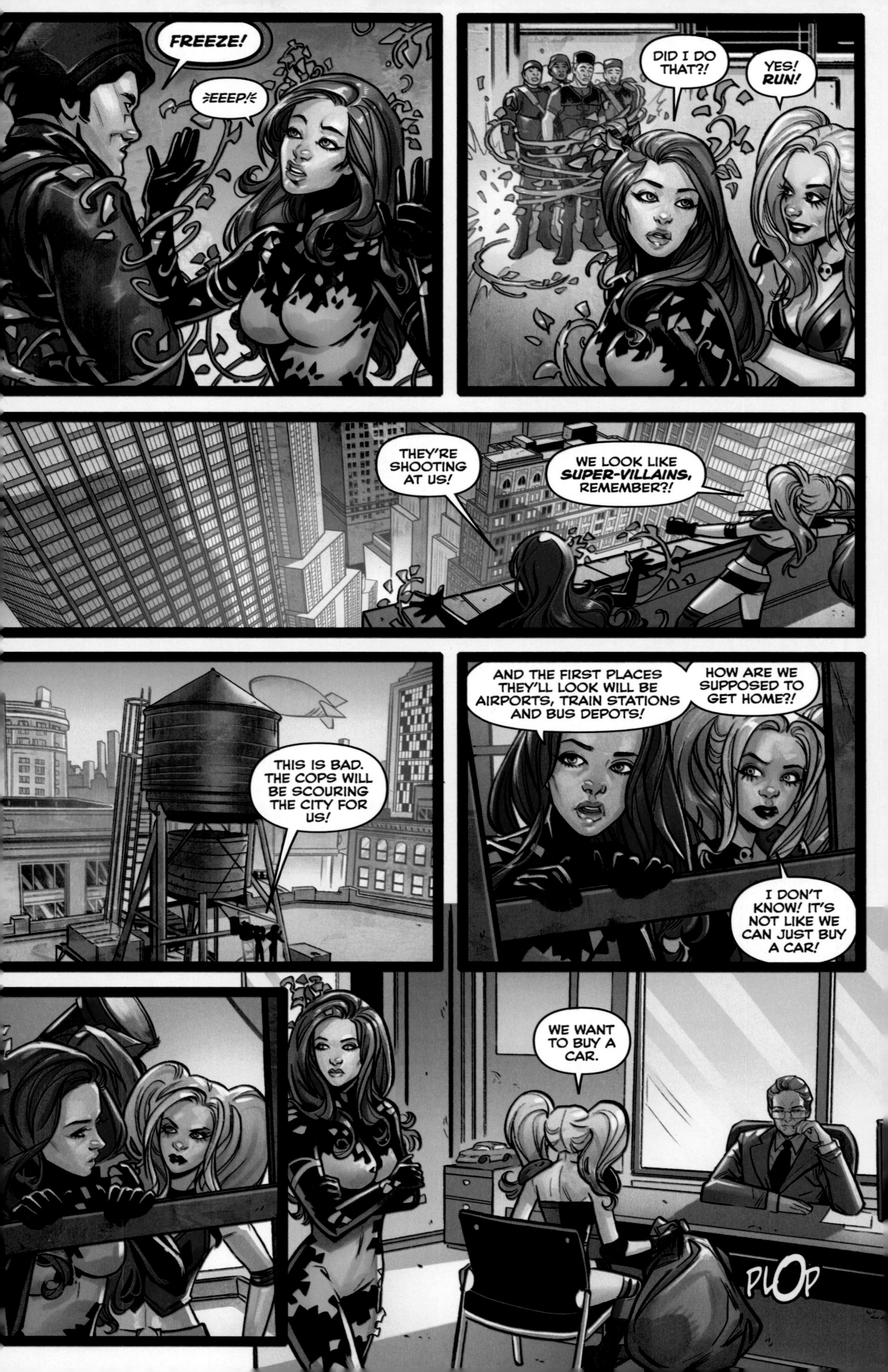
FREEZE!
EEEP!
DID I DO THAT?!
YES! RUN!
THEY'RE SHOOTING AT US!
WE LOOK LIKE SUPER-VILLAINS, REMEMBER?!
THIS IS BAD. THE COPS WILL BE SCOURING THE CITY FOR US!
AND THE FIRST PLACES THEY'LL LOOK WILL BE AIRPORTS, TRAIN STATIONS AND BUS DEPOTS!
HOW ARE WE SUPPOSED TO GET HOME?!
I DON'T KNOW! IT'S NOT LIKE WE CAN JUST BUY A CAR!
WE WANT TO BUY A CAR.
PLOP

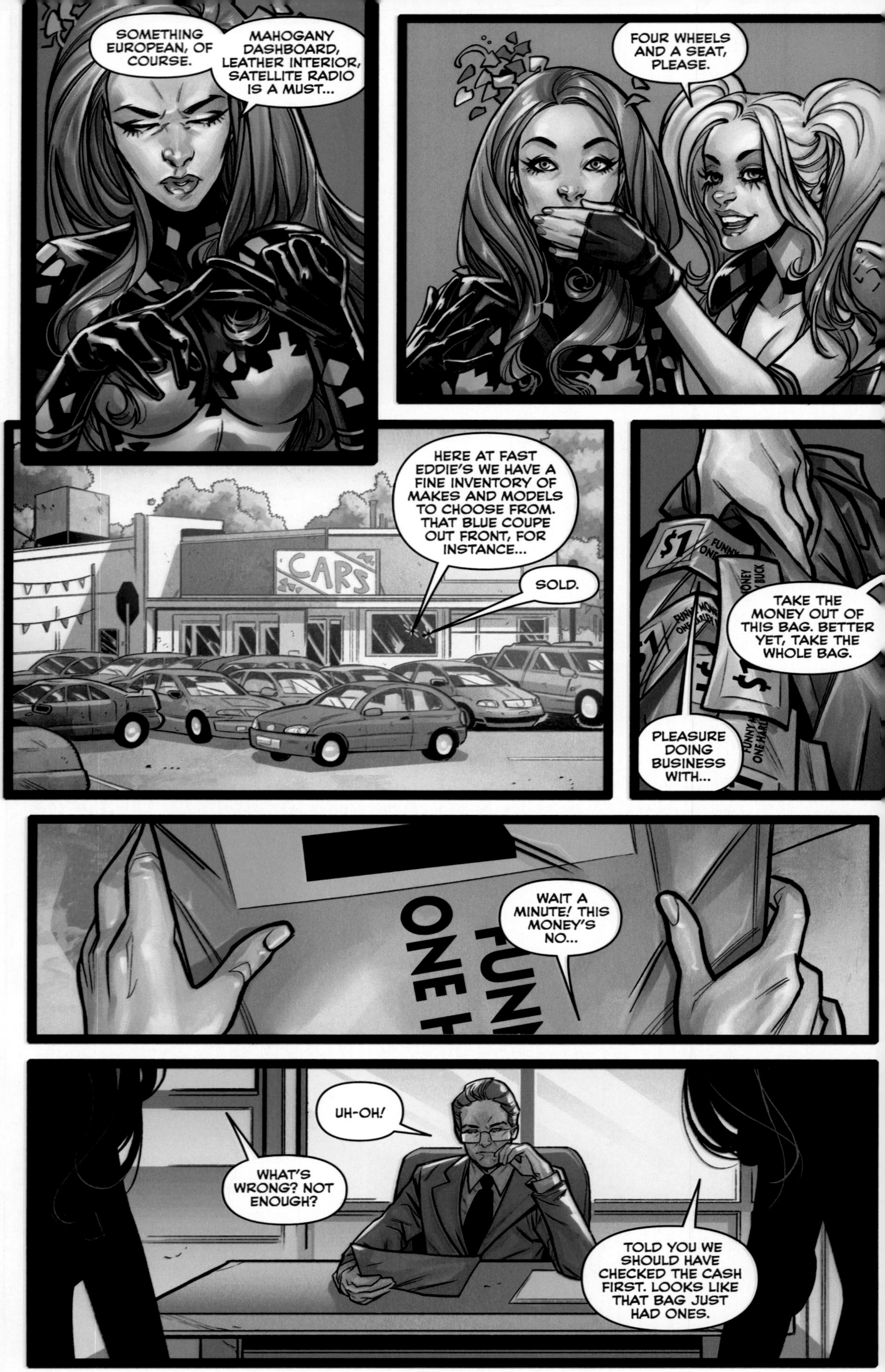
SOMETHING EUROPEAN, OF COURSE.
MAHOGANY DASHBOARD, LEATHER INTERIOR, SATELLITE RADIO IS A MUST...
FOUR WHEELS AND A SEAT, PLEASE.
CARS
HERE AT FAST EDDIE'S WE HAVE A FINE INVENTORY OF MAKES AND MODELS TO CHOOSE FROM. THAT BLUE COUPE OUT FRONT, FOR INSTANCE...
SOLD.
TAKE THE MONEY OUT OF THIS BAG. BETTER YET, TAKE THE WHOLE BAG.
PLEASURE DOING BUSINESS WITH...
WAIT A MINUTE! THIS MONEY'S NO...
UH-OH!
WHAT'S WRONG? NOT ENOUGH?
TOLD YOU WE SHOULD HAVE CHECKED THE CASH FIRST. LOOKS LIKE THAT BAG JUST HAD ONES.

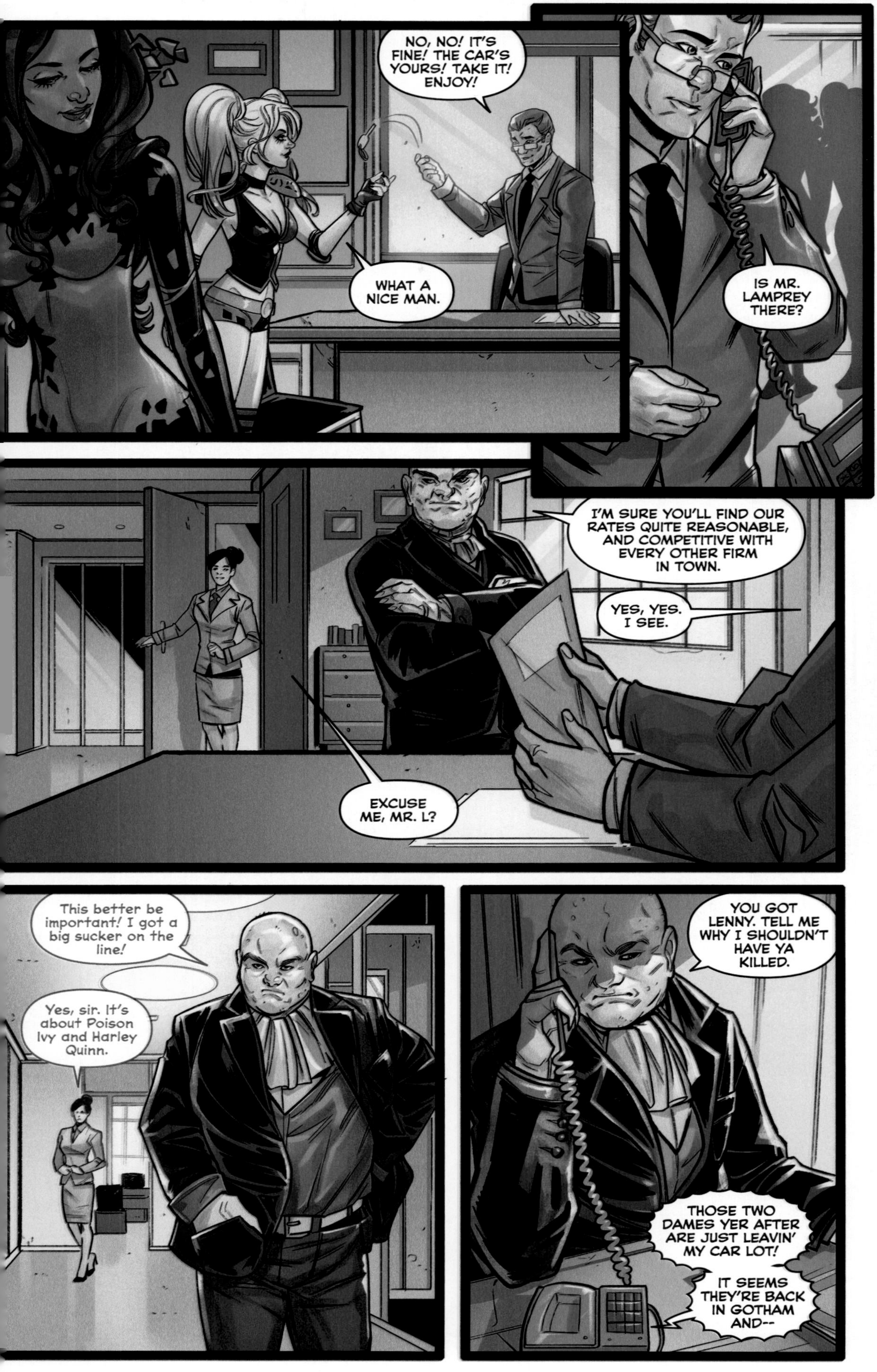
NO, NO! IT'S FINE! THE CAR'S YOURS! TAKE IT! ENJOY!
WHAT A NICE MAN.
IS MR. LAMPREY THERE?
I'M SURE YOU'LL FIND OUR RATES QUITE REASONABLE, AND COMPETITIVE WITH EVERY OTHER FIRM IN TOWN.
YES, YES. I SEE.
EXCUSE ME, MR. L?
This better be important! I got a big sucker on the line!
Yes, sir. It's about Poison Ivy and Harley Quinn.
YOU GOT LENNY. TELL ME WHY I SHOULDN'T HAVE YA KILLED.
THOSE TWO DAMES YER AFTER ARE JUST LEAVIN' MY CAR LOT!
IT SEEMS THEY'RE BACK IN GOTHAM AND--

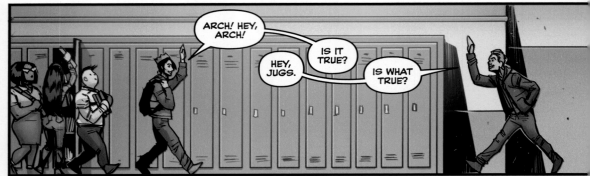

ARCH! HEY, ARCH!

HEY, JUGS.

IS IT TRUE?

IS WHAT TRUE?

THAT BETTY AND VERONICA HAVE GONE MENTAL, THAT'S WHAT! IT'S THE TALK OF RIVERDALE HIGH.

GEEZ, THE GOSSIP TRAIN IS SPEEDY HERE.

THAT'S NOT AN ANSWER.

"MENTAL" IS A STRONG WORD. OKAY, THEY SEEMED A LITTLE...WEIRD...

YOU MEAN "WEIRDER."

WHATEVER... BUT THEY DID HAVE A TOUGH NIGHT. THEY'RE PROBABLY JUST--

--MENTAL! I HEARD OUR FAVORITE FRENEMIES RETURNED A LITTLE BIT...DIFFERENT.

I'M SURE THEY'RE BACK TO NORMAL, YOU GUYS.

LOOK, THERE THEY ARE NOW.

HEY! WHERE DO YA THINK YOU'RE GOIN'? WE WERE TALKIN' HERE!

KEEP YOUR VOICE DOWN!

Is this better?!

MARGINALLY.

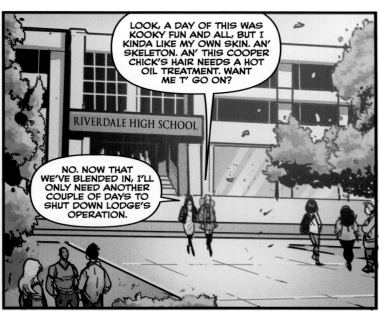

LOOK, A DAY OF THIS WAS KOOKY FUN AND ALL, BUT I KINDA LIKE MY OWN SKIN. AN' SKELETON. AN' THIS COOPER CHICK'S HAIR NEEDS A HOT OIL TREATMENT. WANT ME T' GO ON?

RIVERDALE HIGH SCHOOL

NO. NOW THAT WE'VE BLENDED IN, I'LL ONLY NEED ANOTHER COUPLE OF DAYS TO SHUT DOWN LODGE'S OPERATION.

BESIDES, I'M ACTUALLY HAVING FUN. I FORGOT WHAT BEING A KID FELT LIKE. LET ME HAVE THIS A LITTLE LONGER.

OKAY, FINE, BUT I DON'T WANNA BE HERE TAKING MIDTERMS! ONE MORE DAY AN' THEN WE TRY AND FIGURE OUT HOW TO GET OUR OLD BODS BACK! DEAL?

DEAL.

AND THANK YOU, HARLEY.

OH, YOU KNOW I LOVE YA, RED. I MEAN "TEMPORARILY BRUNETTE!"

OH YEAH. PERFECTLY NORMAL.

GOOD GRIEF! THEY'VE GONE MENTAL!

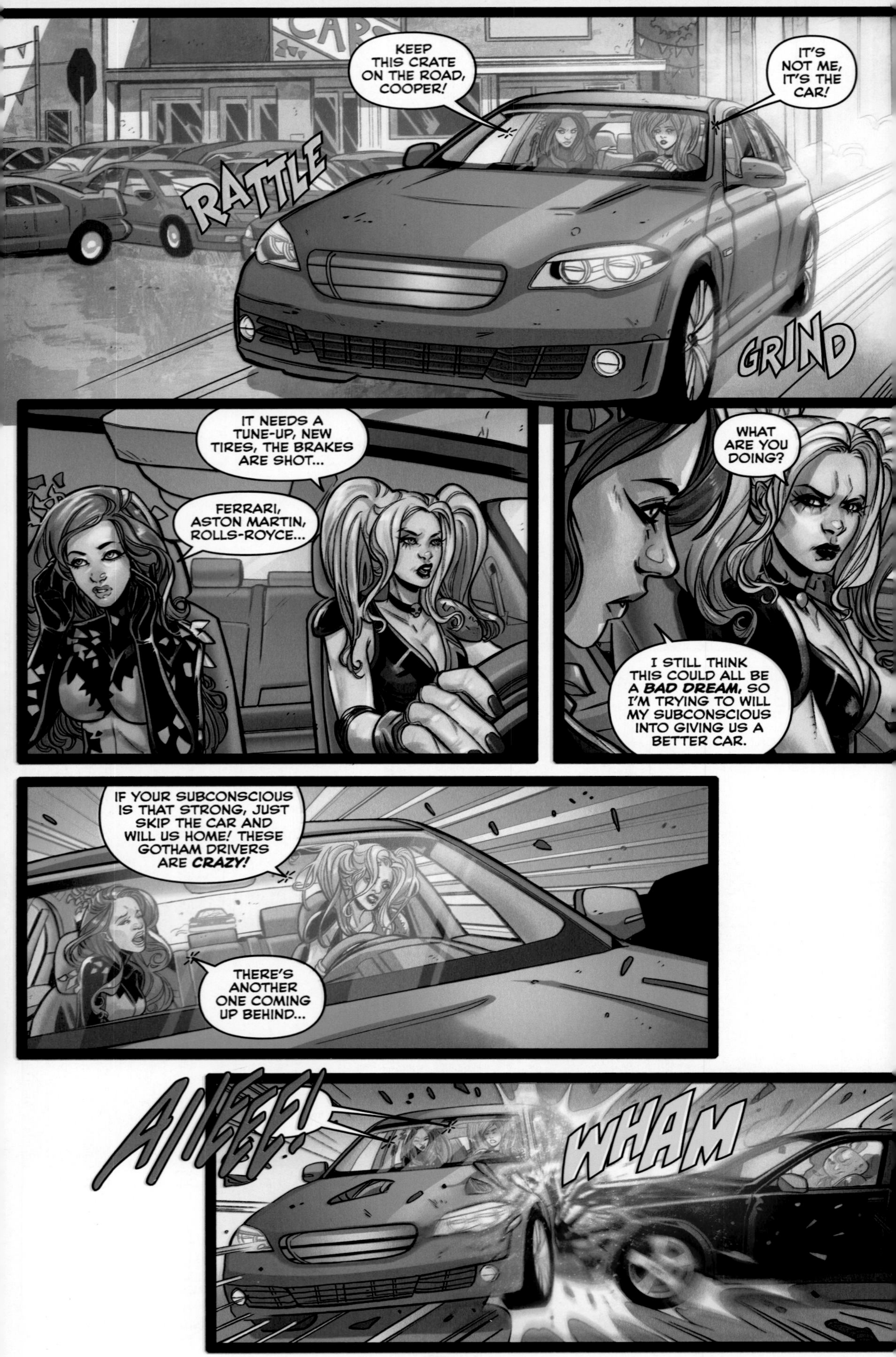
KEEP THIS CRATE ON THE ROAD, COOPER!
IT'S NOT ME, IT'S THE CAR!
RATTLE
GRIND
IT NEEDS A TUNE-UP, NEW TIRES, THE BRAKES ARE SHOT...
FERRARI, ASTON MARTIN, ROLLS-ROYCE...
WHAT ARE YOU DOING?
I STILL THINK THIS COULD ALL BE A **BAD DREAM**, SO I'M TRYING TO WILL MY SUBCONSCIOUS INTO GIVING US A BETTER CAR.
IF YOUR SUBCONSCIOUS IS THAT STRONG, JUST SKIP THE CAR AND WILL US HOME! THESE GOTHAM DRIVERS ARE ***CRAZY!***
THERE'S ANOTHER ONE COMING UP BEHIND...
AIIEEE!
WHAM

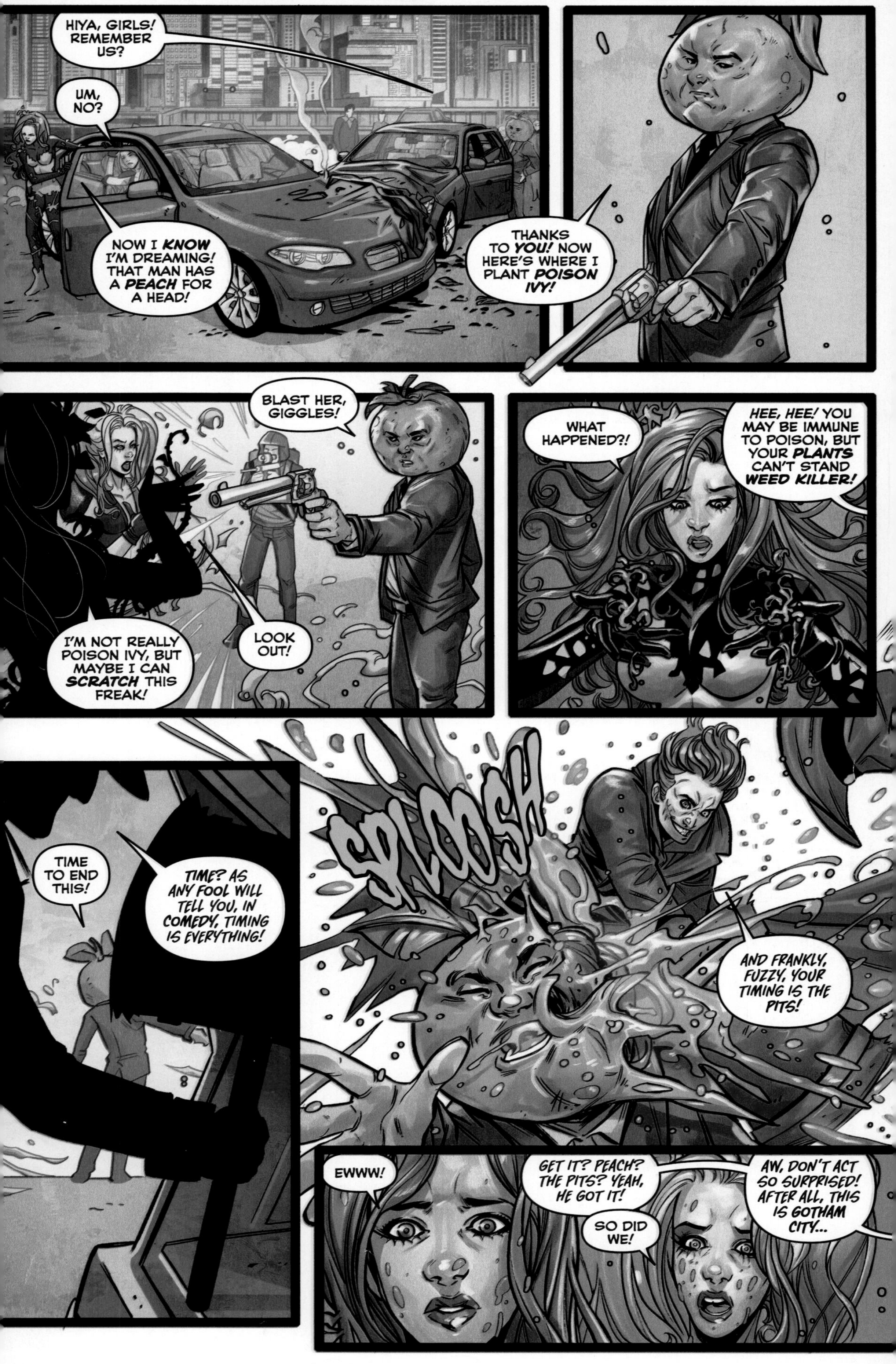
HIYA, GIRLS! REMEMBER US?
UM, NO?
NOW I KNOW I'M DREAMING! THAT MAN HAS A PEACH FOR A HEAD!
THANKS TO YOU! NOW HERE'S WHERE I PLANT POISON IVY!
BLAST HER, GIGGLES!
I'M NOT REALLY POISON IVY, BUT MAYBE I CAN SCRATCH THIS FREAK!
LOOK OUT!
WHAT HAPPENED?!
HEE, HEE! YOU MAY BE IMMUNE TO POISON, BUT YOUR PLANTS CAN'T STAND WEED KILLER!
TIME TO END THIS!
TIME? AS ANY FOOL WILL TELL YOU, IN COMEDY, TIMING IS EVERYTHING!
SPLOOSH
AND FRANKLY, FUZZY, YOUR TIMING IS THE PITS!
EWWW!
GET IT? PEACH? THE PITS? YEAH, HE GOT IT!
SO DID WE!
AW, DON'T ACT SO SURPRISED! AFTER ALL, THIS IS GOTHAM CITY...

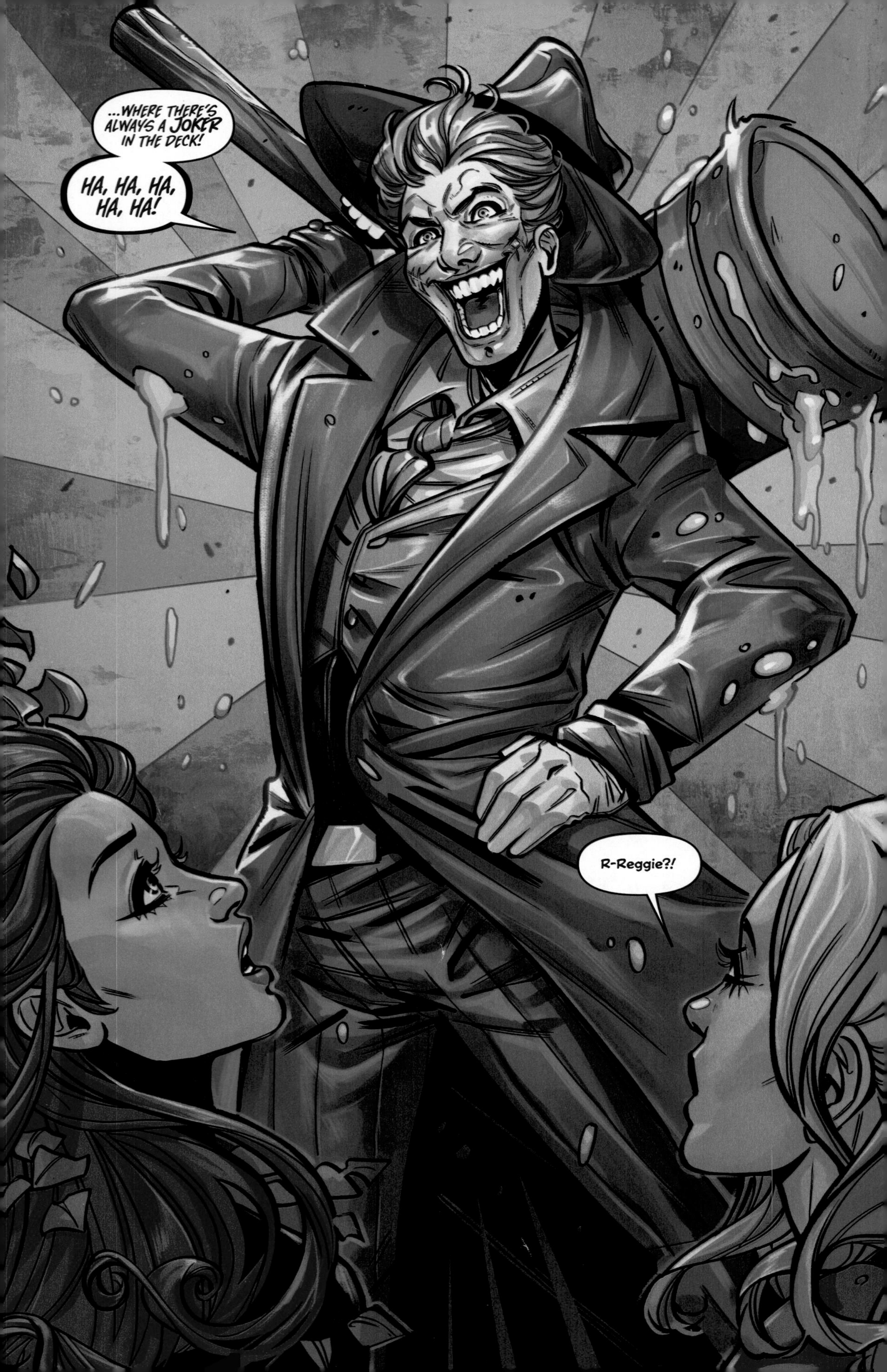
...WHERE THERE'S ALWAYS A JOKER IN THE DECK!
HA, HA, HA, HA, HA!
R-Reggie?!

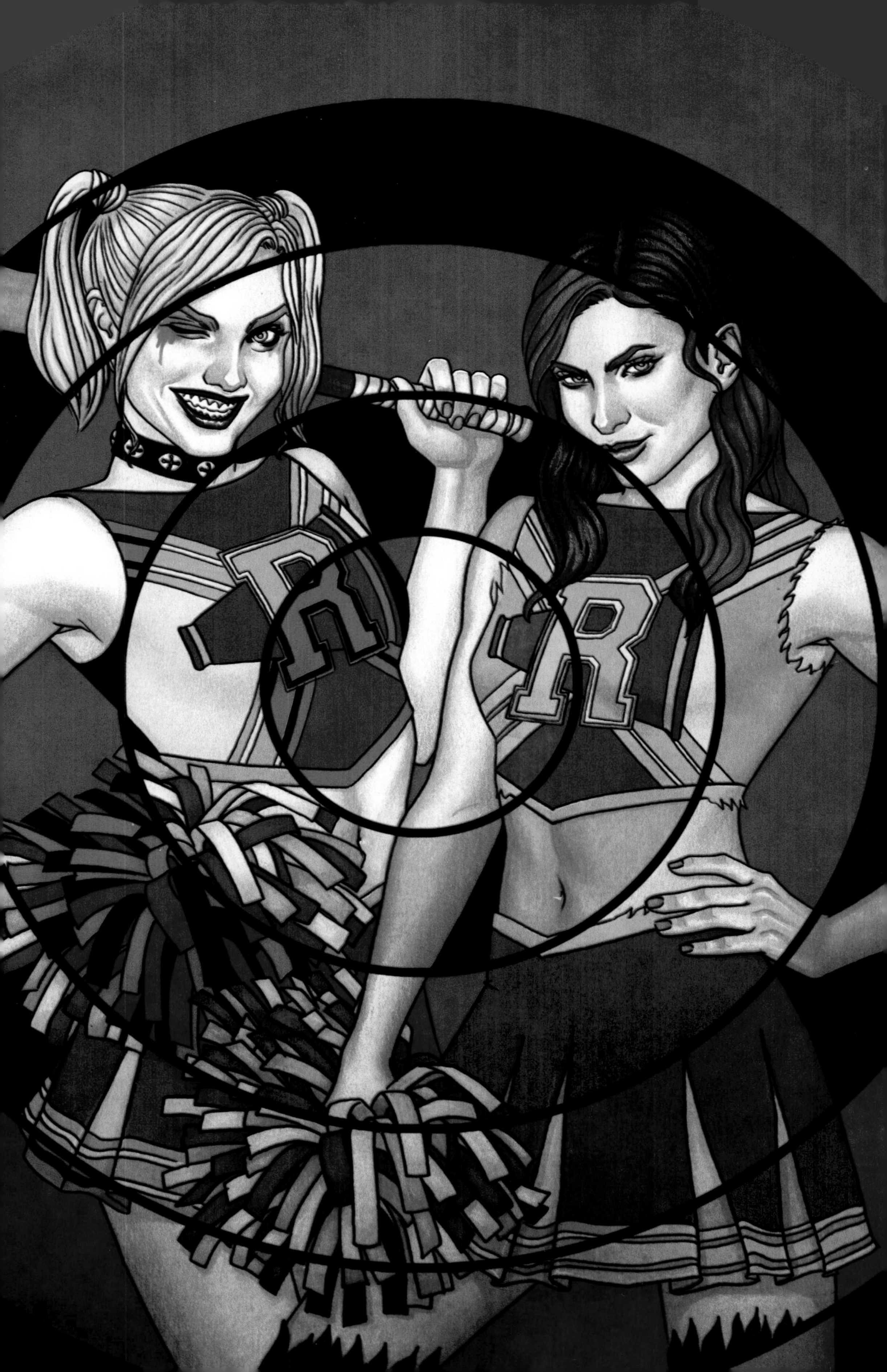

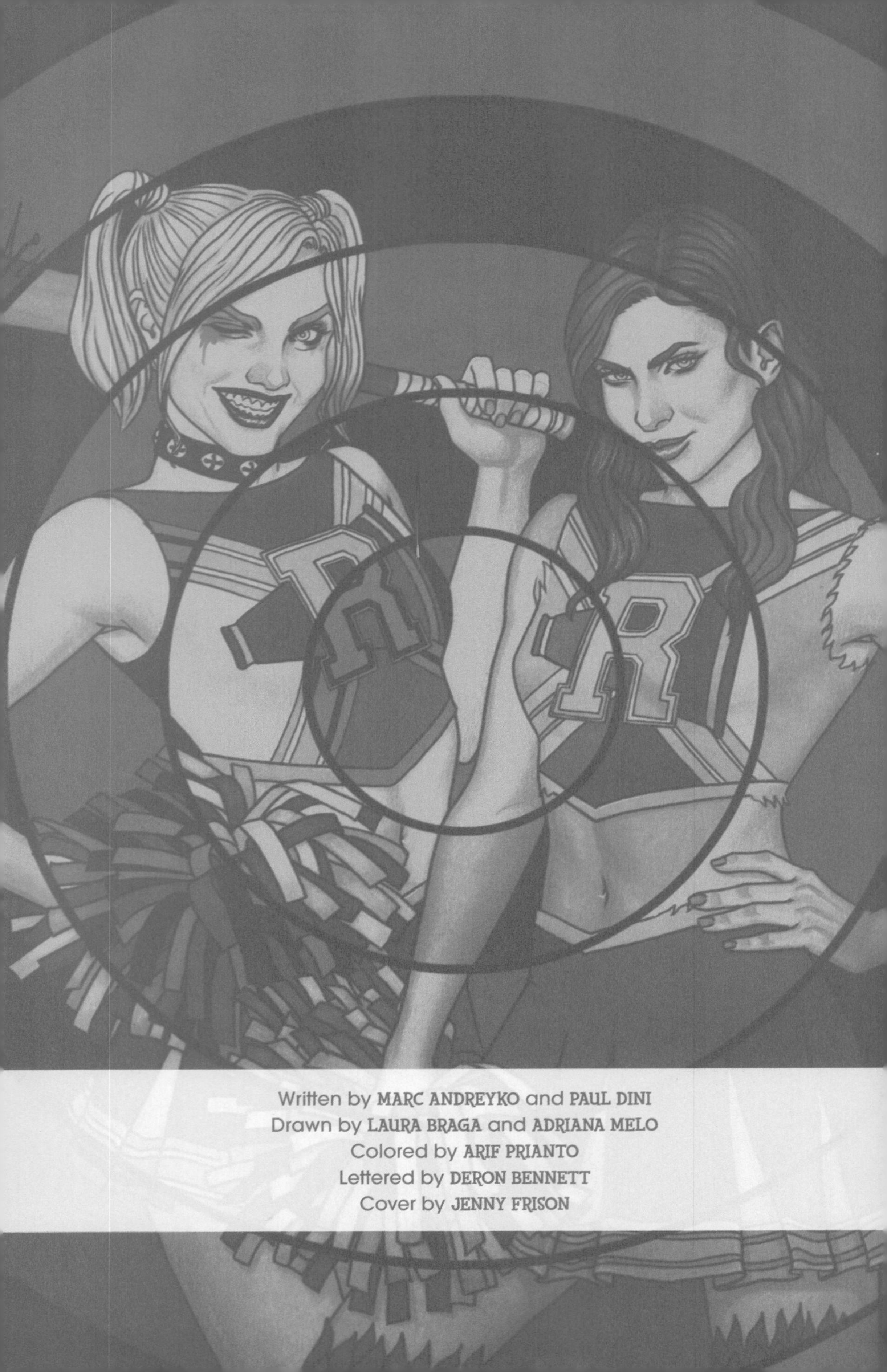

Written by **MARC ANDREYKO** and **PAUL DINI**
Drawn by **LAURA BRAGA** and **ADRIANA MELO**
Colored by **ARIF PRIANTO**
Lettered by **DERON BENNETT**
Cover by **JENNY FRISON**

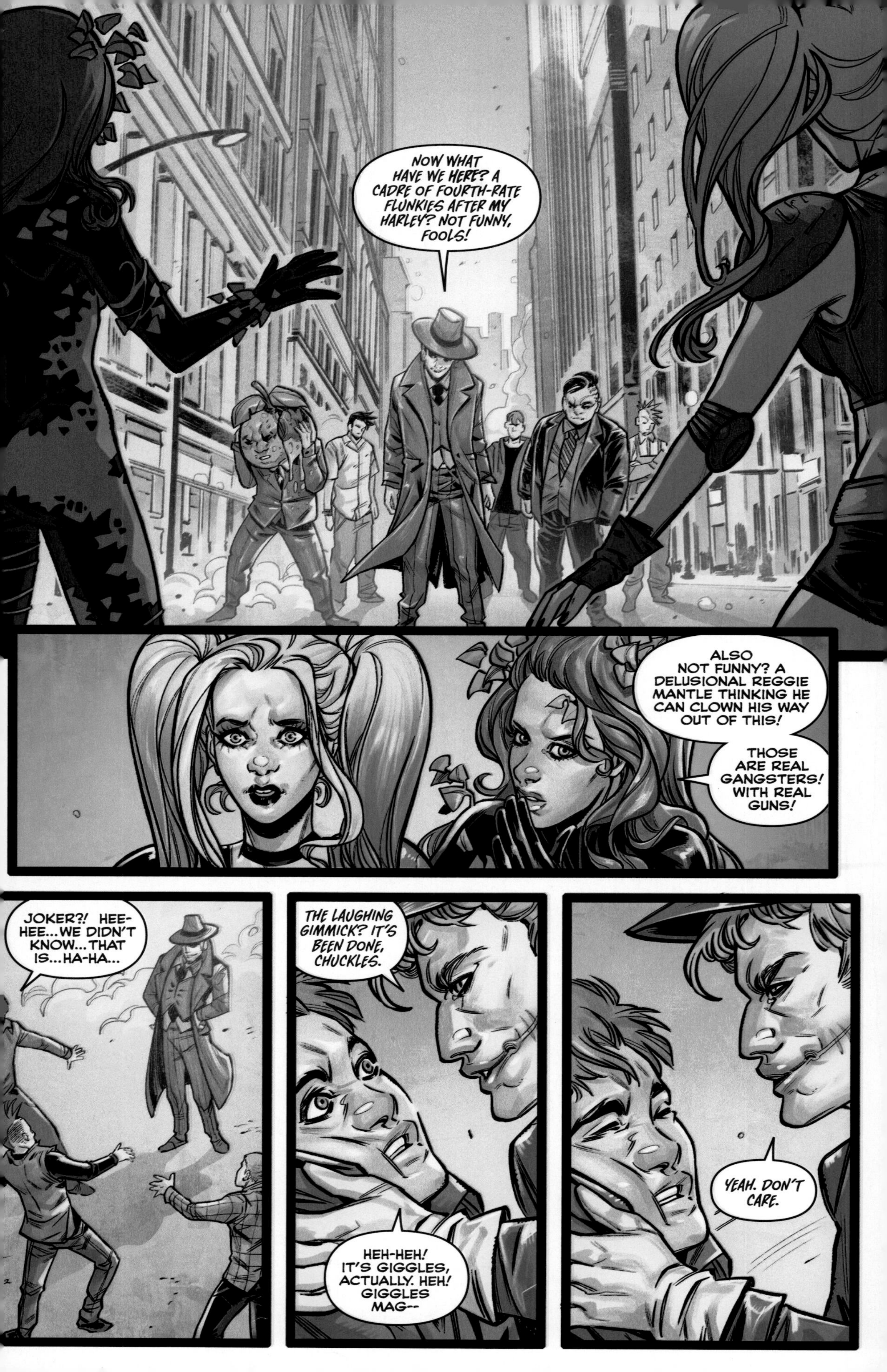
NOW WHAT HAVE WE HERE? A CADRE OF FOURTH-RATE FLUNKIES AFTER MY HARLEY? NOT FUNNY, FOOLS!
ALSO NOT FUNNY? A DELUSIONAL REGGIE MANTLE THINKING HE CAN CLOWN HIS WAY OUT OF THIS!
THOSE ARE REAL GANGSTERS! WITH REAL GUNS!
JOKER?! HEE-HEE...WE DIDN'T KNOW...THAT IS...HA-HA...
THE LAUGHING GIMMICK? IT'S BEEN DONE, CHUCKLES.
HEH-HEH! IT'S GIGGLES, ACTUALLY. HEH! GIGGLES MAG--
YEAH. DON'T CARE.

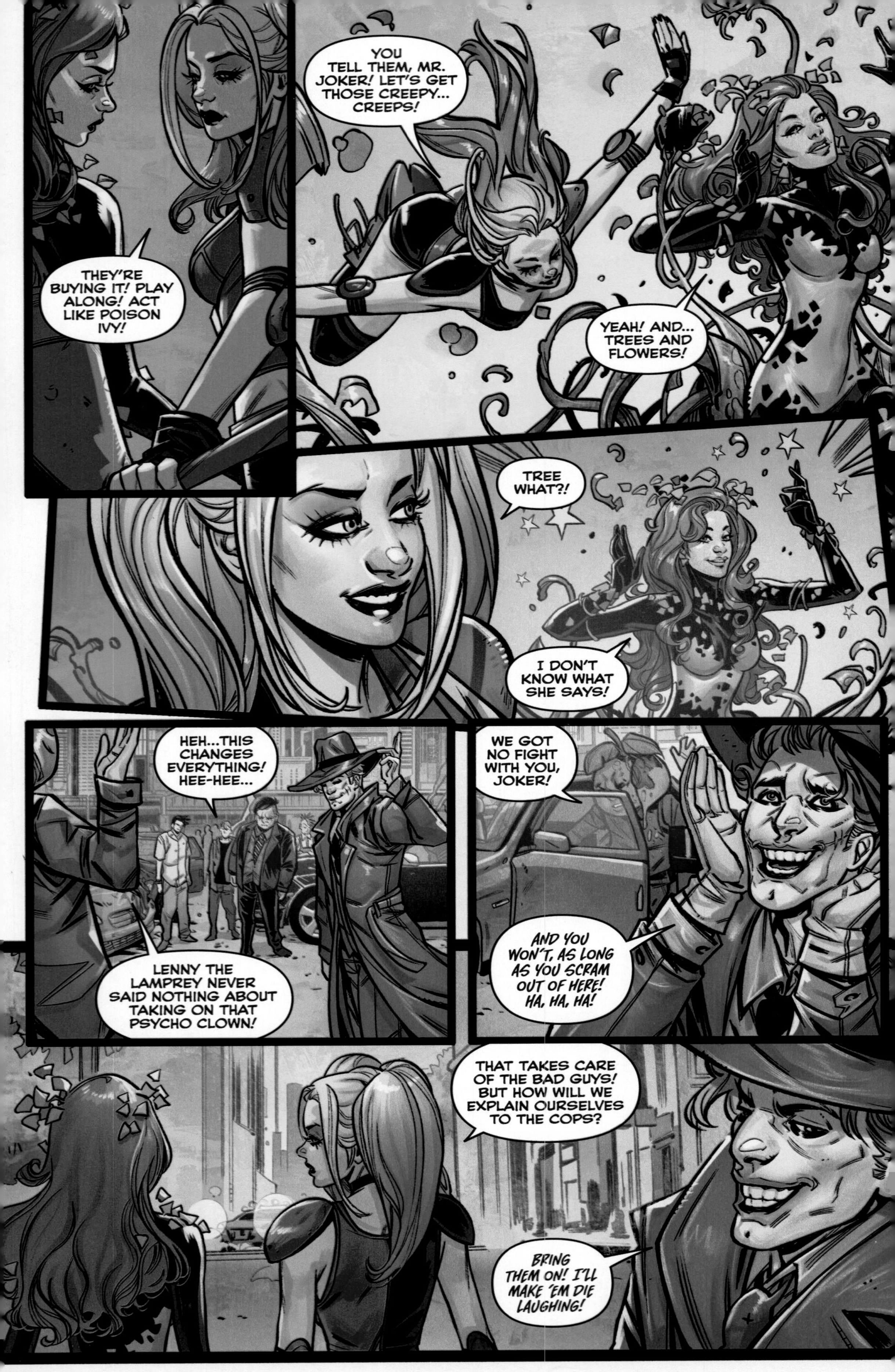
THEY'RE BUYING IT! PLAY ALONG! ACT LIKE POISON IVY!
YOU TELL THEM, MR. JOKER! LET'S GET THOSE CREEPY... CREEPS!
YEAH! AND... TREES AND FLOWERS!
TREE WHAT?!
I DON'T KNOW WHAT SHE SAYS!
HEH...THIS CHANGES EVERYTHING! HEE-HEE...
LENNY THE LAMPREY NEVER SAID NOTHING ABOUT TAKING ON THAT PSYCHO CLOWN!
WE GOT NO FIGHT WITH YOU, JOKER!
AND YOU WON'T, AS LONG AS YOU SCRAM OUT OF HERE! HA, HA, HA!
THAT TAKES CARE OF THE BAD GUYS! BUT HOW WILL WE EXPLAIN OURSELVES TO THE COPS?
BRING THEM ON! I'LL MAKE 'EM DIE LAUGHING!

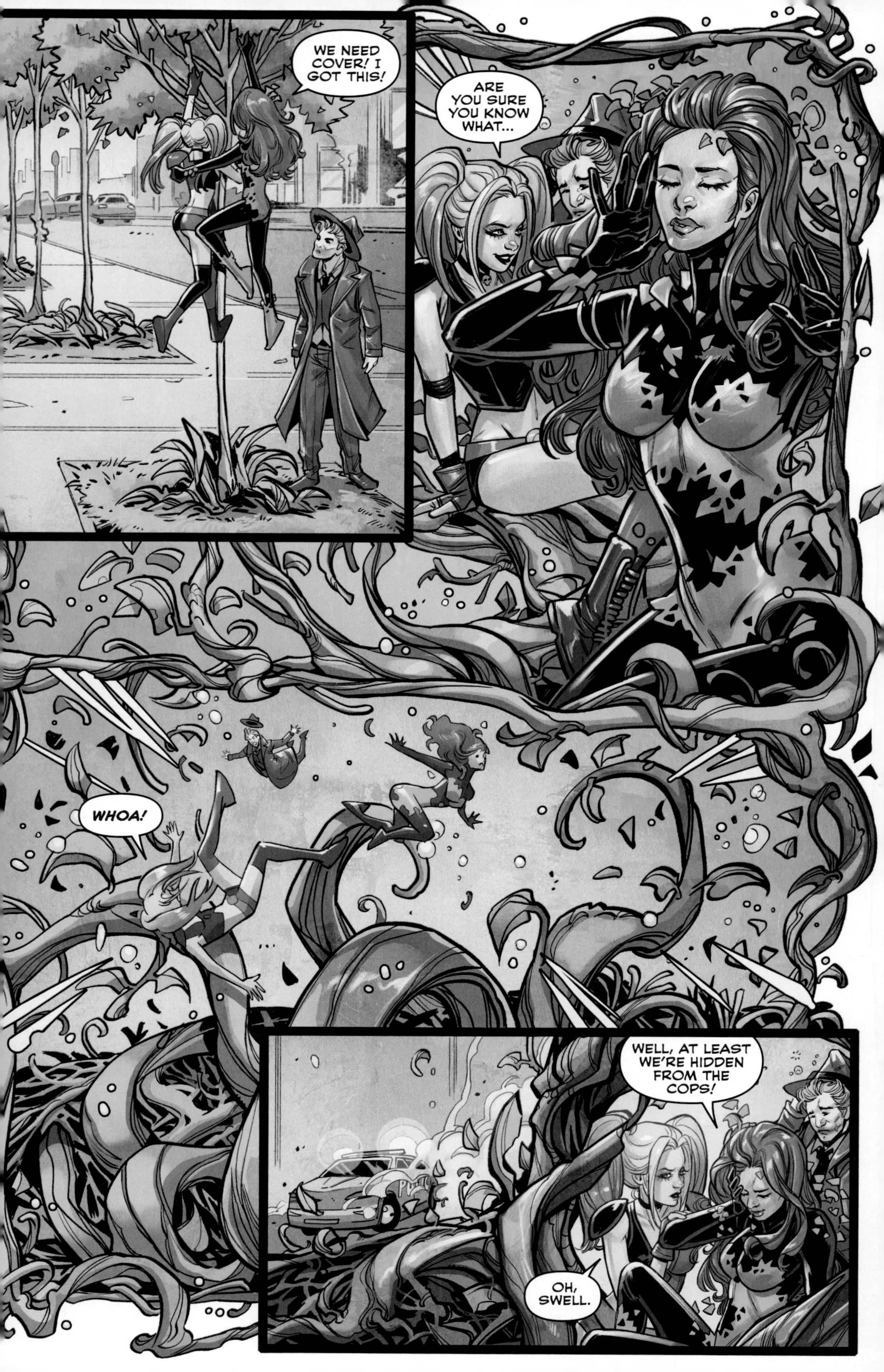

WE NEED COVER! I GOT THIS!
ARE YOU SURE YOU KNOW WHAT...
WHOA!
WELL, AT LEAST WE'RE HIDDEN FROM THE COPS!
OH, SWELL.

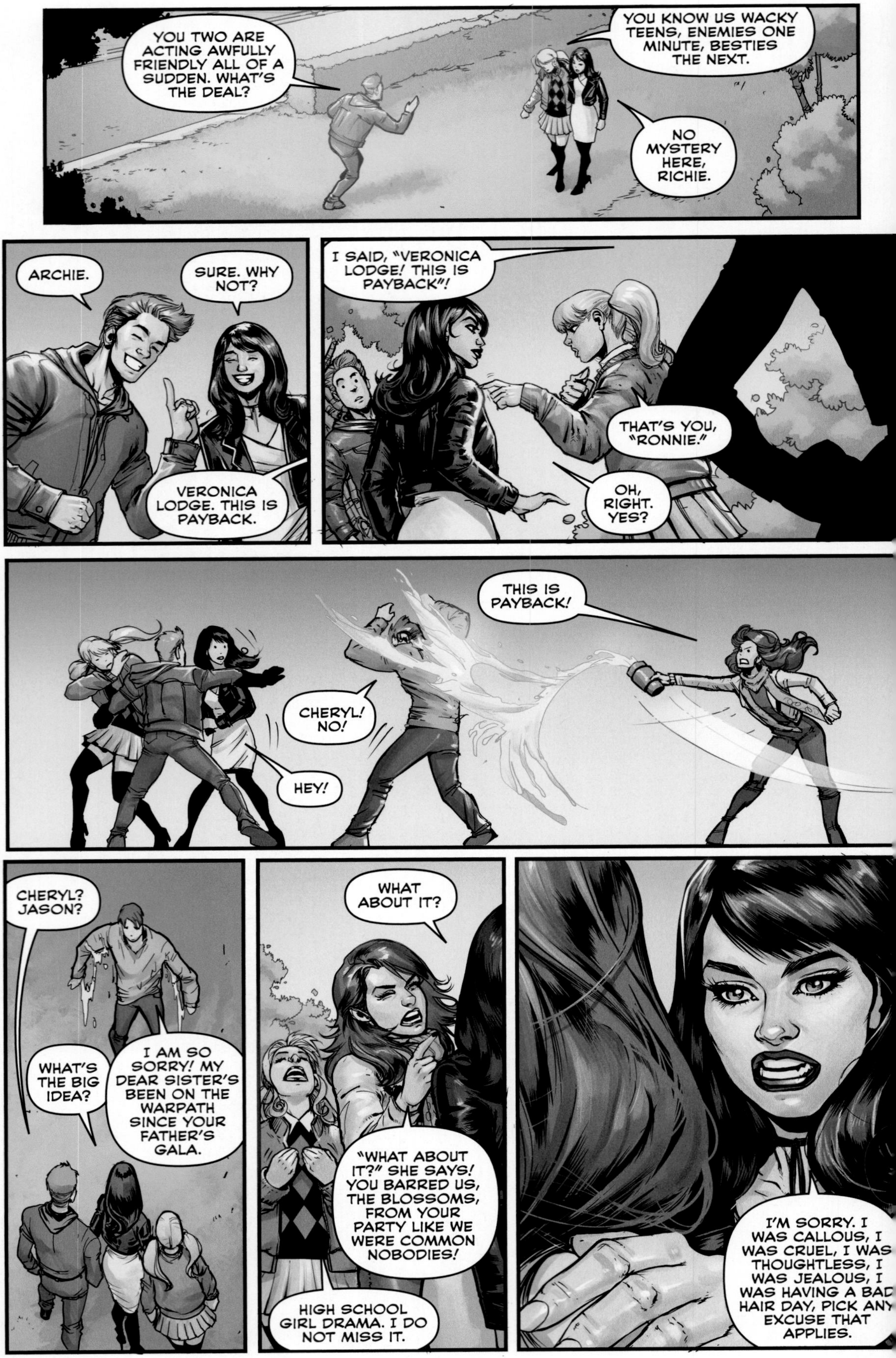
YOU TWO ARE ACTING AWFULLY FRIENDLY ALL OF A SUDDEN. WHAT'S THE DEAL?
YOU KNOW US WACKY TEENS, ENEMIES ONE MINUTE, BESTIES THE NEXT.
NO MYSTERY HERE, RICHIE.
ARCHIE.
SURE. WHY NOT?
VERONICA LODGE. THIS IS PAYBACK.
I SAID, "VERONICA LODGE! THIS IS PAYBACK"!
THAT'S YOU, "RONNIE."
OH, RIGHT. YES?
THIS IS PAYBACK!
CHERYL! NO!
HEY!
CHERYL? JASON?
WHAT'S THE BIG IDEA?
I AM SO SORRY! MY DEAR SISTER'S BEEN ON THE WARPATH SINCE YOUR FATHER'S GALA.
WHAT ABOUT IT?
"WHAT ABOUT IT?" SHE SAYS! YOU BARRED US, THE BLOSSOMS, FROM YOUR PARTY LIKE WE WERE COMMON NOBODIES!
HIGH SCHOOL GIRL DRAMA. I DO NOT MISS IT.
I'M SORRY. I WAS CALLOUS, I WAS CRUEL, I WAS THOUGHTLESS, I WAS JEALOUS, I WAS HAVING A BAD HAIR DAY, PICK ANY EXCUSE THAT APPLIES.

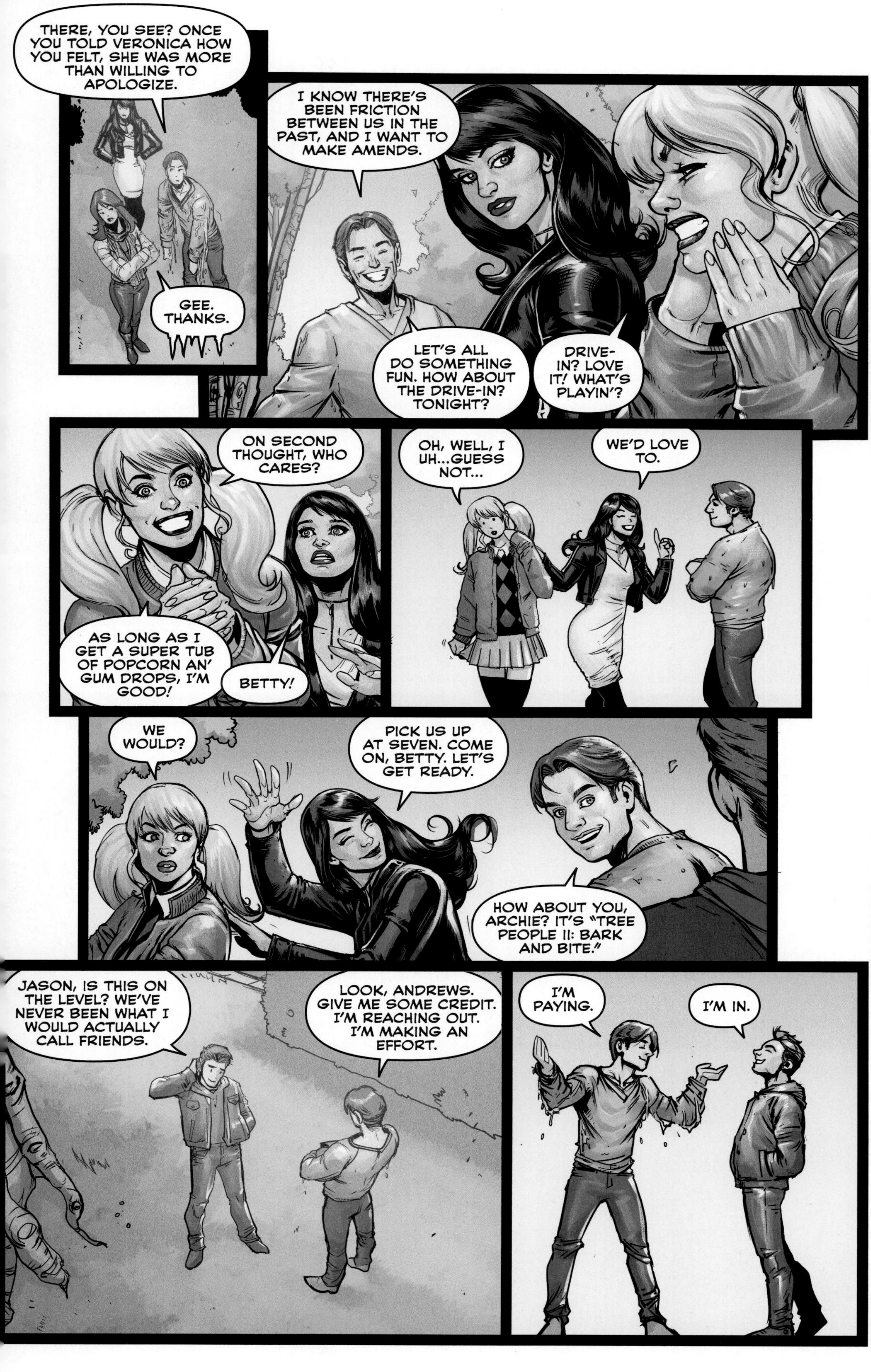
THERE, YOU SEE? ONCE YOU TOLD VERONICA HOW YOU FELT, SHE WAS MORE THAN WILLING TO APOLOGIZE.
GEE. THANKS.
I KNOW THERE'S BEEN FRICTION BETWEEN US IN THE PAST, AND I WANT TO MAKE AMENDS.
LET'S ALL DO SOMETHING FUN. HOW ABOUT THE DRIVE-IN? TONIGHT?
DRIVE-IN? LOVE IT! WHAT'S PLAYIN'?
ON SECOND THOUGHT, WHO CARES?
AS LONG AS I GET A SUPER TUB OF POPCORN AN' GUM DROPS, I'M GOOD!
BETTY!
OH, WELL, I UH...GUESS NOT...
WE'D LOVE TO.
WE WOULD?
PICK US UP AT SEVEN. COME ON, BETTY. LET'S GET READY.
HOW ABOUT YOU, ARCHIE? IT'S "TREE PEOPLE II: BARK AND BITE."
JASON, IS THIS ON THE LEVEL? WE'VE NEVER BEEN WHAT I WOULD ACTUALLY CALL FRIENDS.
LOOK, ANDREWS. GIVE ME SOME CREDIT. I'M REACHING OUT. I'M MAKING AN EFFORT.
I'M PAYING.
I'M IN.

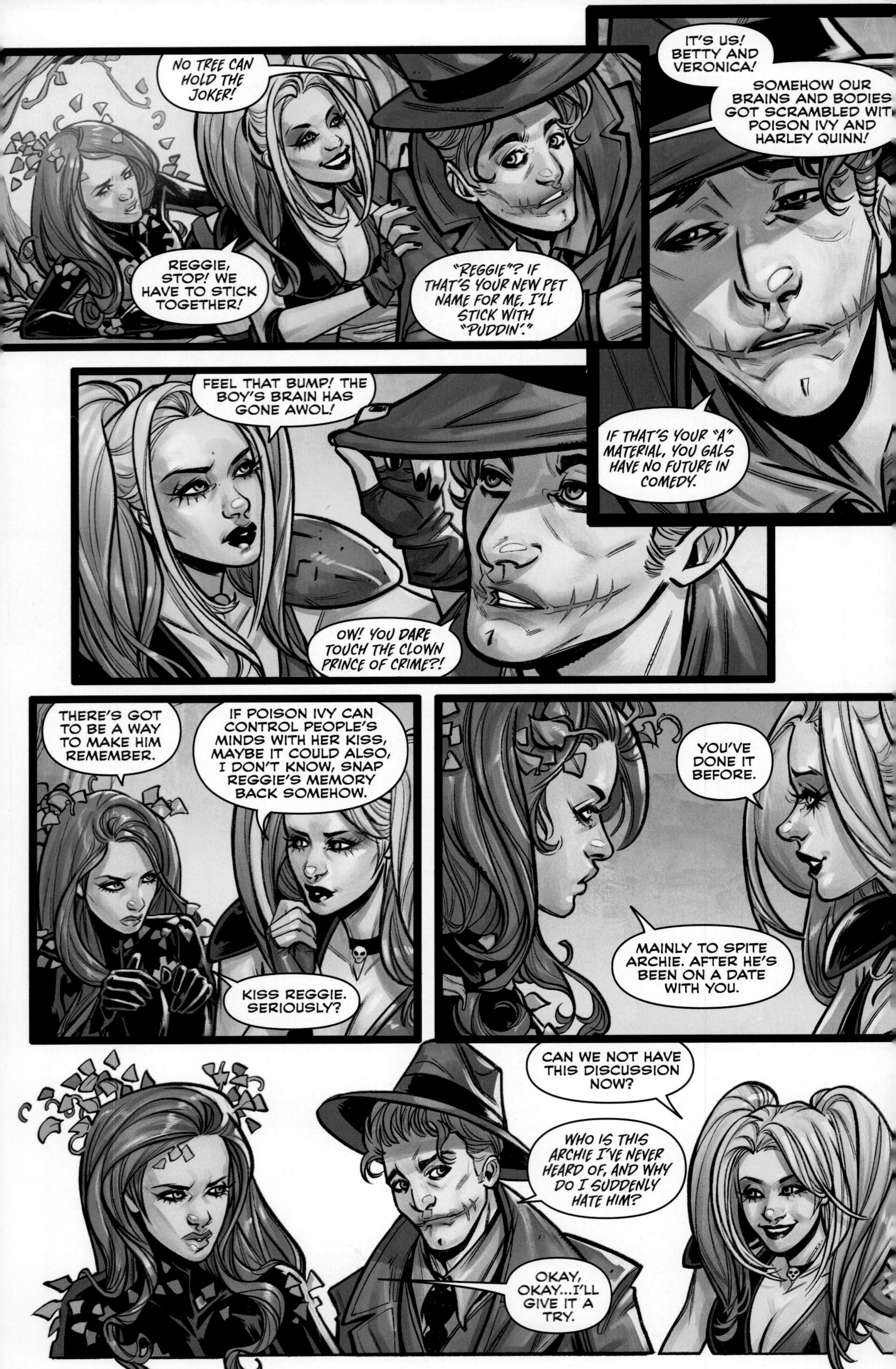

NO TREE CAN HOLD THE JOKER!
REGGIE, STOP! WE HAVE TO STICK TOGETHER!
"REGGIE"? IF THAT'S YOUR NEW PET NAME FOR ME, I'LL STICK WITH "PUDDIN'."
IT'S US! BETTY AND VERONICA!
SOMEHOW OUR BRAINS AND BODIES GOT SCRAMBLED WIT POISON IVY AND HARLEY QUINN!
IF THAT'S YOUR "A" MATERIAL, YOU GALS HAVE NO FUTURE IN COMEDY.
FEEL THAT BUMP! THE BOY'S BRAIN HAS GONE AWOL!
OW! YOU DARE TOUCH THE CLOWN PRINCE OF CRIME?!
THERE'S GOT TO BE A WAY TO MAKE HIM REMEMBER.
IF POISON IVY CAN CONTROL PEOPLE'S MINDS WITH HER KISS, MAYBE IT COULD ALSO, I DON'T KNOW, SNAP REGGIE'S MEMORY BACK SOMEHOW.
KISS REGGIE. SERIOUSLY?
YOU'VE DONE IT BEFORE.
MAINLY TO SPITE ARCHIE. AFTER HE'S BEEN ON A DATE WITH YOU.
CAN WE NOT HAVE THIS DISCUSSION NOW?
WHO IS THIS ARCHIE I'VE NEVER HEARD OF, AND WHY DO I SUDDENLY HATE HIM?
OKAY, OKAY...I'LL GIVE IT A TRY.

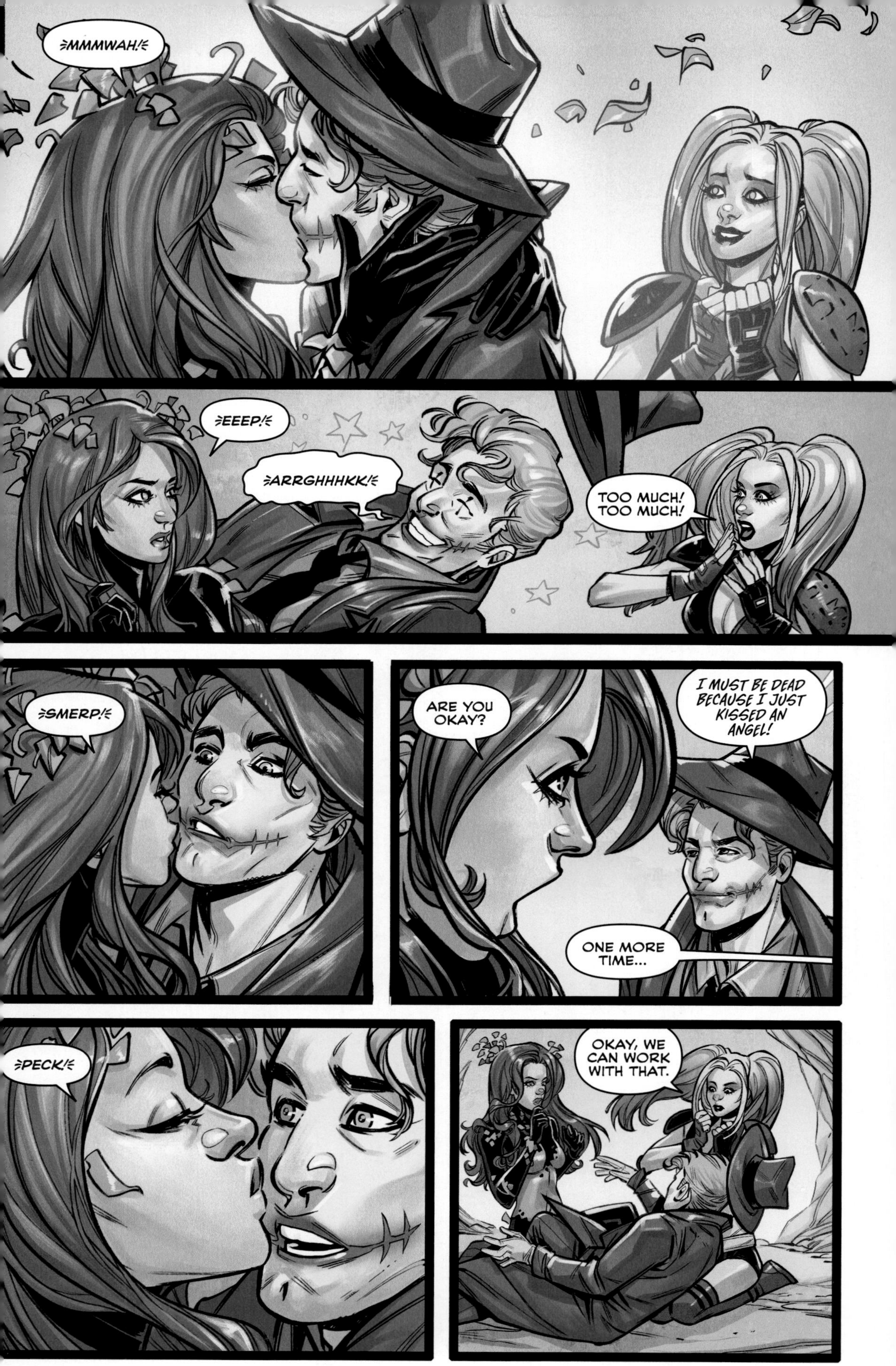

MMMWAH!
EEEP!
ARRGHHHKK!
TOO MUCH! TOO MUCH!
SMERP!
ARE YOU OKAY?
I MUST BE DEAD BECAUSE I JUST KISSED AN ANGEL!
ONE MORE TIME...
PECK!
OKAY, WE CAN WORK WITH THAT.

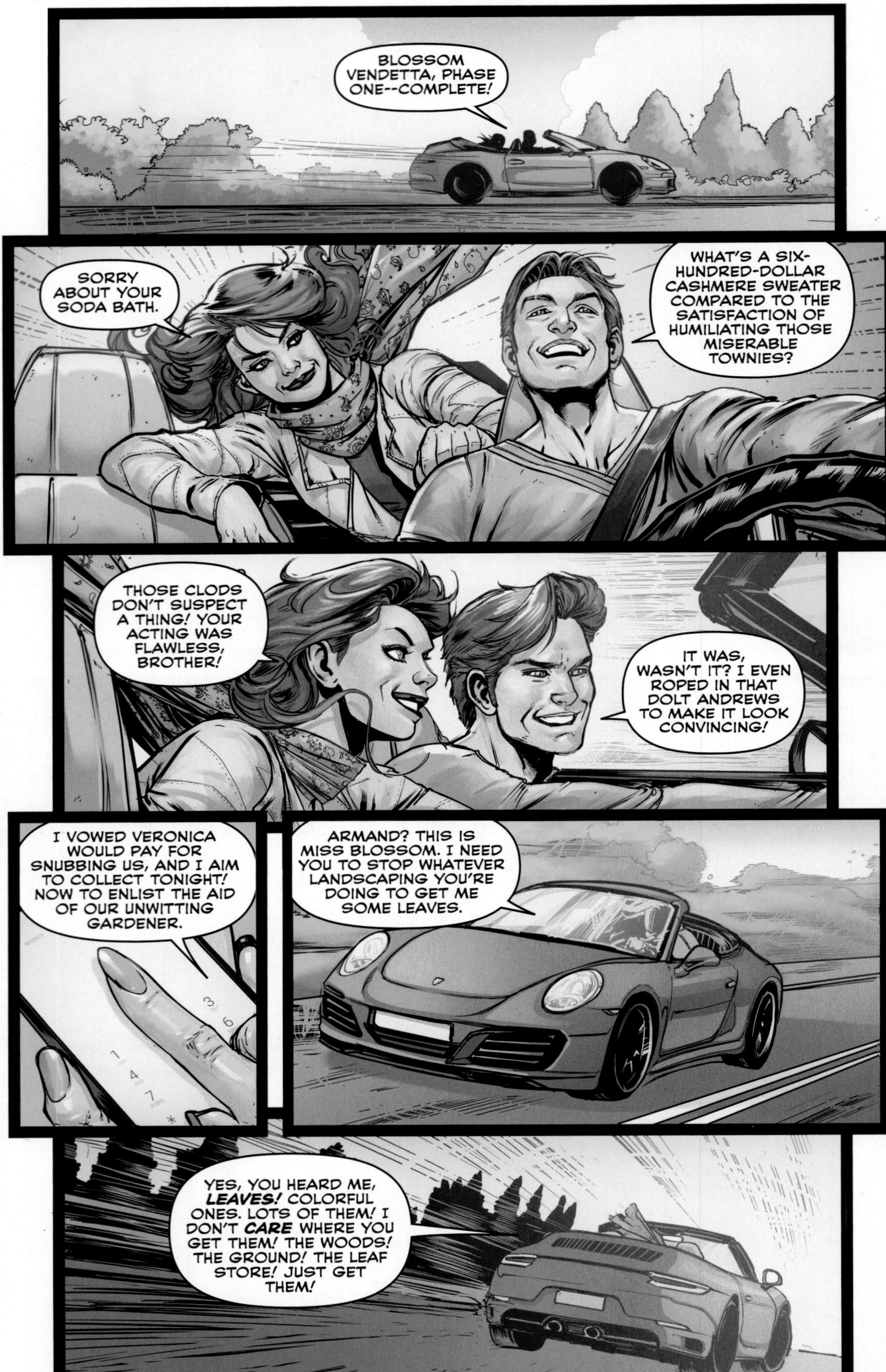
BLOSSOM VENDETTA, PHASE ONE--COMPLETE!
SORRY ABOUT YOUR SODA BATH.
WHAT'S A SIX-HUNDRED-DOLLAR CASHMERE SWEATER COMPARED TO THE SATISFACTION OF HUMILIATING THOSE MISERABLE TOWNIES?
THOSE CLODS DON'T SUSPECT A THING! YOUR ACTING WAS FLAWLESS, BROTHER!
IT WAS, WASN'T IT? I EVEN ROPED IN THAT DOLT ANDREWS TO MAKE IT LOOK CONVINCING!
I VOWED VERONICA WOULD PAY FOR SNUBBING US, AND I AIM TO COLLECT TONIGHT! NOW TO ENLIST THE AID OF OUR UNWITTING GARDENER.
ARMAND? THIS IS MISS BLOSSOM. I NEED YOU TO STOP WHATEVER LANDSCAPING YOU'RE DOING TO GET ME SOME LEAVES.
YES, YOU HEARD ME, ***LEAVES!*** COLORFUL ONES. LOTS OF THEM! I DON'T ***CARE*** WHERE YOU GET THEM! THE WOODS! THE GROUND! THE LEAF STORE! JUST GET THEM!

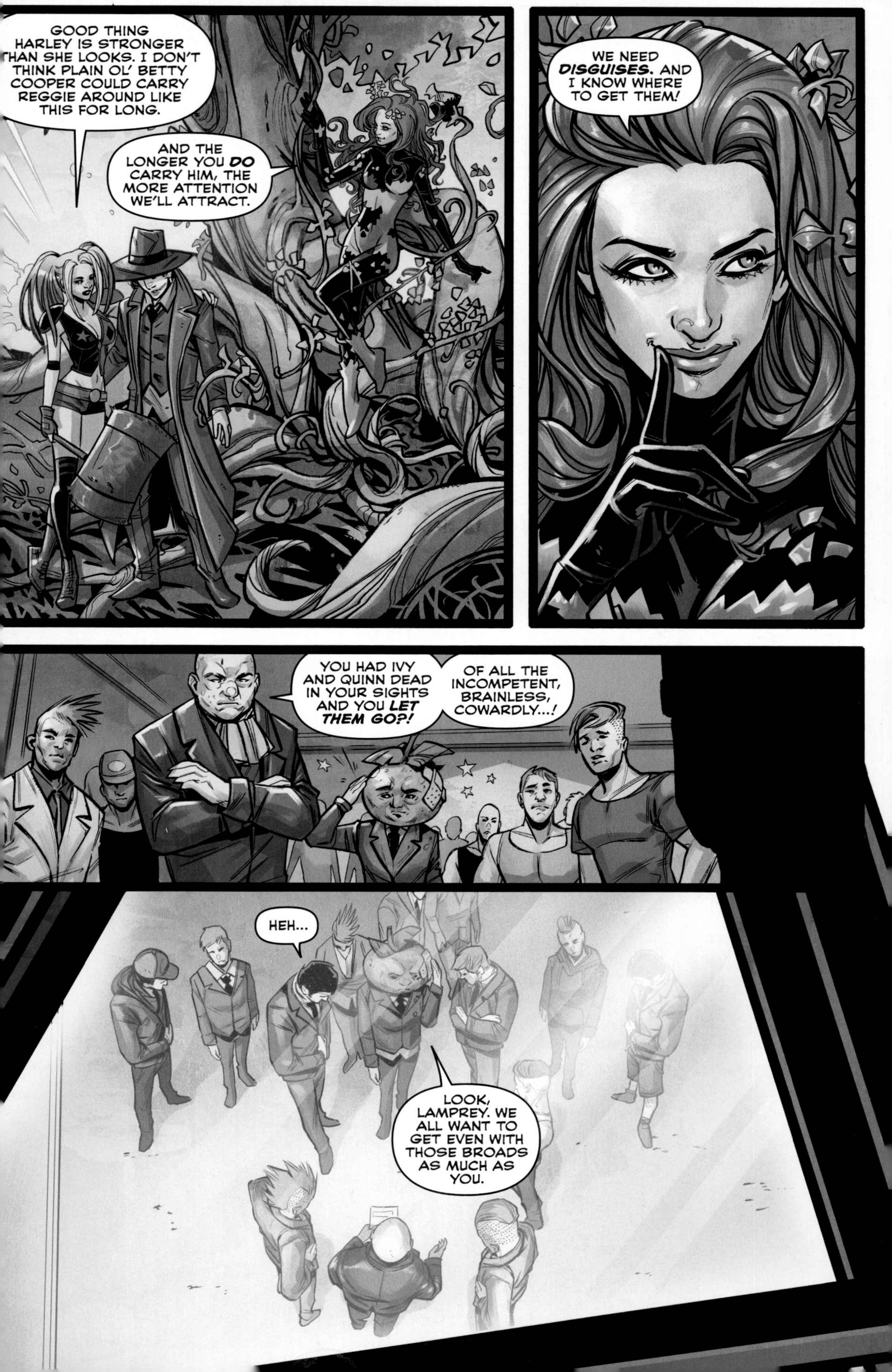
GOOD THING HARLEY IS STRONGER THAN SHE LOOKS. I DON'T THINK PLAIN OL' BETTY COOPER COULD CARRY REGGIE AROUND LIKE THIS FOR LONG.
AND THE LONGER YOU ***DO*** CARRY HIM, THE MORE ATTENTION WE'LL ATTRACT.
WE NEED ***DISGUISES.*** AND I KNOW WHERE TO GET THEM!
YOU HAD IVY AND QUINN DEAD IN YOUR SIGHTS AND YOU ***LET THEM GO?!***
OF ALL THE INCOMPETENT, BRAINLESS, COWARDLY...!
HEH...
LOOK, LAMPREY. WE ALL WANT TO GET EVEN WITH THOSE BROADS AS MUCH AS YOU.

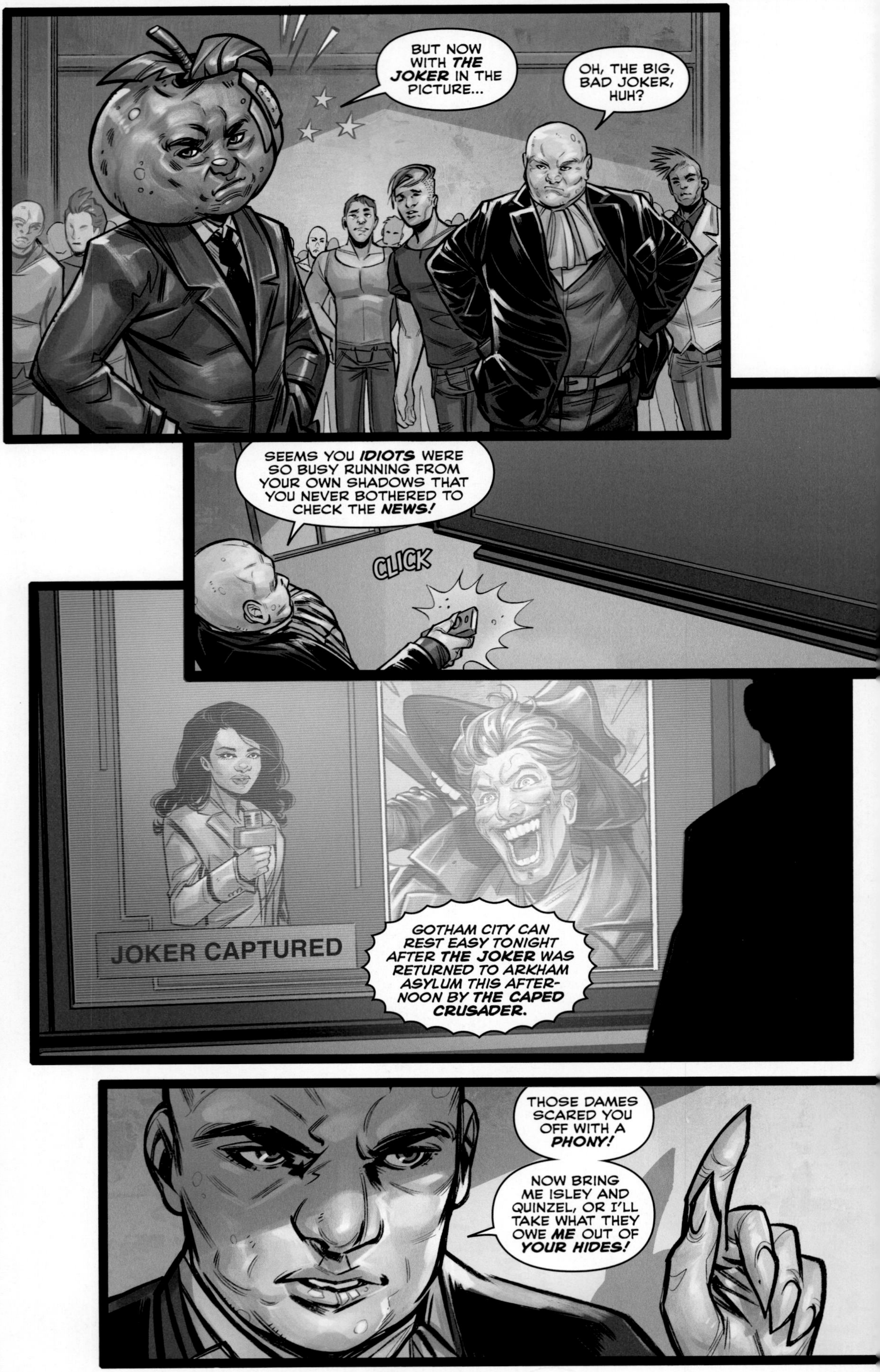
BUT NOW WITH THE JOKER IN THE PICTURE...
OH, THE BIG, BAD JOKER, HUH?
SEEMS YOU IDIOTS WERE SO BUSY RUNNING FROM YOUR OWN SHADOWS THAT YOU NEVER BOTHERED TO CHECK THE NEWS!
CLICK
JOKER CAPTURED
GOTHAM CITY CAN REST EASY TONIGHT AFTER THE JOKER WAS RETURNED TO ARKHAM ASYLUM THIS AFTER-NOON BY THE CAPED CRUSADER.
THOSE DAMES SCARED YOU OFF WITH A PHONY!
NOW BRING ME ISLEY AND QUINZEL, OR I'LL TAKE WHAT THEY OWE ME OUT OF YOUR HIDES!

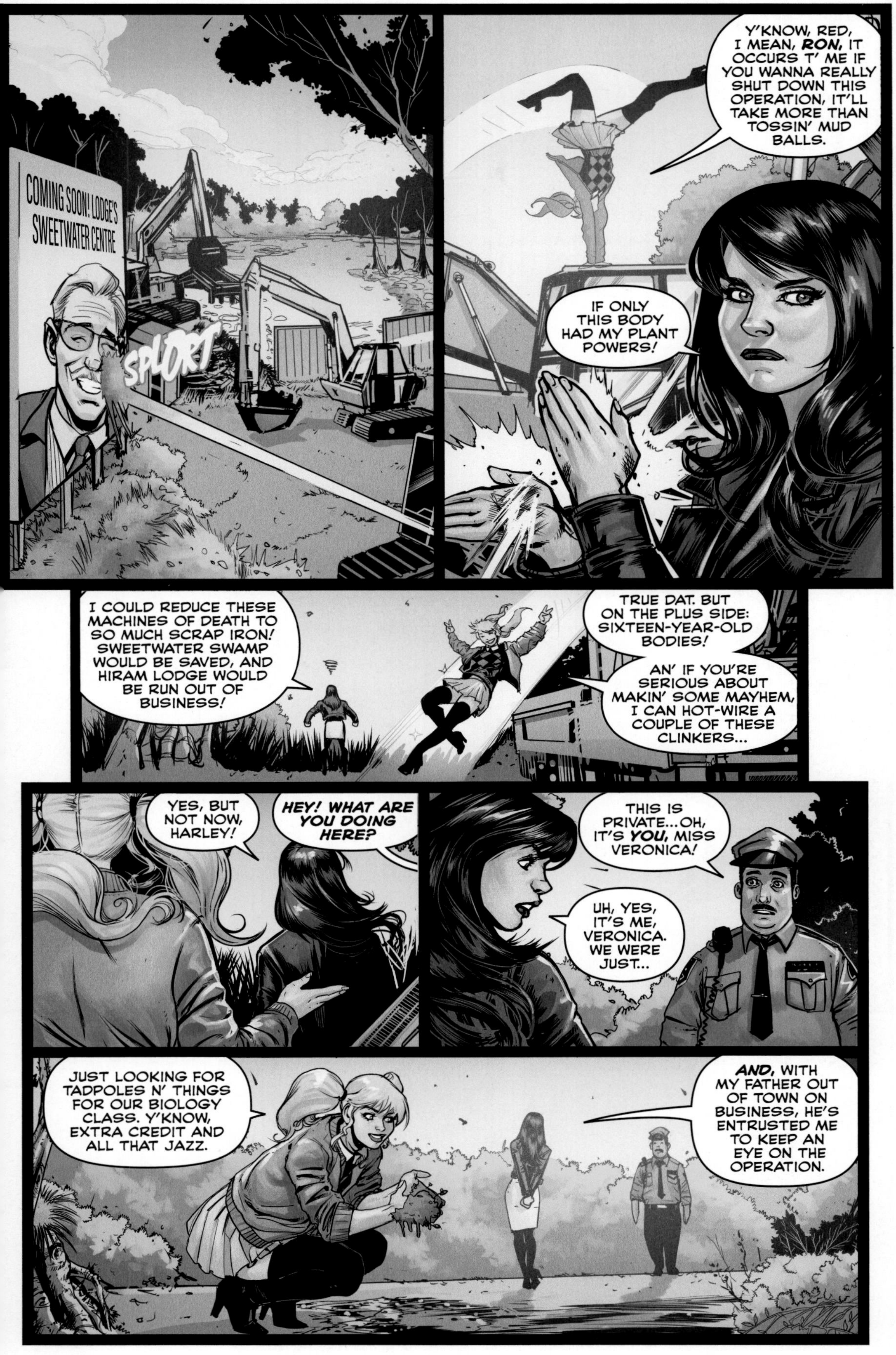
COMING SOON! LODGE'S SWEETWATER CENTRE
SPLORT
Y'KNOW, RED, I MEAN, RON, IT OCCURS T' ME IF YOU WANNA REALLY SHUT DOWN THIS OPERATION, IT'LL TAKE MORE THAN TOSSIN' MUD BALLS.
IF ONLY THIS BODY HAD MY PLANT POWERS!
I COULD REDUCE THESE MACHINES OF DEATH TO SO MUCH SCRAP IRON! SWEETWATER SWAMP WOULD BE SAVED, AND HIRAM LODGE WOULD BE RUN OUT OF BUSINESS!
TRUE DAT. BUT ON THE PLUS SIDE: SIXTEEN-YEAR-OLD BODIES!
AN' IF YOU'RE SERIOUS ABOUT MAKIN' SOME MAYHEM, I CAN HOT-WIRE A COUPLE OF THESE CLINKERS...
YES, BUT NOT NOW, HARLEY!
HEY! WHAT ARE YOU DOING HERE?
THIS IS PRIVATE...OH, IT'S YOU, MISS VERONICA!
UH, YES, IT'S ME, VERONICA. WE WERE JUST...
JUST LOOKING FOR TADPOLES N' THINGS FOR OUR BIOLOGY CLASS. Y'KNOW, EXTRA CREDIT AND ALL THAT JAZZ.
AND, WITH MY FATHER OUT OF TOWN ON BUSINESS, HE'S ENTRUSTED ME TO KEEP AN EYE ON THE OPERATION.

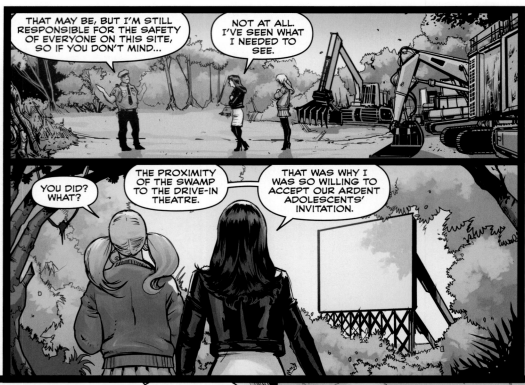

THAT MAY BE, BUT I'M STILL RESPONSIBLE FOR THE SAFETY OF EVERYONE ON THIS SITE, SO IF YOU DON'T MIND...

NOT AT ALL. I'VE SEEN WHAT I NEEDED TO SEE.

YOU DID? WHAT?

THE PROXIMITY OF THE SWAMP TO THE DRIVE-IN THEATRE.

THAT WAS WHY I WAS SO WILLING TO ACCEPT OUR ARDENT ADOLESCENTS' INVITATION.

I GETCHA! AFTER IT'S DARK AN' THE PICTURE STARTS, YOU AN' ME SNEAK OVER, WRECK THE PLACE, AN' SNEAK BACK!

NO WITNESSES, EASY-PEASY!

EXACTLY!

NO ONE CAN PUT TOGETHER A PLOT LIKE YOU, IVY!

LATER THAT NIGHT...

TIGHTER!

ARE YOU SURE? I DON'T WANT TO BREAK ANY RIBS!

SYRUP

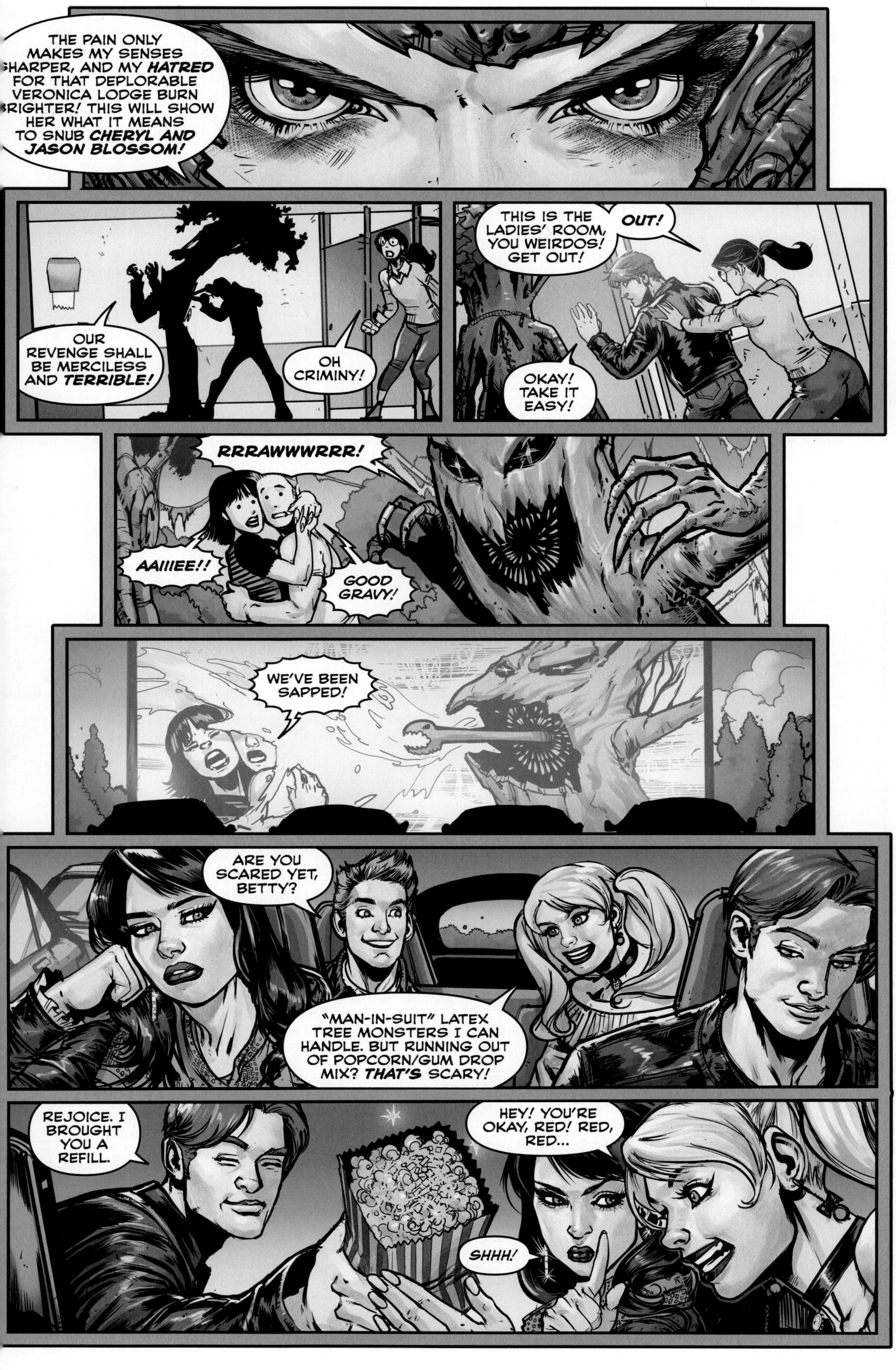
THE PAIN ONLY MAKES MY SENSES SHARPER, AND MY *HATRED* FOR THAT DEPLORABLE VERONICA LODGE BURN BRIGHTER! THIS WILL SHOW HER WHAT IT MEANS TO SNUB *CHERYL AND JASON BLOSSOM!*
OUR REVENGE SHALL BE MERCILESS AND *TERRIBLE!*
OH CRIMINY!
THIS IS THE LADIES' ROOM, YOU WEIRDOS! GET OUT!
OUT!
OKAY! TAKE IT EASY!
RRRAWWWRRR!
AAIIIEE!!
GOOD GRAVY!
WE'VE BEEN SAPPED!
ARE YOU SCARED YET, BETTY?
"MAN-IN-SUIT" LATEX TREE MONSTERS I CAN HANDLE. BUT RUNNING OUT OF POPCORN/GUM DROP MIX? *THAT'S* SCARY!
REJOICE. I BROUGHT YOU A REFILL.
HEY! YOU'RE OKAY, RED! RED, RED...
SHHH!

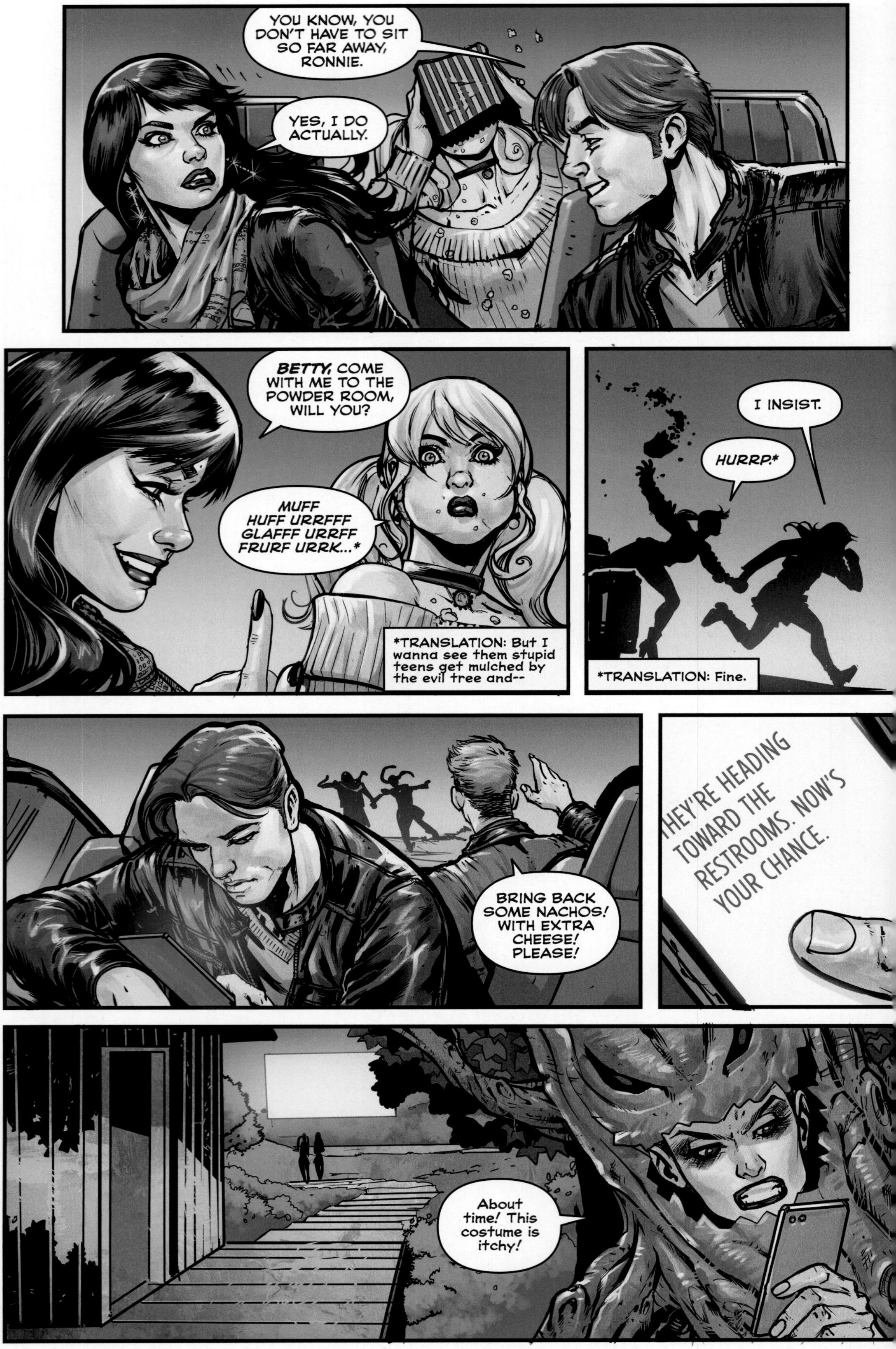
YOU KNOW, YOU DON'T HAVE TO SIT SO FAR AWAY, RONNIE.
YES, I DO ACTUALLY.
BETTY, COME WITH ME TO THE POWDER ROOM, WILL YOU?
MUFF HUFF URRFFF GLAFFF URRFF FRURF URRK...*
*TRANSLATION: But I wanna see them stupid teens get mulched by the evil tree and--
I INSIST.
HURRP.*
*TRANSLATION: Fine.
BRING BACK SOME NACHOS! WITH EXTRA CHEESE! PLEASE!
THEY'RE HEADING TOWARD THE RESTROOMS. NOW'S YOUR CHANCE.
About time! This costume is itchy!

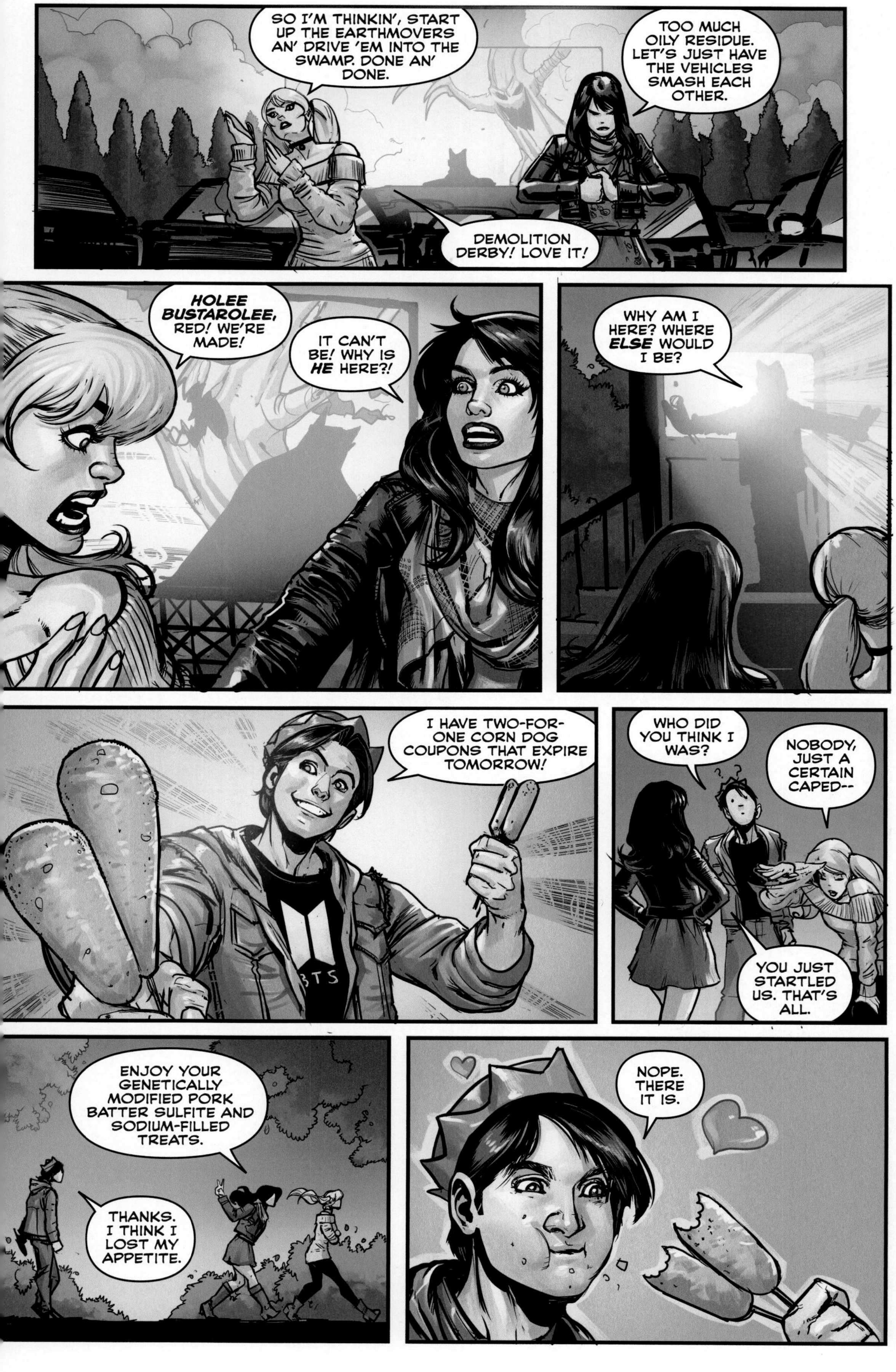

SO I'M THINKIN', START UP THE EARTHMOVERS AN' DRIVE 'EM INTO THE SWAMP. DONE AN' DONE.
TOO MUCH OILY RESIDUE. LET'S JUST HAVE THE VEHICLES SMASH EACH OTHER.
DEMOLITION DERBY! LOVE IT!
HOLEE BUSTAROLEE, RED! WE'RE MADE!
IT CAN'T BE! WHY IS HE HERE?!
WHY AM I HERE? WHERE ELSE WOULD I BE?
I HAVE TWO-FOR-ONE CORN DOG COUPONS THAT EXPIRE TOMORROW!
BTS
WHO DID YOU THINK I WAS?
NOBODY, JUST A CERTAIN CAPED--
YOU JUST STARTLED US. THAT'S ALL.
ENJOY YOUR GENETICALLY MODIFIED PORK BATTER SULFITE AND SODIUM-FILLED TREATS.
THANKS. I THINK I LOST MY APPETITE.
NOPE. THERE IT IS.

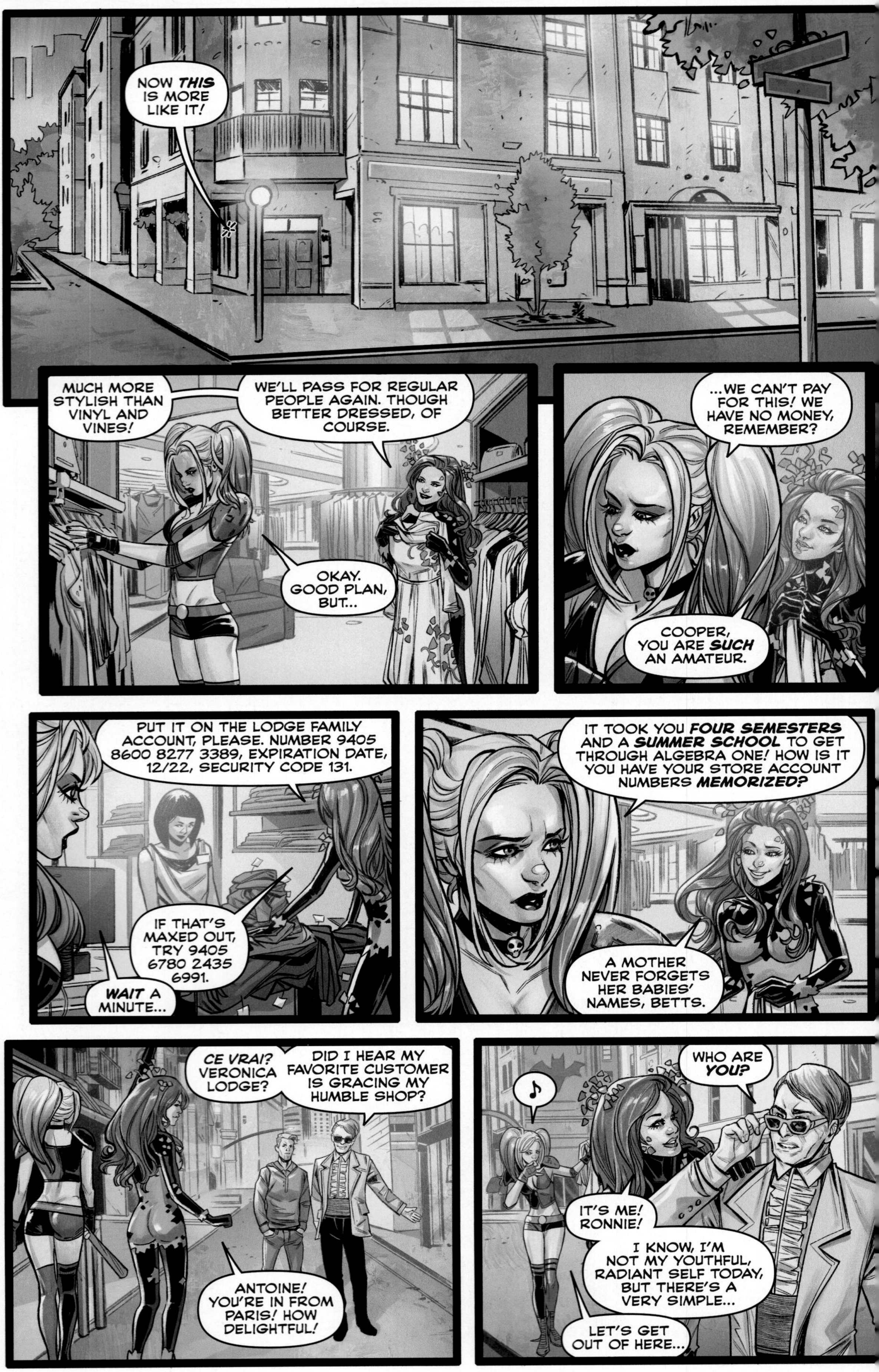

NOW THIS IS MORE LIKE IT!
MUCH MORE STYLISH THAN VINYL AND VINES!
WE'LL PASS FOR REGULAR PEOPLE AGAIN. THOUGH BETTER DRESSED, OF COURSE.
OKAY. GOOD PLAN, BUT...
...WE CAN'T PAY FOR THIS! WE HAVE NO MONEY, REMEMBER?
COOPER, YOU ARE SUCH AN AMATEUR.
PUT IT ON THE LODGE FAMILY ACCOUNT, PLEASE. NUMBER 9405 8600 8277 3389, EXPIRATION DATE, 12/22, SECURITY CODE 131.
IF THAT'S MAXED OUT, TRY 9405 6780 2435 6991.
WAIT A MINUTE...
IT TOOK YOU FOUR SEMESTERS AND A SUMMER SCHOOL TO GET THROUGH ALGEBRA ONE! HOW IS IT YOU HAVE YOUR STORE ACCOUNT NUMBERS MEMORIZED?
A MOTHER NEVER FORGETS HER BABIES' NAMES, BETTS.
CE VRAI? VERONICA LODGE?
DID I HEAR MY FAVORITE CUSTOMER IS GRACING MY HUMBLE SHOP?
ANTOINE! YOU'RE IN FROM PARIS! HOW DELIGHTFUL!
WHO ARE YOU?
♪
IT'S ME! RONNIE!
I KNOW, I'M NOT MY YOUTHFUL, RADIANT SELF TODAY, BUT THERE'S A VERY SIMPLE...
LET'S GET OUT OF HERE...

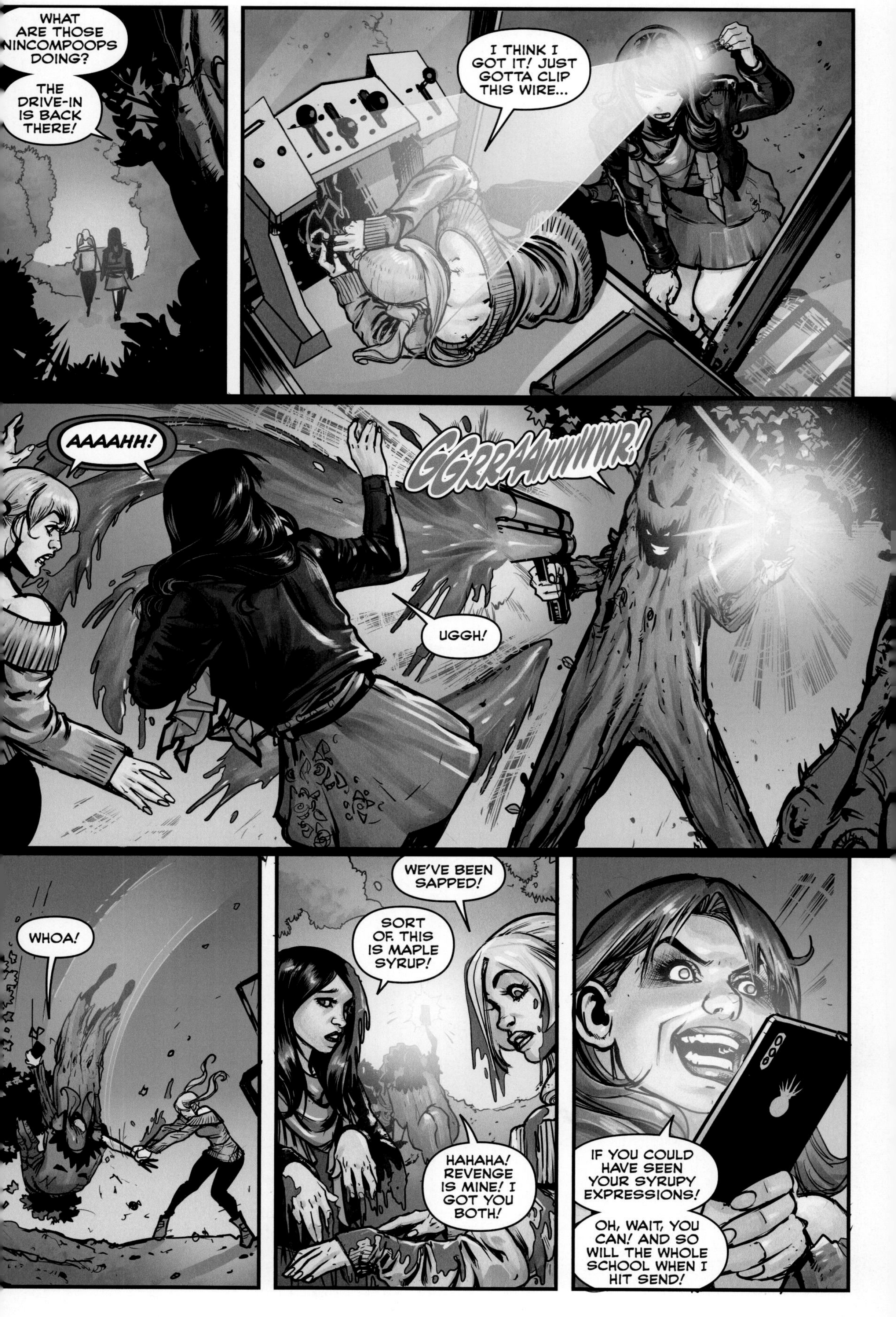
WHAT ARE THOSE NINCOMPOOPS DOING?
THE DRIVE-IN IS BACK THERE!
I THINK I GOT IT! JUST GOTTA CLIP THIS WIRE...
AAAAHH!
GGRRAAWWWWR!
UGGH!
WHOA!
WE'VE BEEN SAPPED!
SORT OF. THIS IS MAPLE SYRUP!
HAHAHA! REVENGE IS MINE! I GOT YOU BOTH!
IF YOU COULD HAVE SEEN YOUR SYRUPY EXPRESSIONS!
OH, WAIT, YOU CAN! AND SO WILL THE WHOLE SCHOOL WHEN I HIT SEND!

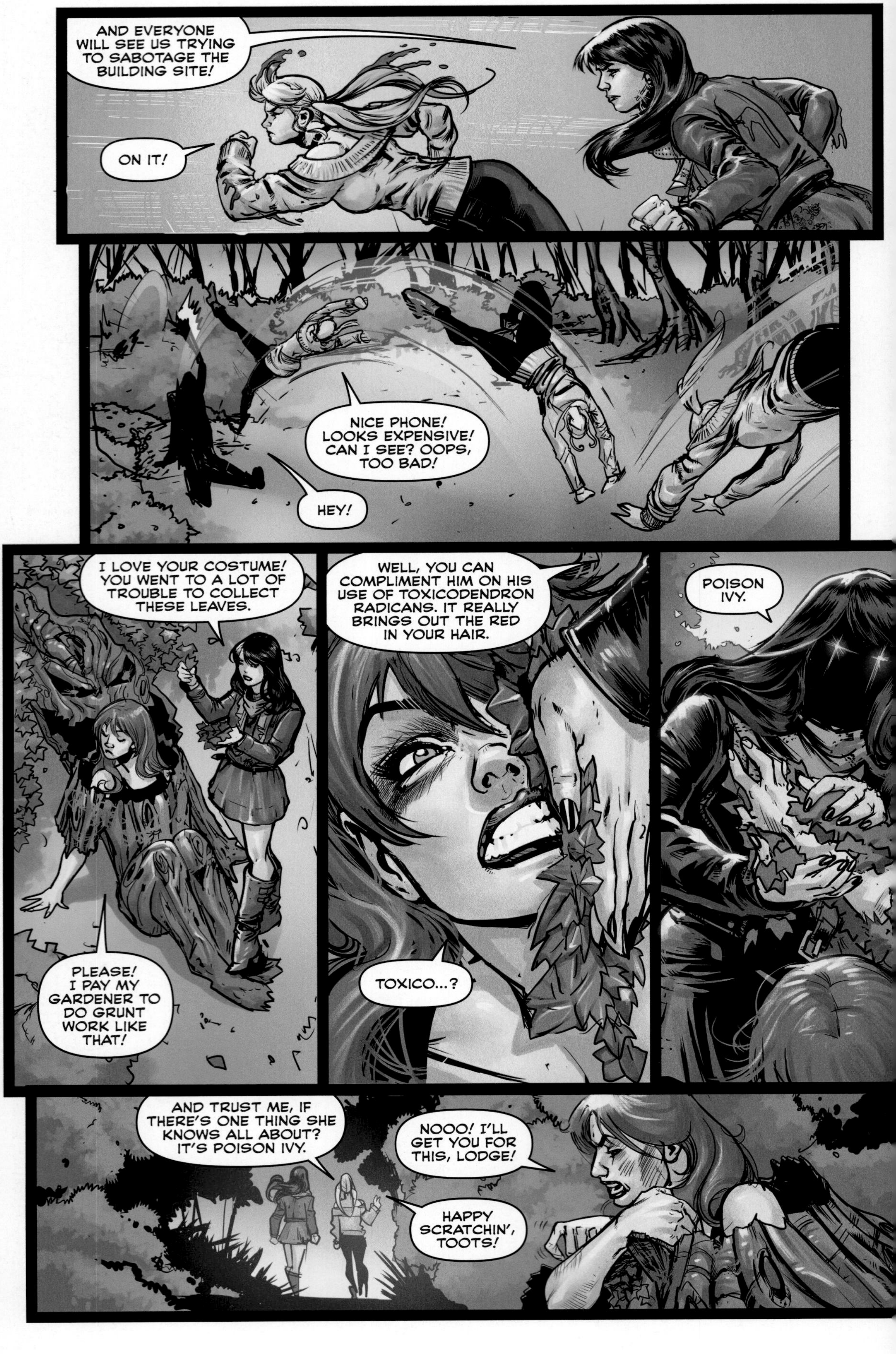
AND EVERYONE WILL SEE US TRYING TO SABOTAGE THE BUILDING SITE!
ON IT!
NICE PHONE! LOOKS EXPENSIVE! CAN I SEE? OOPS, TOO BAD!
HEY!
I LOVE YOUR COSTUME! YOU WENT TO A LOT OF TROUBLE TO COLLECT THESE LEAVES.
PLEASE! I PAY MY GARDENER TO DO GRUNT WORK LIKE THAT!
WELL, YOU CAN COMPLIMENT HIM ON HIS USE OF TOXICODENDRON RADICANS. IT REALLY BRINGS OUT THE RED IN YOUR HAIR.
TOXICO...?
POISON IVY.
AND TRUST ME, IF THERE'S ONE THING SHE KNOWS ALL ABOUT? IT'S POISON IVY.
NOOO! I'LL GET YOU FOR THIS, LODGE!
HAPPY SCRATCHIN', TOOTS!

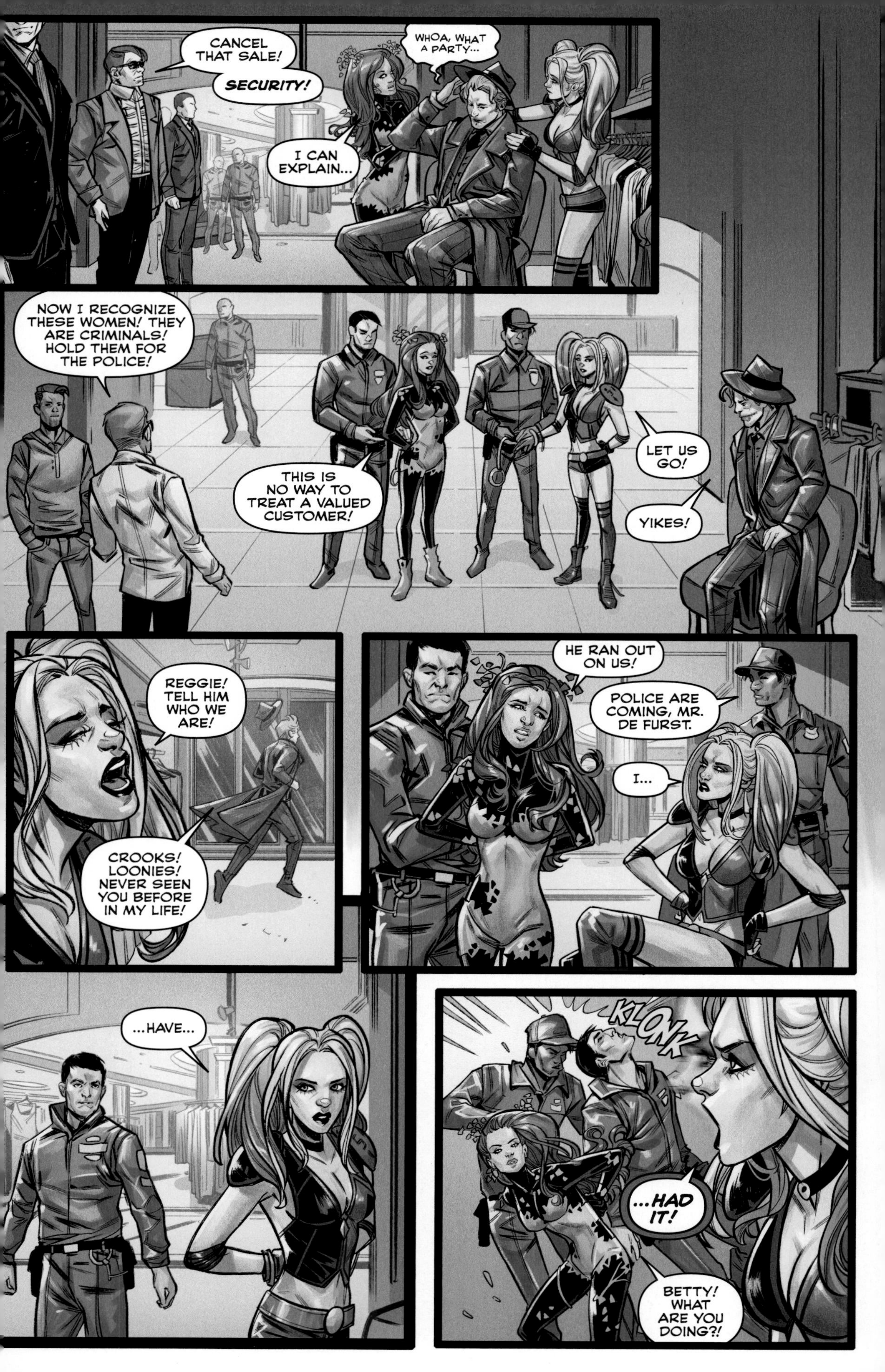
CANCEL THAT SALE!
SECURITY!
WHOA, WHAT A PARTY...
I CAN EXPLAIN...
NOW I RECOGNIZE THESE WOMEN! THEY ARE CRIMINALS! HOLD THEM FOR THE POLICE!
THIS IS NO WAY TO TREAT A VALUED CUSTOMER!
LET US GO!
YIKES!
REGGIE! TELL HIM WHO WE ARE!
CROOKS! LOONIES! NEVER SEEN YOU BEFORE IN MY LIFE!
HE RAN OUT ON US!
POLICE ARE COMING, MR. DE FURST.
I...
...HAVE...
KLONK
...HAD IT!
BETTY! WHAT ARE YOU DOING?!

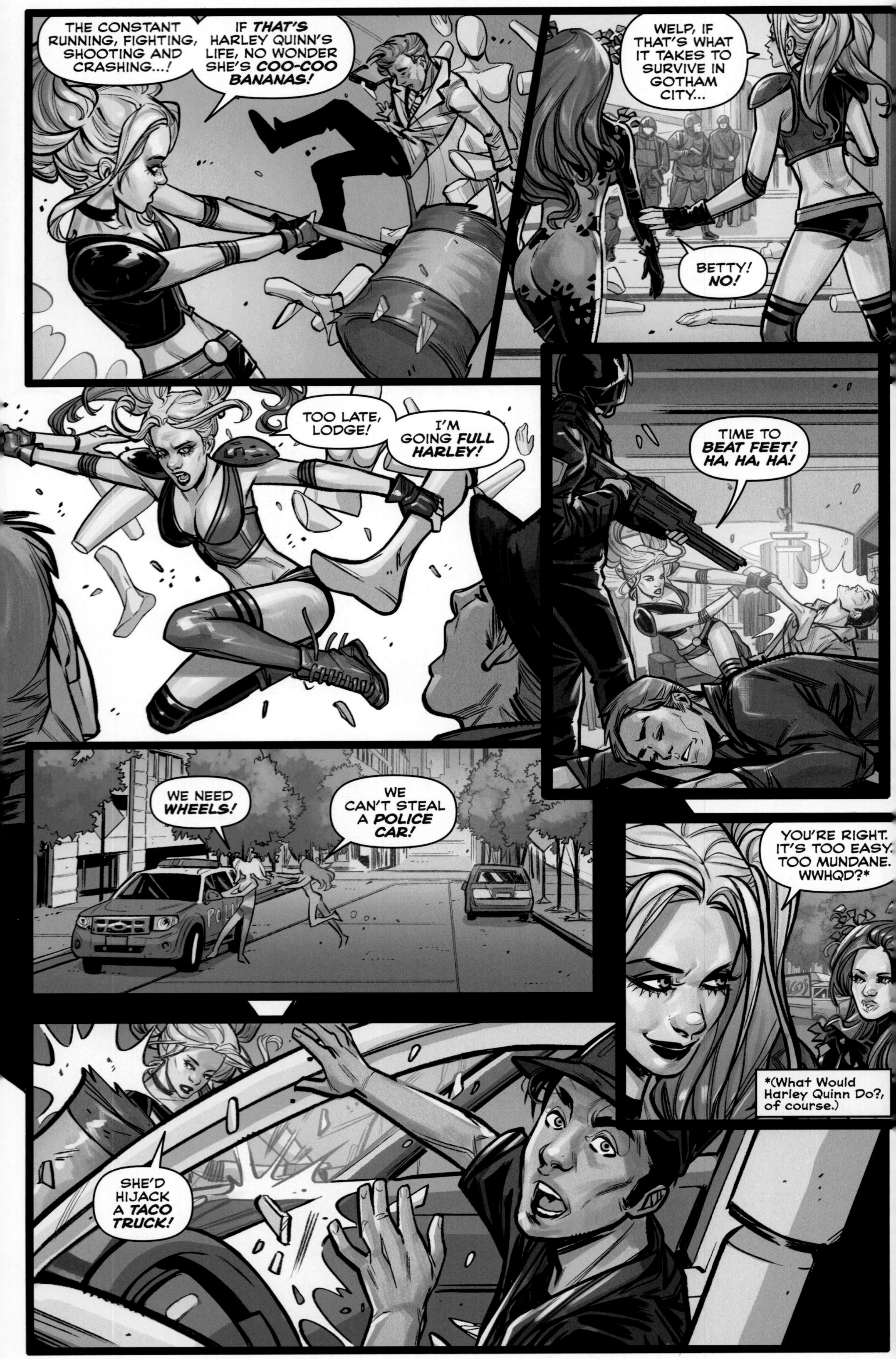
THE CONSTANT RUNNING, FIGHTING, SHOOTING AND CRASHING...!
IF *THAT'S* HARLEY QUINN'S LIFE, NO WONDER SHE'S *COO-COO BANANAS!*
WELP, IF THAT'S WHAT IT TAKES TO SURVIVE IN GOTHAM CITY...
BETTY! *NO!*
TOO LATE, LODGE!
I'M GOING *FULL HARLEY!*
TIME TO *BEAT FEET! HA, HA, HA!*
WE NEED *WHEELS!*
WE CAN'T STEAL A *POLICE CAR!*
YOU'RE RIGHT. IT'S TOO EASY. TOO MUNDANE. WWHQD?*
*(What Would Harley Quinn Do?, of course.)
SHE'D HIJACK A *TACO TRUCK!*

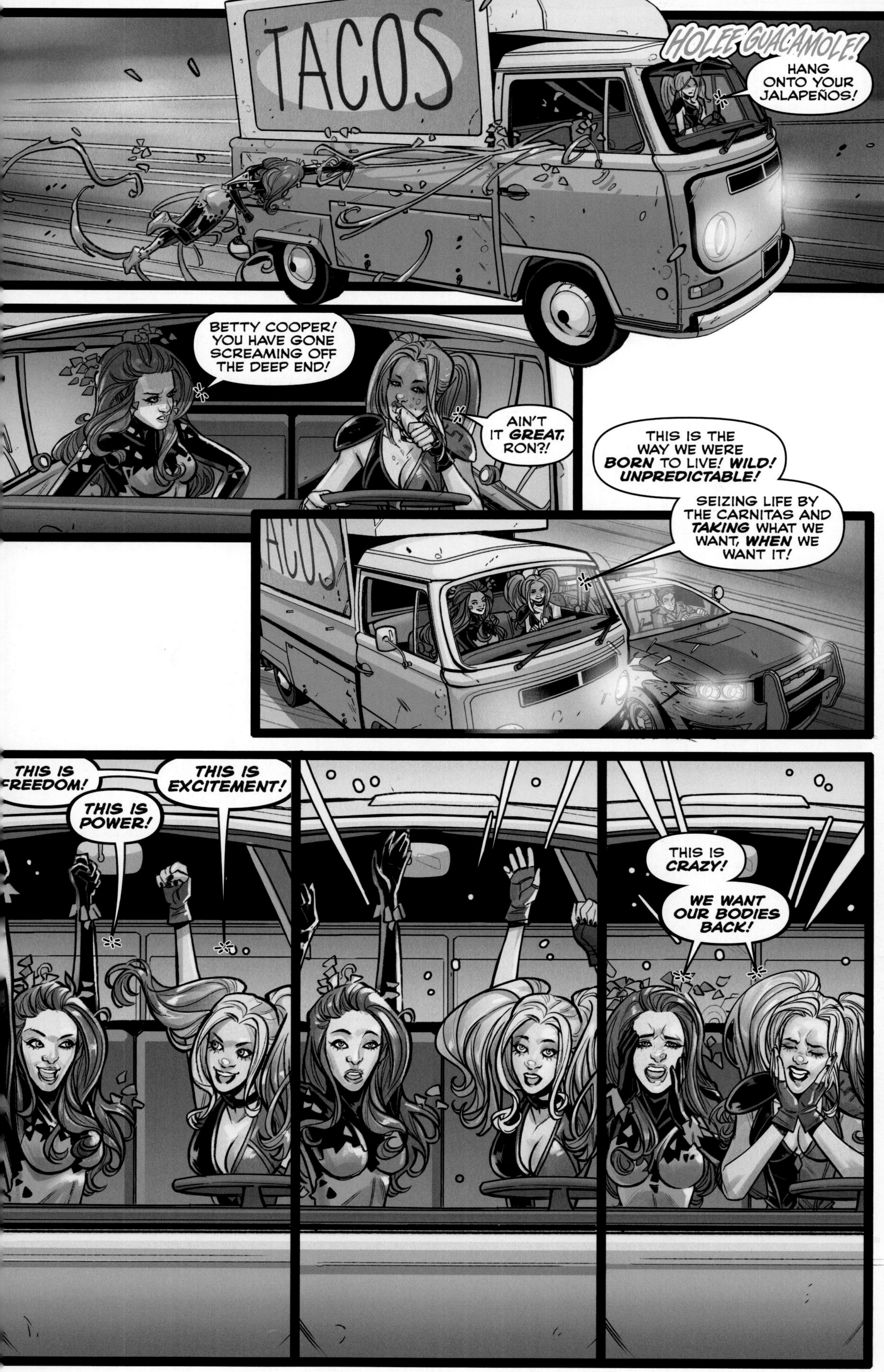
HOLEE GUACAMOLE!
HANG ONTO YOUR JALAPEÑOS!
BETTY COOPER! YOU HAVE GONE SCREAMING OFF THE DEEP END!
AIN'T IT GREAT, RON?!
THIS IS THE WAY WE WERE BORN TO LIVE! WILD! UNPREDICTABLE!
SEIZING LIFE BY THE CARNITAS AND TAKING WHAT WE WANT, WHEN WE WANT IT!
THIS IS FREEDOM!
THIS IS POWER!
THIS IS EXCITEMENT!
THIS IS CRAZY!
WE WANT OUR BODIES BACK!

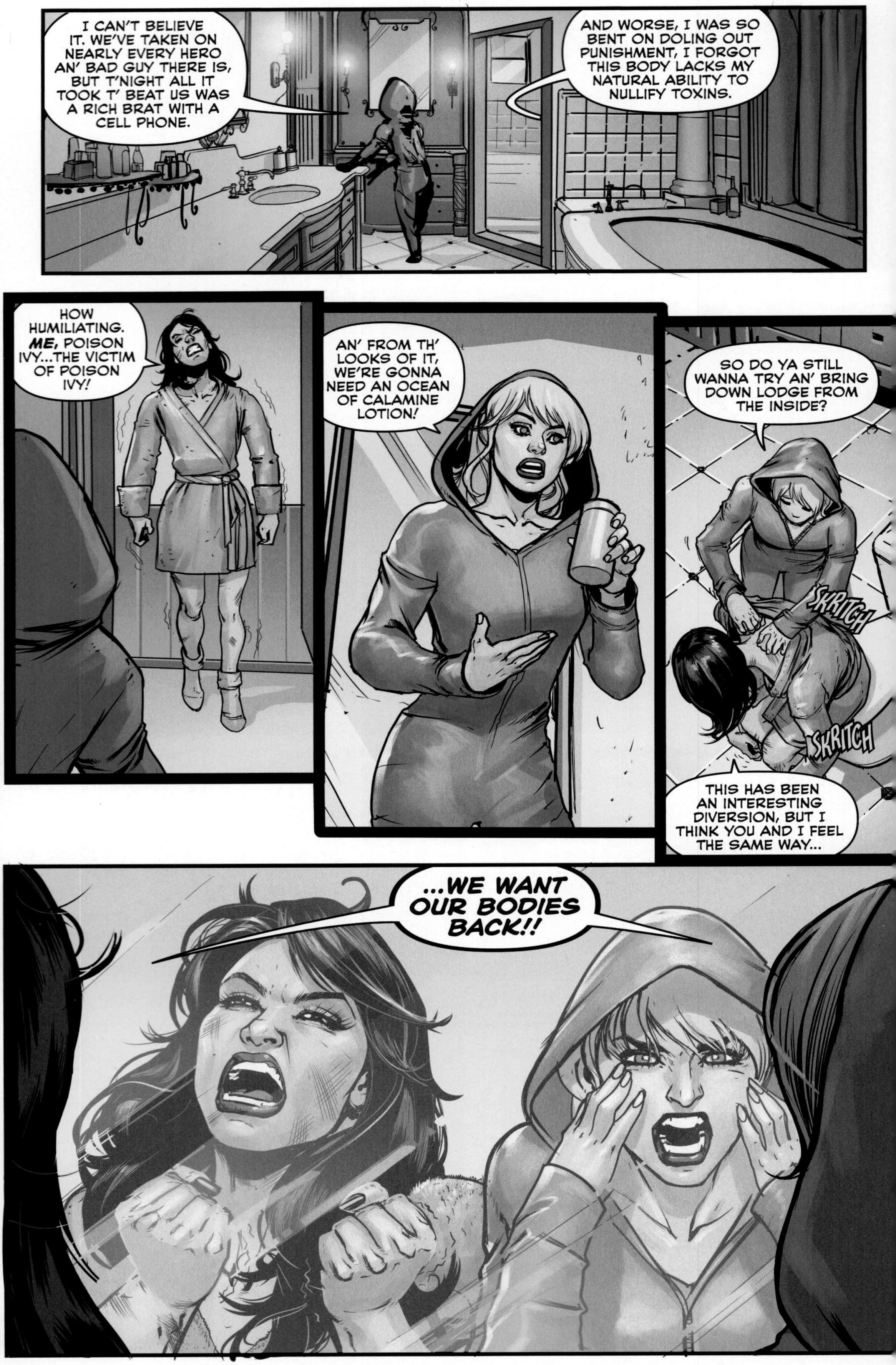

I CAN'T BELIEVE IT. WE'VE TAKEN ON NEARLY EVERY HERO AN' BAD GUY THERE IS, BUT T'NIGHT ALL IT TOOK T' BEAT US WAS A RICH BRAT WITH A CELL PHONE.
AND WORSE, I WAS SO BENT ON DOLING OUT PUNISHMENT, I FORGOT THIS BODY LACKS MY NATURAL ABILITY TO NULLIFY TOXINS.
HOW HUMILIATING. ME, POISON IVY...THE VICTIM OF POISON IVY!
AN' FROM TH' LOOKS OF IT, WE'RE GONNA NEED AN OCEAN OF CALAMINE LOTION!
SO DO YA STILL WANNA TRY AN' BRING DOWN LODGE FROM THE INSIDE?
SKRITCH
SKRITCH
THIS HAS BEEN AN INTERESTING DIVERSION, BUT I THINK YOU AND I FEEL THE SAME WAY...
...WE WANT OUR BODIES BACK!!

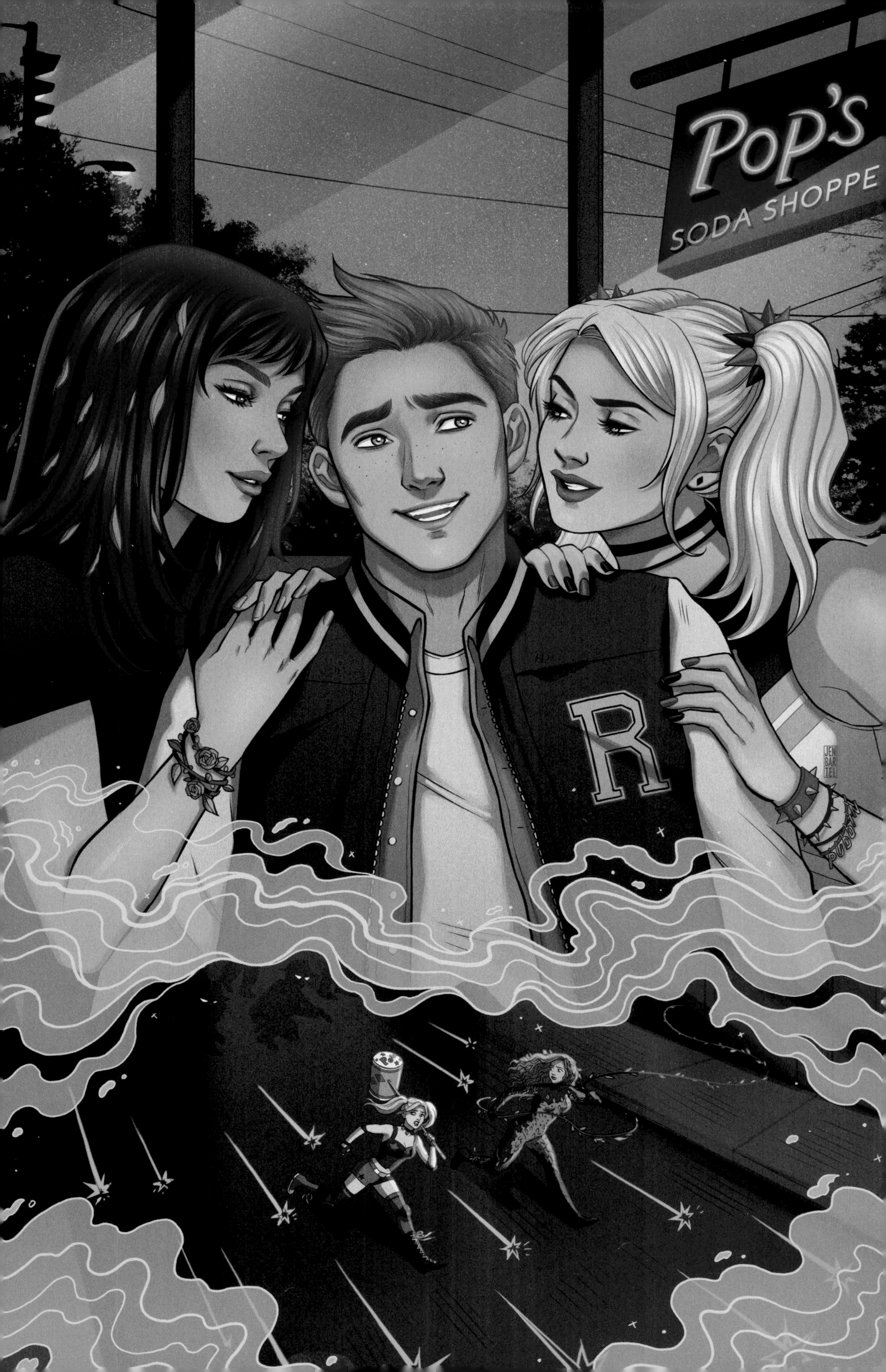

Pop's
SODA SHOPPE
R
JEN BAR TEL

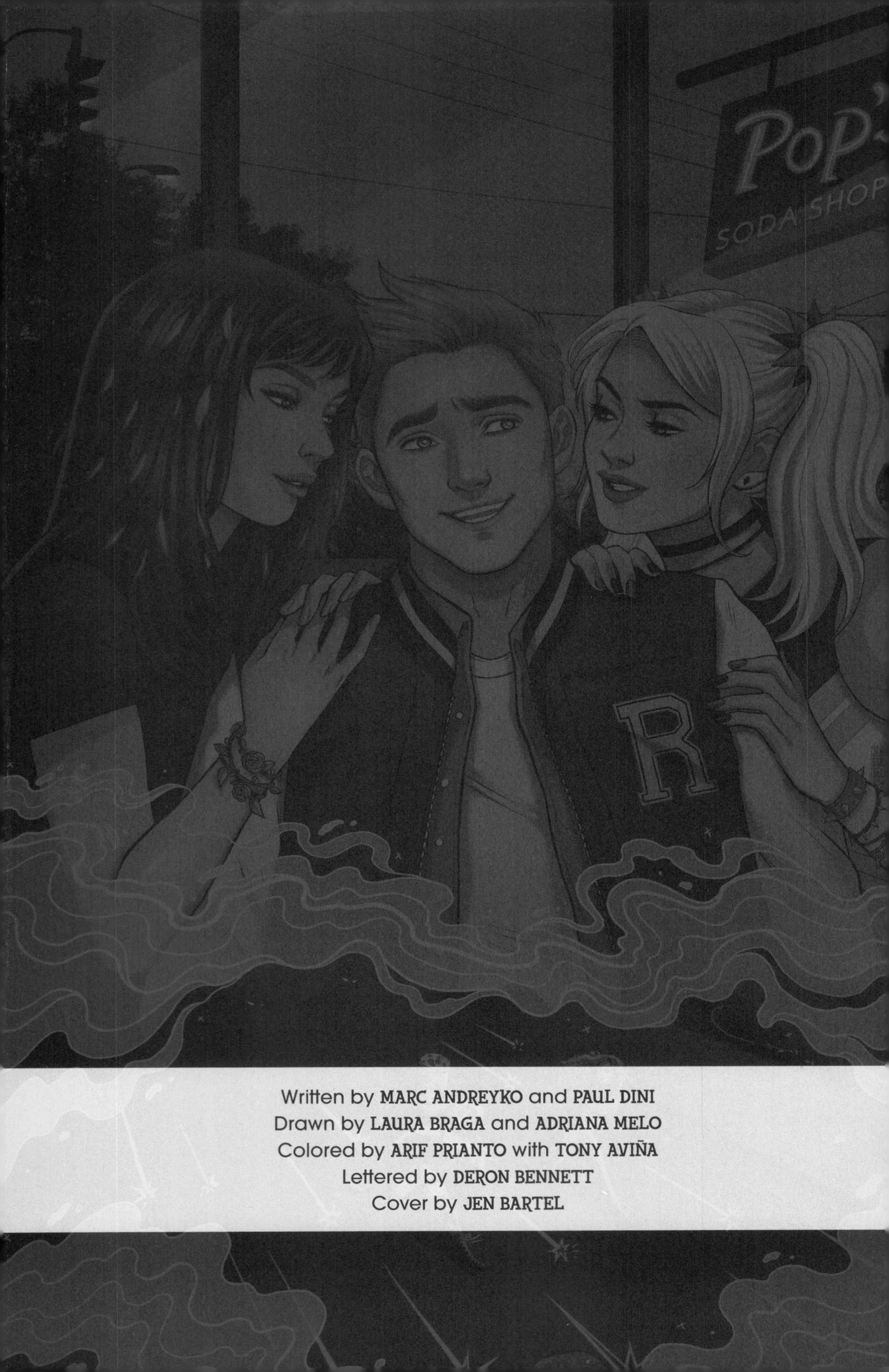
SODA SHOP

Written by **MARC ANDREYKO** and **PAUL DINI**
Drawn by **LAURA BRAGA** and **ADRIANA MELO**
Colored by **ARIF PRIANTO** with **TONY AVIÑA**
Lettered by **DERON BENNETT**
Cover by **JEN BARTEL**

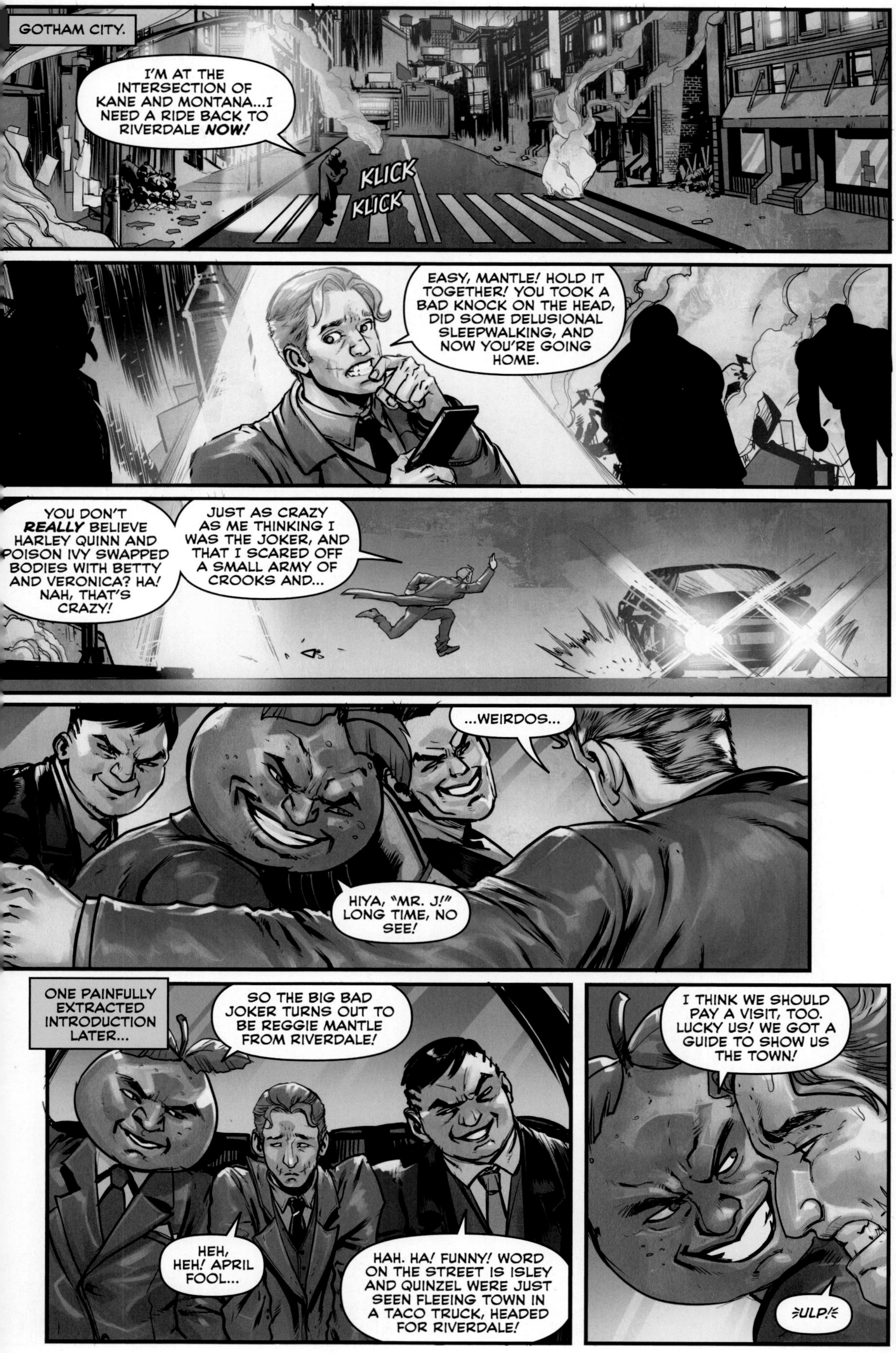
GOTHAM CITY.
I'M AT THE INTERSECTION OF KANE AND MONTANA...I NEED A RIDE BACK TO RIVERDALE NOW!
KLICK
KLICK
EASY, MANTLE! HOLD IT TOGETHER! YOU TOOK A BAD KNOCK ON THE HEAD, DID SOME DELUSIONAL SLEEPWALKING, AND NOW YOU'RE GOING HOME.
YOU DON'T REALLY BELIEVE HARLEY QUINN AND POISON IVY SWAPPED BODIES WITH BETTY AND VERONICA? HA! NAH, THAT'S CRAZY!
JUST AS CRAZY AS ME THINKING I WAS THE JOKER, AND THAT I SCARED OFF A SMALL ARMY OF CROOKS AND...
...WEIRDOS...
HIYA, "MR. J!" LONG TIME, NO SEE!
ONE PAINFULLY EXTRACTED INTRODUCTION LATER...
SO THE BIG BAD JOKER TURNS OUT TO BE REGGIE MANTLE FROM RIVERDALE!
HEH, HEH! APRIL FOOL...
HAH. HA! FUNNY! WORD ON THE STREET IS ISLEY AND QUINZEL WERE JUST SEEN FLEEING TOWN IN A TACO TRUCK, HEADED FOR RIVERDALE!
I THINK WE SHOULD PAY A VISIT, TOO. LUCKY US! WE GOT A GUIDE TO SHOW US THE TOWN!
ULP!

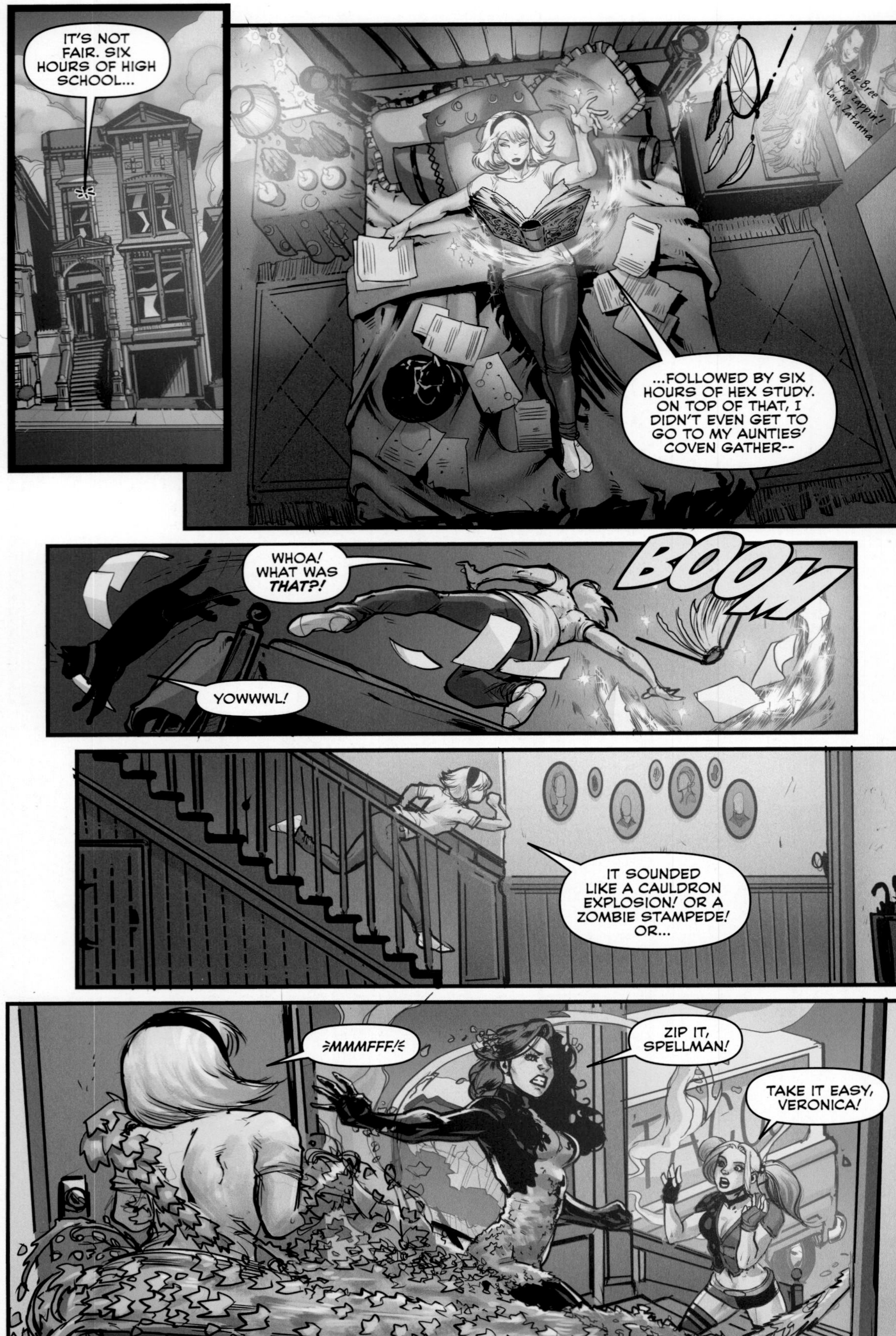
IT'S NOT FAIR. SIX HOURS OF HIGH SCHOOL...
For Bree — Keep zappin'! Love, Zatanna
...FOLLOWED BY SIX HOURS OF HEX STUDY. ON TOP OF THAT, I DIDN'T EVEN GET TO GO TO MY AUNTIES' COVEN GATHER--
WHOA! WHAT WAS *THAT?!*
BOOM
YOWWWL!
IT SOUNDED LIKE A CAULDRON EXPLOSION! OR A ZOMBIE STAMPEDE! OR...
MMMFFF!
ZIP IT, SPELLMAN!
TAKE IT EASY, VERONICA!

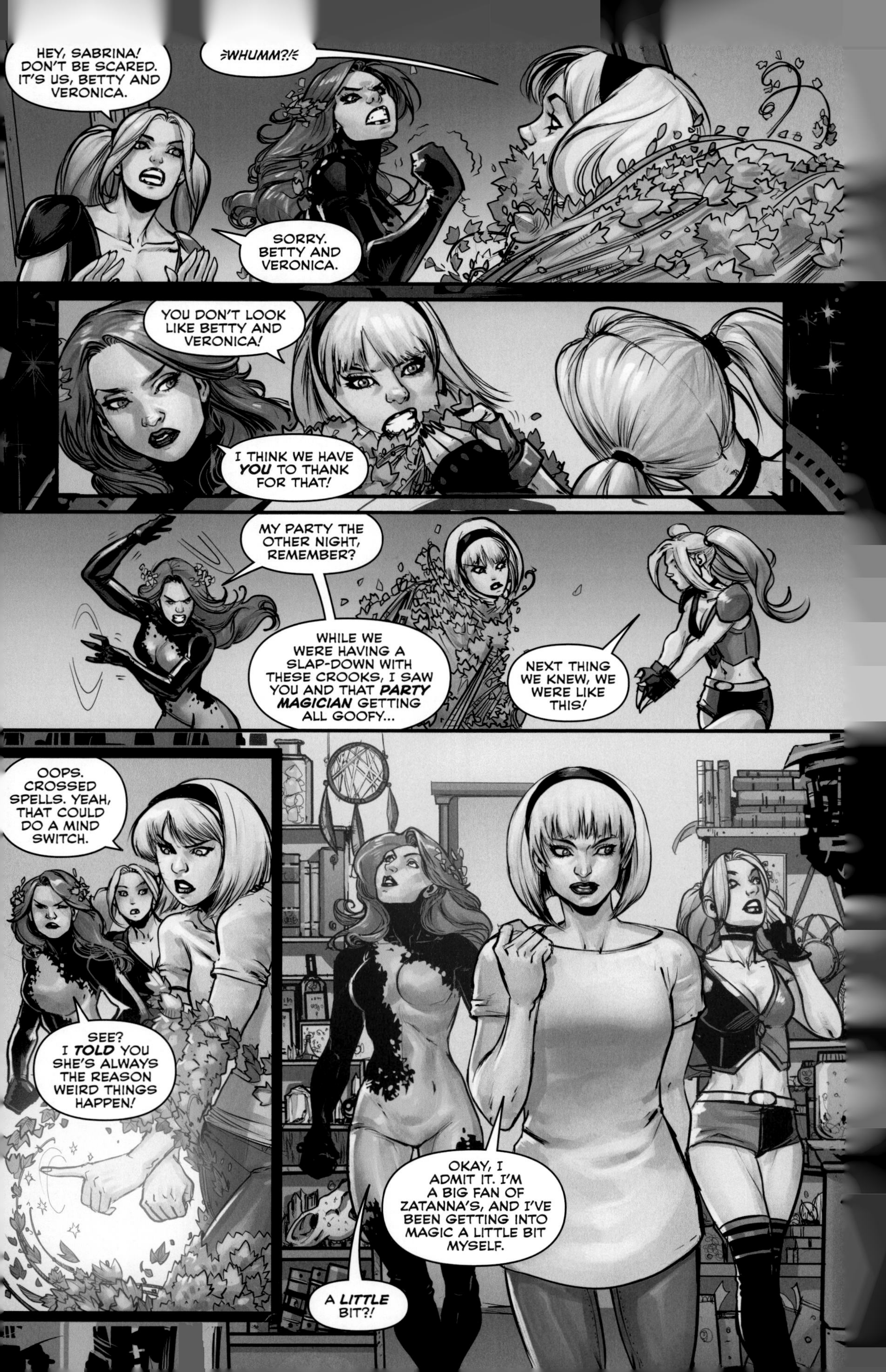
HEY, SABRINA! DON'T BE SCARED. IT'S US, BETTY AND VERONICA.
WHUMM?!
SORRY. BETTY AND VERONICA.
YOU DON'T LOOK LIKE BETTY AND VERONICA!
I THINK WE HAVE YOU TO THANK FOR THAT!
MY PARTY THE OTHER NIGHT, REMEMBER?
WHILE WE WERE HAVING A SLAP-DOWN WITH THESE CROOKS, I SAW YOU AND THAT PARTY MAGICIAN GETTING ALL GOOFY...
NEXT THING WE KNEW, WE WERE LIKE THIS!
OOPS. CROSSED SPELLS. YEAH, THAT COULD DO A MIND SWITCH.
SEE? I TOLD YOU SHE'S ALWAYS THE REASON WEIRD THINGS HAPPEN!
OKAY, I ADMIT IT. I'M A BIG FAN OF ZATANNA'S, AND I'VE BEEN GETTING INTO MAGIC A LITTLE BIT MYSELF.
A LITTLE BIT?!

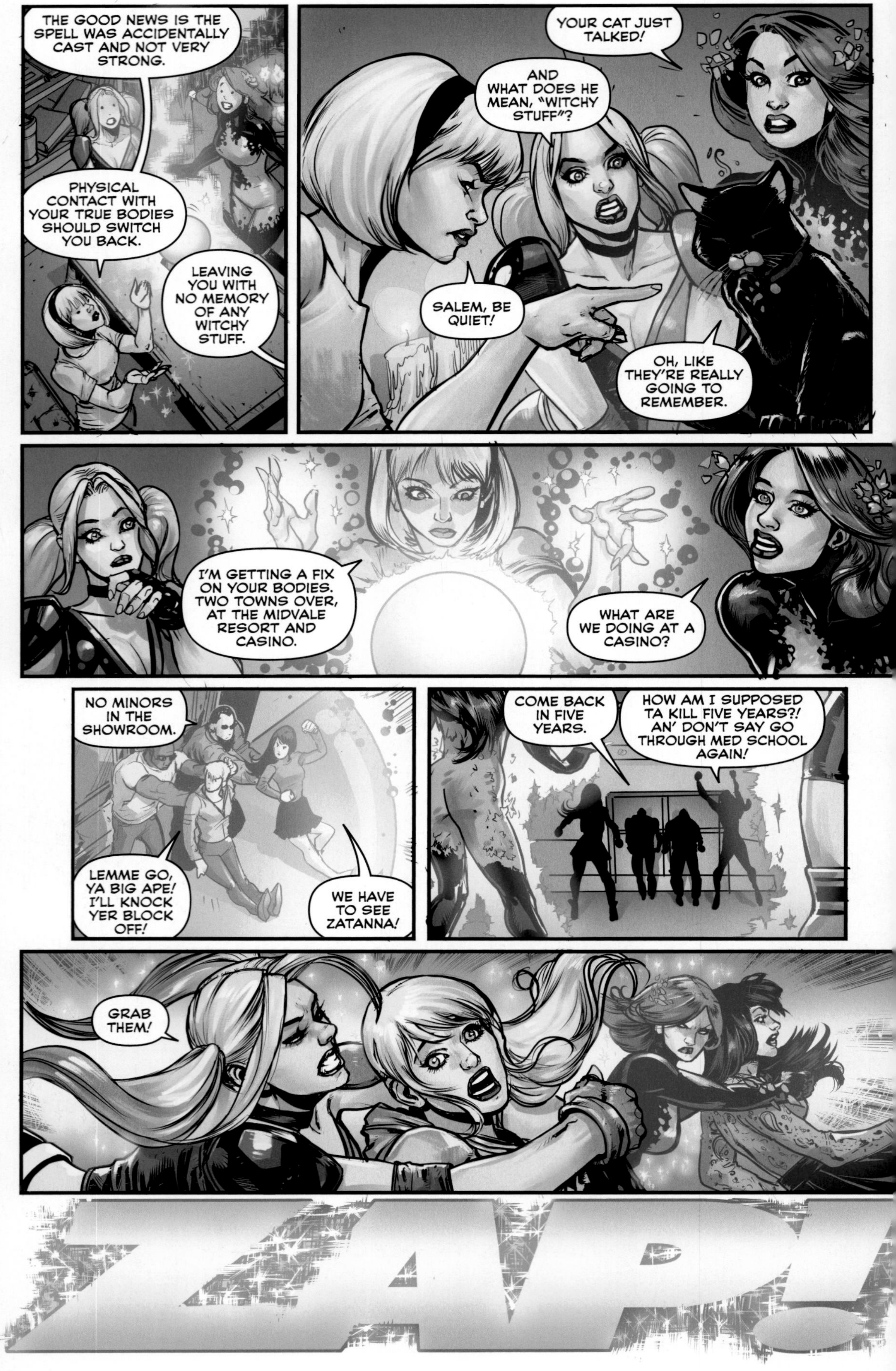
THE GOOD NEWS IS THE SPELL WAS ACCIDENTALLY CAST AND NOT VERY STRONG.
PHYSICAL CONTACT WITH YOUR TRUE BODIES SHOULD SWITCH YOU BACK.
LEAVING YOU WITH NO MEMORY OF ANY WITCHY STUFF.
YOUR CAT JUST TALKED!
AND WHAT DOES HE MEAN, "WITCHY STUFF"?
SALEM, BE QUIET!
OH, LIKE THEY'RE REALLY GOING TO REMEMBER.
I'M GETTING A FIX ON YOUR BODIES. TWO TOWNS OVER, AT THE MIDVALE RESORT AND CASINO.
WHAT ARE WE DOING AT A CASINO?
NO MINORS IN THE SHOWROOM.
LEMME GO, YA BIG APE! I'LL KNOCK YER BLOCK OFF!
WE HAVE TO SEE ZATANNA!
COME BACK IN FIVE YEARS.
HOW AM I SUPPOSED TA KILL FIVE YEARS?! AN' DON'T SAY GO THROUGH MED SCHOOL AGAIN!
GRAB THEM!
ZAP!

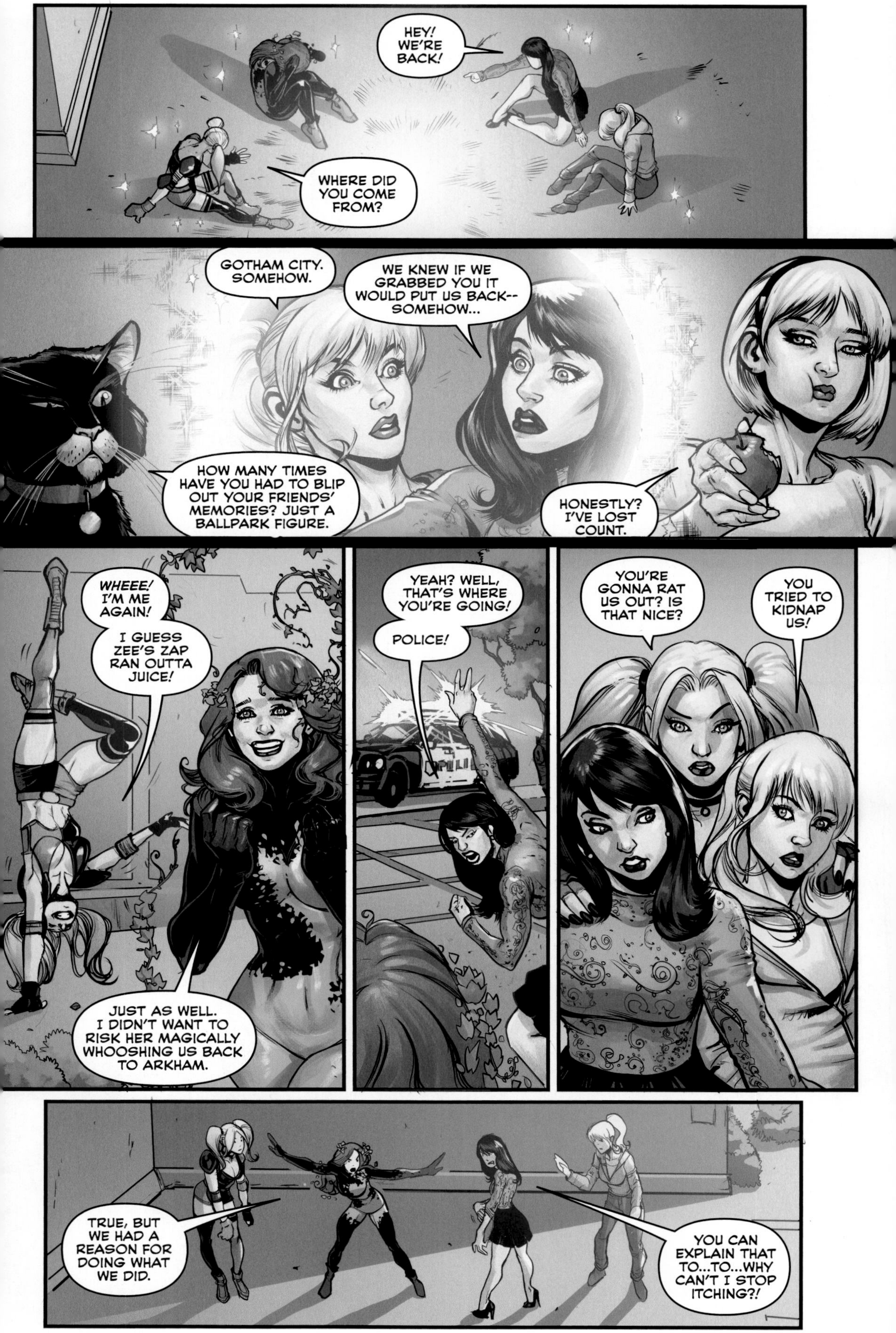
HEY! WE'RE BACK!
WHERE DID YOU COME FROM?
GOTHAM CITY. SOMEHOW.
WE KNEW IF WE GRABBED YOU IT WOULD PUT US BACK-- SOMEHOW...
HOW MANY TIMES HAVE YOU HAD TO BLIP OUT YOUR FRIENDS' MEMORIES? JUST A BALLPARK FIGURE.
HONESTLY? I'VE LOST COUNT.
WHEEE! I'M ME AGAIN!
I GUESS ZEE'S ZAP RAN OUTTA JUICE!
JUST AS WELL. I DIDN'T WANT TO RISK HER MAGICALLY WHOOSHING US BACK TO ARKHAM.
YEAH? WELL, THAT'S WHERE YOU'RE GOING!
POLICE!
YOU'RE GONNA RAT US OUT? IS THAT NICE?
YOU TRIED TO KIDNAP US!
TRUE, BUT WE HAD A REASON FOR DOING WHAT WE DID.
YOU CAN EXPLAIN THAT TO...TO...WHY CAN'T I STOP ITCHING?!

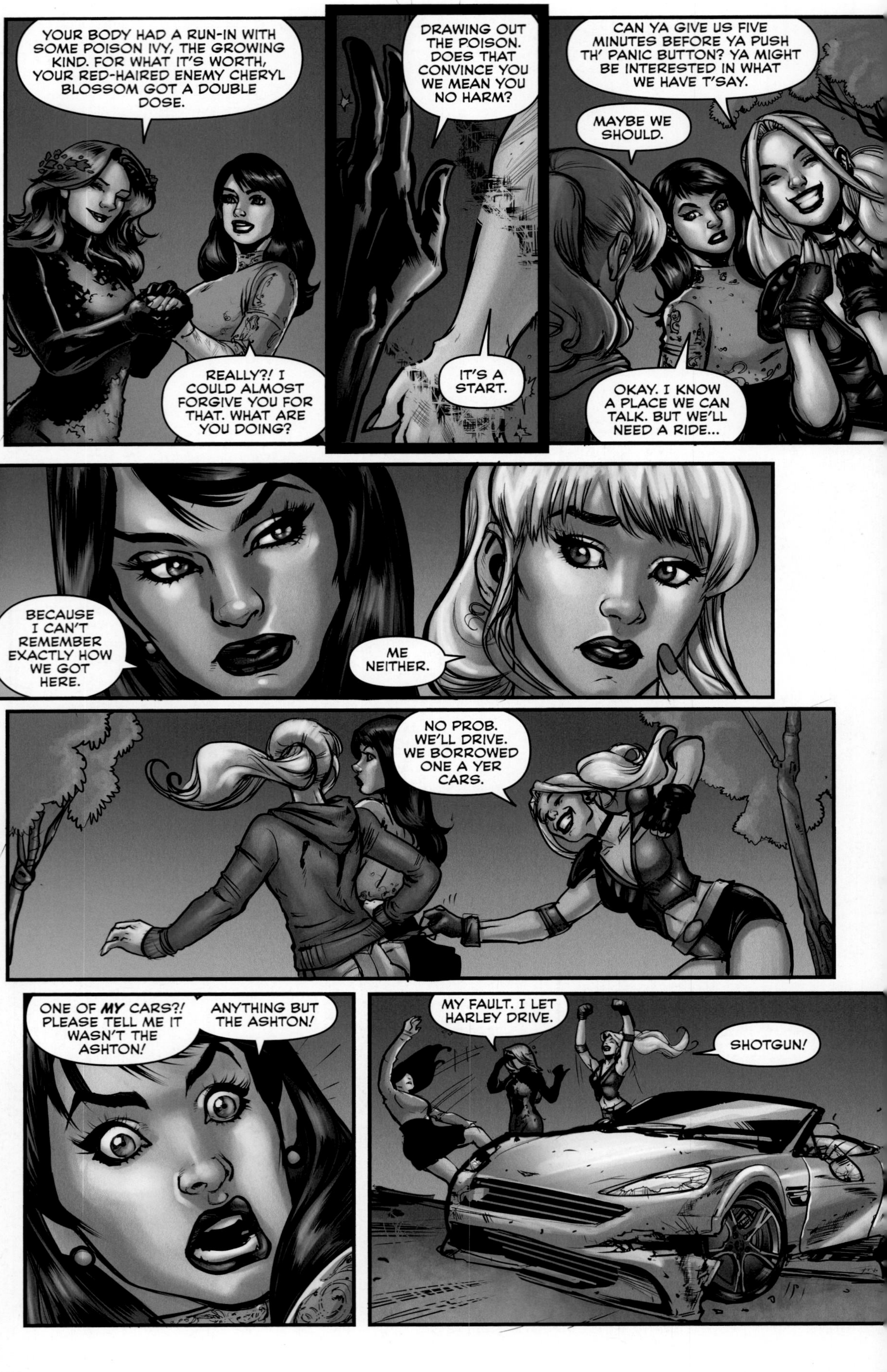
YOUR BODY HAD A RUN-IN WITH SOME POISON IVY, THE GROWING KIND. FOR WHAT IT'S WORTH, YOUR RED-HAIRED ENEMY CHERYL BLOSSOM GOT A DOUBLE DOSE.
REALLY?! I COULD ALMOST FORGIVE YOU FOR THAT. WHAT ARE YOU DOING?
DRAWING OUT THE POISON. DOES THAT CONVINCE YOU WE MEAN YOU NO HARM?
IT'S A START.
CAN YA GIVE US FIVE MINUTES BEFORE YA PUSH TH' PANIC BUTTON? YA MIGHT BE INTERESTED IN WHAT WE HAVE T'SAY.
MAYBE WE SHOULD.
OKAY. I KNOW A PLACE WE CAN TALK. BUT WE'LL NEED A RIDE...
BECAUSE I CAN'T REMEMBER EXACTLY HOW WE GOT HERE.
ME NEITHER.
NO PROB. WE'LL DRIVE. WE BORROWED ONE A YER CARS.
ONE OF *MY* CARS?! PLEASE TELL ME IT WASN'T THE ASHTON!
ANYTHING BUT THE ASHTON!
MY FAULT. I LET HARLEY DRIVE.
SHOTGUN!

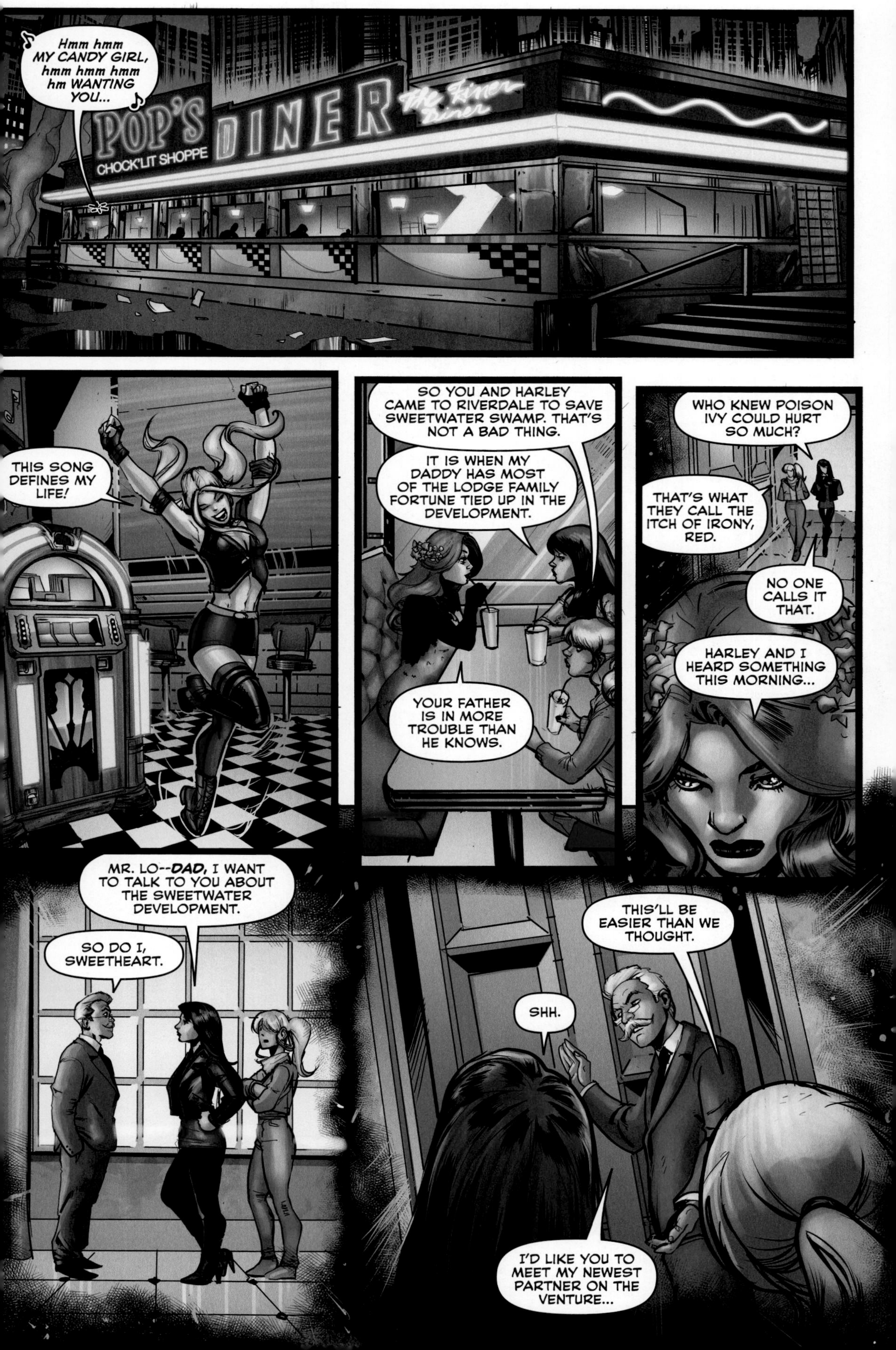
Hmm hmm MY CANDY GIRL, hmm hmm hmm hm WANTING YOU...
POP'S
CHOCK'LIT SHOPPE
DINER
the Finer Diner
THIS SONG DEFINES MY LIFE!
SO YOU AND HARLEY CAME TO RIVERDALE TO SAVE SWEETWATER SWAMP. THAT'S NOT A BAD THING.
IT IS WHEN MY DADDY HAS MOST OF THE LODGE FAMILY FORTUNE TIED UP IN THE DEVELOPMENT.
YOUR FATHER IS IN MORE TROUBLE THAN HE KNOWS.
WHO KNEW POISON IVY COULD HURT SO MUCH?
THAT'S WHAT THEY CALL THE ITCH OF IRONY, RED.
NO ONE CALLS IT THAT.
HARLEY AND I HEARD SOMETHING THIS MORNING...
MR. LO--DAD, I WANT TO TALK TO YOU ABOUT THE SWEETWATER DEVELOPMENT.
SO DO I, SWEETHEART.
THIS'LL BE EASIER THAN WE THOUGHT.
SHH.
I'D LIKE YOU TO MEET MY NEWEST PARTNER ON THE VENTURE...

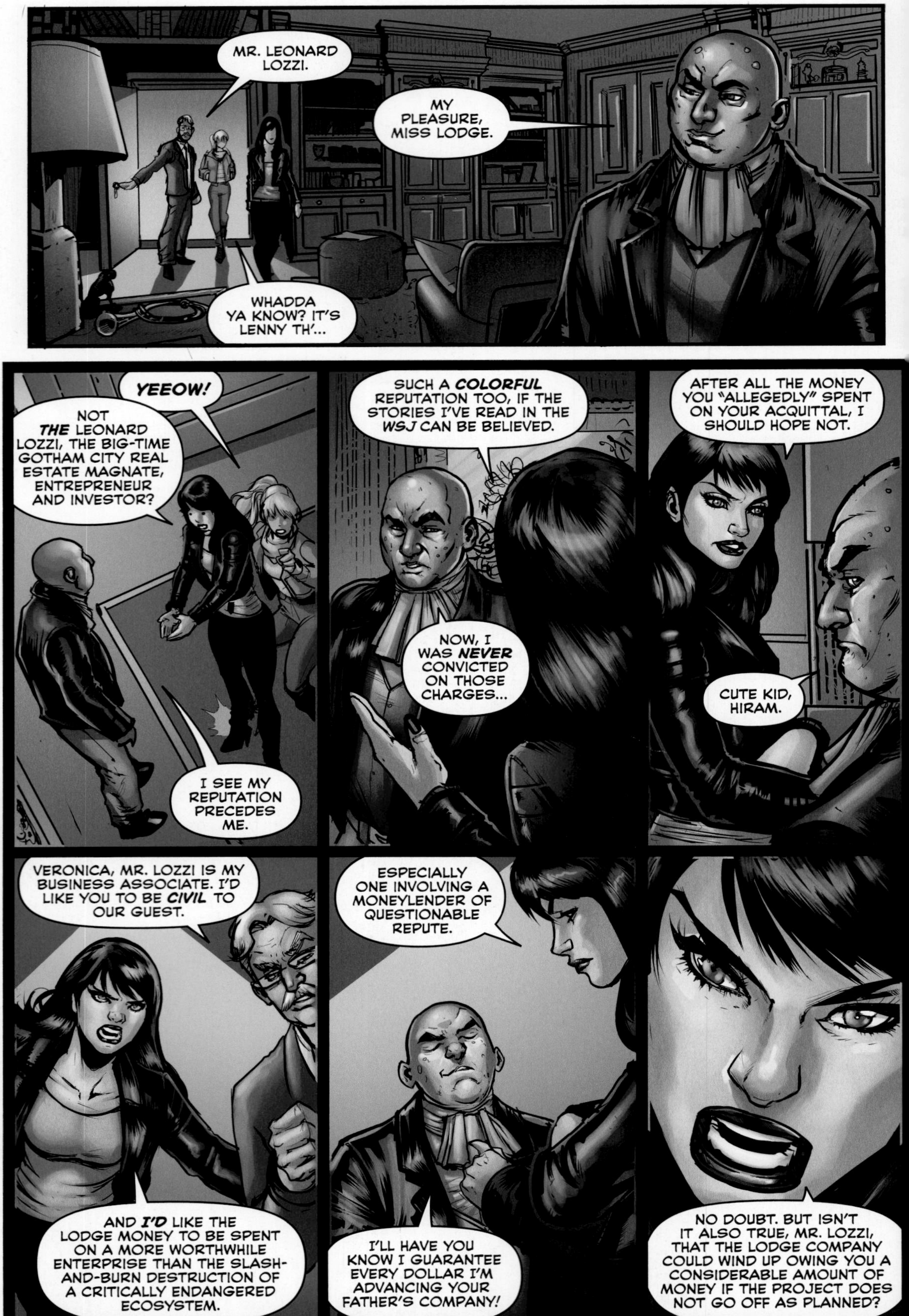
MR. LEONARD LOZZI.
MY PLEASURE, MISS LODGE.
WHADDA YA KNOW? IT'S LENNY TH'...
YEEOW!
NOT THE LEONARD LOZZI, THE BIG-TIME GOTHAM CITY REAL ESTATE MAGNATE, ENTREPRENEUR AND INVESTOR?
I SEE MY REPUTATION PRECEDES ME.
SUCH A COLORFUL REPUTATION TOO, IF THE STORIES I'VE READ IN THE WSJ CAN BE BELIEVED.
NOW, I WAS NEVER CONVICTED ON THOSE CHARGES...
AFTER ALL THE MONEY YOU "ALLEGEDLY" SPENT ON YOUR ACQUITTAL, I SHOULD HOPE NOT.
CUTE KID, HIRAM.
VERONICA, MR. LOZZI IS MY BUSINESS ASSOCIATE. I'D LIKE YOU TO BE CIVIL TO OUR GUEST.
AND I'D LIKE THE LODGE MONEY TO BE SPENT ON A MORE WORTHWHILE ENTERPRISE THAN THE SLASH-AND-BURN DESTRUCTION OF A CRITICALLY ENDANGERED ECOSYSTEM.
ESPECIALLY ONE INVOLVING A MONEYLENDER OF QUESTIONABLE REPUTE.
I'LL HAVE YOU KNOW I GUARANTEE EVERY DOLLAR I'M ADVANCING YOUR FATHER'S COMPANY!
NO DOUBT. BUT ISN'T IT ALSO TRUE, MR. LOZZI, THAT THE LODGE COMPANY COULD WIND UP OWING YOU A CONSIDERABLE AMOUNT OF MONEY IF THE PROJECT DOES NOT GO OFF AS PLANNED?

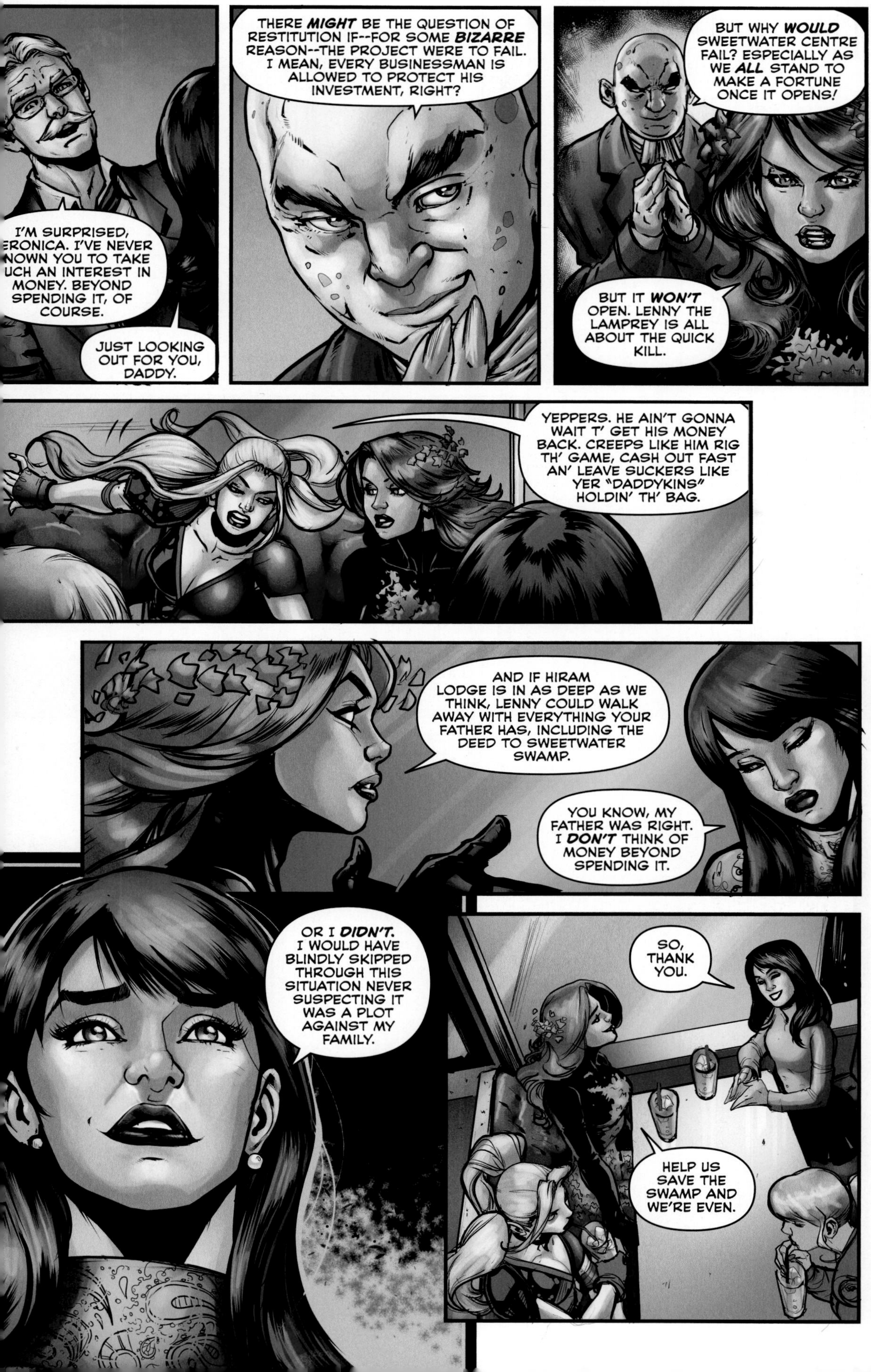
I'M SURPRISED, ERONICA. I'VE NEVER NOWN YOU TO TAKE UCH AN INTEREST IN MONEY. BEYOND SPENDING IT, OF COURSE.
JUST LOOKING OUT FOR YOU, DADDY.
THERE MIGHT BE THE QUESTION OF RESTITUTION IF--FOR SOME BIZARRE REASON--THE PROJECT WERE TO FAIL. I MEAN, EVERY BUSINESSMAN IS ALLOWED TO PROTECT HIS INVESTMENT, RIGHT?
BUT WHY WOULD SWEETWATER CENTRE FAIL? ESPECIALLY AS WE ALL STAND TO MAKE A FORTUNE ONCE IT OPENS!
BUT IT WON'T OPEN. LENNY THE LAMPREY IS ALL ABOUT THE QUICK KILL.
YEPPERS. HE AIN'T GONNA WAIT T' GET HIS MONEY BACK. CREEPS LIKE HIM RIG TH' GAME, CASH OUT FAST AN' LEAVE SUCKERS LIKE YER "DADDYKINS" HOLDIN' TH' BAG.
AND IF HIRAM LODGE IS IN AS DEEP AS WE THINK, LENNY COULD WALK AWAY WITH EVERYTHING YOUR FATHER HAS, INCLUDING THE DEED TO SWEETWATER SWAMP.
YOU KNOW, MY FATHER WAS RIGHT. I DON'T THINK OF MONEY BEYOND SPENDING IT.
OR I DIDN'T. I WOULD HAVE BLINDLY SKIPPED THROUGH THIS SITUATION NEVER SUSPECTING IT WAS A PLOT AGAINST MY FAMILY.
SO, THANK YOU.
HELP US SAVE THE SWAMP AND WE'RE EVEN.

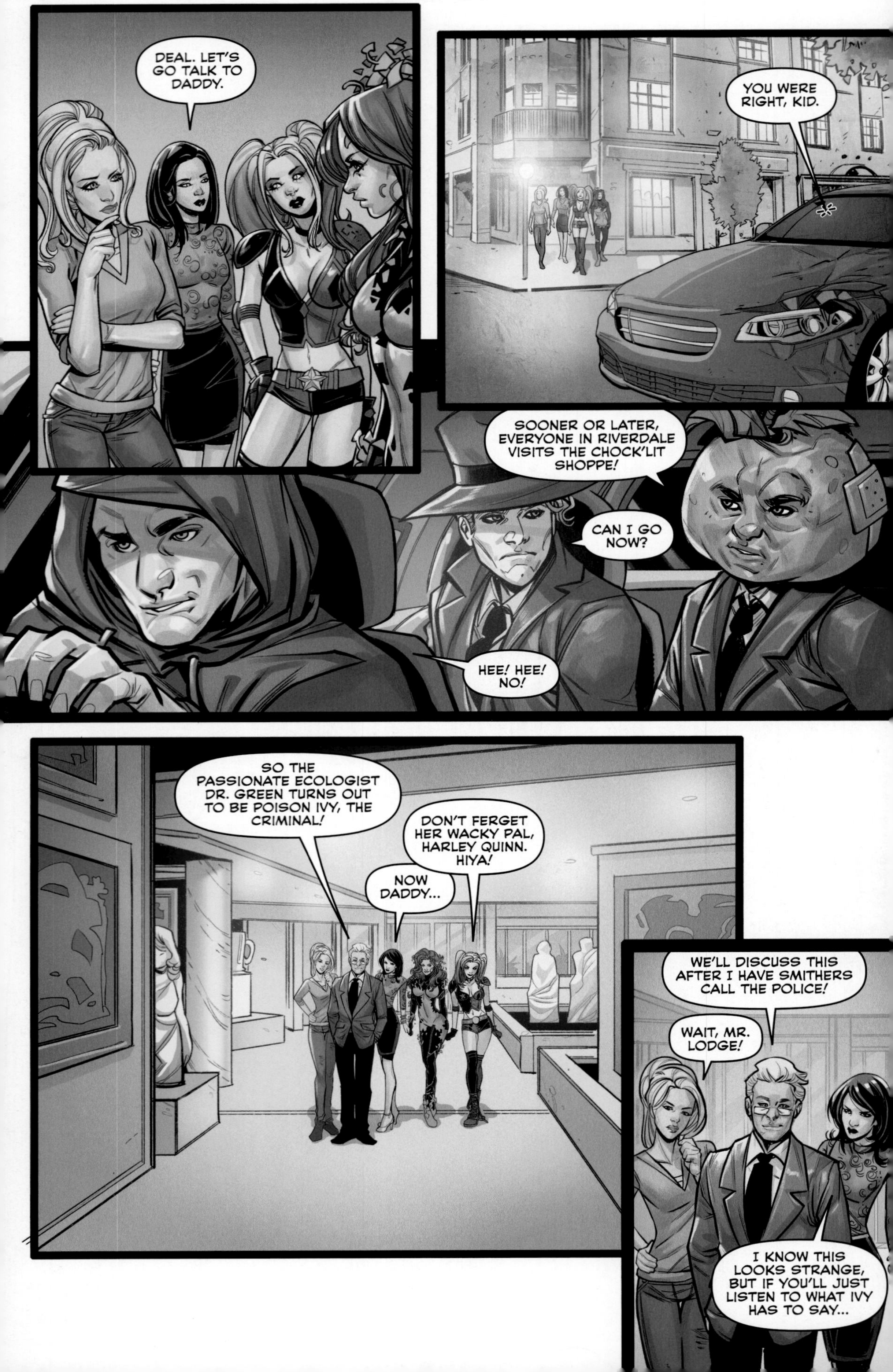
DEAL. LET'S GO TALK TO DADDY.
YOU WERE RIGHT, KID.
SOONER OR LATER, EVERYONE IN RIVERDALE VISITS THE CHOCK'LIT SHOPPE!
CAN I GO NOW?
HEE! HEE! NO!
SO THE PASSIONATE ECOLOGIST DR. GREEN TURNS OUT TO BE POISON IVY, THE CRIMINAL!
DON'T FERGET HER WACKY PAL, HARLEY QUINN. HIYA!
NOW DADDY...
WE'LL DISCUSS THIS AFTER I HAVE SMITHERS CALL THE POLICE!
WAIT, MR. LODGE!
I KNOW THIS LOOKS STRANGE, BUT IF YOU'LL JUST LISTEN TO WHAT IVY HAS TO SAY...

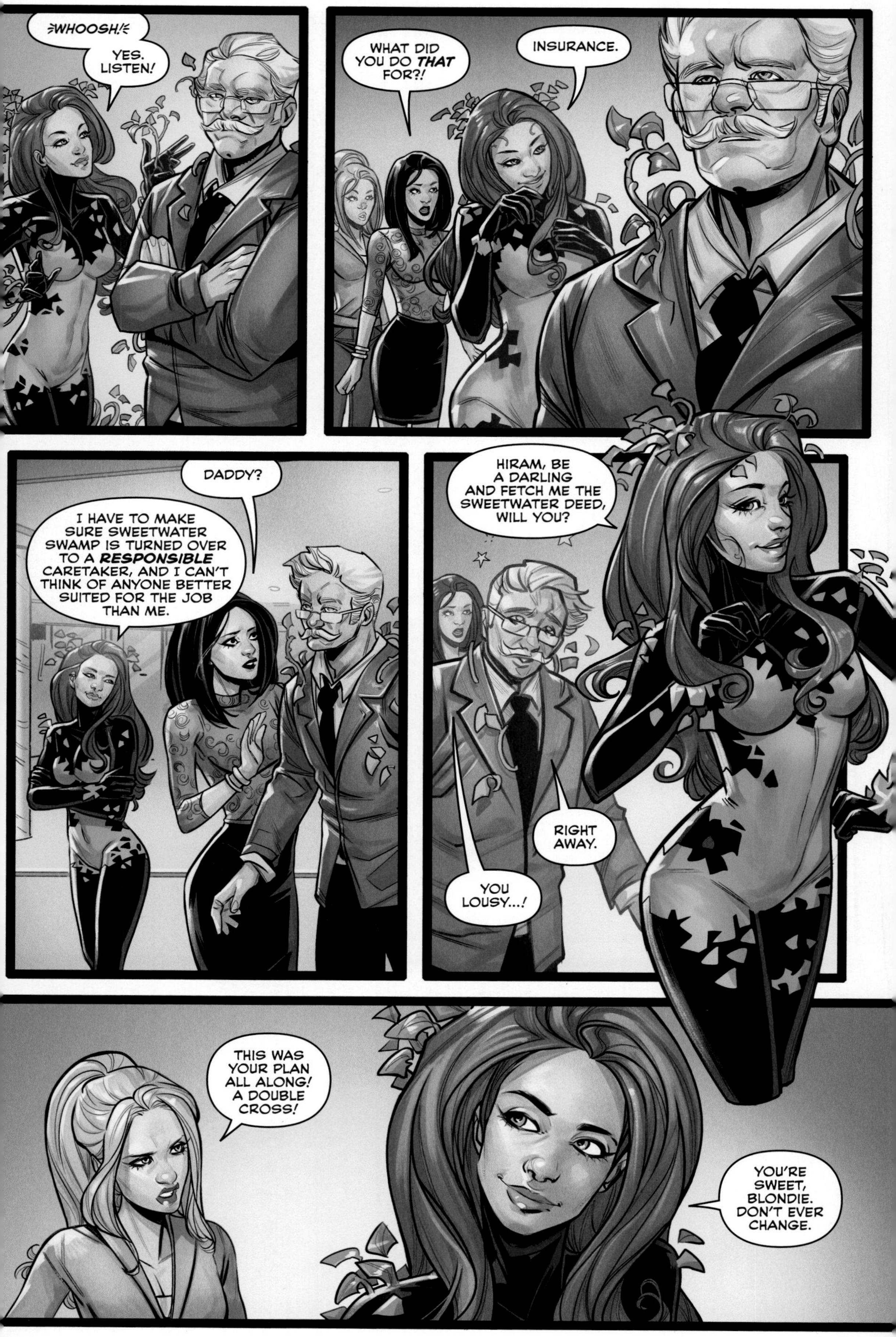

WHOOSH!
YES. LISTEN!
WHAT DID YOU DO THAT FOR?!
INSURANCE.
DADDY?
I HAVE TO MAKE SURE SWEETWATER SWAMP IS TURNED OVER TO A RESPONSIBLE CARETAKER, AND I CAN'T THINK OF ANYONE BETTER SUITED FOR THE JOB THAN ME.
HIRAM, BE A DARLING AND FETCH ME THE SWEETWATER DEED, WILL YOU?
RIGHT AWAY.
YOU LOUSY...!
THIS WAS YOUR PLAN ALL ALONG! A DOUBLE CROSS!
YOU'RE SWEET, BLONDIE. DON'T EVER CHANGE.

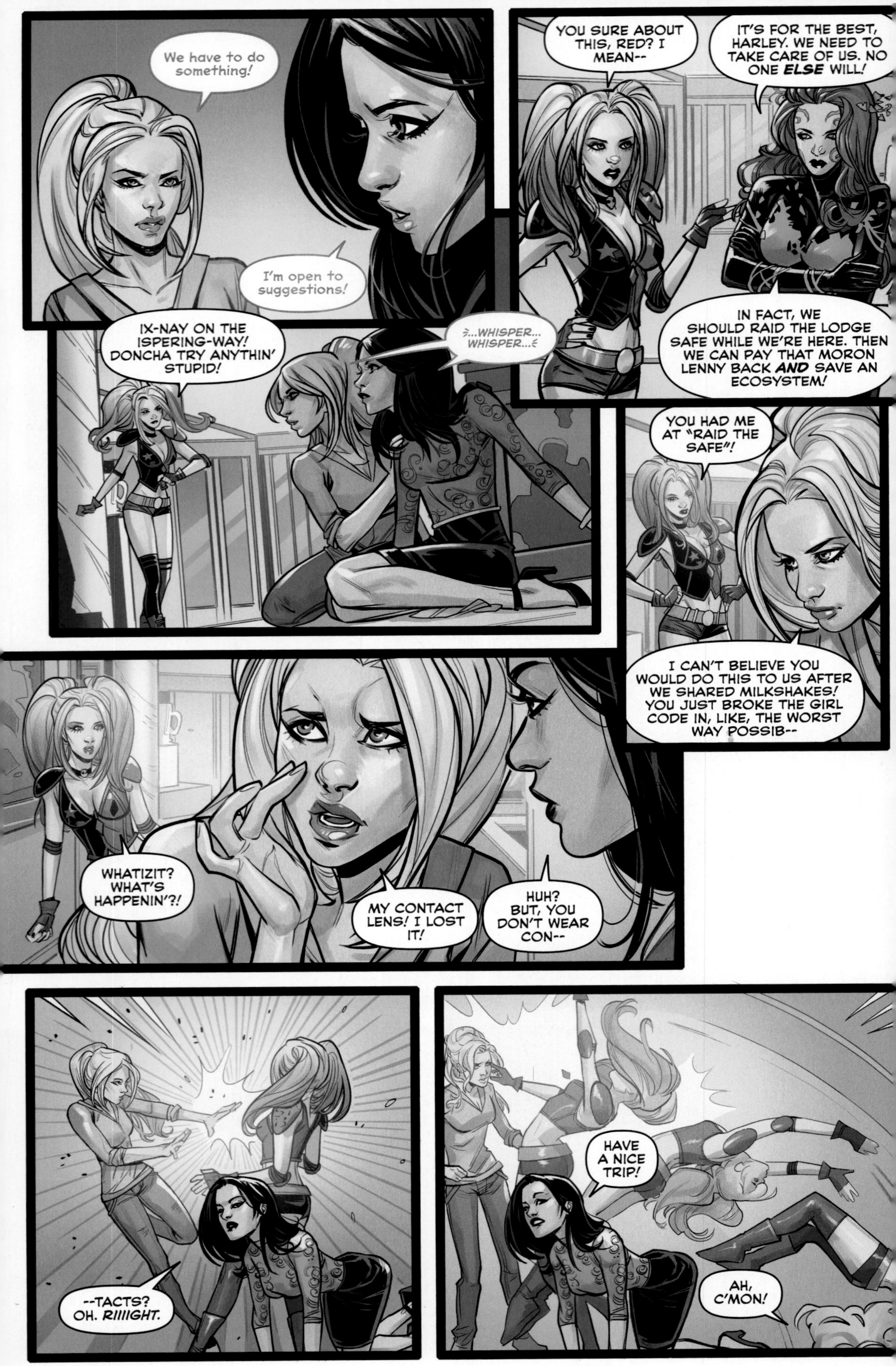

We have to do something!
I'm open to suggestions!
YOU SURE ABOUT THIS, RED? I MEAN--
IT'S FOR THE BEST, HARLEY. WE NEED TO TAKE CARE OF US. NO ONE ELSE WILL!
IX-NAY ON THE ISPERING-WAY! DONCHA TRY ANYTHIN' STUPID!
...WHISPER... WHISPER...
IN FACT, WE SHOULD RAID THE LODGE SAFE WHILE WE'RE HERE. THEN WE CAN PAY THAT MORON LENNY BACK AND SAVE AN ECOSYSTEM!
YOU HAD ME AT "RAID THE SAFE"!
I CAN'T BELIEVE YOU WOULD DO THIS TO US AFTER WE SHARED MILKSHAKES! YOU JUST BROKE THE GIRL CODE IN, LIKE, THE WORST WAY POSSIB--
WHATIZIT? WHAT'S HAPPENIN'?!
MY CONTACT LENS! I LOST IT!
HUH? BUT, YOU DON'T WEAR CON--
--TACTS? OH. RIIIGHT.
HAVE A NICE TRIP!
AH, C'MON!

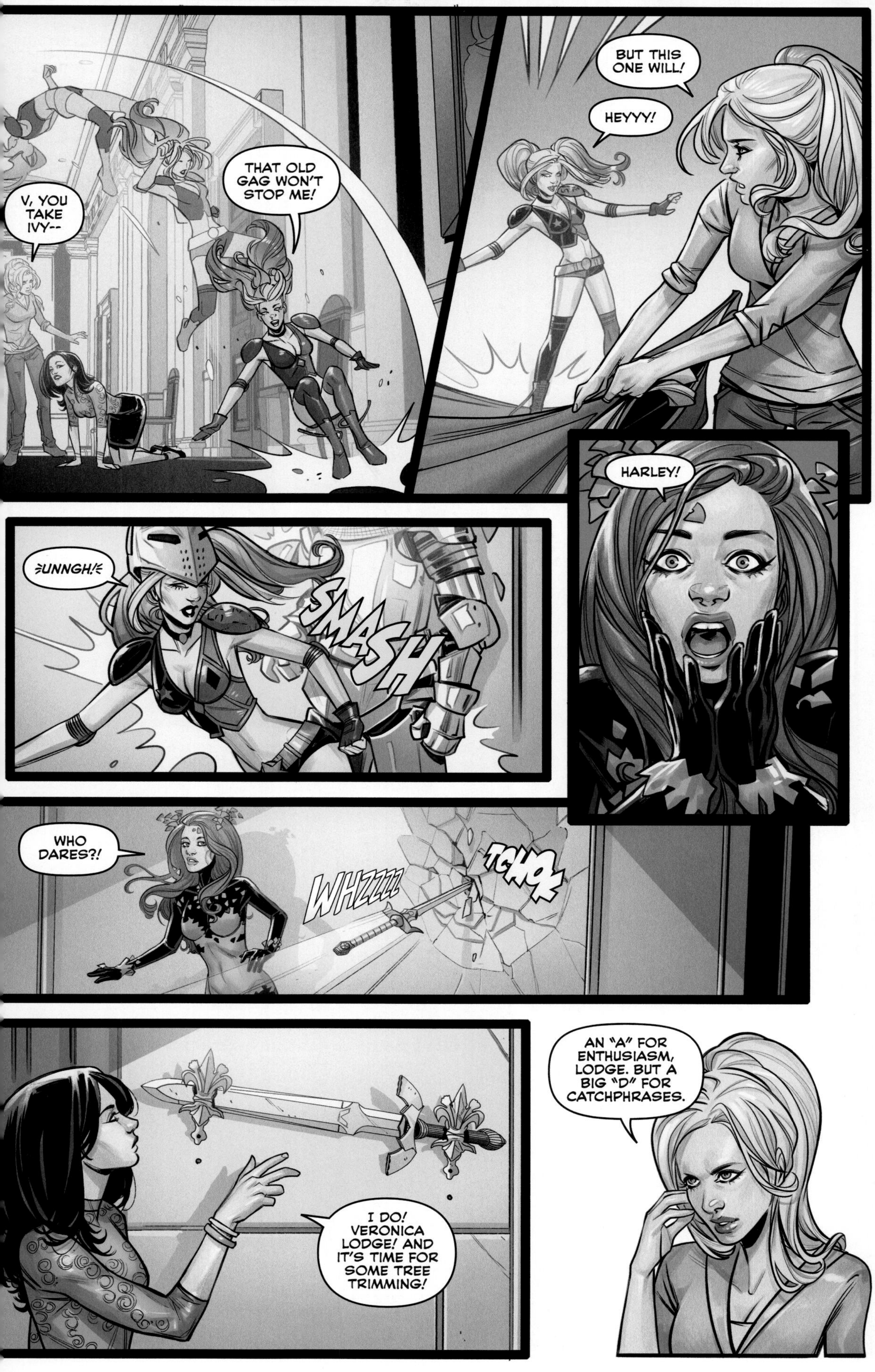
V, YOU TAKE IVY--
THAT OLD GAG WON'T STOP ME!
BUT THIS ONE WILL!
HEYYY!
UNNGH!
SMASH
HARLEY!
WHO DARES?!
WHZZZZ
TCHOK
I DO! VERONICA LODGE! AND IT'S TIME FOR SOME TREE TRIMMING!
AN "A" FOR ENTHUSIASM, LODGE. BUT A BIG "D" FOR CATCHPHRASES.

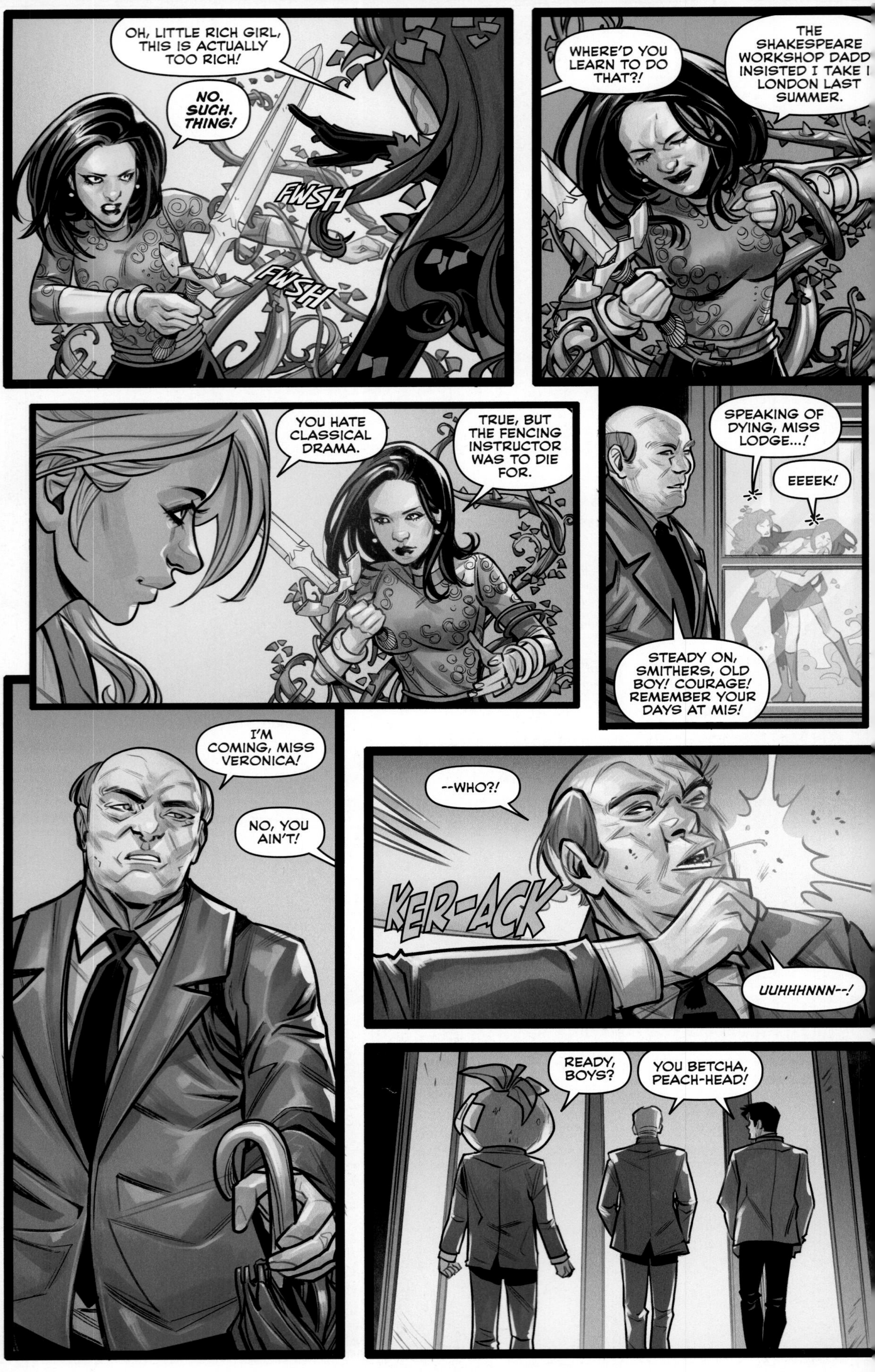
OH, LITTLE RICH GIRL, THIS IS ACTUALLY TOO RICH!
NO. SUCH. THING!
FWSH
FWSH
WHERE'D YOU LEARN TO DO THAT?!
THE SHAKESPEARE WORKSHOP DADD INSISTED I TAKE I LONDON LAST SUMMER.
YOU HATE CLASSICAL DRAMA.
TRUE, BUT THE FENCING INSTRUCTOR WAS TO DIE FOR.
SPEAKING OF DYING, MISS LODGE...!
EEEEK!
STEADY ON, SMITHERS, OLD BOY! COURAGE! REMEMBER YOUR DAYS AT MI5!
I'M COMING, MISS VERONICA!
NO, YOU AIN'T!
--WHO?!
KER-ACK
UUHHHNNN--!
READY, BOYS?
YOU BETCHA, PEACH-HEAD!

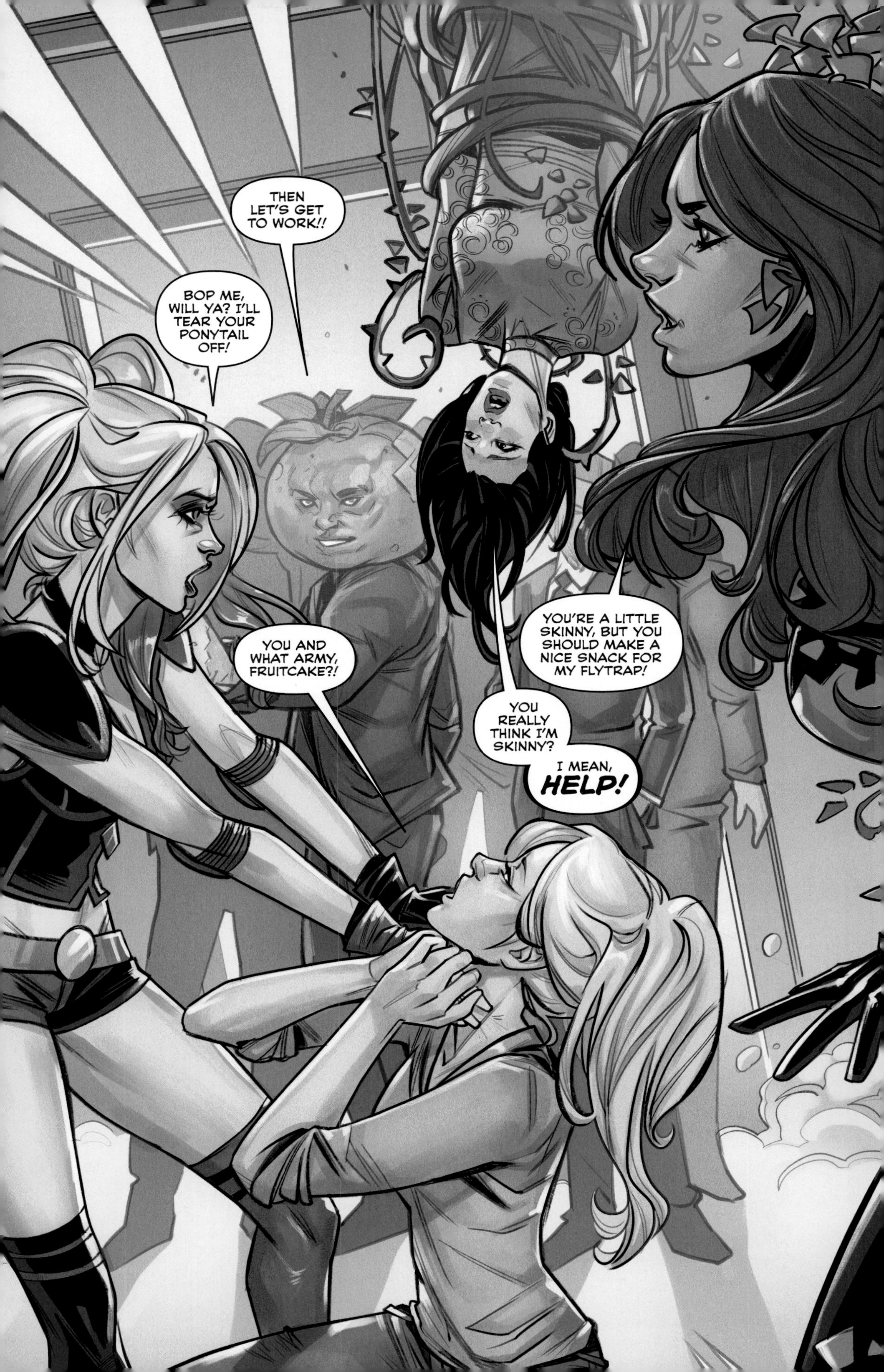
THEN LET'S GET TO WORK!!
BOP ME, WILL YA? I'LL TEAR YOUR PONYTAIL OFF!
YOU AND WHAT ARMY, FRUITCAKE?!
YOU'RE A LITTLE SKINNY, BUT YOU SHOULD MAKE A NICE SNACK FOR MY FLYTRAP!
YOU REALLY THINK I'M SKINNY?
I MEAN, HELP!

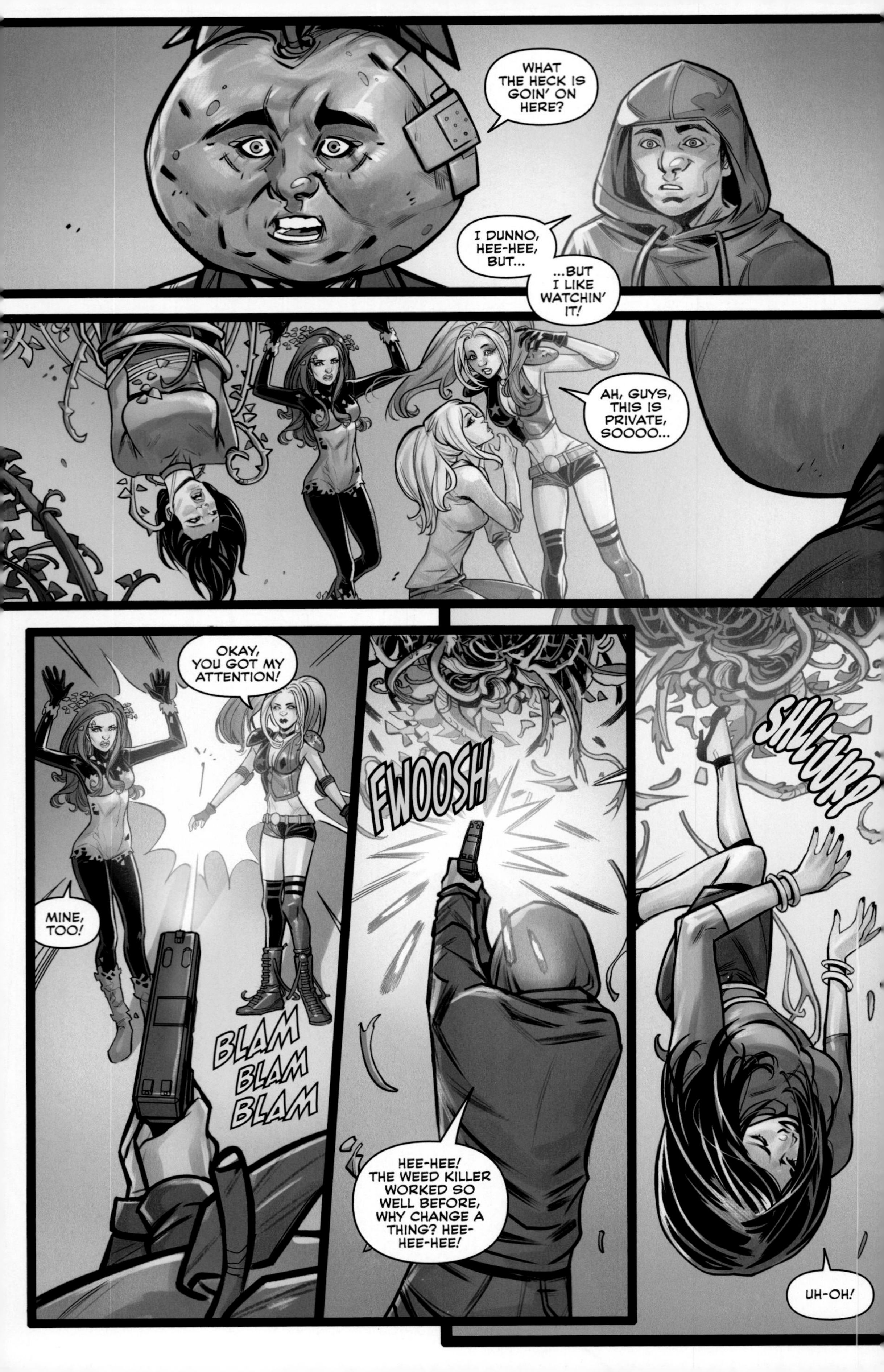
WHAT THE HECK IS GOIN' ON HERE?
I DUNNO, HEE-HEE, BUT...
...BUT I LIKE WATCHIN' IT!
AH, GUYS, THIS IS PRIVATE, SOOOO...
OKAY, YOU GOT MY ATTENTION!
MINE, TOO!
BLAM BLAM BLAM
FWOOSH
HEE-HEE! THE WEED KILLER WORKED SO WELL BEFORE, WHY CHANGE A THING? HEE-HEE-HEE!
SHLURP!
UH-OH!

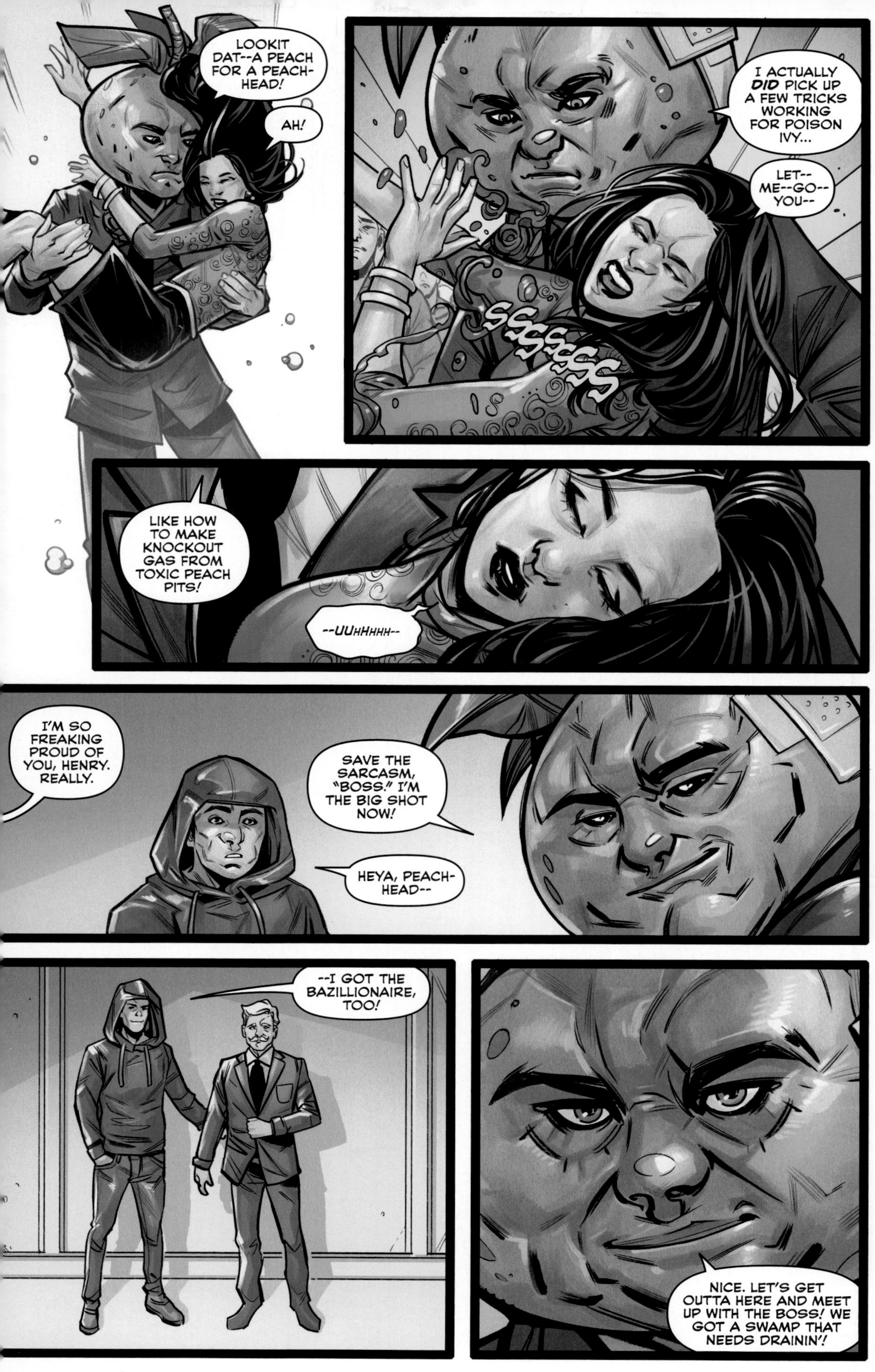
LOOKIT DAT--A PEACH FOR A PEACH-HEAD!
AH!
I ACTUALLY DID PICK UP A FEW TRICKS WORKING FOR POISON IVY...
LET--ME--GO--YOU--
SSSSSSS
LIKE HOW TO MAKE KNOCKOUT GAS FROM TOXIC PEACH PITS!
--UUHHHHH--
I'M SO FREAKING PROUD OF YOU, HENRY. REALLY.
SAVE THE SARCASM, "BOSS." I'M THE BIG SHOT NOW!
HEYA, PEACH-HEAD--
--I GOT THE BAZILLIONAIRE, TOO!
NICE. LET'S GET OUTTA HERE AND MEET UP WITH THE BOSS! WE GOT A SWAMP THAT NEEDS DRAININ'!

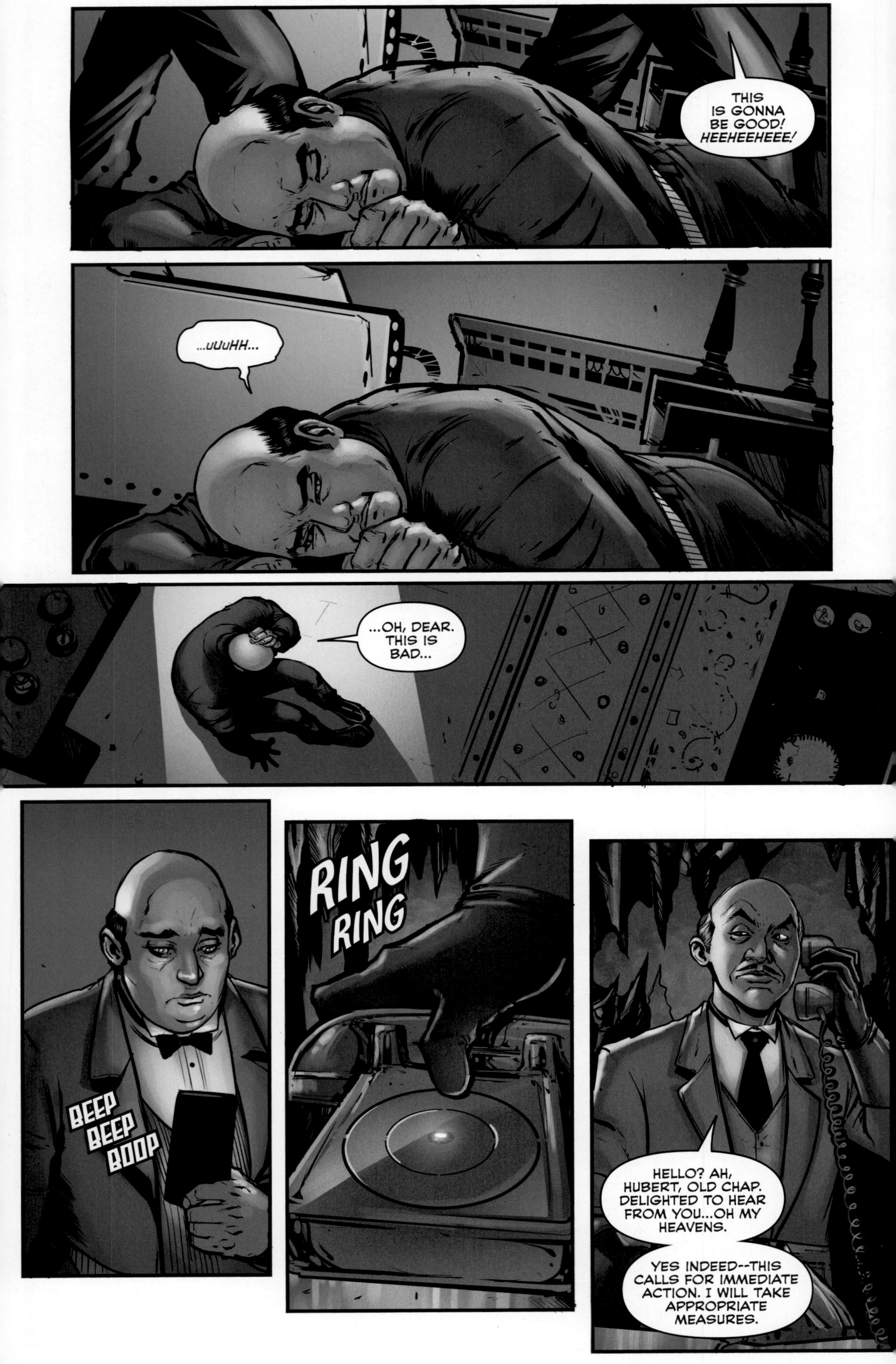
THIS IS GONNA BE GOOD! HEEHEEHEEE!
...uuuHH...
...OH, DEAR. THIS IS BAD...
BEEP BEEP BOOP
RING RING
HELLO? AH, HUBERT, OLD CHAP. DELIGHTED TO HEAR FROM YOU...OH MY HEAVENS.
YES INDEED--THIS CALLS FOR IMMEDIATE ACTION. I WILL TAKE APPROPRIATE MEASURES.

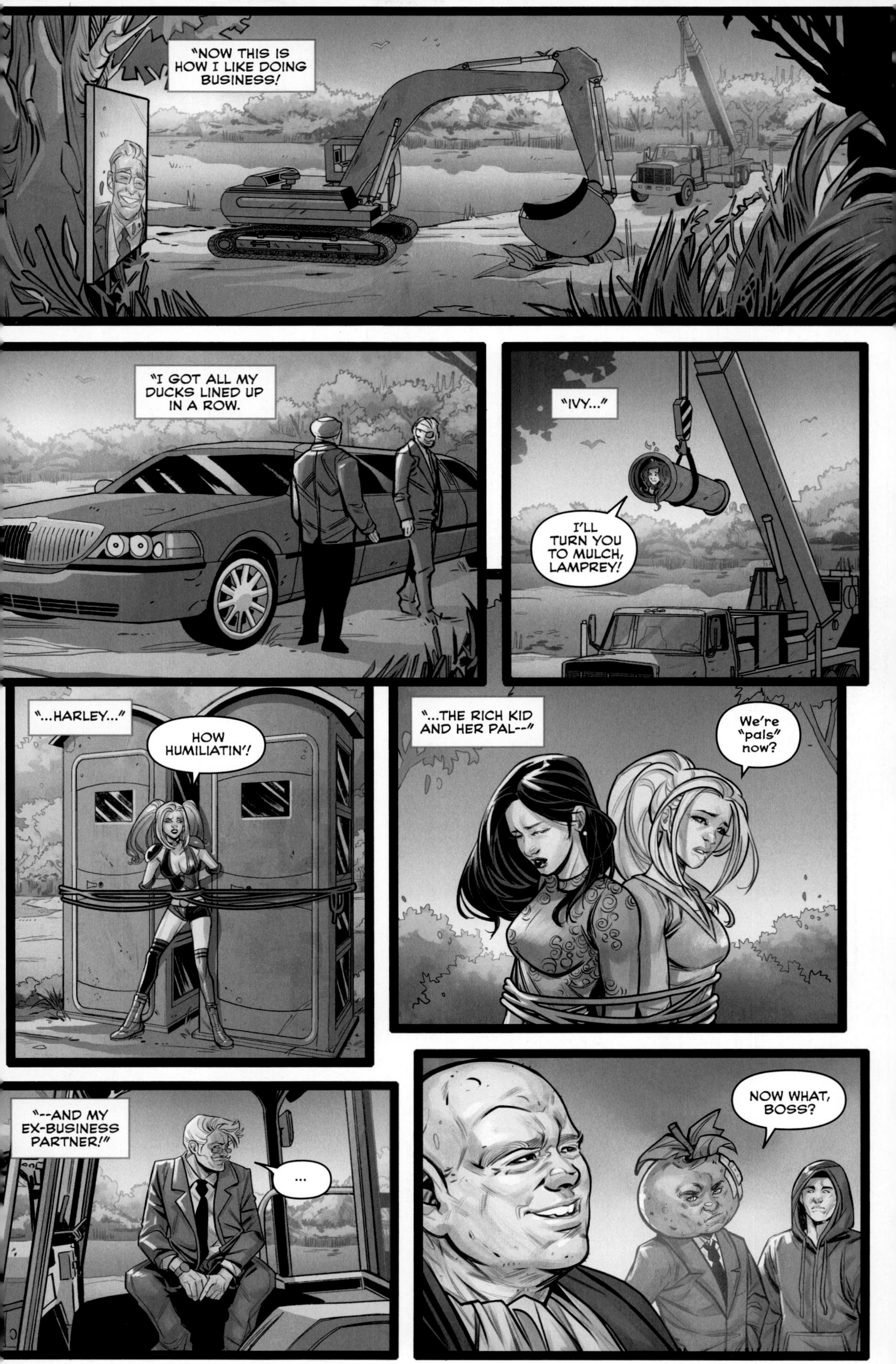
"NOW THIS IS HOW I LIKE DOING BUSINESS!
"I GOT ALL MY DUCKS LINED UP IN A ROW.
"IVY..."
I'LL TURN YOU TO MULCH, LAMPREY!
"...HARLEY..."
HOW HUMILIATIN'!
"...THE RICH KID AND HER PAL--"
We're "pals" now?
"--AND MY EX-BUSINESS PARTNER!"
...
NOW WHAT, BOSS?

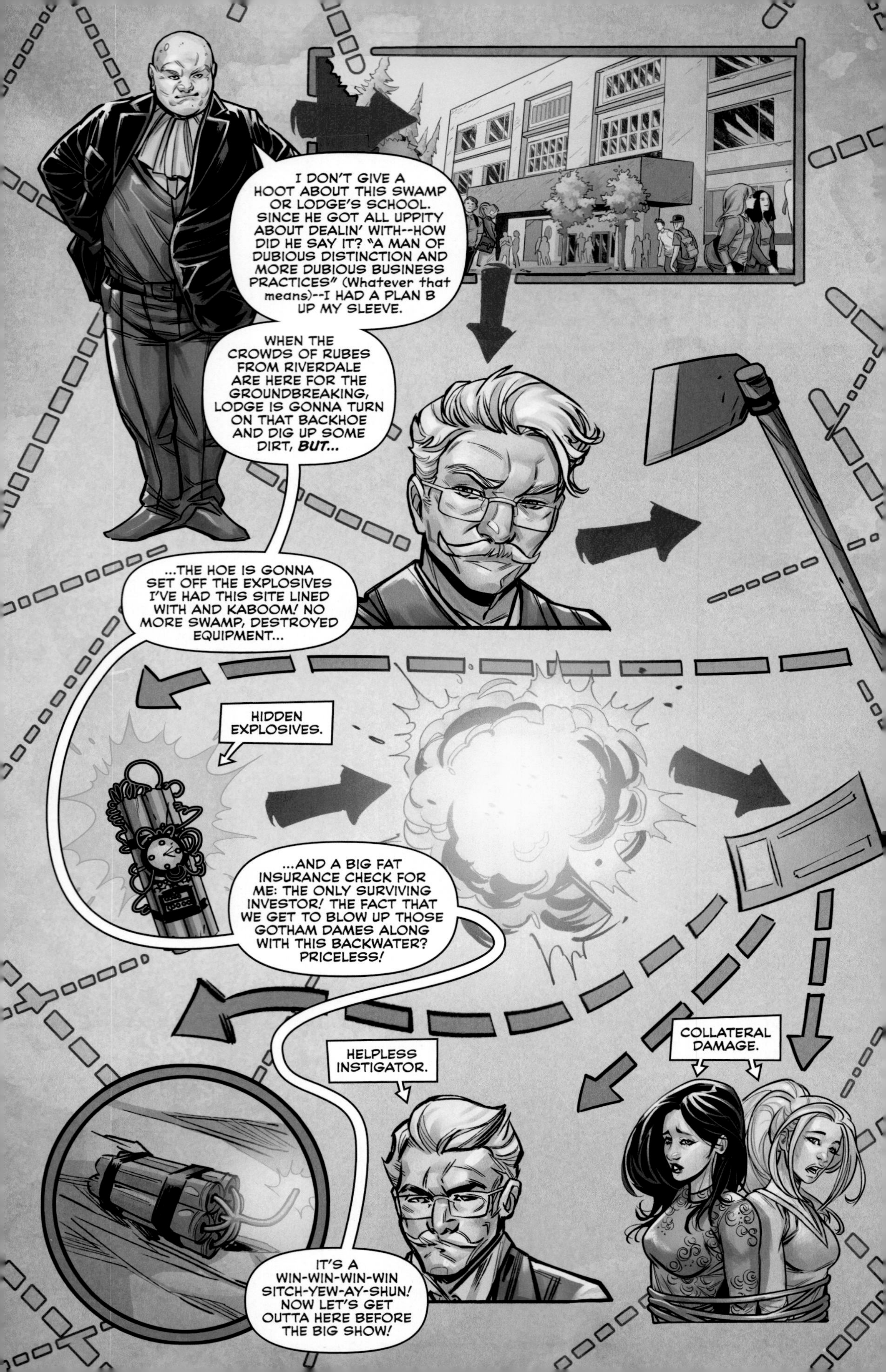
I DON'T GIVE A HOOT ABOUT THIS SWAMP OR LODGE'S SCHOOL. SINCE HE GOT ALL UPPITY ABOUT DEALIN' WITH--HOW DID HE SAY IT? "A MAN OF DUBIOUS DISTINCTION AND MORE DUBIOUS BUSINESS PRACTICES" (Whatever that means)--I HAD A PLAN B UP MY SLEEVE.
WHEN THE CROWDS OF RUBES FROM RIVERDALE ARE HERE FOR THE GROUNDBREAKING, LODGE IS GONNA TURN ON THAT BACKHOE AND DIG UP SOME DIRT, BUT...
...THE HOE IS GONNA SET OFF THE EXPLOSIVES I'VE HAD THIS SITE LINED WITH AND KABOOM! NO MORE SWAMP, DESTROYED EQUIPMENT...
HIDDEN EXPLOSIVES.
...AND A BIG FAT INSURANCE CHECK FOR ME: THE ONLY SURVIVING INVESTOR! THE FACT THAT WE GET TO BLOW UP THOSE GOTHAM DAMES ALONG WITH THIS BACKWATER? PRICELESS!
HELPLESS INSTIGATOR.
COLLATERAL DAMAGE.
IT'S A WIN-WIN-WIN-WIN SITCH-YEW-AY-SHUN! NOW LET'S GET OUTTA HERE BEFORE THE BIG SHOW!

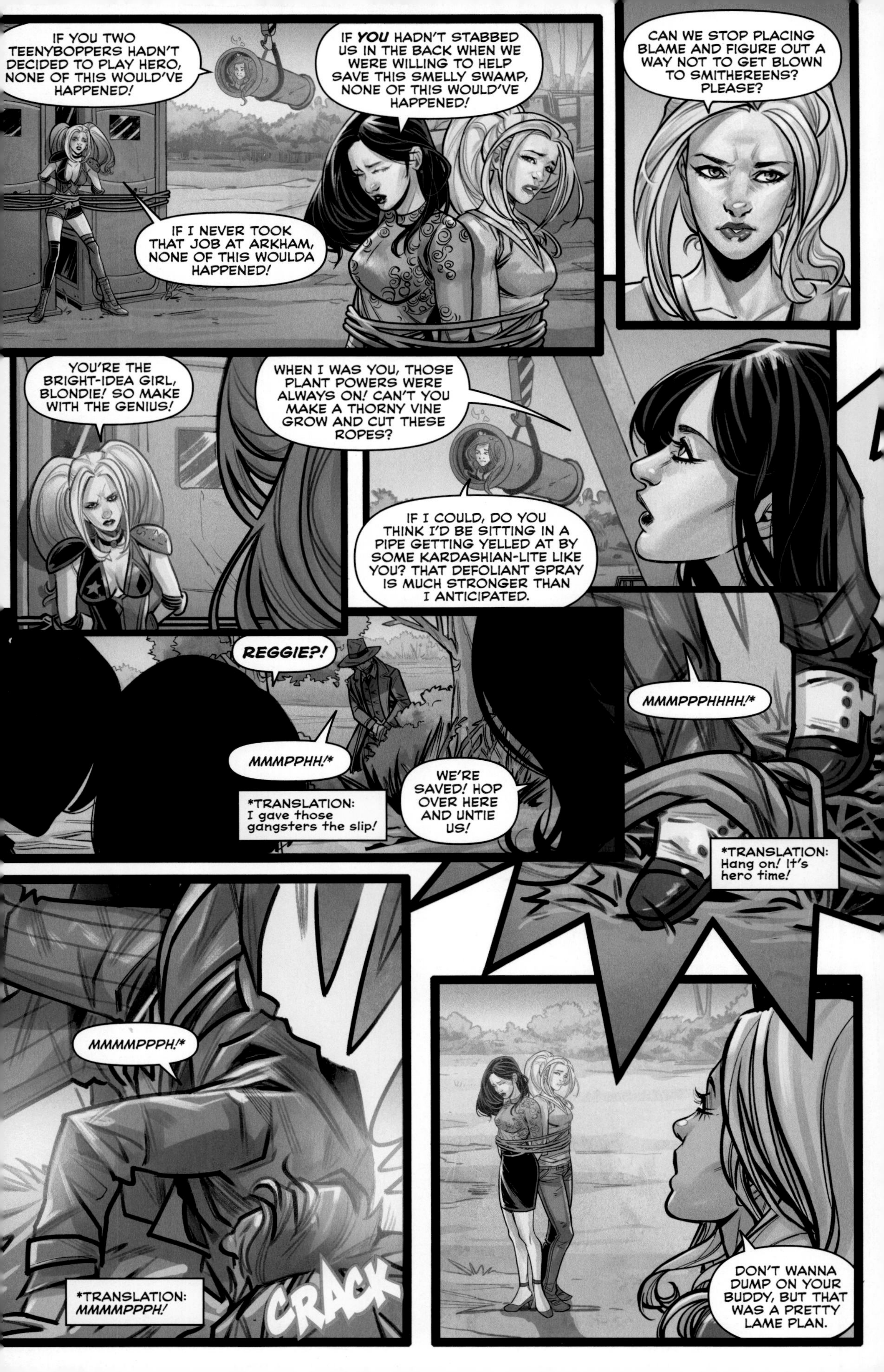
IF YOU TWO TEENYBOPPERS HADN'T DECIDED TO PLAY HERO, NONE OF THIS WOULD'VE HAPPENED!
IF YOU HADN'T STABBED US IN THE BACK WHEN WE WERE WILLING TO HELP SAVE THIS SMELLY SWAMP, NONE OF THIS WOULD'VE HAPPENED!
IF I NEVER TOOK THAT JOB AT ARKHAM, NONE OF THIS WOULDA HAPPENED!
CAN WE STOP PLACING BLAME AND FIGURE OUT A WAY NOT TO GET BLOWN TO SMITHEREENS? PLEASE?
YOU'RE THE BRIGHT-IDEA GIRL, BLONDIE! SO MAKE WITH THE GENIUS!
WHEN I WAS YOU, THOSE PLANT POWERS WERE ALWAYS ON! CAN'T YOU MAKE A THORNY VINE GROW AND CUT THESE ROPES?
IF I COULD, DO YOU THINK I'D BE SITTING IN A PIPE GETTING YELLED AT BY SOME KARDASHIAN-LITE LIKE YOU? THAT DEFOLIANT SPRAY IS MUCH STRONGER THAN I ANTICIPATED.
REGGIE?!
MMMPPH!*
*TRANSLATION: I gave those gangsters the slip!
WE'RE SAVED! HOP OVER HERE AND UNTIE US!
MMMPPPHHHH!*
*TRANSLATION: Hang on! It's hero time!
MMMMPPPH!*
*TRANSLATION: MMMMPPPH!
CRACK
DON'T WANNA DUMP ON YOUR BUDDY, BUT THAT WAS A PRETTY LAME PLAN.

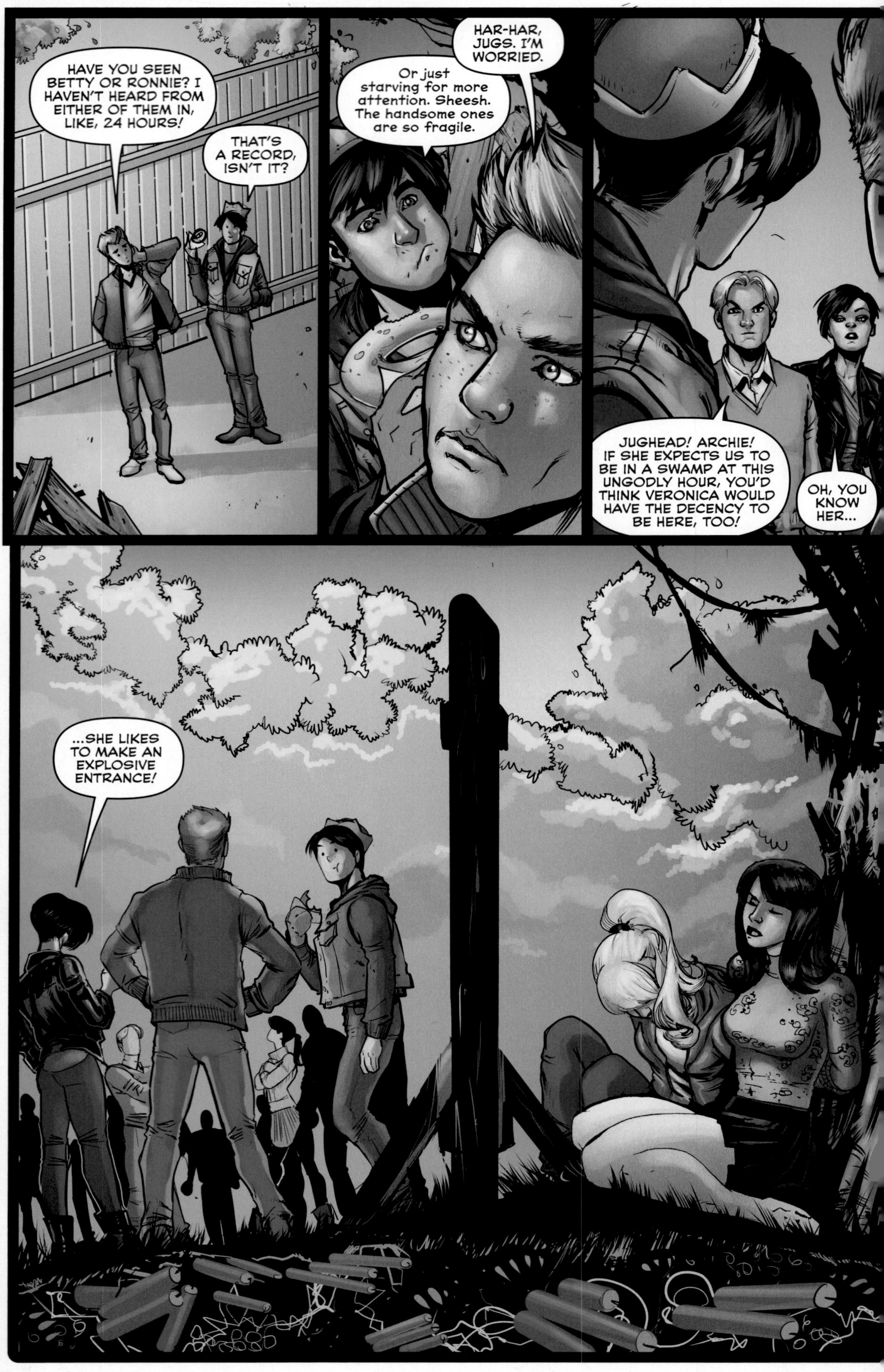
HAVE YOU SEEN BETTY OR RONNIE? I HAVEN'T HEARD FROM EITHER OF THEM IN, LIKE, 24 HOURS!
THAT'S A RECORD, ISN'T IT?
HAR-HAR, JUGS. I'M WORRIED.
Or just starving for more attention. Sheesh. The handsome ones are so fragile.
JUGHEAD! ARCHIE! IF SHE EXPECTS US TO BE IN A SWAMP AT THIS UNGODLY HOUR, YOU'D THINK VERONICA WOULD HAVE THE DECENCY TO BE HERE, TOO!
OH, YOU KNOW HER...
...SHE LIKES TO MAKE AN EXPLOSIVE ENTRANCE!

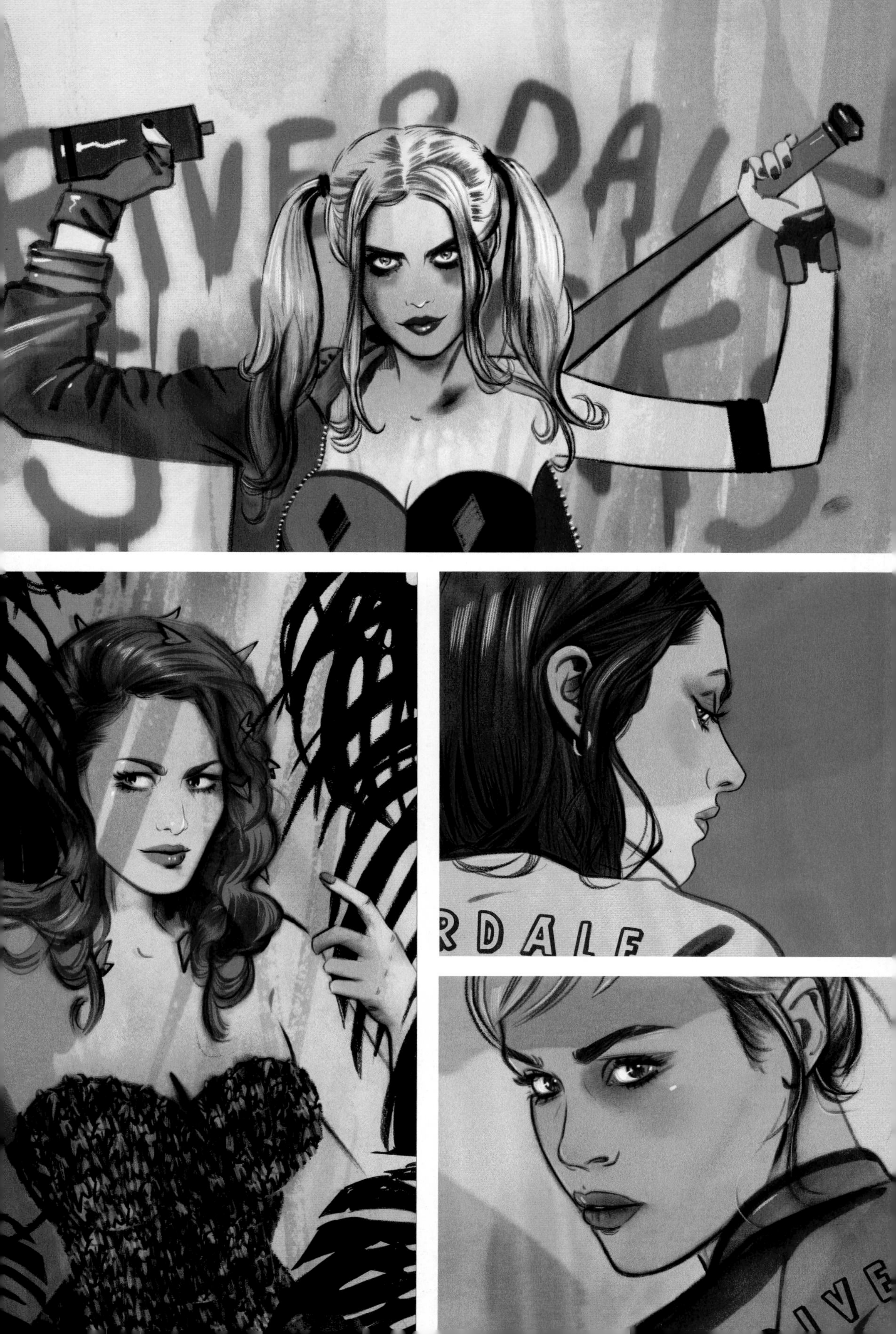
RDALE
IVE

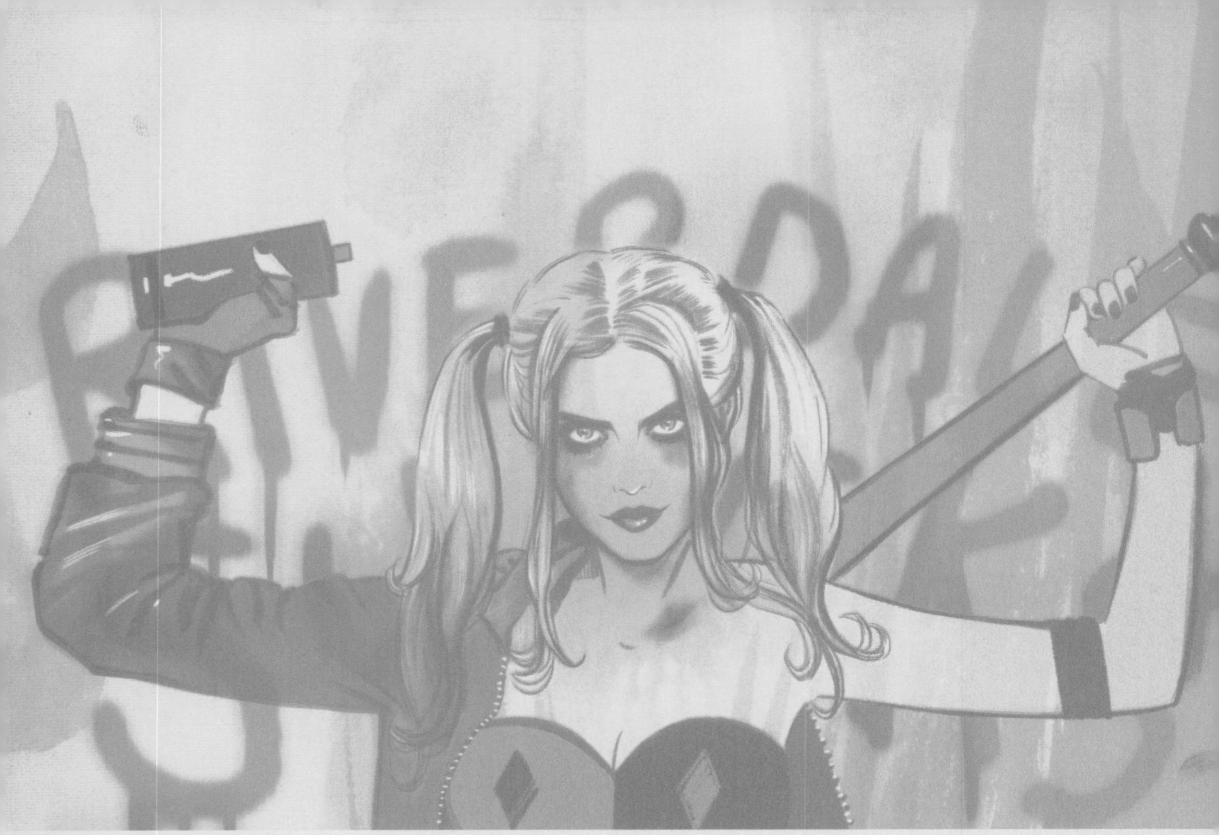

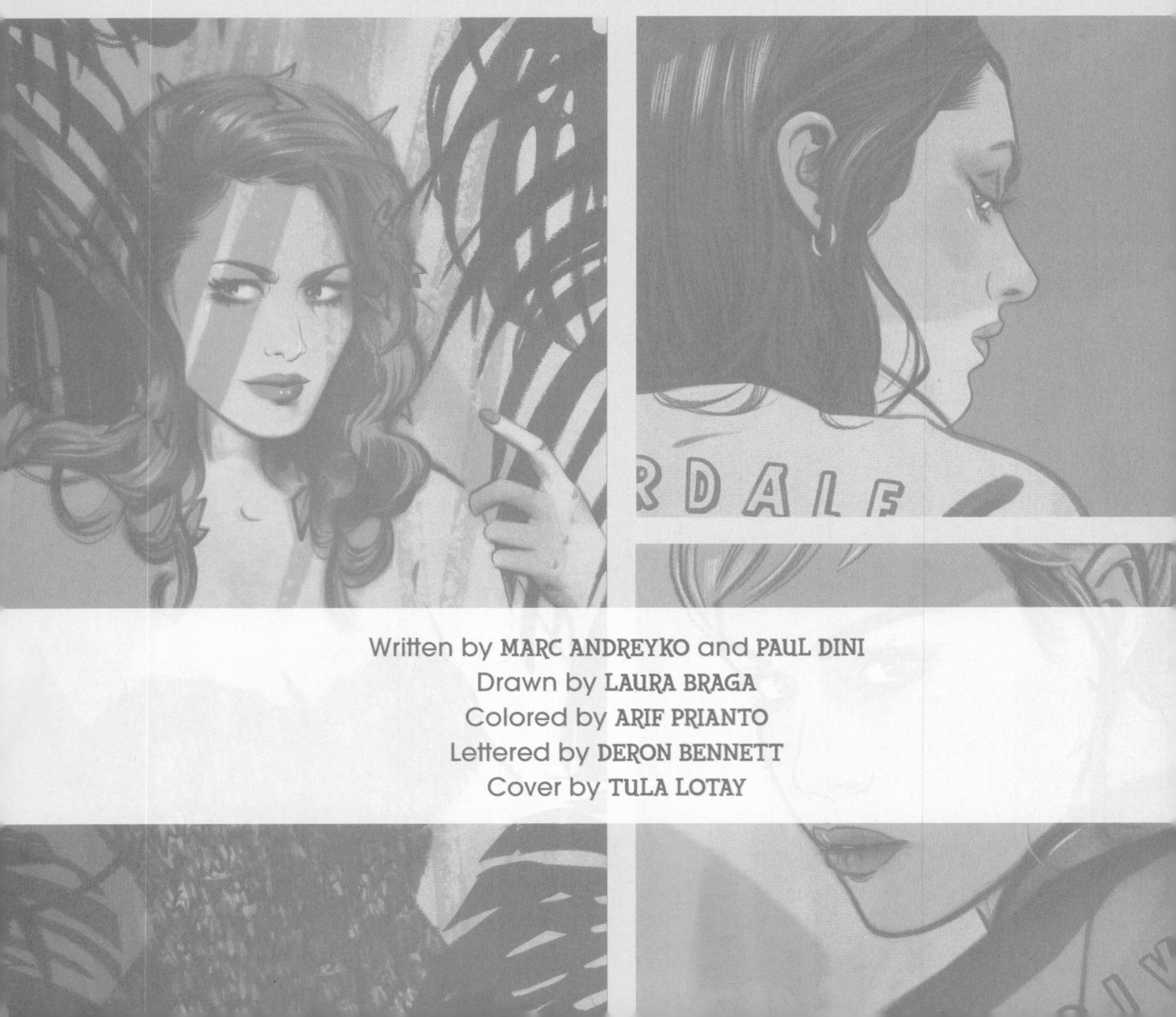
RDALE

Written by **MARC ANDREYKO** and **PAUL DINI**
Drawn by **LAURA BRAGA**
Colored by **ARIF PRIANTO**
Lettered by **DERON BENNETT**
Cover by **TULA LOTAY**

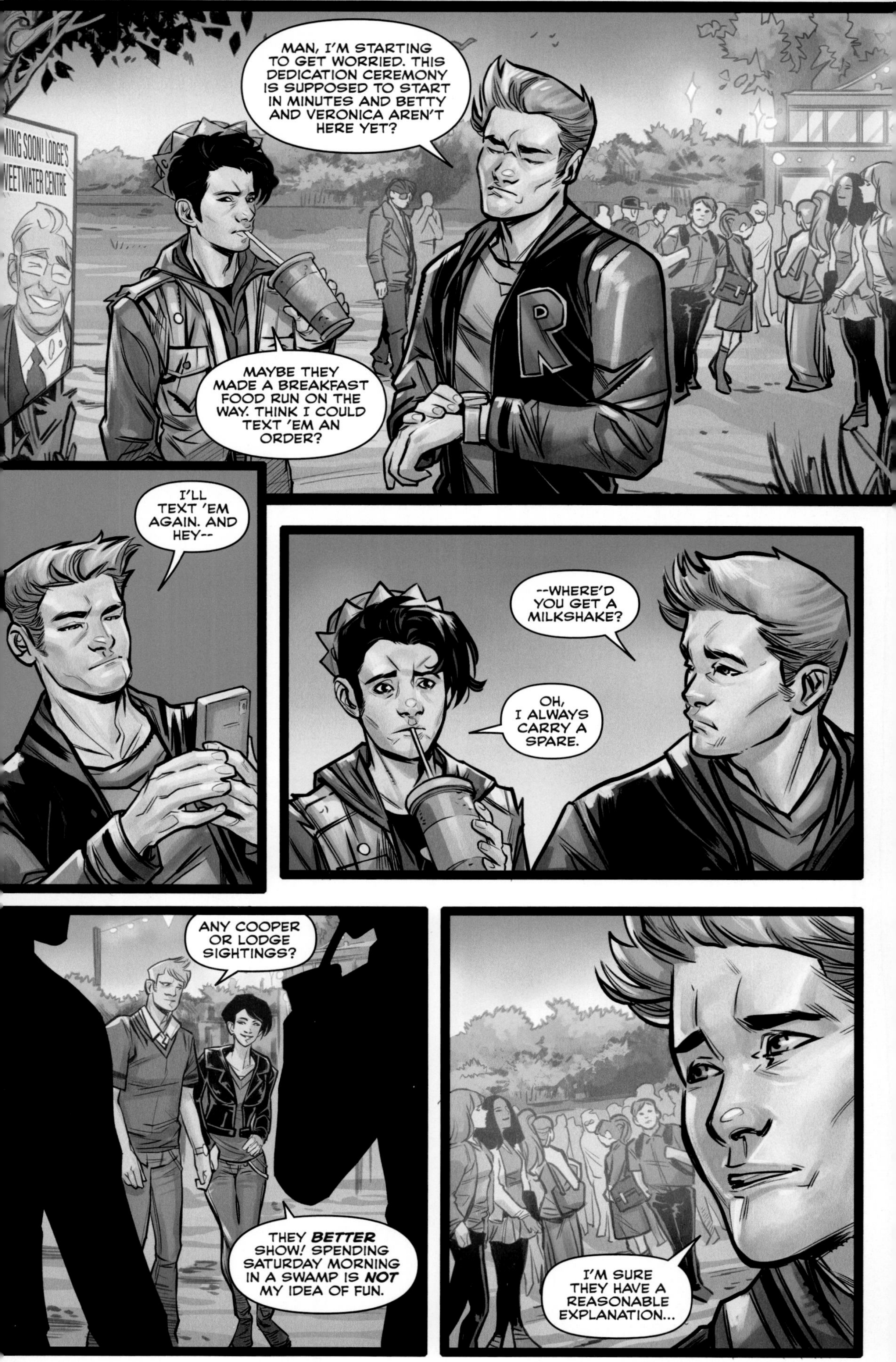
COMING SOON! LODGE'S SWEETWATER CENTRE
MAN, I'M STARTING TO GET WORRIED. THIS DEDICATION CEREMONY IS SUPPOSED TO START IN MINUTES AND BETTY AND VERONICA AREN'T HERE YET?
MAYBE THEY MADE A BREAKFAST FOOD RUN ON THE WAY. THINK I COULD TEXT 'EM AN ORDER?
I'LL TEXT 'EM AGAIN. AND HEY--
--WHERE'D YOU GET A MILKSHAKE?
OH, I ALWAYS CARRY A SPARE.
ANY COOPER OR LODGE SIGHTINGS?
THEY **BETTER** SHOW! SPENDING SATURDAY MORNING IN A SWAMP IS **NOT** MY IDEA OF FUN.
I'M SURE THEY HAVE A REASONABLE EXPLANATION...

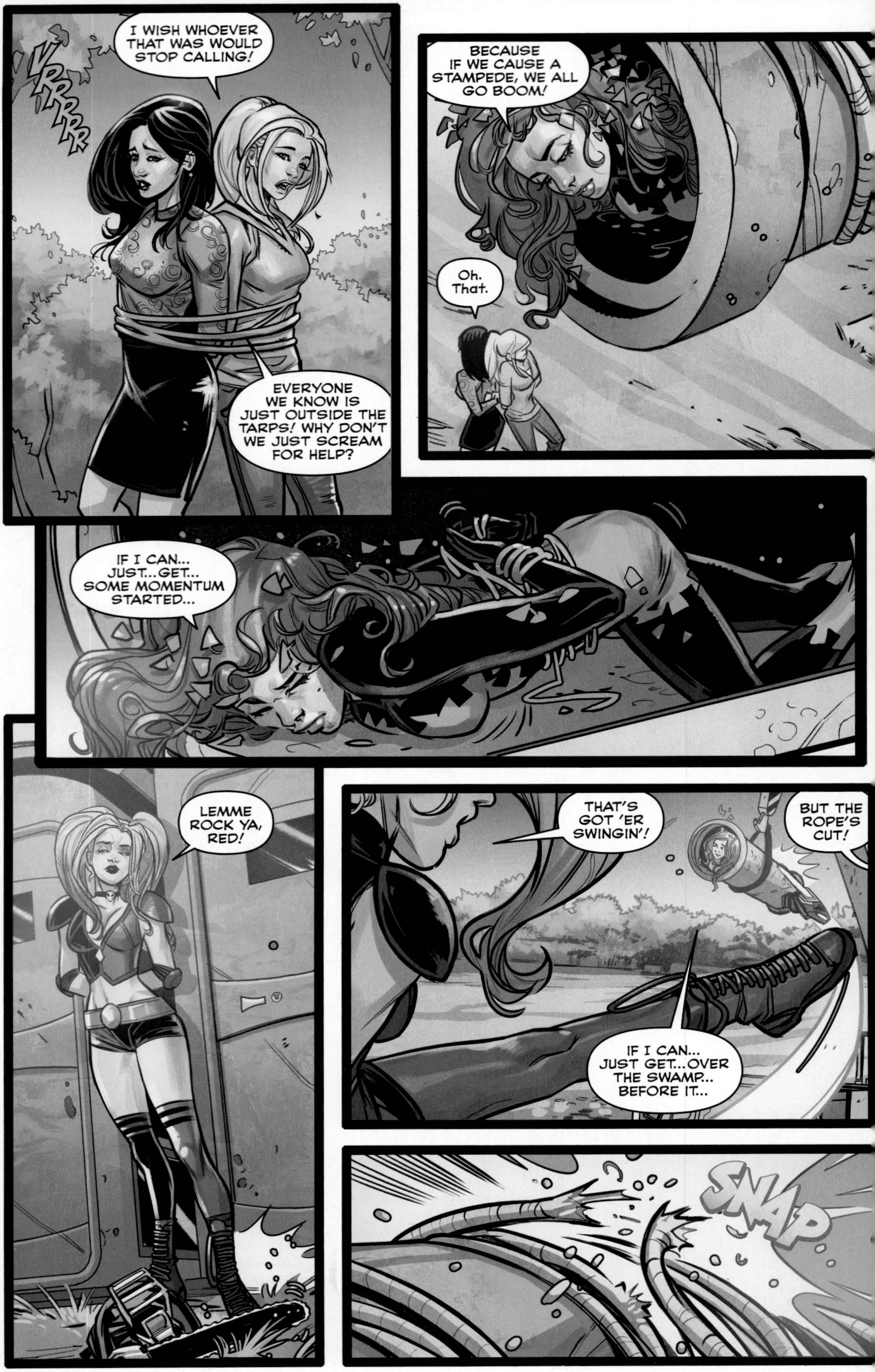
VRRRRR
I WISH WHOEVER THAT WAS WOULD STOP CALLING!
EVERYONE WE KNOW IS JUST OUTSIDE THE TARPS! WHY DON'T WE JUST SCREAM FOR HELP?
BECAUSE IF WE CAUSE A STAMPEDE, WE ALL GO BOOM!
Oh. That.
IF I CAN... JUST...GET... SOME MOMENTUM STARTED...
LEMME ROCK YA, RED!
THAT'S GOT 'ER SWINGIN'!
BUT THE ROPE'S CUT!
IF I CAN... JUST GET...OVER THE SWAMP... BEFORE IT...
SNAP

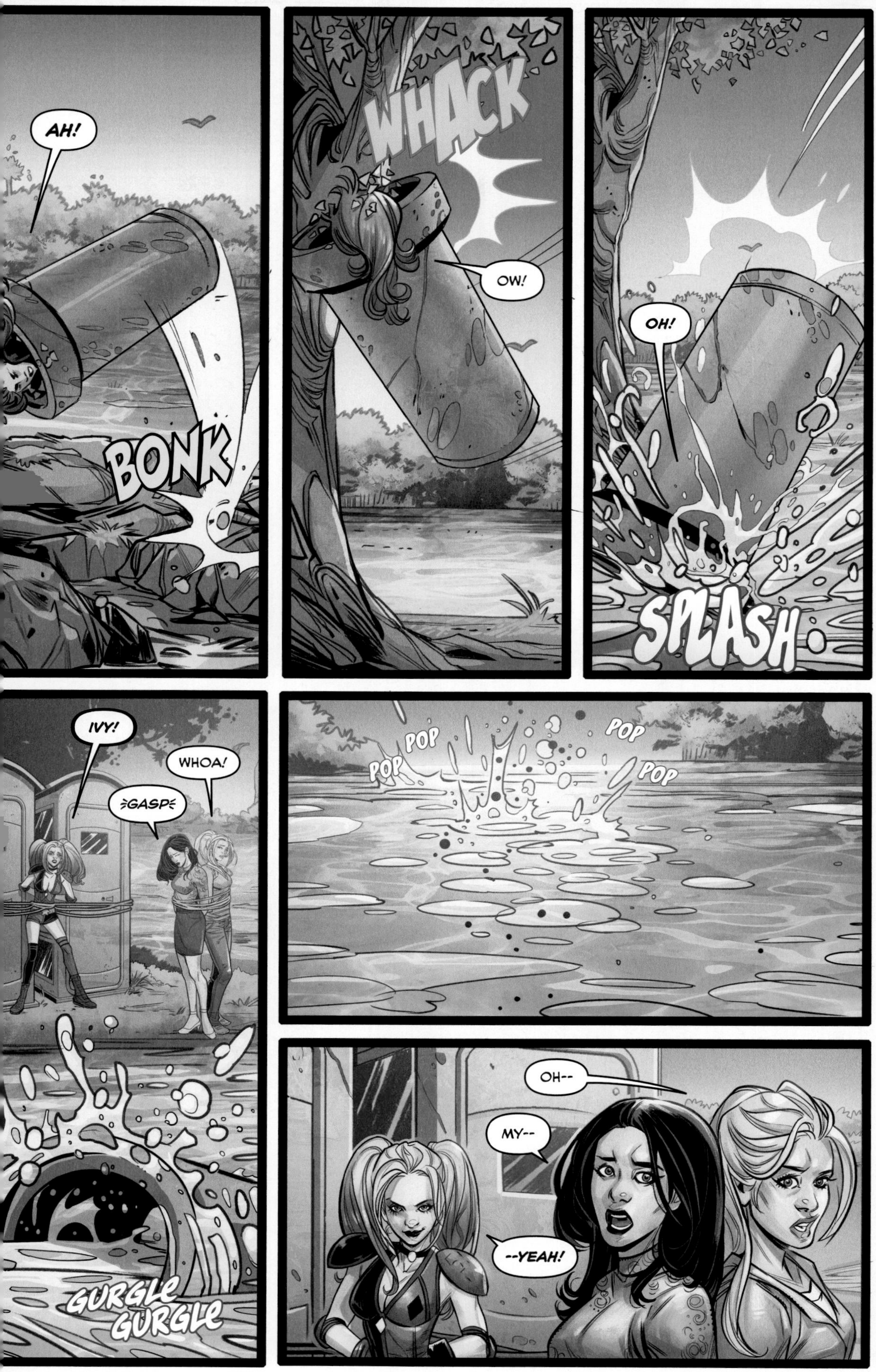

AH!
BONK
WHACK
OW!
OH!
SPLASH
IVY!
WHOA!
GASP
GURGLE
GURGLE
POP
POP
POP
POP
OH--
MY--
--YEAH!

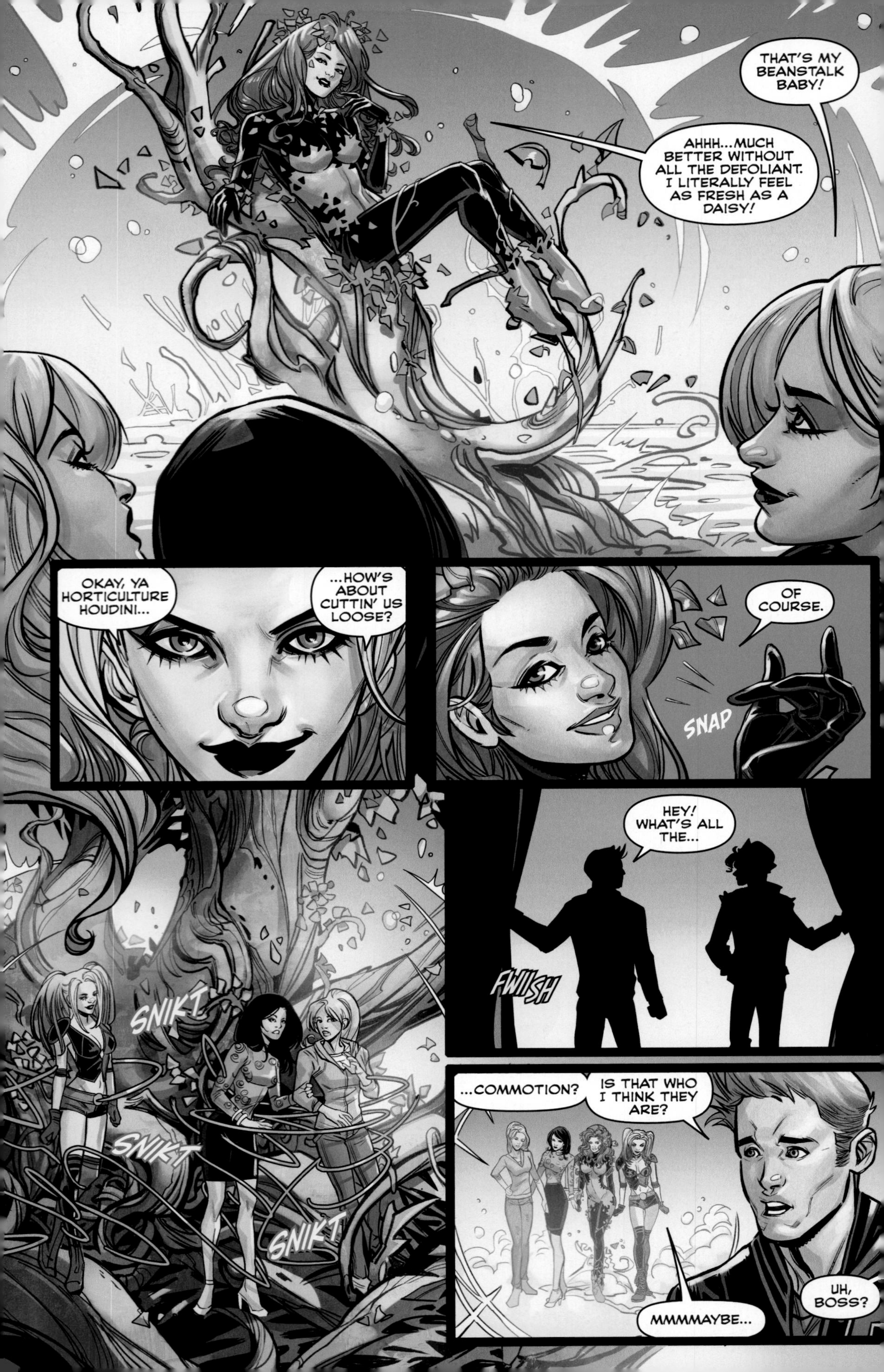
THAT'S MY BEANSTALK BABY!
AHHH...MUCH BETTER WITHOUT ALL THE DEFOLIANT. I LITERALLY FEEL AS FRESH AS A DAISY!
OKAY, YA HORTICULTURE HOUDINI...
...HOW'S ABOUT CUTTIN' US LOOSE?
OF COURSE.
SNAP
SNIKT
SNIKT
SNIKT
HEY! WHAT'S ALL THE...
FWIISH
...COMMOTION?
IS THAT WHO I THINK THEY ARE?
MMMMAYBE...
UH, BOSS?

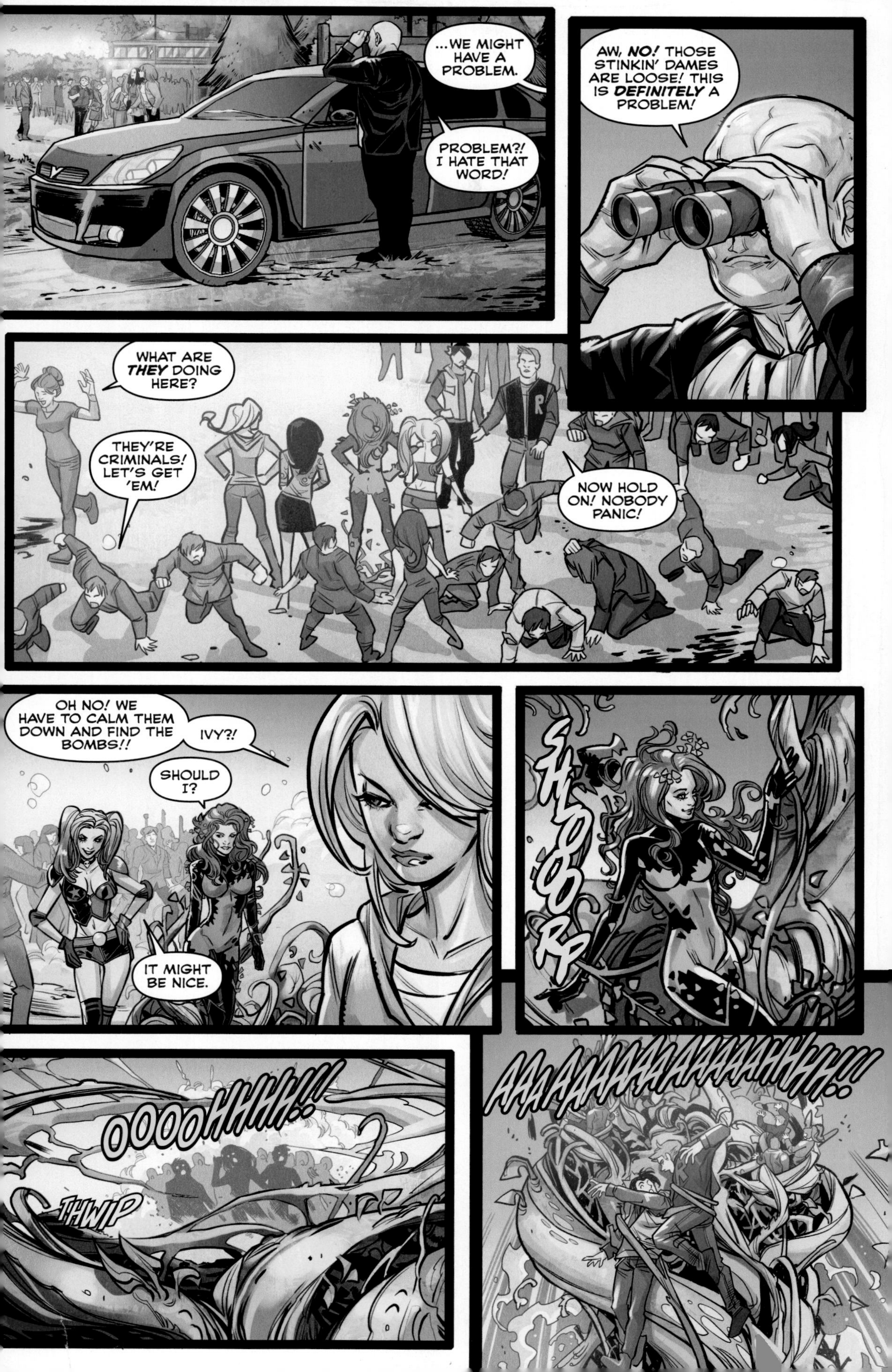
...WE MIGHT HAVE A PROBLEM.
PROBLEM?! I HATE THAT WORD!
AW, NO! THOSE STINKIN' DAMES ARE LOOSE! THIS IS DEFINITELY A PROBLEM!
WHAT ARE THEY DOING HERE?
THEY'RE CRIMINALS! LET'S GET 'EM!
NOW HOLD ON! NOBODY PANIC!
OH NO! WE HAVE TO CALM THEM DOWN AND FIND THE BOMBS!!
IVY?!
SHOULD I?
IT MIGHT BE NICE.
SHOOORP
OOOOHHHH!!
THWIP
AAAAAAAAAAAAAHHHH!!

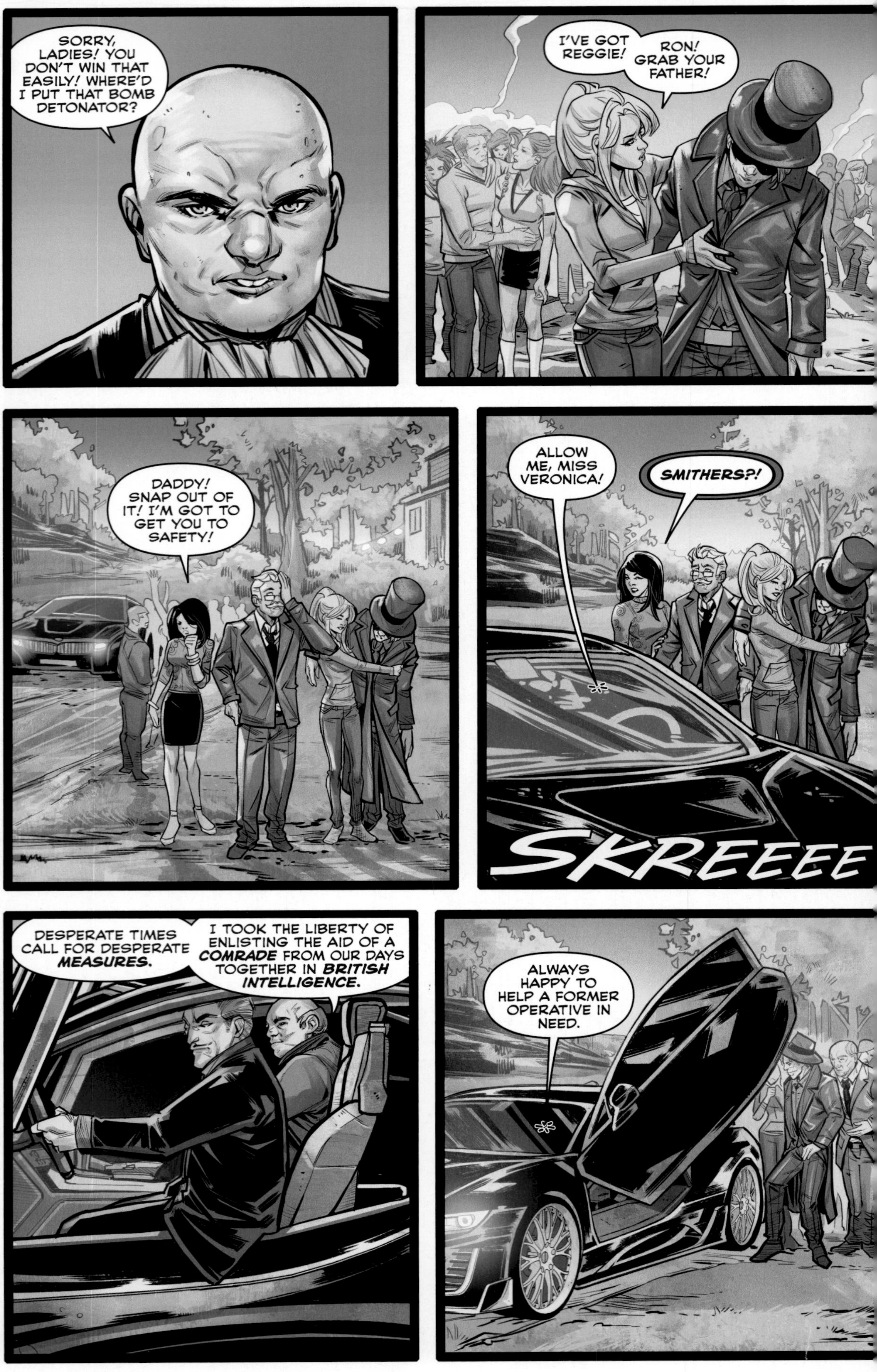
SORRY, LADIES! YOU DON'T WIN THAT EASILY! WHERE'D I PUT THAT BOMB DETONATOR?
I'VE GOT REGGIE!
RON! GRAB YOUR FATHER!
DADDY! SNAP OUT OF IT! I'M GOT TO GET YOU TO SAFETY!
ALLOW ME, MISS VERONICA!
SMITHERS?!
SKREEEE
DESPERATE TIMES CALL FOR DESPERATE MEASURES.
I TOOK THE LIBERTY OF ENLISTING THE AID OF A COMRADE FROM OUR DAYS TOGETHER IN BRITISH INTELLIGENCE.
ALWAYS HAPPY TO HELP A FORMER OPERATIVE IN NEED.

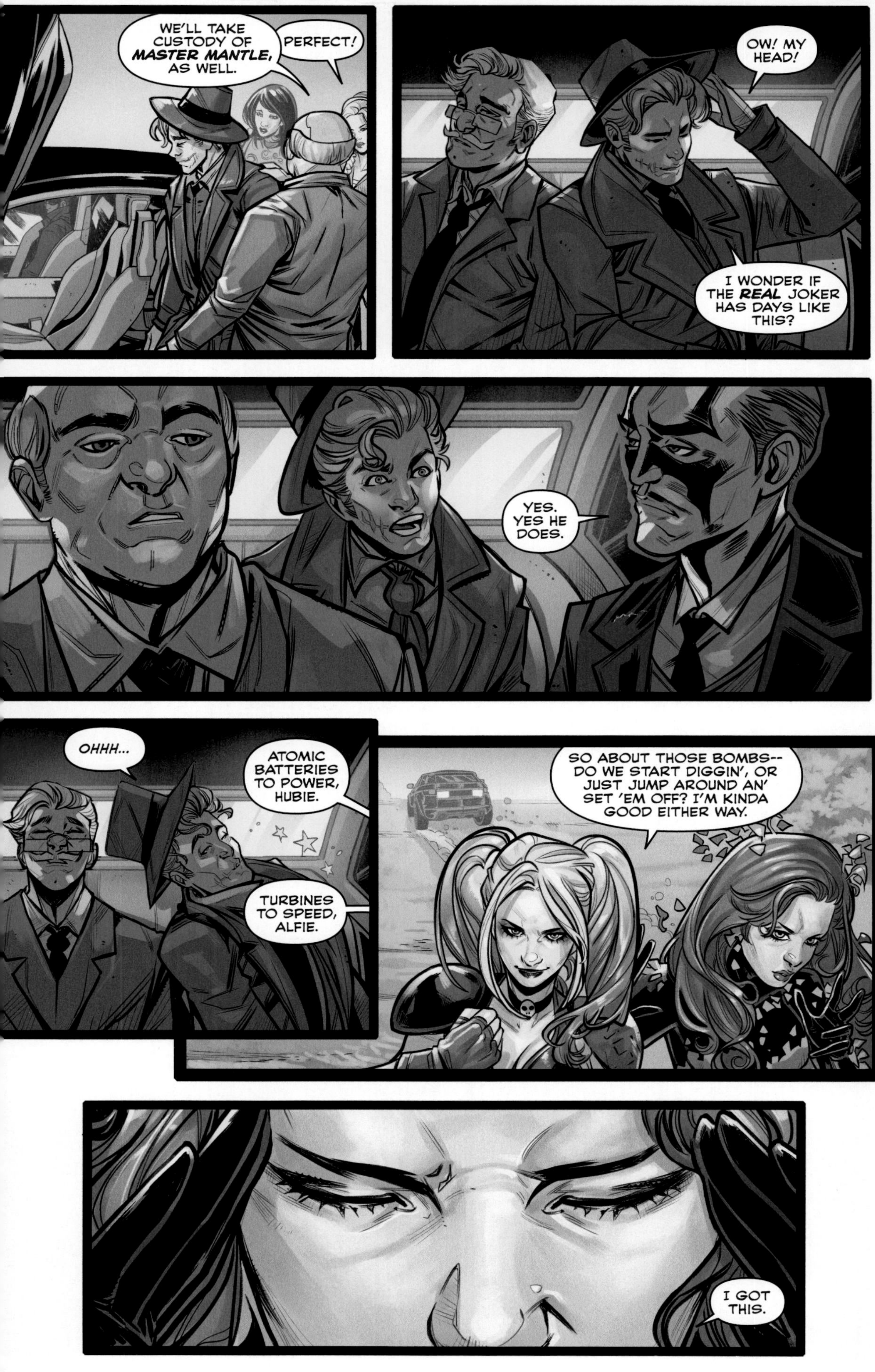

WE'LL TAKE CUSTODY OF MASTER MANTLE, AS WELL.
PERFECT!
OW! MY HEAD!
I WONDER IF THE REAL JOKER HAS DAYS LIKE THIS?
YES. YES HE DOES.
OHHH...
ATOMIC BATTERIES TO POWER, HUBIE.
TURBINES TO SPEED, ALFIE.
SO ABOUT THOSE BOMBS-- DO WE START DIGGIN', OR JUST JUMP AROUND AN' SET 'EM OFF? I'M KINDA GOOD EITHER WAY.
I GOT THIS.

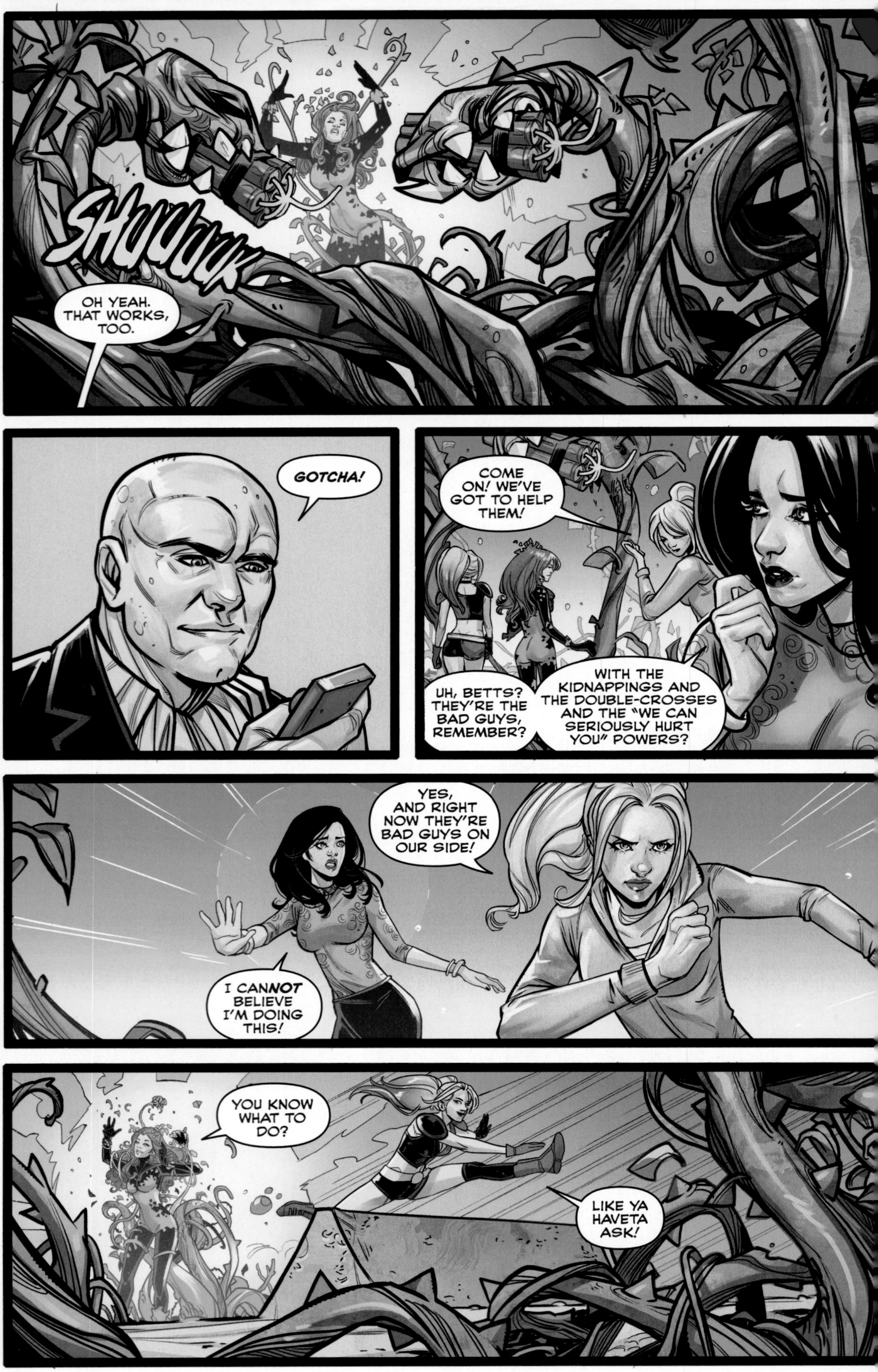
SHUUUUK
OH YEAH. THAT WORKS, TOO.
GOTCHA!
COME ON! WE'VE GOT TO HELP THEM!
UH, BETTS? THEY'RE THE BAD GUYS, REMEMBER?
WITH THE KIDNAPPINGS AND THE DOUBLE-CROSSES AND THE "WE CAN SERIOUSLY HURT YOU" POWERS?
YES, AND RIGHT NOW THEY'RE BAD GUYS ON OUR SIDE!
I CANNOT BELIEVE I'M DOING THIS!
YOU KNOW WHAT TO DO?
LIKE YA HAVETA ASK!

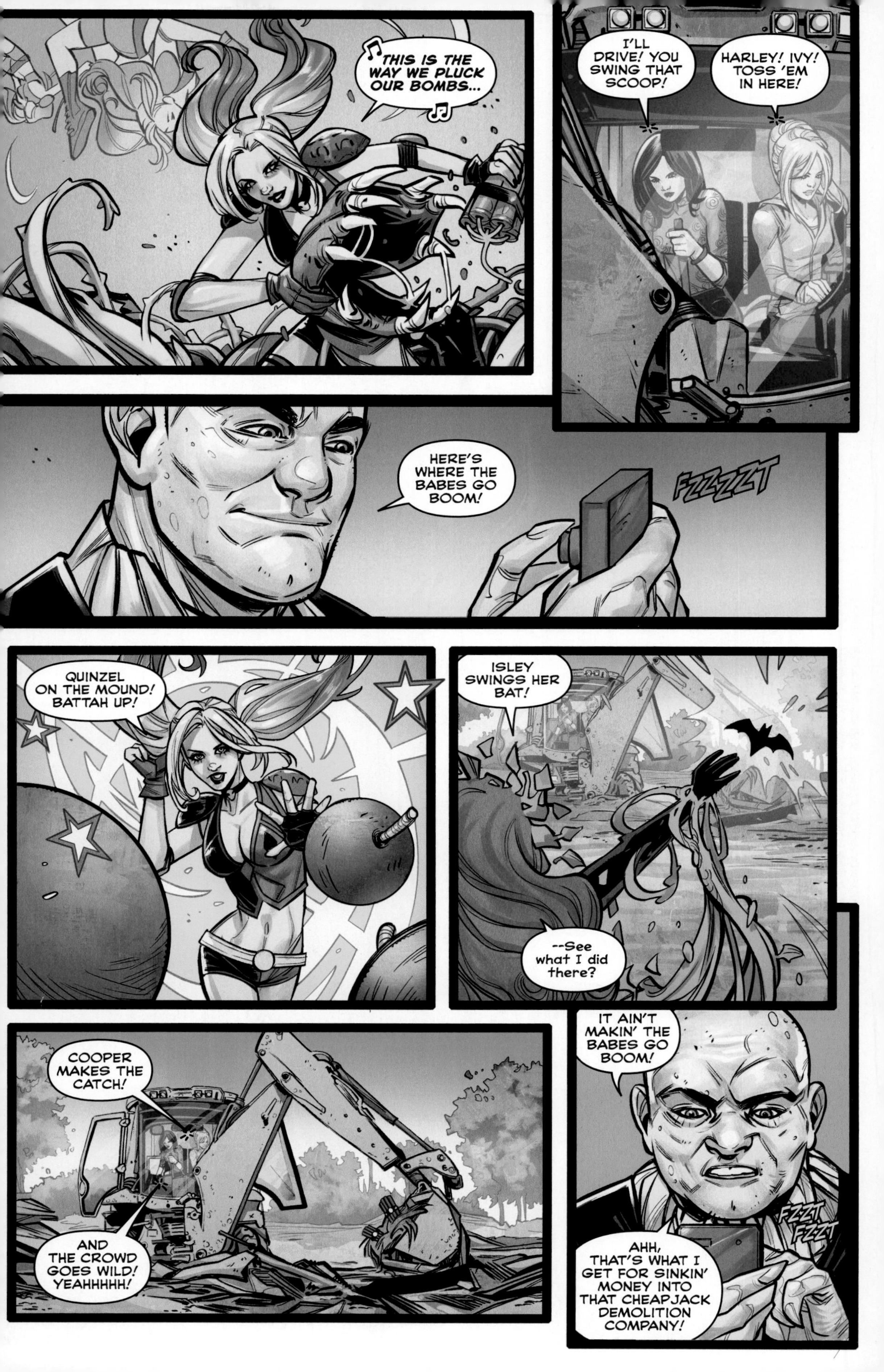
THIS IS THE WAY WE PLUCK OUR BOMBS...
I'LL DRIVE! YOU SWING THAT SCOOP!
HARLEY! IVY! TOSS 'EM IN HERE!
HERE'S WHERE THE BABES GO BOOM!
FZZZZT
QUINZEL ON THE MOUND! BATTAH UP!
ISLEY SWINGS HER BAT!
--See what I did there?
COOPER MAKES THE CATCH!
AND THE CROWD GOES WILD! YEAHHHHH!
IT AIN'T MAKIN' THE BABES GO BOOM!
FZZT FZZT
AHH, THAT'S WHAT I GET FOR SINKIN' MONEY INTO THAT CHEAPJACK DEMOLITION COMPANY!

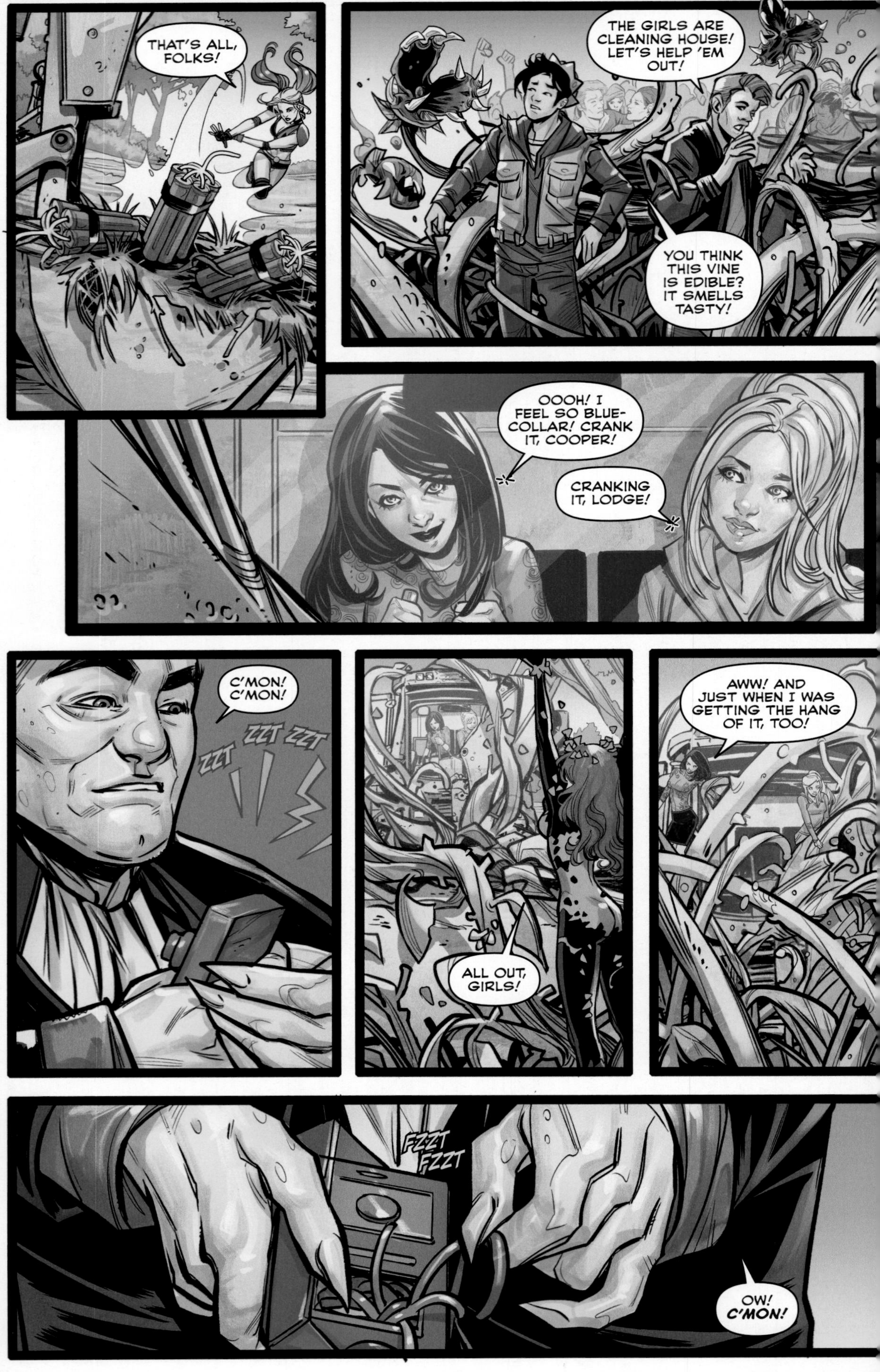
THAT'S ALL, FOLKS!
THE GIRLS ARE CLEANING HOUSE! LET'S HELP 'EM OUT!
YOU THINK THIS VINE IS EDIBLE? IT SMELLS TASTY!
OOOH! I FEEL SO BLUE-COLLAR! CRANK IT, COOPER!
CRANKING IT, LODGE!
C'MON! C'MON!
ZZT ZZT ZZT
ALL OUT, GIRLS!
AWW! AND JUST WHEN I WAS GETTING THE HANG OF IT, TOO!
FZZT FZZT
OW! C'MON!

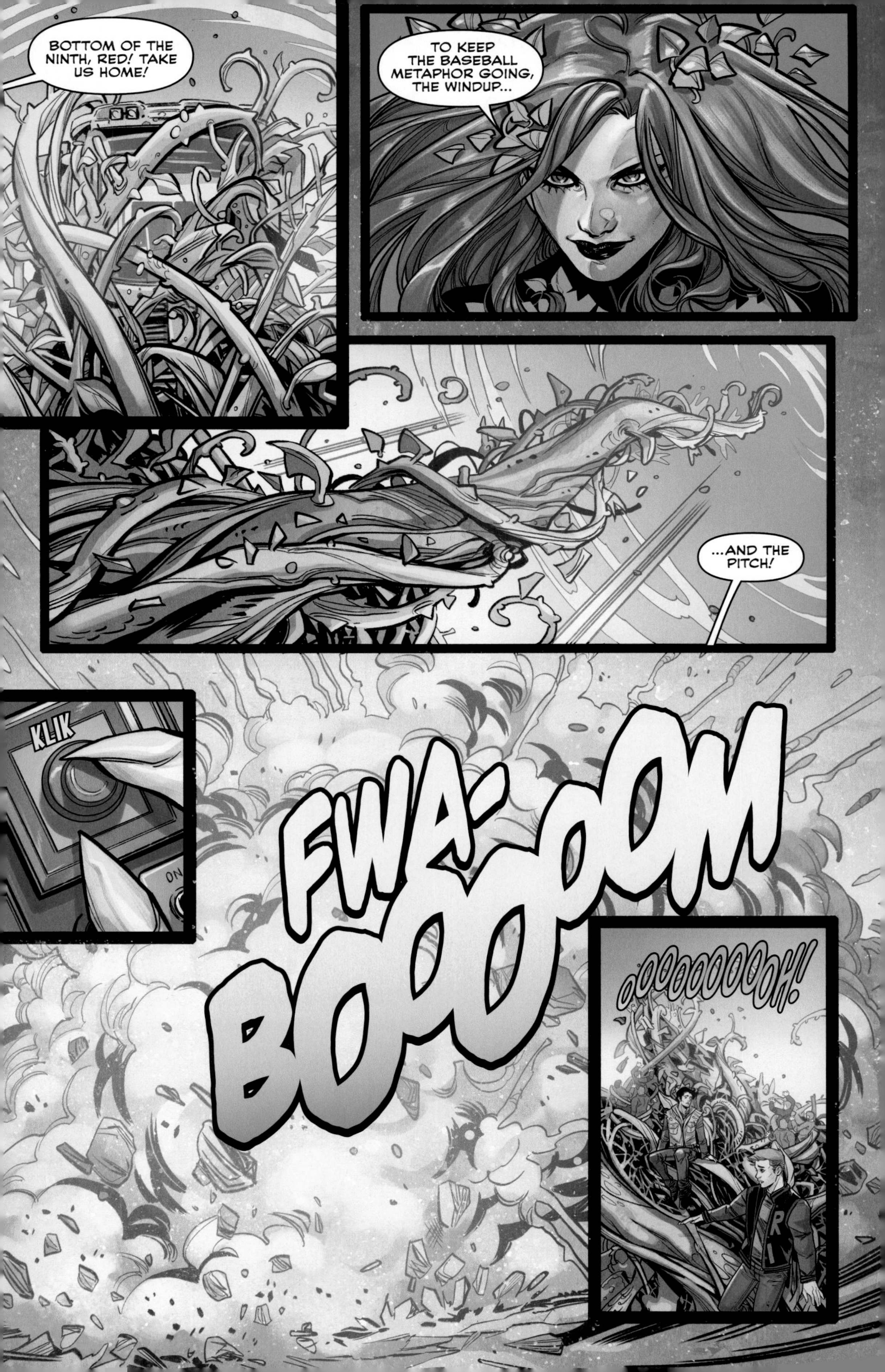
BOTTOM OF THE NINTH, RED! TAKE US HOME!
TO KEEP THE BASEBALL METAPHOR GOING, THE WINDUP...
...AND THE PITCH!
KLIK
ON
FWA-BOOOOOM
OOOOOOOOOH!

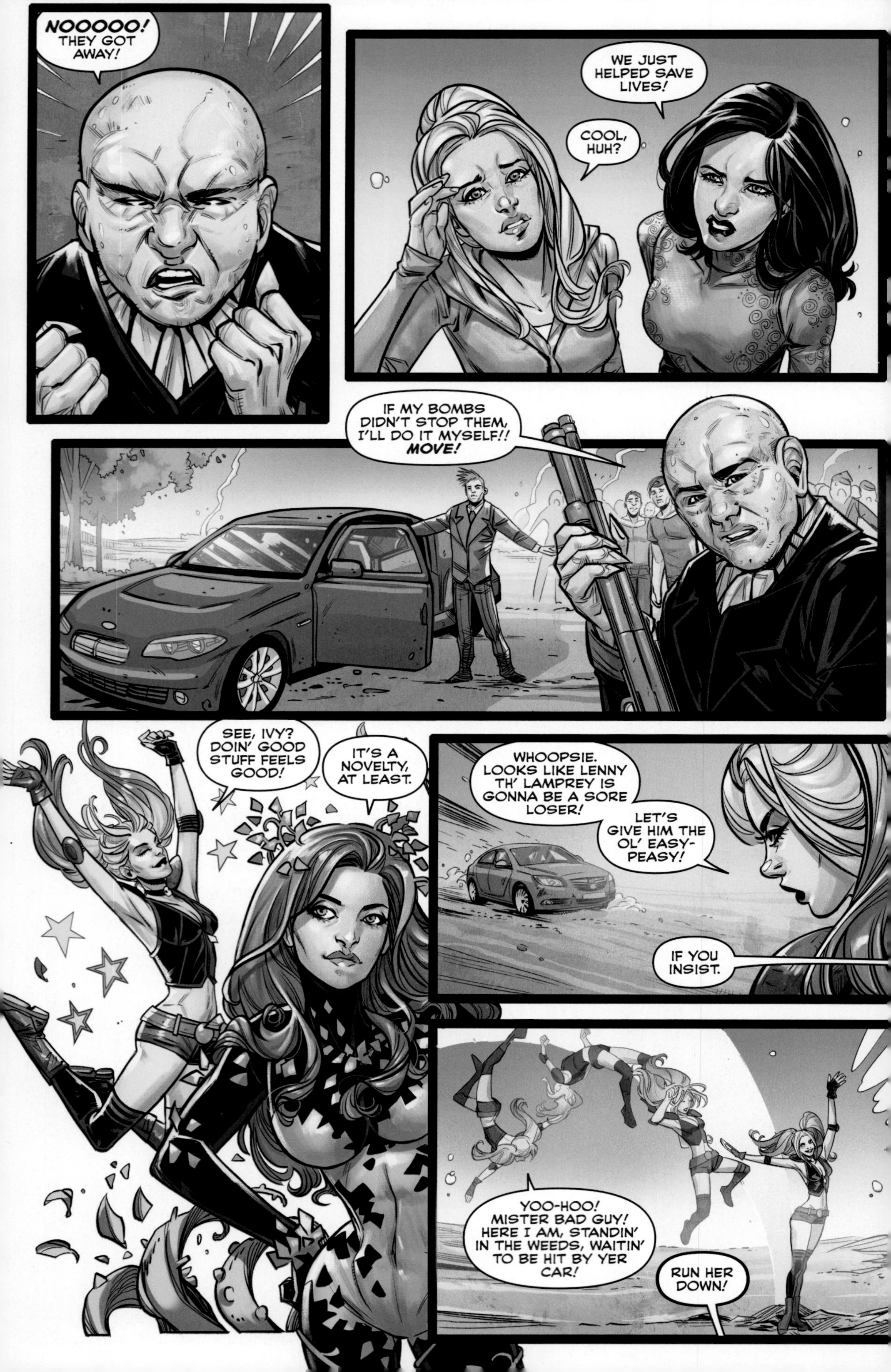
NOOOOO! THEY GOT AWAY!
WE JUST HELPED SAVE LIVES!
COOL, HUH?
IF MY BOMBS DIDN'T STOP THEM, I'LL DO IT MYSELF!! MOVE!
SEE, IVY? DOIN' GOOD STUFF FEELS GOOD!
IT'S A NOVELTY, AT LEAST.
WHOOPSIE. LOOKS LIKE LENNY TH' LAMPREY IS GONNA BE A SORE LOSER!
LET'S GIVE HIM THE OL' EASY-PEASY!
IF YOU INSIST.
YOO-HOO! MISTER BAD GUY! HERE I AM, STANDIN' IN THE WEEDS, WAITIN' TO BE HIT BY YER CAR!
RUN HER DOWN!

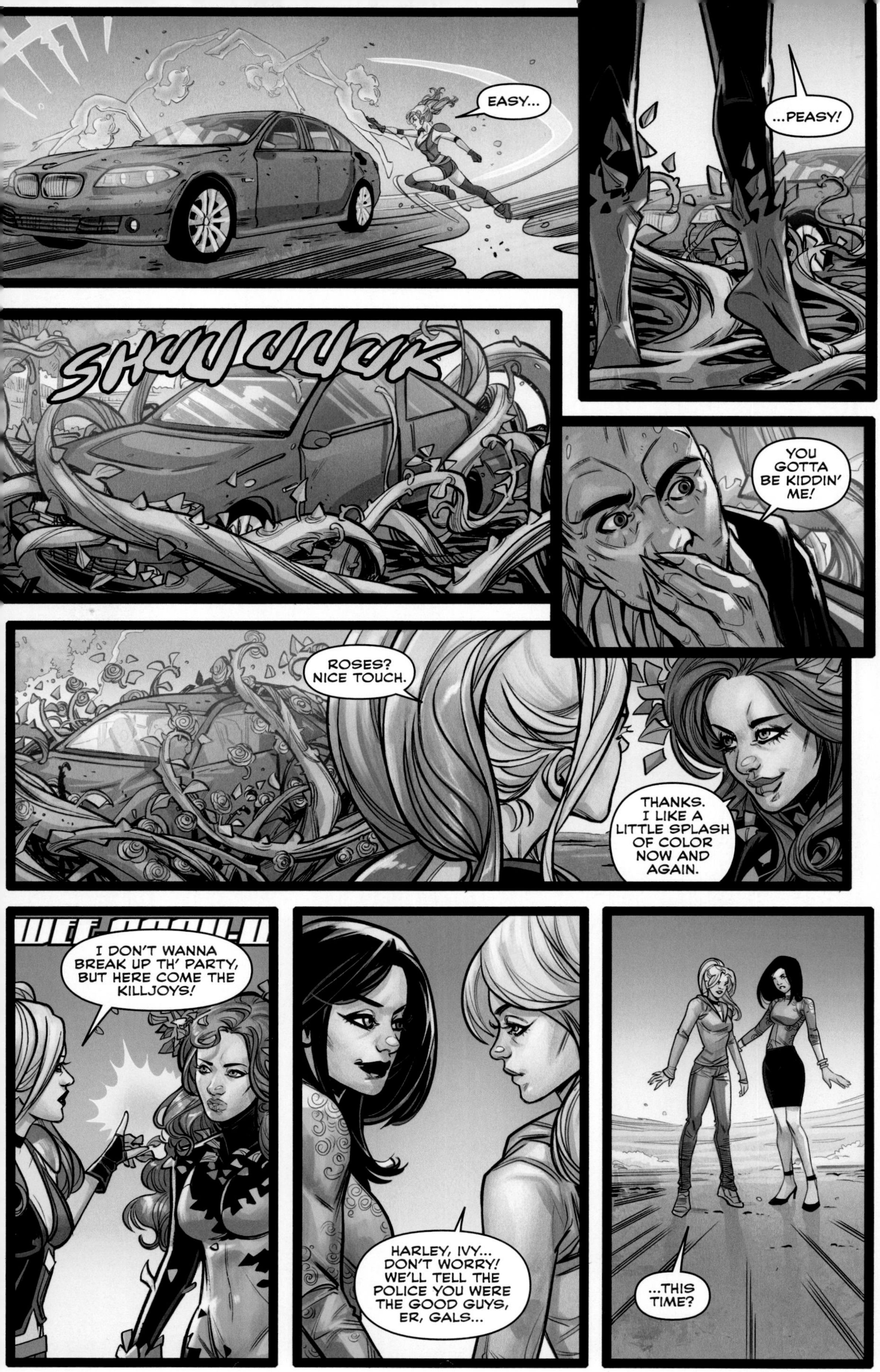
EASY...
...PEASY!
YOU GOTTA BE KIDDIN' ME!
ROSES? NICE TOUCH.
THANKS. I LIKE A LITTLE SPLASH OF COLOR NOW AND AGAIN.
I DON'T WANNA BREAK UP TH' PARTY, BUT HERE COME THE KILLJOYS!
HARLEY, IVY... DON'T WORRY! WE'LL TELL THE POLICE YOU WERE THE GOOD GUYS, ER, GALS...
...THIS TIME?

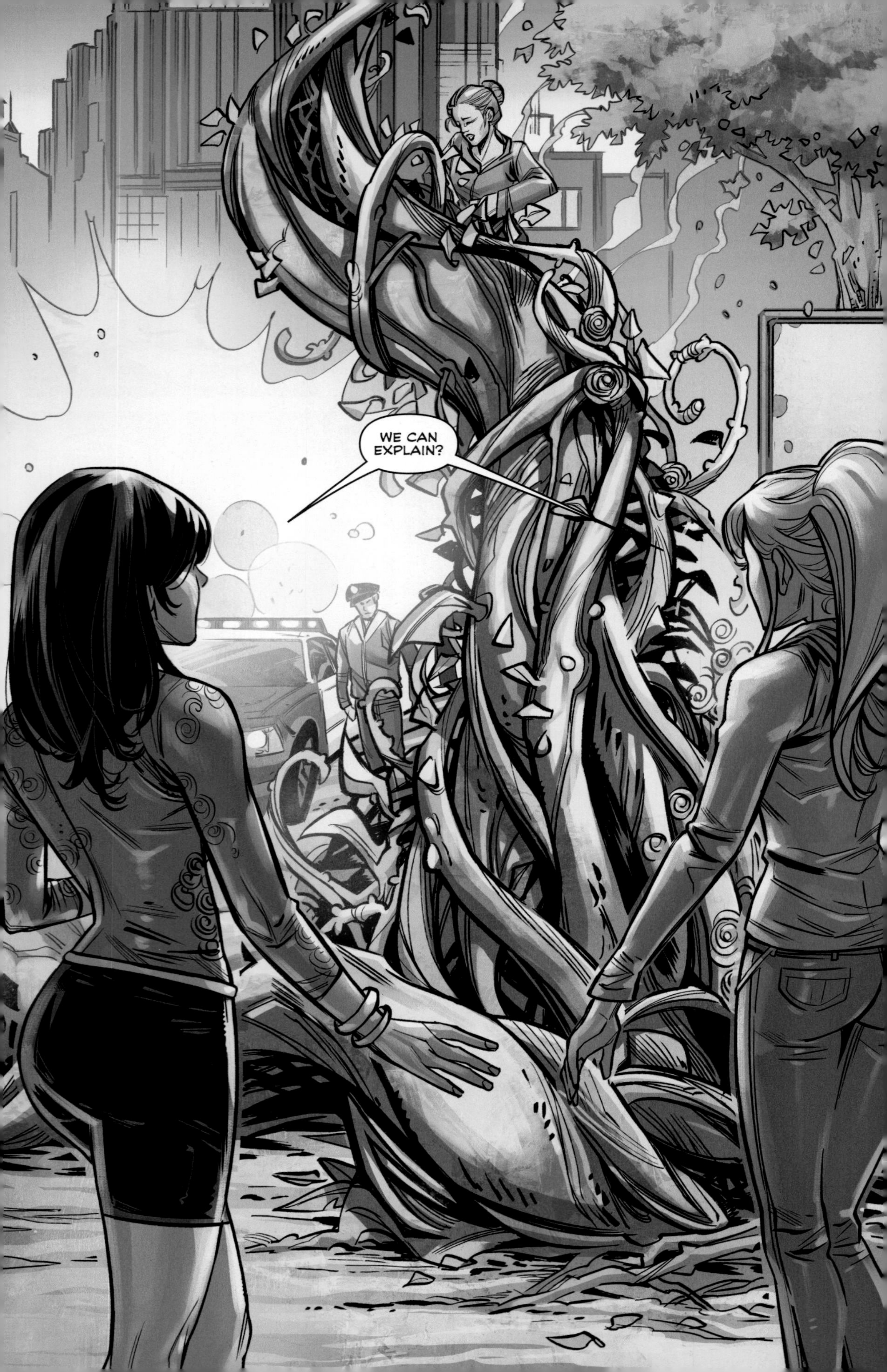
WE CAN EXPLAIN?

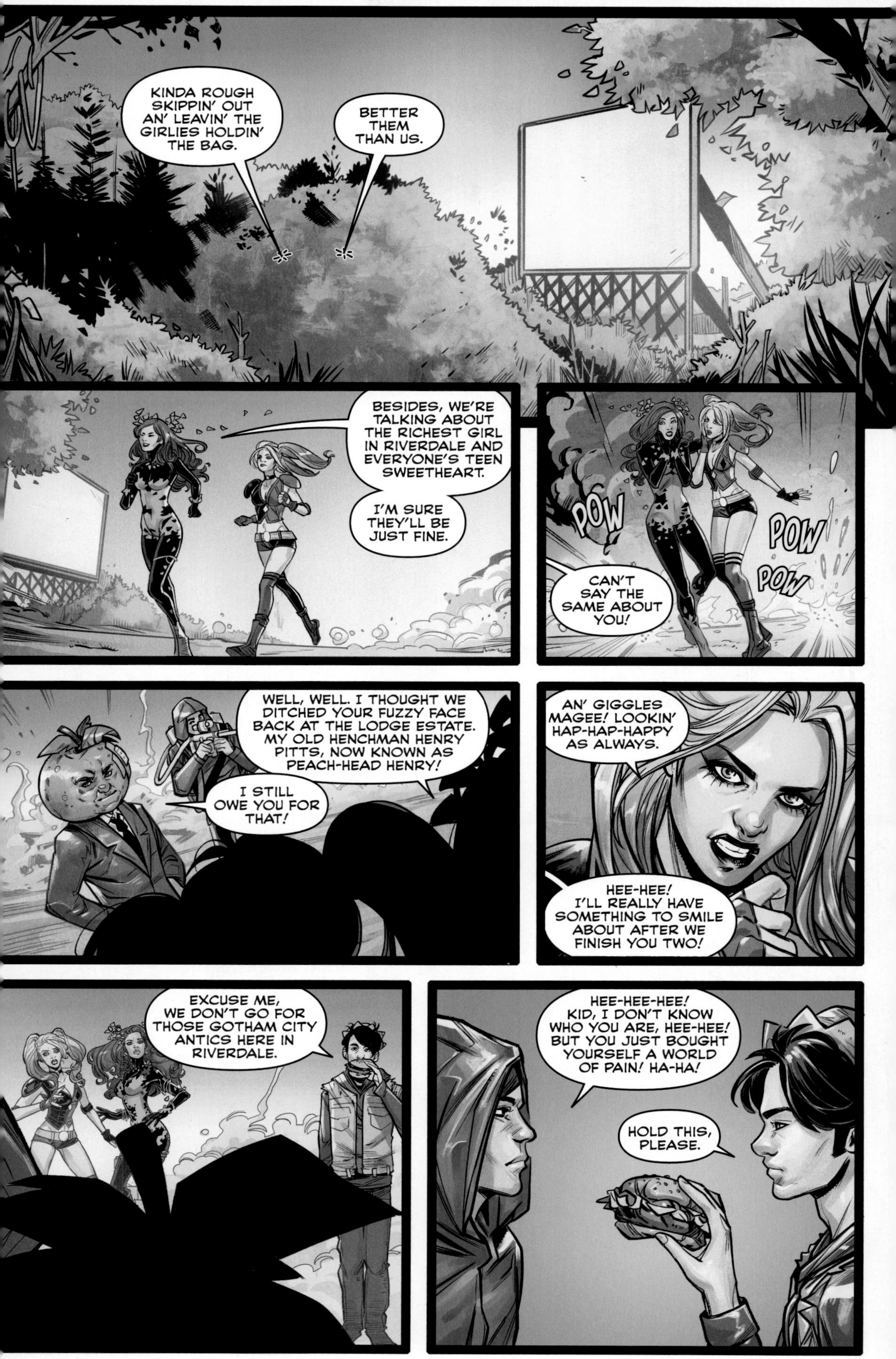
KINDA ROUGH SKIPPIN' OUT AN' LEAVIN' THE GIRLIES HOLDIN' THE BAG.
BETTER THEM THAN US.
BESIDES, WE'RE TALKING ABOUT THE RICHEST GIRL IN RIVERDALE AND EVERYONE'S TEEN SWEETHEART.
I'M SURE THEY'LL BE JUST FINE.
POW
POW
POW
CAN'T SAY THE SAME ABOUT YOU!
WELL, WELL. I THOUGHT WE DITCHED YOUR FUZZY FACE BACK AT THE LODGE ESTATE. MY OLD HENCHMAN HENRY PITTS, NOW KNOWN AS PEACH-HEAD HENRY!
I STILL OWE YOU FOR THAT!
AN' GIGGLES MAGEE! LOOKIN' HAP-HAP-HAPPY AS ALWAYS.
HEE-HEE! I'LL REALLY HAVE SOMETHING TO SMILE ABOUT AFTER WE FINISH YOU TWO!
EXCUSE ME, WE DON'T GO FOR THOSE GOTHAM CITY ANTICS HERE IN RIVERDALE.
HEE-HEE-HEE! KID, I DON'T KNOW WHO YOU ARE, HEE-HEE! BUT YOU JUST BOUGHT YOURSELF A WORLD OF PAIN! HA-HA!
HOLD THIS, PLEASE.

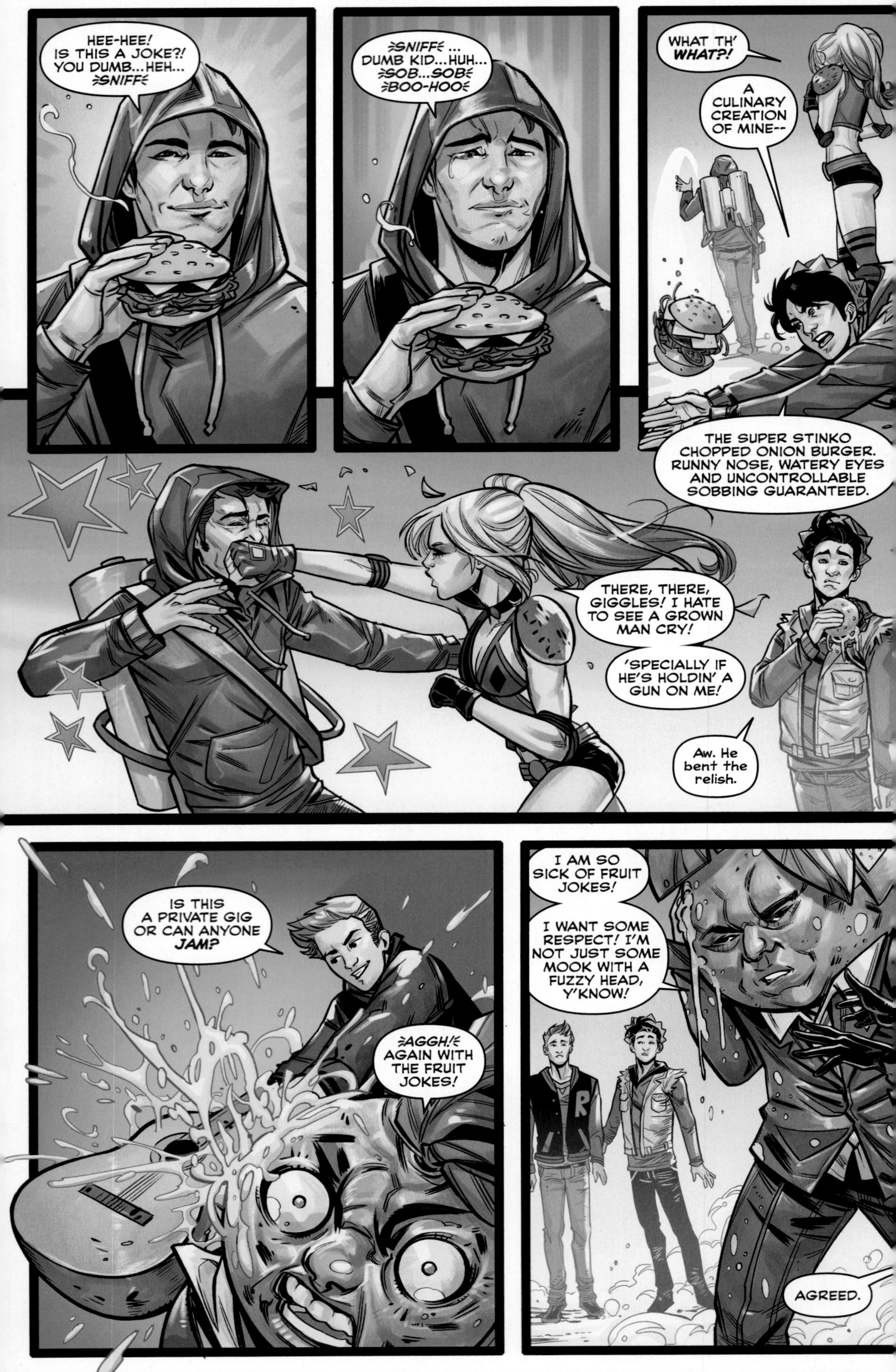
HEE-HEE! IS THIS A JOKE?! YOU DUMB...HEH... SNIFF
SNIFF ... DUMB KID...HUH... SOB...SOB BOO-HOO
WHAT TH' WHAT?!
A CULINARY CREATION OF MINE--
THE SUPER STINKO CHOPPED ONION BURGER. RUNNY NOSE, WATERY EYES AND UNCONTROLLABLE SOBBING GUARANTEED.
THERE, THERE, GIGGLES! I HATE TO SEE A GROWN MAN CRY!
'SPECIALLY IF HE'S HOLDIN' A GUN ON ME!
Aw. He bent the relish.
IS THIS A PRIVATE GIG OR CAN ANYONE JAM?
AGGH! AGAIN WITH THE FRUIT JOKES!
I AM SO SICK OF FRUIT JOKES!
I WANT SOME RESPECT! I'M NOT JUST SOME MOOK WITH A FUZZY HEAD, Y'KNOW!
AGREED.

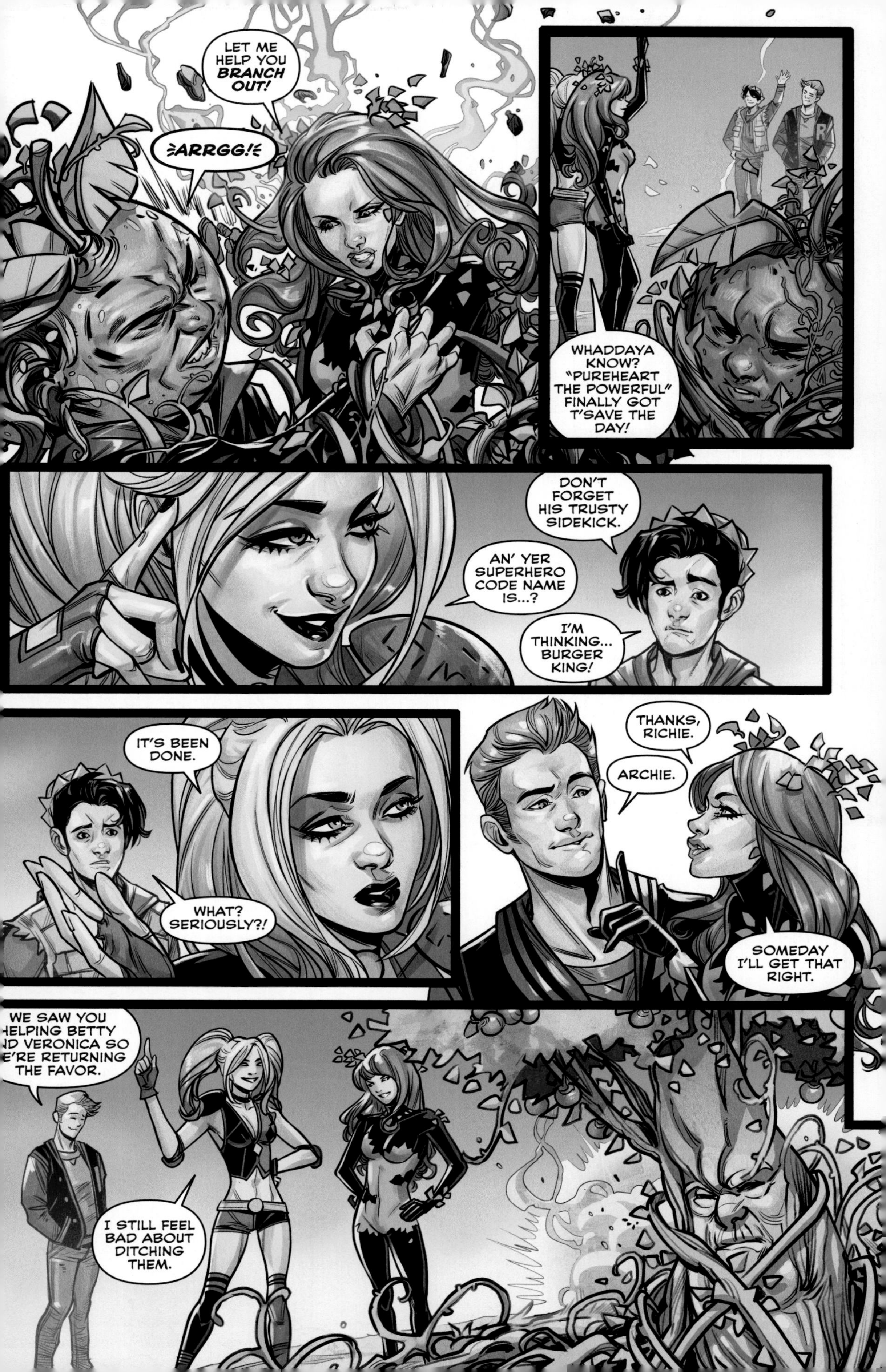
LET ME HELP YOU BRANCH OUT!
ARRGG!
WHADDAYA KNOW? "PUREHEART THE POWERFUL" FINALLY GOT T'SAVE THE DAY!
DON'T FORGET HIS TRUSTY SIDEKICK.
AN' YER SUPERHERO CODE NAME IS...?
I'M THINKING... BURGER KING!
IT'S BEEN DONE.
WHAT? SERIOUSLY?!
THANKS, RICHIE.
ARCHIE.
SOMEDAY I'LL GET THAT RIGHT.
WE SAW YOU HELPING BETTY AND VERONICA SO WE'RE RETURNING THE FAVOR.
I STILL FEEL BAD ABOUT DITCHING THEM.

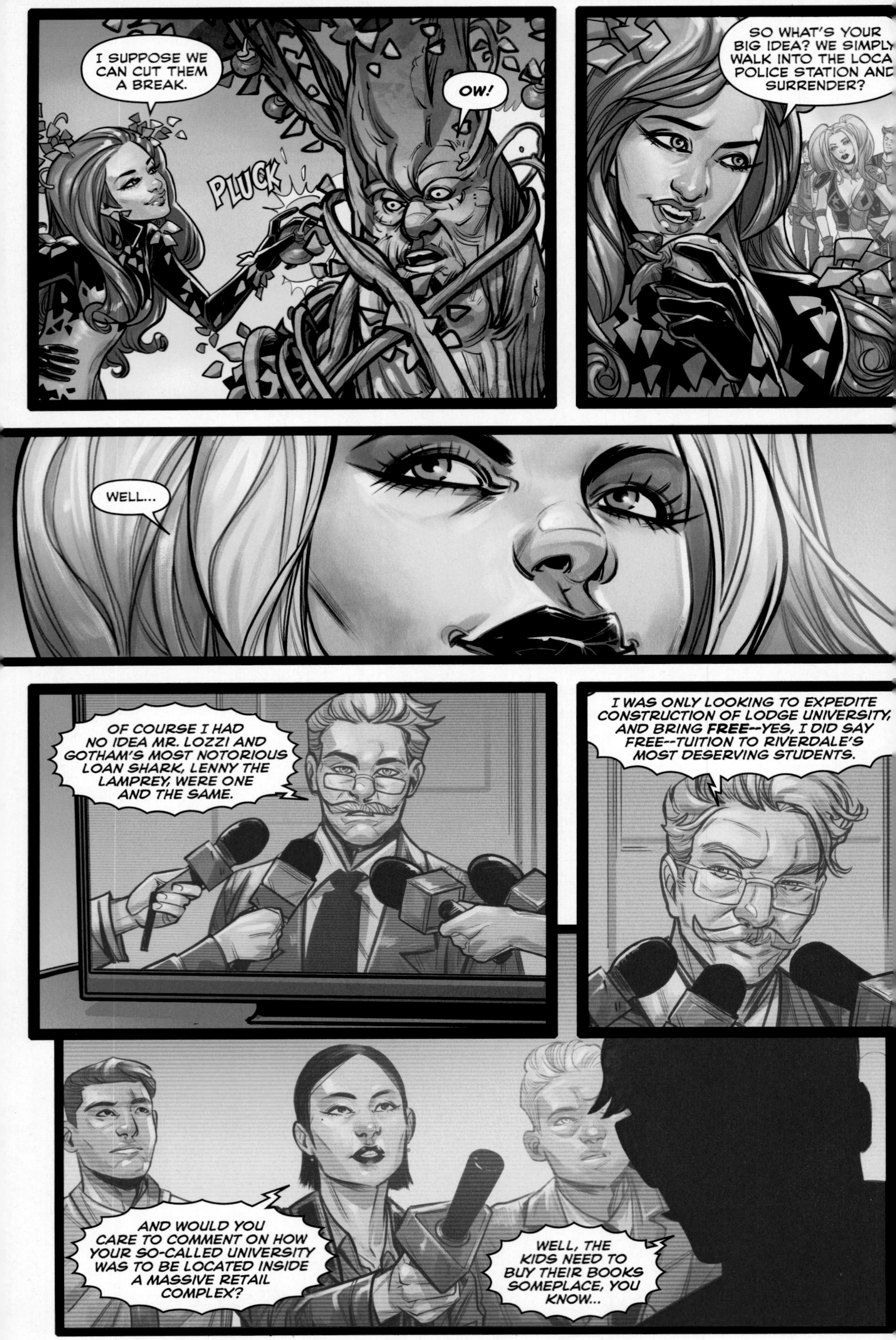
I SUPPOSE WE CAN CUT THEM A BREAK.
PLUCK
OW!
SO WHAT'S YOUR BIG IDEA? WE SIMPLY WALK INTO THE LOCA POLICE STATION AND SURRENDER?
WELL...
OF COURSE I HAD NO IDEA MR. LOZZI AND GOTHAM'S MOST NOTORIOUS LOAN SHARK, LENNY THE LAMPREY, WERE ONE AND THE SAME.
I WAS ONLY LOOKING TO EXPEDITE CONSTRUCTION OF LODGE UNIVERSITY, AND BRING FREE--YES, I DID SAY FREE--TUITION TO RIVERDALE'S MOST DESERVING STUDENTS.
AND WOULD YOU CARE TO COMMENT ON HOW YOUR SO-CALLED UNIVERSITY WAS TO BE LOCATED INSIDE A MASSIVE RETAIL COMPLEX?
WELL, THE KIDS NEED TO BUY THEIR BOOKS SOMEPLACE, YOU KNOW...

BUT THAT'S ALL WATER UNDER THE BRIDGE. AT THE URGING OF MY DAUGHTER AND, AH, ADVICE OF MY LEGAL TEAM, I AM DONATING FULL AND PERMANENT POSSESSION OF SWEETWATER SWAMP TO THE RIVERDALE PRESERVATION SOCIETY...

YAY! DUCKIES!

...WHILE LOSING A CONSIDERABLE FORTUNE MYSELF, I MIGHT ADD.

BOO-HOO. POOR WIDDLE BILLIONAIRE.

SALEM!

HENCEFORTH IT SHALL BE KNOWN AS THE SWEETWATER WETLANDS CONSERVANCY, A BIODIVERSITY REFUGE DEVOTED TO THE AREA'S UNIQUE ANIMAL AND PLANT LIFE.

OW!

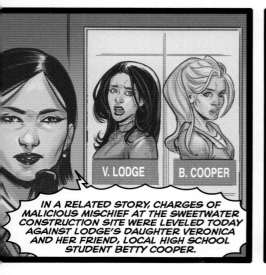

V. LODGE

B. COOPER

IN A RELATED STORY, CHARGES OF MALICIOUS MISCHIEF AT THE SWEETWATER CONSTRUCTION SITE WERE LEVELED TODAY AGAINST LODGE'S DAUGHTER VERONICA AND HER FRIEND, LOCAL HIGH SCHOOL STUDENT BETTY COOPER.

HOWEVER, THOSE CHARGES WERE SUBSEQUENTLY DROPPED DUE TO THE SURPRISE SURRENDER OF GOTHAM CITY CRIMINALS POISON IVY AND HARLEY QUINN...

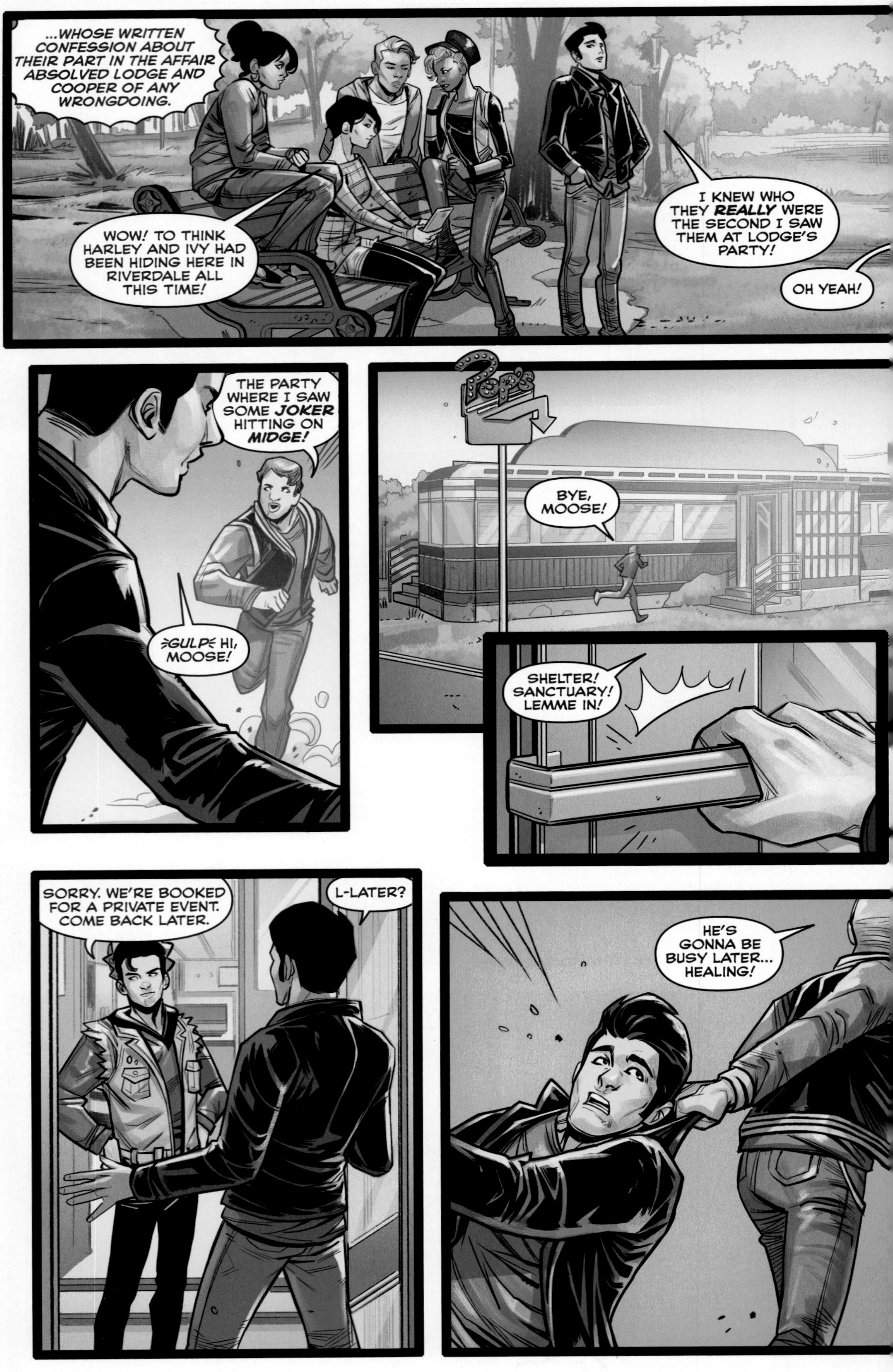
...WHOSE WRITTEN CONFESSION ABOUT THEIR PART IN THE AFFAIR ABSOLVED LODGE AND COOPER OF ANY WRONGDOING.
WOW! TO THINK HARLEY AND IVY HAD BEEN HIDING HERE IN RIVERDALE ALL THIS TIME!
I KNEW WHO THEY REALLY WERE THE SECOND I SAW THEM AT LODGE'S PARTY!
OH YEAH!
THE PARTY WHERE I SAW SOME JOKER HITTING ON MIDGE!
GULP HI, MOOSE!
POP'S
BYE, MOOSE!
SHELTER! SANCTUARY! LEMME IN!
SORRY. WE'RE BOOKED FOR A PRIVATE EVENT. COME BACK LATER.
L-LATER?
HE'S GONNA BE BUSY LATER... HEALING!

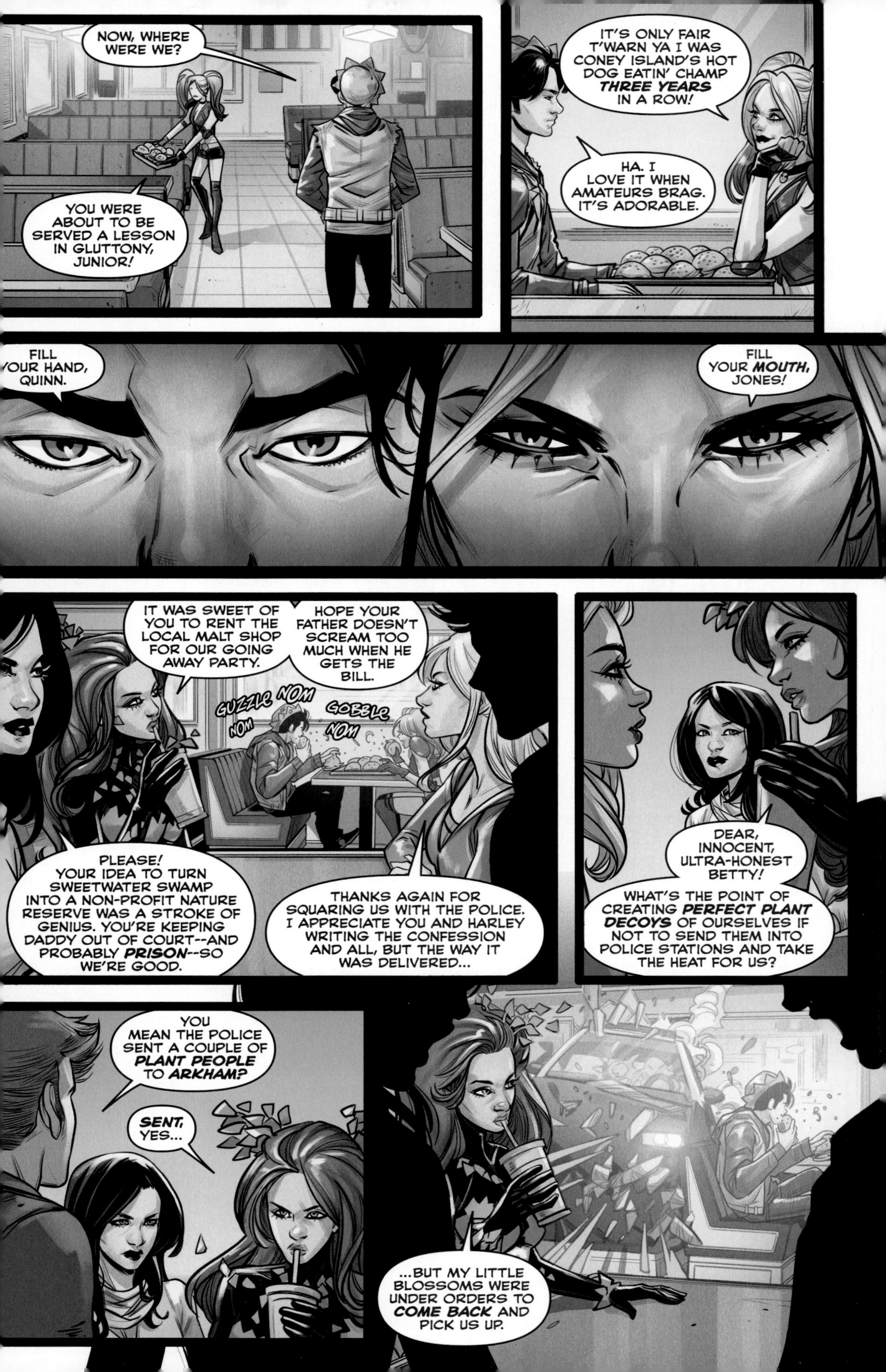
NOW, WHERE WERE WE?
YOU WERE ABOUT TO BE SERVED A LESSON IN GLUTTONY, JUNIOR!
IT'S ONLY FAIR T'WARN YA I WAS CONEY ISLAND'S HOT DOG EATIN' CHAMP THREE YEARS IN A ROW!
HA. I LOVE IT WHEN AMATEURS BRAG. IT'S ADORABLE.
FILL YOUR HAND, QUINN.
FILL YOUR MOUTH, JONES!
IT WAS SWEET OF YOU TO RENT THE LOCAL MALT SHOP FOR OUR GOING AWAY PARTY.
HOPE YOUR FATHER DOESN'T SCREAM TOO MUCH WHEN HE GETS THE BILL.
GUZZLE NOM NOM GOBBLE NOM
PLEASE! YOUR IDEA TO TURN SWEETWATER SWAMP INTO A NON-PROFIT NATURE RESERVE WAS A STROKE OF GENIUS. YOU'RE KEEPING DADDY OUT OF COURT--AND PROBABLY PRISON--SO WE'RE GOOD.
THANKS AGAIN FOR SQUARING US WITH THE POLICE. I APPRECIATE YOU AND HARLEY WRITING THE CONFESSION AND ALL, BUT THE WAY IT WAS DELIVERED...
DEAR, INNOCENT, ULTRA-HONEST BETTY!
WHAT'S THE POINT OF CREATING PERFECT PLANT DECOYS OF OURSELVES IF NOT TO SEND THEM INTO POLICE STATIONS AND TAKE THE HEAT FOR US?
YOU MEAN THE POLICE SENT A COUPLE OF PLANT PEOPLE TO ARKHAM?
SENT, YES...
...BUT MY LITTLE BLOSSOMS WERE UNDER ORDERS TO COME BACK AND PICK US UP.

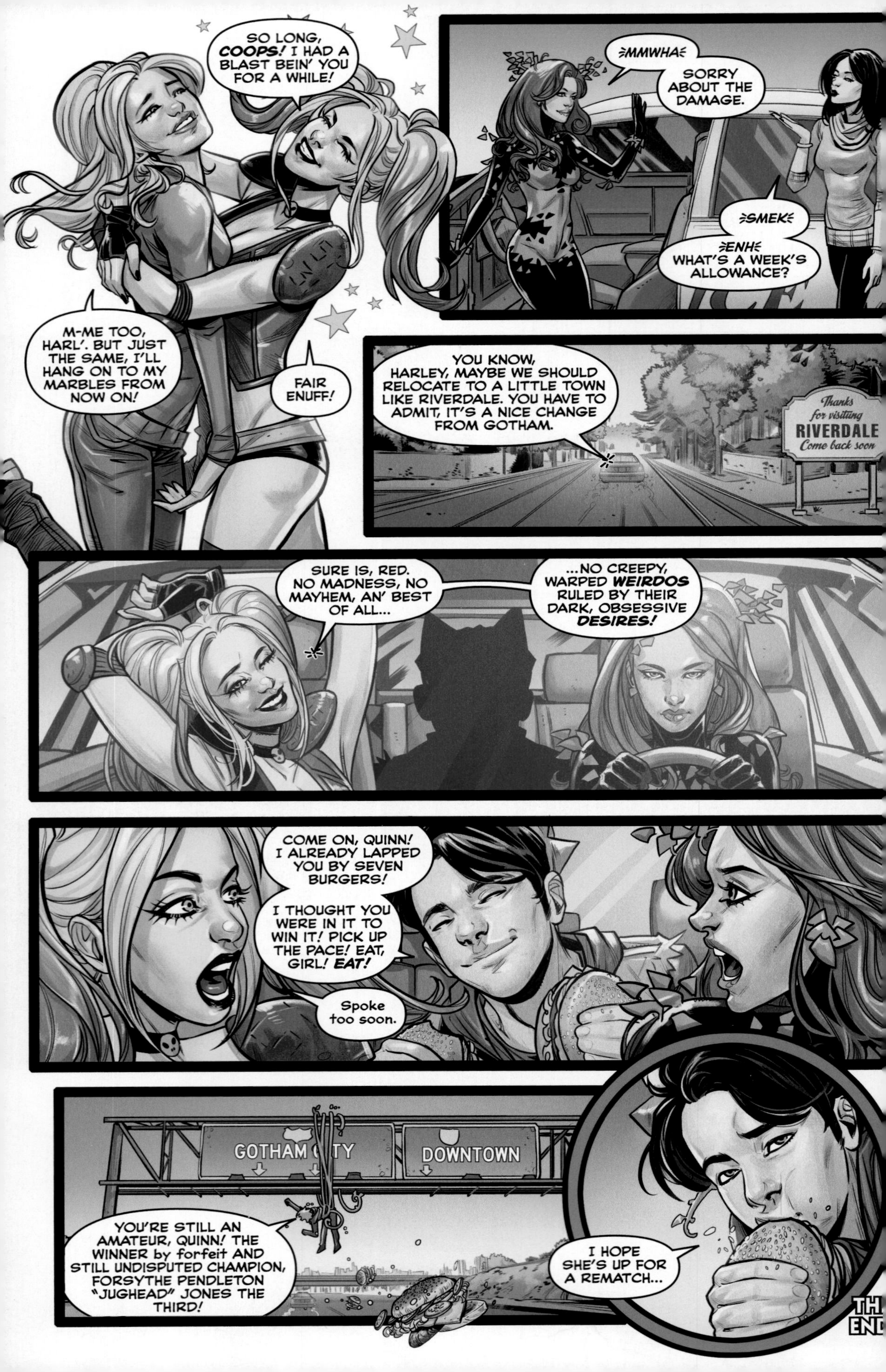
SO LONG, COOPS! I HAD A BLAST BEIN' YOU FOR A WHILE!
M-ME TOO, HARL'. BUT JUST THE SAME, I'LL HANG ON TO MY MARBLES FROM NOW ON!
FAIR ENUFF!
MMWHA
SORRY ABOUT THE DAMAGE.
SMEK
ENH WHAT'S A WEEK'S ALLOWANCE?
YOU KNOW, HARLEY, MAYBE WE SHOULD RELOCATE TO A LITTLE TOWN LIKE RIVERDALE. YOU HAVE TO ADMIT, IT'S A NICE CHANGE FROM GOTHAM.
Thanks for visiting RIVERDALE Come back soon
SURE IS, RED. NO MADNESS, NO MAYHEM, AN' BEST OF ALL...
...NO CREEPY, WARPED WEIRDOS RULED BY THEIR DARK, OBSESSIVE DESIRES!
COME ON, QUINN! I ALREADY LAPPED YOU BY SEVEN BURGERS!
I THOUGHT YOU WERE IN IT TO WIN IT! PICK UP THE PACE! EAT, GIRL! EAT!
Spoke too soon.
DOWNTOWN
YOU'RE STILL AN AMATEUR, QUINN! THE WINNER by forfeit AND STILL UNDISPUTED CHAMPION, FORSYTHE PENDLETON "JUGHEAD" JONES THE THIRD!
I HOPE SHE'S UP FOR A REMATCH...

VARIANT COVER GALLERY

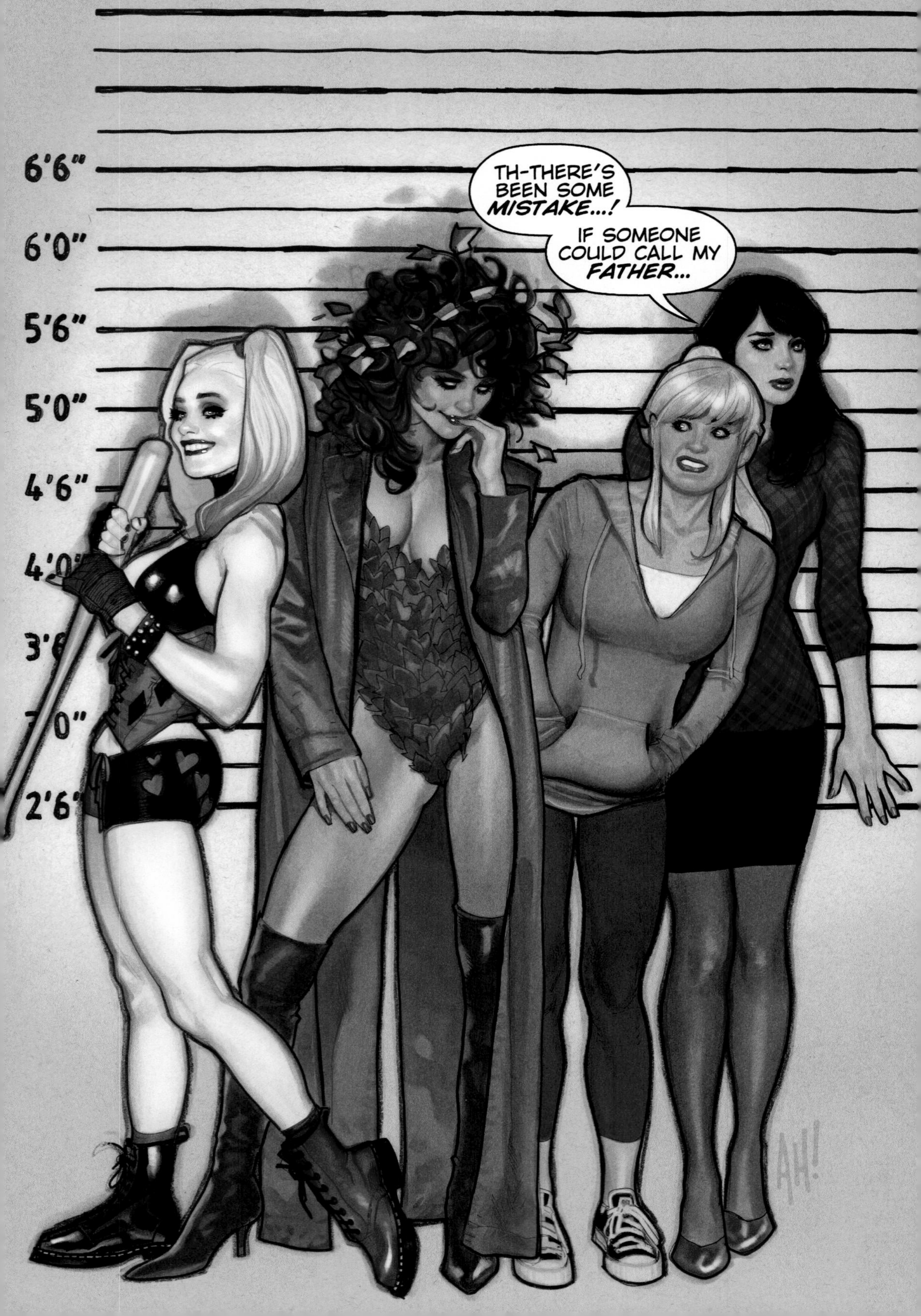
6'6"
6'0"
5'6"
5'0"
4'6"
2'6"
TH-THERE'S BEEN SOME *MISTAKE*...!
IF SOMEONE COULD CALL MY *FATHER*...
AH!

HARLEY AND IVY MEET BETTY AND VERONICA #1 variant cover
by ADAM HUGHES

HARLEY AND IVY MEET BETTY AND VERONICA #2 variant cover
by DAN PARENT

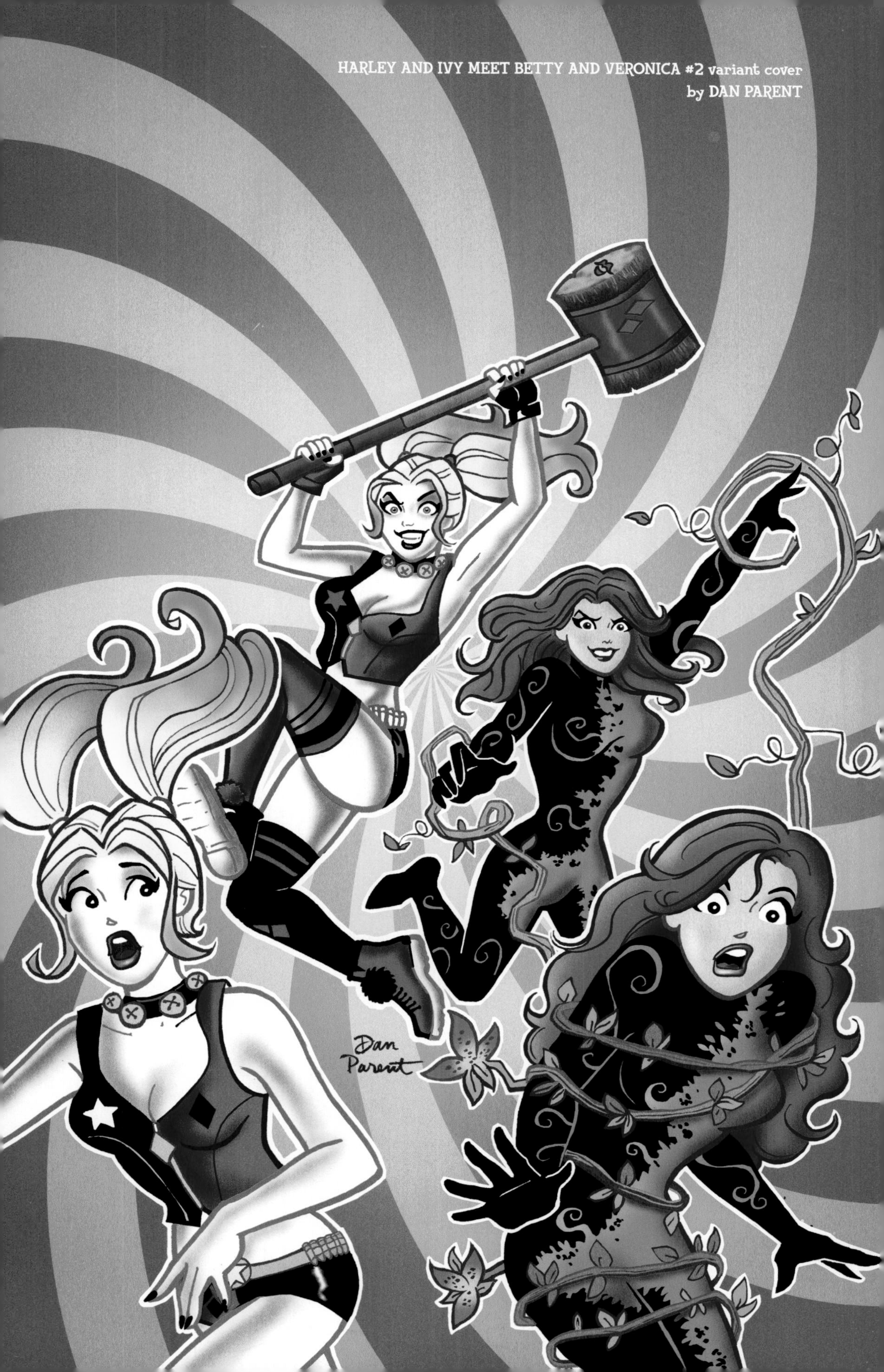
Dan Parent

HARLEY AND IVY MEET BETTY AND VERONICA #3 variant cover
by STEPHANIE HANS

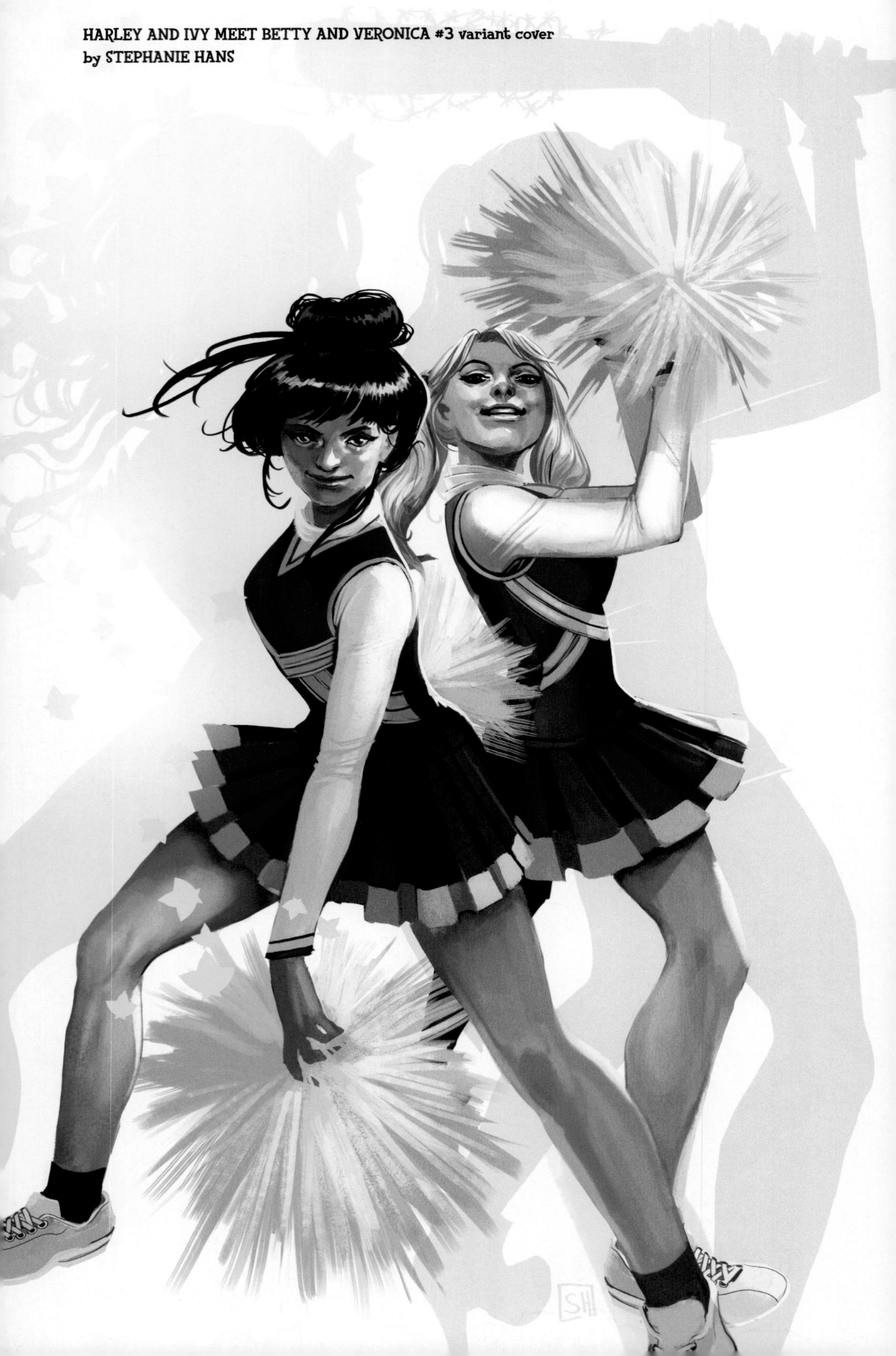

HARLEY AND IVY MEET BETTY AND VERONICA #4 variant cover
by GENE HA

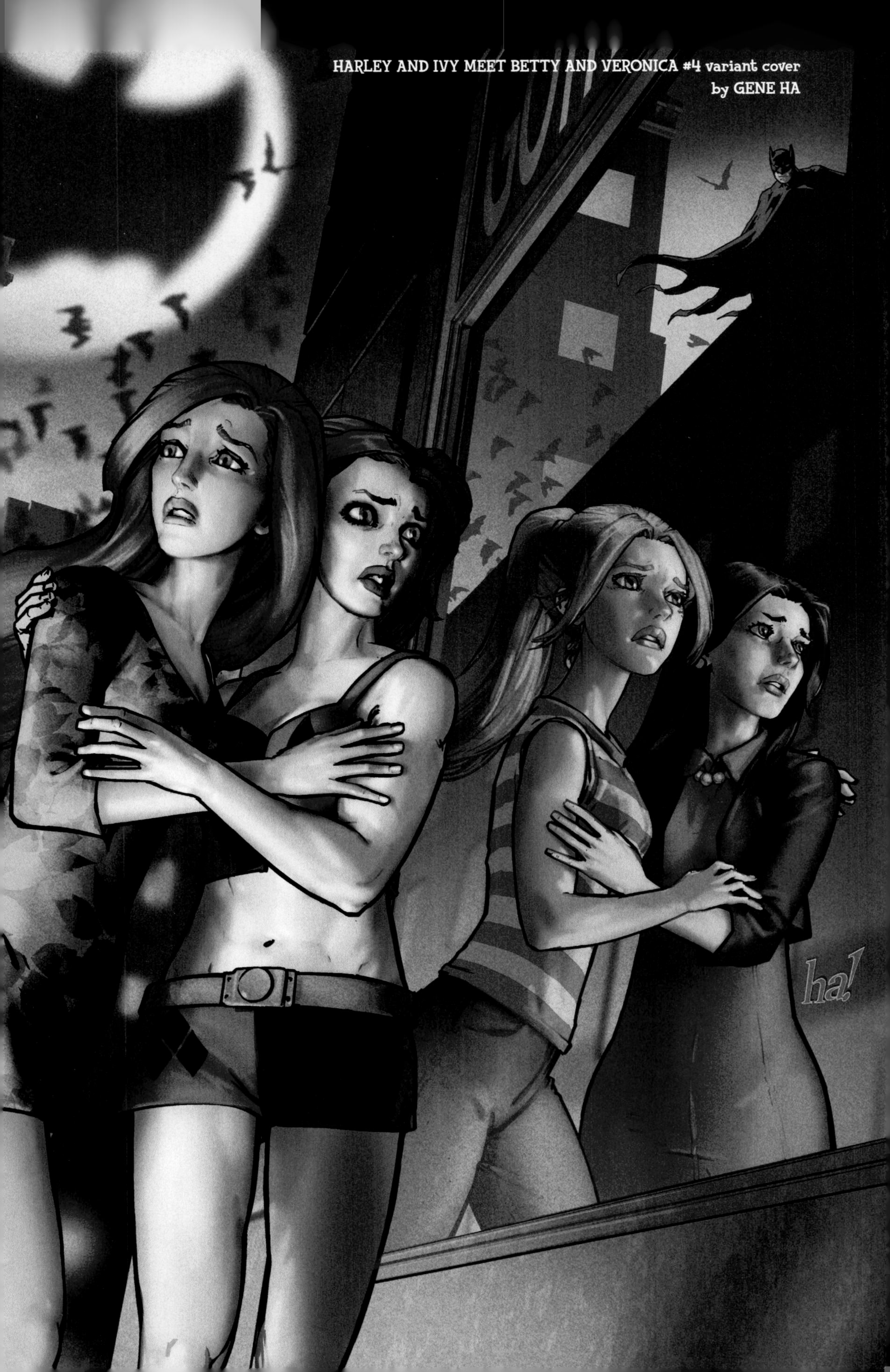
ha!

HARLEY AND IVY MEET BETTY AND VERONICA #5 variant cover
by BILQUIS EVELY and MAT LOPES

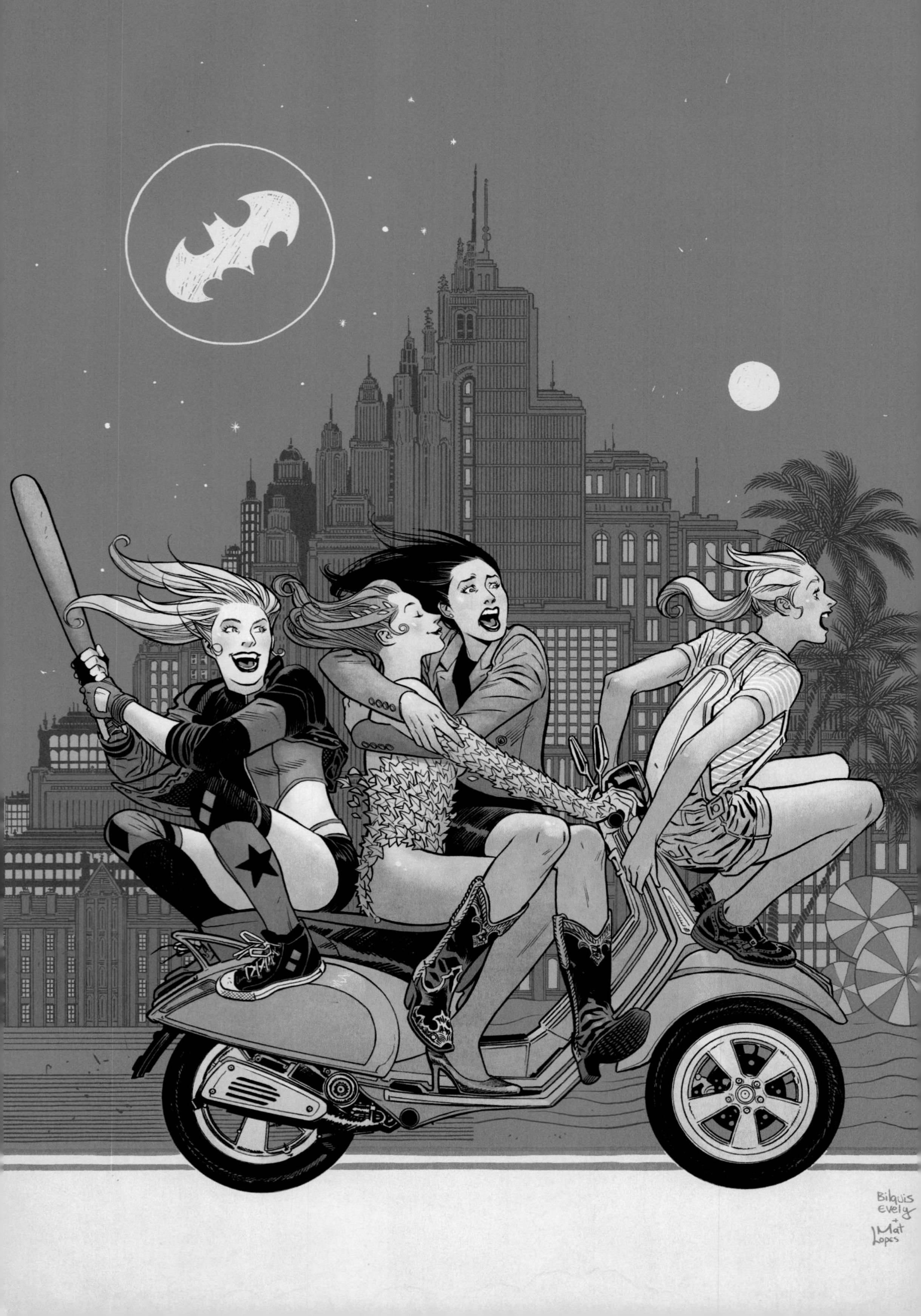
Bilquis
Evely
+
Mat
Lopes

HARLEY AND IVY MEET BETTY AND VERONICA #6 variant cover
by JAE LEE with JUNE CHUNG

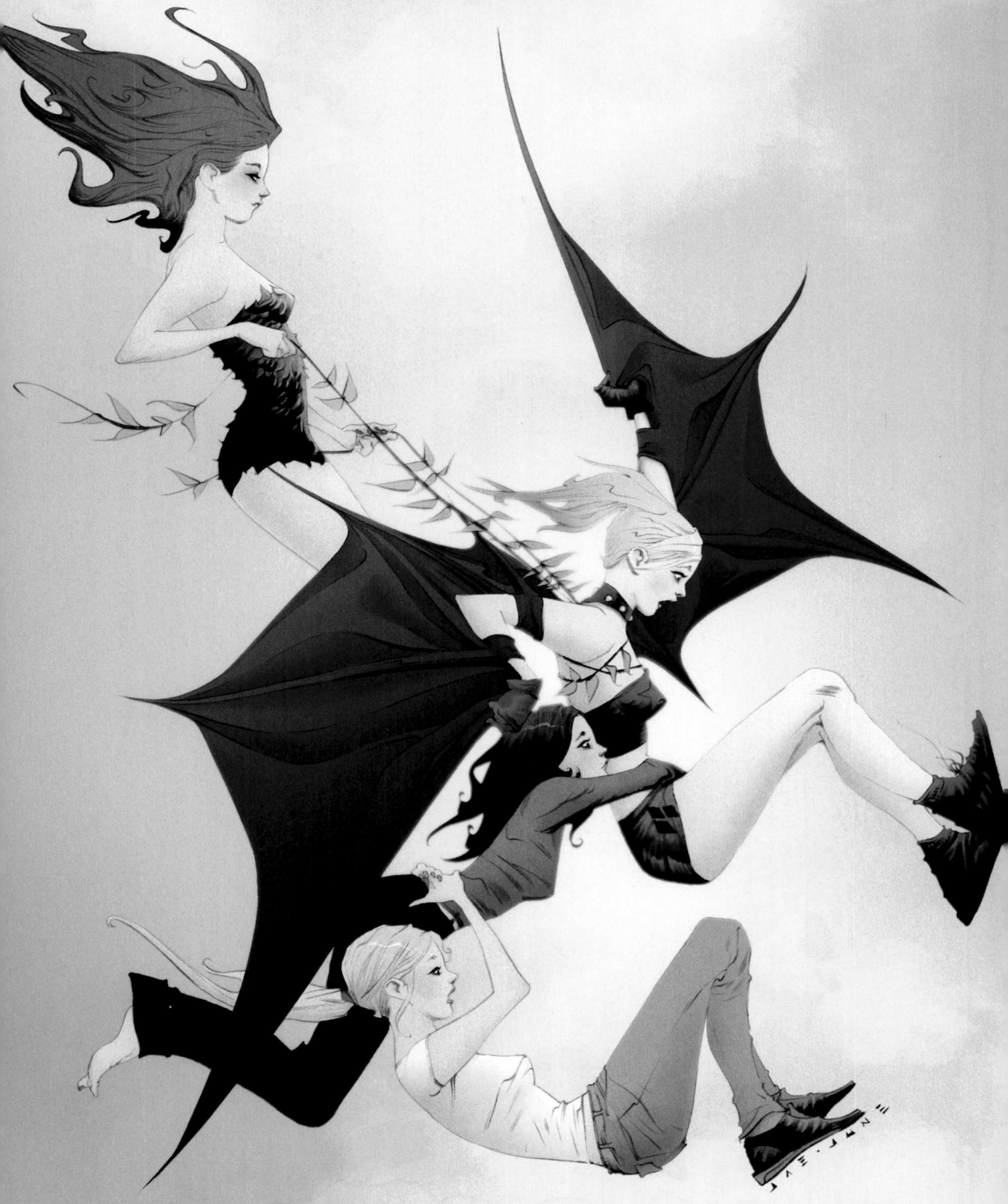

HARLEY AND IVY MEET BETTY AND VERONICA #1 cover sketches
by AMANDA CONNER

HARLEY AND IVY MEET BETTY AND VERONICA #2 variant cover sketches
by DAN PARENT

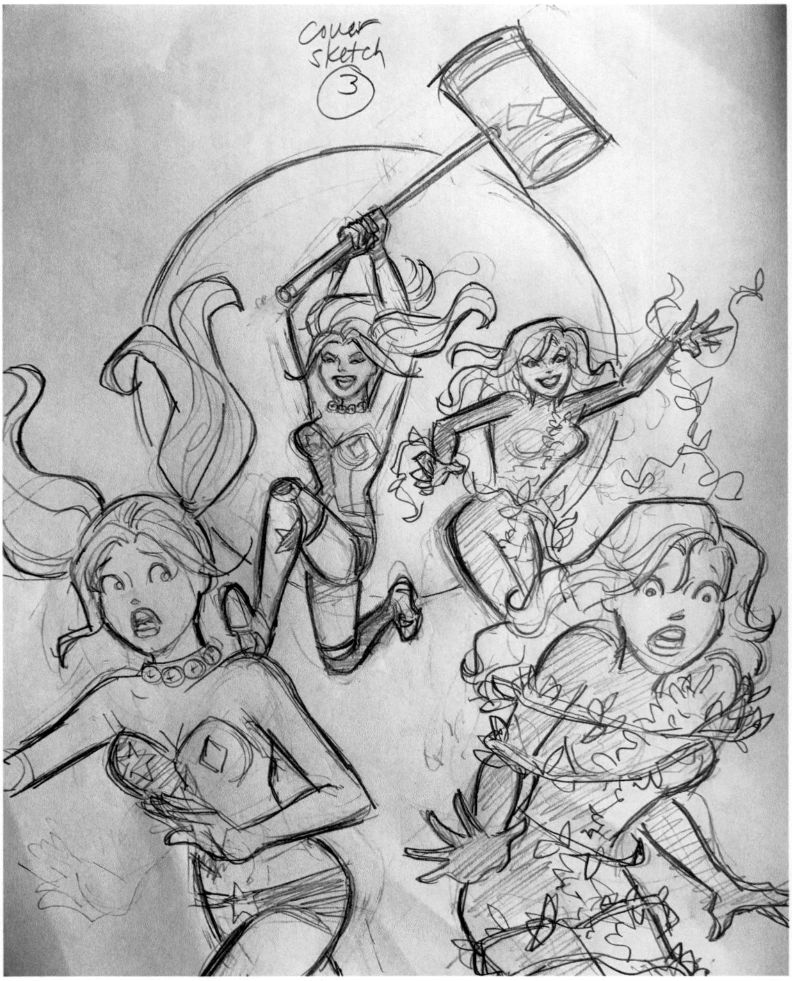
cover sketch
3

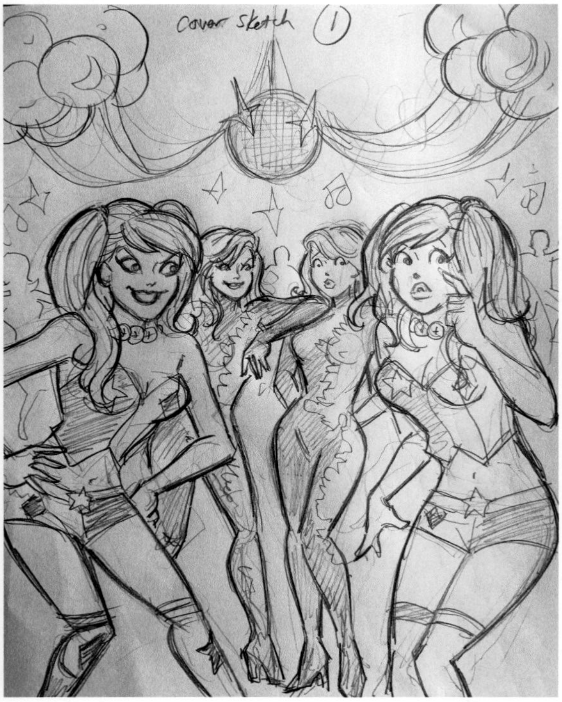
cover sketch 1

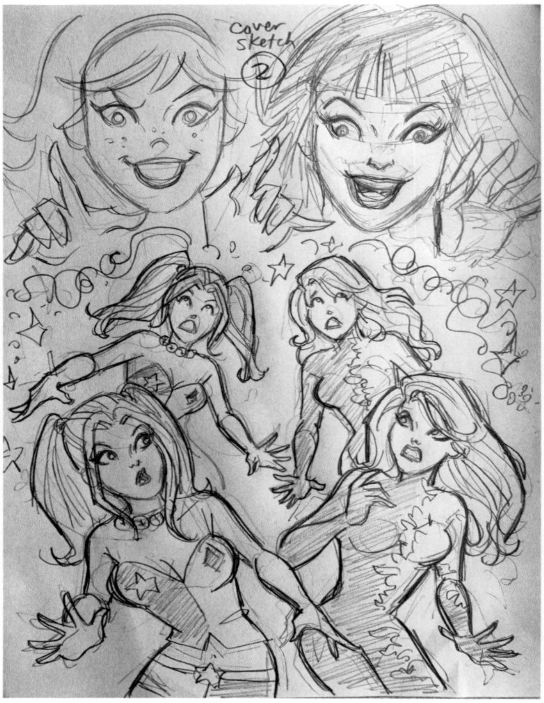
cover sketch
2

HARLEY AND IVY MEET BETTY AND VERONICA #3 variant cover sketches
by STEPHANIE HANS

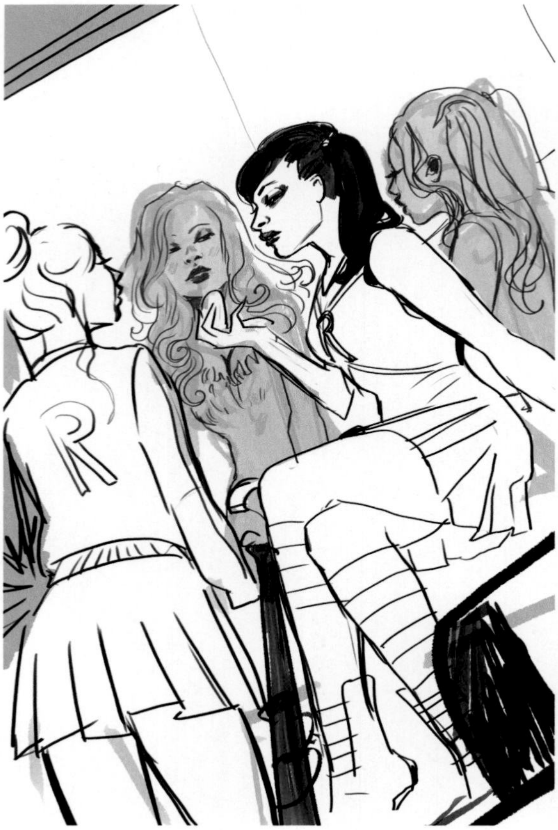

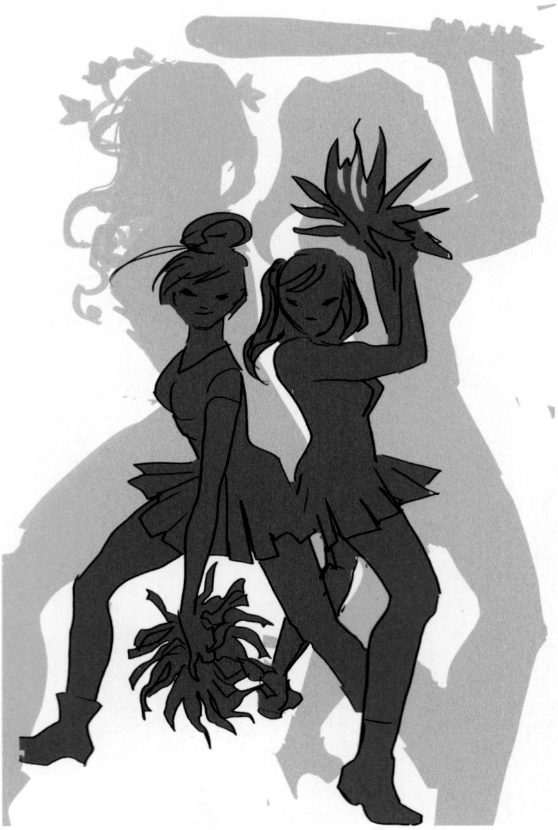

HARLEY AND IVY MEET BETTY AND VERONICA #4 cover sketches
by JENNY FRISON

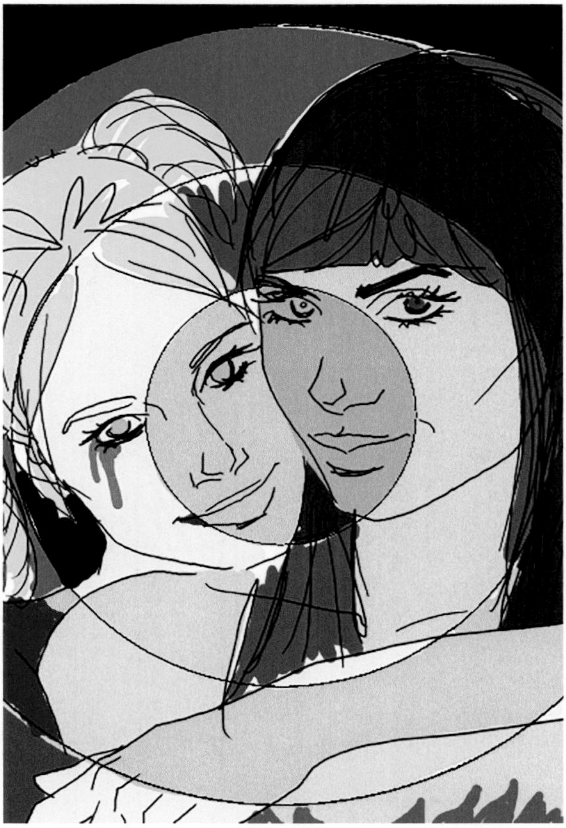

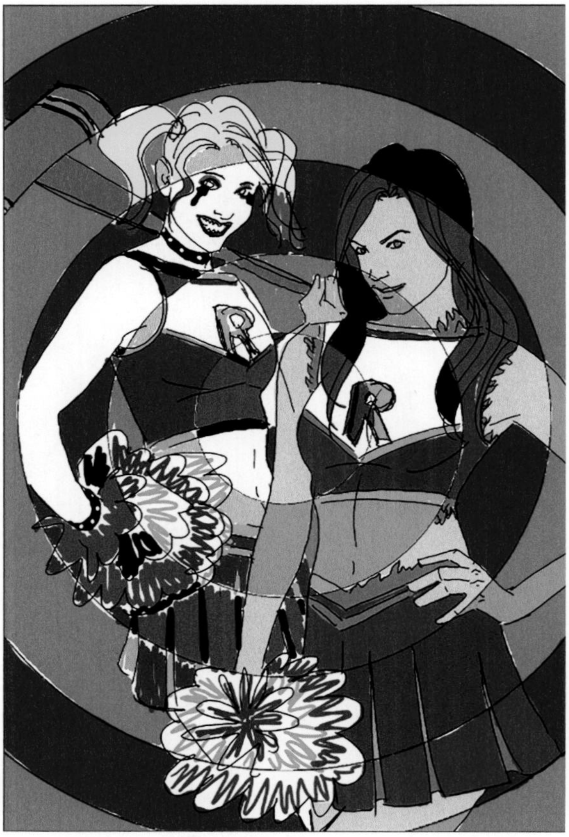

HARLEY AND IVY MEET BETTY AND VERONICA #5 cover sKetches
by JEN BARTEL

A. BETTY AS HARLEY, VERONICA AS IVY – GOTHAM.

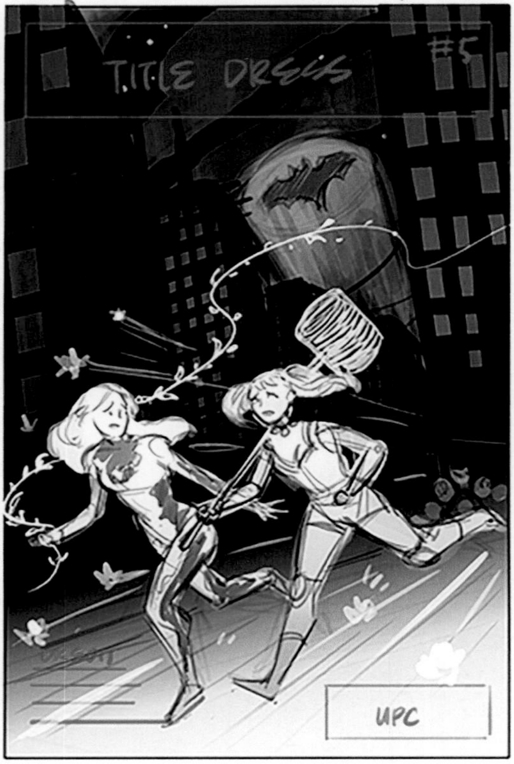
TITLE DRESS
#5
UPC

B. IVY AS BETTY, HARLEY AS VERONICA – RIVERDALE.

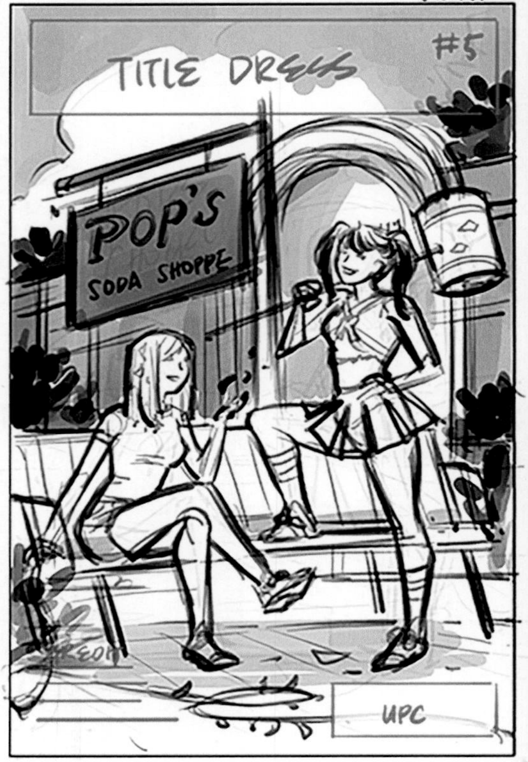
TITLE DRESS
#5
POP'S
SODA SHOPPE
UPC

C. X4 GROUP NARRATIVE

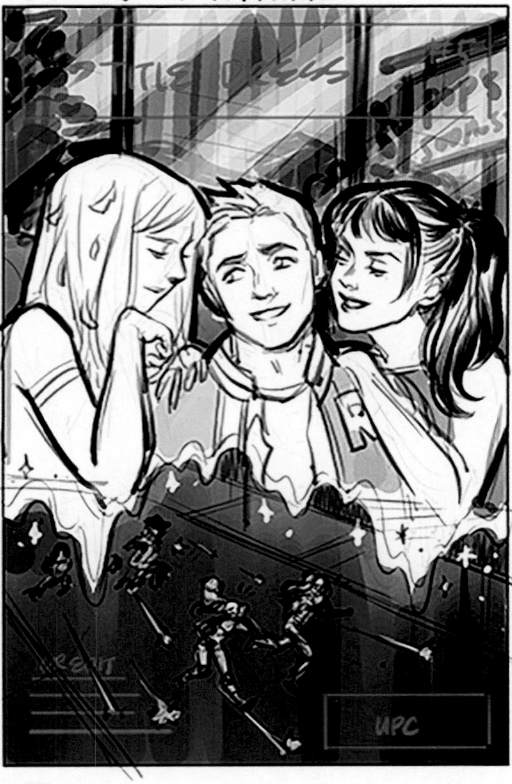
TITLE DRESS
CREDIT
UPC

D. X4 GROUP

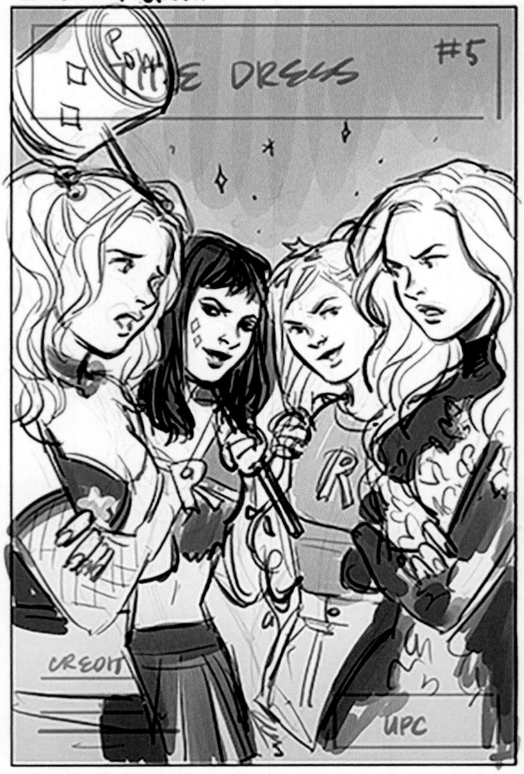
TITLE DRESS
#5
CREDIT
UPC